# Integrating the Language Arts in the Elementary School

# Integrating the Language Arts in the Elementary School

Edited by

**Beverly A. Busching**
University of South Carolina

**Judith I. Schwartz**
Queens College, Flushing, New York

National Council of Teachers of English
1111 Kenyon Road, Urbana, Illinois 61801

The editors wish to express their appreciation to the following persons for their thoughtful assistance in the review of manuscripts: Beverly Altschuler, Lee J. Garfield, Edith Grossman, Sydell Kane, Marcia Knoll, Norman Najimy, Linda Philips, Jean Stanton.


NCTE Editorial Board: Marilyn Hanf Buckley, Thomas L. Clark, Jane Hornburger, Elisabeth McPherson, Zora Rashkis, John C. Maxwell, *ex officio,* Paul O'Dea, *ex officio*

Book Design: Tom Kovacs for TGK Design

NCTE Stock Number 23511

**Library of Congress Cataloging in Publication Data**

Main entry under title:

Integrating the language arts in the elementary school.

   A project of NCTE Committee on Integrating the
Language Arts in the Elementary School.
   Includes bibliographies.
   1. Language arts (Elementary)—United States—
Curricula—Addresses, essays, lectures.  I. Busching,
Beverly A., 1937–   .  II. Schwartz, Judy I.  III. NCTE
Committee on Integrating the Language Arts in the
Elementary School.
LB1576.I66   1983       372.6′043       83-25099
ISBN 0-8141-2351-1

# Contents

**Part Three: Integration with Other Subject Matter**

# Preface

The idea for this book emerged from conversations with troubled teachers and supervisors. In a convention workshop, after several speakers had made a strong case for reading and writing as active mental and social experiences, a teacher spoke. "I agree with you. I think we *should* integrate, but I need help. I need to know *how*." A supervisor of a large metropolitan school district agreed, and spoke of her need for a strong professional support. "I need something I can take to my superintendent to support what I think we should do." It is our hope that this book will support efforts to keep communication going in elementary classrooms despite the pressures of basic skill testing and competency sequences.

As the NCTE Committee on Integrating the Language Arts in the Elementary School began discussions on integration, and as we listened to invited speakers and interested auditors, we discovered that one single definition of integration was not possible. Integrated language arts learning takes many different forms, some of which are controversial. In our lively discussions, we agreed that meaningful learning was the central issue, but opinion differed on how meaningful learning is best structured in the classroom. We have tried to represent the variety of professional opinion in the selection of articles presented here.

The combined efforts of members of the Committee on Integrating the Language Arts in the Elementary School and those who worked with us over the past few years made this book possible. The ideas of all committee members are represented here. In keeping with our purpose of giving assistance to schools, representatives of several public school districts were asked to help screen proposed contributions. All of the articles included in this publication have had a strong vote of approval from these representatives.

# Introduction

Here is a book for teachers who want their elementary school pupils to be eager to learn and to be equally eager to work. It is for teachers who want their pupils to grow in the many aspects of literacy and in those skills that enable them to learn independently. And, above all, it is a book for those who want their pupils to love both language and learning.

Dozens of ways are graphically described for accomplishing these goals. Children are shown in situations that call for thinking, talking, listening, reading, writing, painting, modeling, mounting exhibits of their work, dramatizing. Many different teachers present their ways of working and show the results of these efforts. The arts and skills of language are related vigorously to one another and, indeed, to the entire curriculum. The authors show instances as specific as how teachers support the learning motivation of slow learners, how singing games engage children's energies, how drama can begin with spontaneous improvisation of the tribal life of Native Americans and move on to study, reading, writing, talking. The authors present demonstrations of colorful, fulfilling classroom practices, but they also clarify the theoretical groundwork that underlies such activities. And further, the organization of the contents makes it easy for inquiring readers to find discussions related to their particular interests, whether it be how to engage parents in home response to the language arts program or an analysis of the meaning-building learnings in infant "speech."

Seldom since the turn of the century has there been so urgent a need to look critically at problems of integrating language arts instruction. Increased use of machines, conveniently available printed exercises, widespread emphasis upon testing for discrete items of behavioral objectives, and ever greater crowding of the curriculum with increasing demands and time pressures—all too often, these result in isolating specific bits of information in skill-drills to achieve test gains rather than real understanding in a genuine communications context. In the world of work—in industry and the professions, in communications among departments and with the public—reading writing, talking, and listening occur simultaneously. In the nation at large, whether raising funds for a new park or arranging an art exhibit, the language arts must operate together in order to be effective, not merely in general, but with respect to given content and audience.

In classrooms, too, when children work for goals they understand, when obvious changes or visible results occur, children are caught up in the importance of the task. This book gives a wealth of examples of how such vigor is accomplished. Further, it illuminates the broad educational spectrum in which language arts integration is essential. Schools with a strict academic, subject-centered program can find suggestions for combining some subjects (as a time saver if for no other reason). Almost surely, teachers will find encouragement for moving towards an integration of the language arts with the entire curriculum.

The many contributors to this book offer a broad array of suggestions both immediate and specific along with an over-arching philosophy based upon today's research and knowledge. Children and teachers should benefit from their concerted efforts to relate integrated language arts programs to today's many demands, not least among them the renewed call for *excellence*.

Alvina Treut Burrows

# I   Foundations

Teachers and children together create the moments that encourage integrated learning. A textbook cannot do it for them, nor a curriculum guide. But teachers and children need assistance to make integration work in the classroom. They need organizational structures, curriculum frameworks, and supportive services that encourage purposefulness and coherence across large spans of time and subject matter.

This section offers a look at the theoretical and practical frameworks that support integration. What understanding must teachers have in order to make instructional choices? What are the characteristics of children and their language that give rise to integrated learning? What planning structures support it?

Beverly Busching and Sara Lundsteen examine alternative curriculum models, past and present, and suggest guiding principles for building integrated curricula. Conscious selection of a variety of cognitive, social, and personally expressive contexts for language use is essential. Models are available that emphasize frameworks for spontaneous attainment of instructional goals as well as models that emphasize teacher planning of specific language forms and functions.

To help teachers who have difficulty keeping the flow of learning moving forward in many different areas, Laura R. Roehler provides an easy-to-use framework for creating teacher-planned experiences that integrate language arts with subject matter. Roehler's model might help curriculum planning groups avoid one of the pitfalls of interdisciplinary programs noted by Busching and Lundsteen, the downgrading of one subject in service to another. In Roehler's model, neither language arts nor subject matter is used merely to support the other; one plays a supportive role in one combination, and then a dominant role in another combination.

Judith I. Schwartz invites us to consider the single most important impetus for integration: *the child is a meaning-seeking creature.* Children learn to use language as part of the process of making sense of the world and the language that surrounds them. They do not wait passively to be "taught." Schwartz suggests seven conditions that can be created in schools to encourage children to be mentally active, purposeful learners.

# 1 Curriculum Models for Integrating the Language Arts

Beverly A. Busching
University of South Carolina

Sara W. Lundsteen
North Texas State University and Creative Studies Institute

> There is widespread concern about how the "language arts"—reading, writing, speaking, the comprehension of speech, and possibly also the appreciation of literature—should be integrated in the school curriculum. . . . The question is not how the language arts should be brought together in the learner's mind, but why they should ever be separated. (Smith, 1979)

Dividing classroom instruction into separate classes, textbooks, and lessons for individual language skills is a violation of how we use language, whether we be adult or child. When children use language, they do not divide it up into its many individual skills, using each one separately. Nevertheless, some educators have strongly defended classroom separate skill instruction on the grounds that children supposedly *learn* language in small individual bits, then later put the bits back together in use. This assumption about language learning, although widely held, is suspect. The past two decades of school experience and child language research gives impressive support to what many other educators have always believed: Children learn language, by and large, in the same way that they use it. It is the children's doing, their active social experience, their own thinking that are the chief means of their education. Optimally, children will themselves suggest, listen, comment, question, speculate, recapitulate, evaluate, construct relationships, and teach one another in a language arts program.

The nationwide investment in subskill instruction has yielded discouraging results. Test scores have not risen to the extent expected. Achievement gains that have occurred were due to the introduction of *any kind* of systematic attention to language arts instruction, rather than to the particular method being used. New evaluation programs that sample stu-

dents' actual writing and talking have exposed the failure of subskill textbook exercises to build clear and forceful speaking and writing. Concern
is widespread about even more pervasive losses: low student morale,
inadequate thinking abilities, and the loss of broader learnings in social
studies, science, and the arts as these subjects are crowded out of the
elementary school curriculum. It appears to be time to look again at integrated curricula in the light of current research and school experience.

If teachers eliminate a fixed, orderly sequence of subskills as the basis
of the language arts curriculum, what can take its place? What kinds of
comprehensive planning can provide coherence in a program to promote
communication abilities through thinking, expressiveness, and social
participation? We believe that there is no one answer to these questions,
but that there are many alternatives available to meet the particular needs
of a school.

In this chapter we have three purposes. First, we place current development of language arts programs in its broader educational context,
surveying various patterns of curriculum integration that began early in
this century and have persisted today despite recent opposing forces.
Second, we discuss principles of language learning that can serve as
guides for integrated language arts curriculum planning. Third, we show
how these principles can be applied to three different kinds of integration.

How do we define the three kinds of integration? The narrowest, but
most basic kind of integration proposed here is the meaningful integration of the subskills within each language mode, i.e., that children will
actually speak, write, listen, or read rather than practice a fragment of
writing in a skill-book exercise. The second kind of integration is broader.
The various language arts can be integrated with each other, as when
writing is combined with interactive listening and speaking in discussions.
Last, and most broadly, the language arts can be integrated with other
subjects in the elementary curriculum.

## Unified Instruction: Past and Present

### Where We Began: Separate Subject Organization

The fragmentation of instruction that currently plagues our schools is not
a new creation of our times, but a grotesque exaggeration of patterns
rooted deeply in our past. Separate subjects were the first basis for
organizing instruction (Regan and Shephard, 1977).

Each subject was viewed as a discipline, an organized body of knowledge about a unique domain of things and events with defined boundaries. It followed logically that each subject be taught separately. The

subjects of elementary education were few—reading, writing, arithmetic, and perhaps some geography and history—and separate instruction was a natural way to meet the limited goals of schooling in our young nation. Today, when the curriculum has expanded to include a confusing array of subjects, separation no longer has the persuasiveness of a simple solution to a simple problem.

## Another Way: Unified Subject-Based Organization

By the end of the nineteenth century separation of subjects was already under criticism as an impediment to the fullest development of each subject and to the broader intellectual, psychological, and social development of students (Regan and Shephard, 1977; Cremin, 1964).

In 1963 an enterprising reporter fueled the controversy by reporting on his tour of elementary schools in thirty-six cities. He decried the narrowness of instruction he found, including what he called singsong drill, rote repetition, and meaningless verbiage. He praised the few examples of "all-sided" education of children. He praised teachers who introduced "the idea of unification" into the curriculum, to combine the several subjects "so they may acquire more meaning by being seen in their relation to one another" (Cremin, 1964, p.5).

## Broad Fields Approach

One response to these criticisms unifies naturally related subjects within a larger area of study. Longer stretches of time are planned, and related skills are connected in instruction. Social studies or language arts programs are popular examples of the broad field approach.

The unit teaching method is a traditional, often effective way for schools or individual teachers to create new, meaningful instructional interrelationships. Ideally, objectives from each subarea can be reorganized to increase their interrelatedness. Many such integrated language arts programs are available for early childhood from commercial and noncommercial sources. But for teachers of older elementary students, available sources are slim. (Two excellent programs, the Nebraska Curriculum Development Center's *A Curriculum for English* and Holt, Rinehart's *Sounds of Language,* are no longer available.)

Language arts and reading texts, even though labeled "integrated," may be little more than pasted-together activities on related subjects. Students may read a story about animals, then be asked to write a poem about animals, study adverbs in sentences about animals, and act out animal movements, but there may be no thread of discovery or purposefulness tying the sequence together. Admittedly, an integrated language

arts program based on purposeful and intrinsic relationships is a difficult
task. Lacking outside help, most teachers have continued to teach subjects separately in order to use available textbooks. Teachers who are
willing to construct their own integrated curriculum are hampered by the
way in which each area of study is defined. A meaningful integrated program cannot be built upon objectives that are not worth teaching in the
first place. In recent times, the trend to define each subject area by a
lengthy list of minute objectives virtually eliminates the possibility of
unifying similar language subjects.

Critics of the broad fields organization pattern point out that, even at
its best, instruction is still artificially subject-centered, failing to encourage the natural connections between disciplines that result in true human-
istic or scientific education. For language arts, the criticism is especially
telling. Shouldn't children write about *something*? Shouldn't they learn to
write observations, evaluations, descriptions? If so, why not do it in social
studies or science class?

## Interdisciplinary Organizational Patterns

Unifying broad fields such as language arts and social studies is a more
ambitious approach. Most interdisciplinary programs solve the complexities of joining disparate curriculum structures by using the scope and
sequence of one discipline as a skeleton on which to attach skills and
concepts from other disciplines. Thus one discipline serves as the principal organizer, with other disciplines serving as vital, yet supplementary
adjuncts. A more daring approach is to create unification by reinterpret-
ing content and processes from different fields to create what can be considered a "new" curriculum.

The interdisciplinary approach has united selected language arts objectives in commercial programs such as *Science, A Process Approach*
(1974), which features conscious development of scientific language functions such as recording observations, hypothesizing, comparing, and
evaluating. Local school curricula have also united selected language arts
objectives in units of study with other subjects, particularly social studies.
Because much of the "content" of language arts as a separate subject area
consists of skills used in other subjects, these interdisciplinary curricula
have been seen as promising ways to teach language arts effectively.

Critics of interdisciplinary approaches to teaching the language arts
point out that these programs tend to *teach* content and processes from
social studies or science, *using* language arts abilities without intentional
long-range development. Language arts are short-changed. Another criticism of interdisciplinary programs is that they tend to reduce language
learning to a limited set of utilitarian communication skills. Literature

and the expressive power of language as areas of extensive study in themselves tend to get crowded out of the curriculum. It appears to be a difficult task to combine learning across subject matter boundaries in ways that preserve a deep experience in communication.

### Daring to Be Different: Nonsubject-Based Organization

Some integrated curricula reject subject matter as an organizing framework, turning instead to other perspectives to achieve the fullest cognitive, social, emotional, and psycho-motor development of students. Two approaches that eliminate subjects and disciplines as organizational centers are the *Experience Curriculum* and the *Societal Problems Curriculum*. These curricula constitute the second major form of unified curricula, the nonsubject-oriented approach. Human activities and concerns, rather than skill sequences, provide their organizing structures.

*The Experience Curriculum* begins with children and their interests, activities, and needs. The Experience Curriculum approach has a long history, most notably beginning with John Dewey's school at the University of Chicago in 1896. He organized learning around four human impulses: the social impulse, the constructive impulse, the impulse to investigate and experiment, and the expressive or artistic impulse (Regan and Shephard, 1977). In recent history the Open Classroom movement and the Integrated Day approach have given similar strong emphasis to processes such as thinking, feeling, creating, and investigating as foci of learning.

Sometimes attainment of instructional objectives in these programs is *spontaneous*. Objectives are achieved, not as they occur in the workbook, but when they become relevant to the activity at hand. "Curriculum planning," or conscious attainment of goals can occur on the spot in response to ongoing interests of children. For example, a group of first graders makes "cameras," and wants to sell them. As the teacher helps the children devise a system of money, set prices, and make advertising signs, he or she consciously teaches and assesses writing and mathematics learning.

Other programs feature *teacher-planned* areas of activity or projects in line with anticipated child interests and curriculum goals. For example, in an English Integrated Day program, seven-to-eight-year-olds interested in the nearby harbor observe the movement of the boats, monitor shipping schedules, and make related calculations, graphs, pictures, and compositions. They later study geographical features. Teachers have a firm notion of the learning objectives to be attained by the children, and set tasks accordingly. Children who do not study the harbor are guided to other projects through which they can accomplish these objectives (Nuffield Mathematics Project, 1967). Whichever approach is used, spontaneous or teacher-planned attainment of goals, in the Experience Curriculum learning is primarily dependent on the purposeful participation of children in activities that are in line with their felt needs.

Another type of curriculum organization that eliminates subjects as an organizing guide is one that uses *societal functions* as centers of study. Societal function curricula (or units) are based on the belief that although the facts, concepts, and skills of a discipline are worthwhile for children to learn, schools have broader and more significant functions—helping children develop "an understanding of who we are" (Skeel, 1979). For example, a unit of study organized around the westward movement of pioneers in this country might examine pertinent historical, geographical, and social questions. Weather, animal life, and machinery might be studied. Comparisons could be drawn to migrations in other countries or in other times. Instruction in all the language arts takes place based on diagnosed needs while children utilize a variety of study and reporting skills. Societal functions curricula may be organized around many different concepts and schemes. Teachers have used current social problems or events and projections into the future as sources of integrated societal function units (Allain, 1970). Stratemeyer and others in the 1950s proposed a curriculum based on situations, which recur in many different ways in the life of individuals as they grow from infancy to maturity. *Man: A Course of Study* (MACOS) uses organizing concepts from biology (life cycle, adaptation, and so forth) and from the humanities and social sciences to help students understand the forces that have shaped their own culture and behavior patterns.

During the last thirty years, at the same time as some of the most interesting of these integrated curricula were being shaped, the move back toward individually taught subject matter has taken place. Few of the old integrated curricula are still being taught. Some critics were disillusioned when promising curricula actually took form in the classroom. Many teachers were not prepared for the amount of planning, on-the-spot diagnosis, and instructional flexibility needed to keep learning moving ahead. Teachers felt overburdened. Demands for more effective language arts instruction in the late 1960s coincided with a professional concentration on defining the processes of reading, writing, listening, and speaking in terms of complex lists of subskills. Schools accepted the belief that learning would be maximized if each of these identified subskills were taught separately. As mentioned earlier, once a subskill sequence is in place, integration is virtually impossible. Thus, many schools are now left with each individual language subject fragmented into isolated skill exercises.

We are now in a new era of language arts research and theory. The processes of learning to read and write, to speak and listen, are recognized as wholistic processes in which the child is actively seeking out and constructing meanings. Schools with elaborate subskill sequences are looking for more promising approaches. This is the time to build new, more effective integrated language arts curricula based on well-grounded principles. In the remaining sections of this article we will provide a theoretical basis for such new integrated curricula. We will review three crucial "principles" of language learning, and then apply them to curriculum building.

## Principles to Guide Integration

*Principle One: Broad communication effectiveness*
*as the goal of elementary language arts.*

Children need significant, applicable language skills, processes, knowledge, and attitudes as they go on learning and communicating for a lifetime. They need to understand and to come to terms with their complex world. They need to negotiate decisions at home and at work. They need to express personal meanings joyfully and forcefully.

We are not talking about knowledge *about* language; nor are we talking about a demonstration of a single isolated skill drawn from a list of other isolated skills. Skilled communicators not only know about language, they can use language appropriately in many real life situations. Competent language users make appropriate choices among the available linguistic alternatives. These choices arise from extensive, flexible, social and linguistic sensitivity (Shuy, 1980; Wieman and Backlund, 1980).

If we take communication effectiveness seriously as the major goal of language arts instruction, we can use it as a powerful screen through which to examine that instruction. Will teaching about language remain comfortably entrenched at the heart of the program? No, professionals in the fields of language may need such information, but other communicators need very little of it. Once we decide that information about language is not a goal in itself, we must ask rigorous questions about retaining such a heavy dose of subskill and grammar teaching.

*Principle Two: Situation language learning in context.*

Perhaps the most fundamental integrative principle is that language learning is optimal when it is situated in meaningful contexts. Children's doing, their active social experience, and their own thinking create the occasions for becoming more perceptive readers and listeners, more eloquent speakers and writers. Children want to understand the world and to achieve their own ends, and they learn to understand and produce language as it fulfills their own purposes. Language only becomes complicated and difficult to learn when it is separated from more general non-language events in the world. In fact, when language does not make sense or has no apparent purpose, children will fail to learn it (Smith, 1979). As Smith points out, it is because children are concerned about the purposes of language that they grow up speaking language and not imitating the noise of the vacuum cleaner. The "context" principle applies to the more detached, descriptive, and impersonal language of school as well as the interactive language of social relationships.

Children do not first learn language as an abstraction or a "skill," which they then employ later. They find out about language as they use it. In fact, language learning has been described by Smith and others as a trial-and-error and problem-solving process. Children hypothesize about what is appropriate, act on the basis of their guesses, then observe to see if they are right. And always they relate what they have learned to what they already know (see, for example, Clay, 1975; Dyson, 1982; Smith, Goodman, and Meredith, 1978). Children do profit from direct instruction and mature models of language in order to progress toward mature language themselves, but adult support of this nature is most effective when it is closely tied to children's intentions and actions.

Recent investigations of the process of language learning—what actually happens when children write or read—stress the crucial role of the learning context, or situation, as a force to impede or encourage learning. These studies have found that language flourishes in settings where children are exposed to mature language models and have the opportunity to create and receive messages in many different tasks (Graves, 1981). For example, one of the strikingly consistent findings of the nationwide comparison of first grade reading programs was the differences in later writing abilities associated with the Language Experience Approach method as compared to basal reader programs (Spache and Spache, 1977). Apparently, the experience of reading many examples of their own original dictated writing encouraged children's ability to write fluently and complexly, whereas the experience of reading the simplistic prose of basal readers had a negative effect on writing. In other studies, the development of syntactic maturity of oral language (Paley, 1978), discussion skills (Wilcox, 1976), and composing skills (Yatvin, in Haley-James, 1981) have been observed in programs of active communicative exchanges.

Why do "language in use" programs provide such a rich soil for learning? Opportunities for problem-solving learning are abundant. Each child, faced with a need to communicate, can concentrate on improving his or her own "hard spots." No diagnostic program can compete with children's own sensitivities as they pursue their purposes.

Additionally, the forms of language are extremely sensitive to specific social and mental contexts. We were reminded of this basic characteristic that separates language arts from, for instance, mathematics, when one of us attempted to gather a language sample from a five-year-old child. Kristi had happily given her writing earlier, and I thought it was time for more samples. I asked Kristi's mother to ask her to write me a letter. But I had made the mistake of violating her communicative competence. "What does she want a letter for?" Kristi asked suspiciously. Knowing the social role that letters play in our society, she was unable to complete a task that conflicted with her knowledge.

Different *purposes* of communication, such as complaint letter vs. assembly announcement, or narration vs. exposition, have their own characteristic vocabulary, organization, and style. Different *subjects*, such as "Invertebrates" vs. "My Pets," will also trigger different linguistic styles, usually a different level of formality in word choice. Different *audiences,* such as a manager of a grocery store vs. classmates, will also trigger different organizational patterns and word choices.

Many purposes and settings for language use are readily available in school. The language of problem solving can be learned when children address actual problems (spontaneous table talk may not provide such a beneficial setting). Oral reports will help children learn to sustain monologues, using forms that later will influence their expository writing. Standard English usage is especially sensitive to context changes. Nonstandard English speakers will learn the more formal styles associated with Standard English when they undertake social roles that require formal English.

Thoughtful and systematic selection of contexts is essential to building an effective school language arts program. By "thoughtful and systematic selection," we do not mean a regimented sequence of contexts to replace a regimented sequence of subskill exercises. Rather, school personnel can reflect on the goals that are important in their schools, and then select categories of purpose, subject, and audience appropriate for these goals. Room must be left for spontaneous child choice, and for teachers to create schedules suited to life in their classrooms. Thoughtful planning at the total school level can work to avoid one-sided learning experiences—all practical social exchanges and no introspective mental journeys, for instance—which limit a child's fullest development.

At a minimum, an integrated elementary language arts curriculum needs to provide instructional tasks/activities for the following three different kinds of contexts: expressive, cognitive, and social. These three categories seem to us to be useful for school planning. They are readily understandable without specialized training; they are already represented in most school curricula to some extent; and, together, they provide a very broadly applicable language experience. Examples of possibilities in each of these broad categories are explored in the succeeding paragraphs. (It must be noted that any such separation of the purposes of communication creates false divisions. All expression of language is to some extent social—an audience, internal or external, remembered or imagined, is always to some extent present. Likewise, all communication to some extent involves thinking and to some extent involves the expression of personal feelings. Nevertheless, many situations do have an emphasis in one direction or another and therefore call up different forms and processes of language.)

*Expressive contexts.* We use the term expressive contexts to refer to situations in which children give voice to personal feelings and perceptions or respond personally to the expressions of others. For example, in a kindergarten Kim writes below her picture that she is going to get into trouble because she broke a window. Her shared words help to ease her anxiety about this problem. Jose storms across the classroom, in large boots roaring his anger, looking in every corner for a trembling Jack, who has invaded his giant's castle. Expressive uses of language include poetry, spontaneous monologues during free play, creative dramatics, even choral readings and acted plays (if children used these structures for their own personal expression). In these imaginary and artistic productions the cognitive and social overtones are secondary, and satisfying oneself overrides social communication concerns. Similarly, when young children write, their feelings and perceptions are the predominent message and the primary audience is self. When older children write, their sensitivity to different audiences and functions broadens their writing to other contexts.

*Cognitive contexts.* Language may be considered inseparable from thinking. For instance, mental patterns guide reading comprehension; reading material influences and guides mental patterns. A policy statement issued jointly by professional educational organizations, "The Essentials of Education," emphasizes this interdependence by urging schools to unite the disciplines in order to foster mental skills, processes, and abilities along with broader understandings and appreciations. (See Appendix B for the entire statement.)

> . . . in all subjects, students develop skills in using language and other symbol systems; they develop the ability to reason; they undergo experiences that lead to emotional and social maturity. Students master these skills and abilities through observing, listening, reading, talking, and writing *about* science, mathematics, history, and the social sciences, the arts, and other aspects of our intellectual, social, and cultural heritage. As they learn about their world and its heritage, they necessarily deepen their skills in language and

reasoning and acquire the basis for emotional aesthetic and social growth. They also become aware of the world around them and develop an understanding and appreciation of the interdependence of the many facets of that world.

A child learns anything, including language, by autonomously constructing relationships as he or she acts on the world and experiences reactions. For example, a young child manipulates objects that float and that do not float in a water table and begins to abstract principles of buoyancy. An older child ponders several fiction books about interracial friendships and similarly abstracts principles of human relationships. This same type of autonomous construction of relationships slowly and lastingly paves the road for comprehension in all subject areas. As children observe, describe, ponder, question, and explain, they learn the vocabulary, the discourse structures, the syntax, and the interpersonal communication that shape and guide thinking. Little or no cognitive development can occur in an environment of isolated, minimal skills, e.g., ditto sheet after ditto sheet for circling consonants and pictures. A language-in-use curriculum model, which interlaces language learning with all learning, gives the children the chance to engage in mental journeys on their own terms.

*Social contexts.* Children use language to create and continue social interactions. From their earliest years, children communicate in social context. By the time they enter school, children are competent talkers and listeners in many different social situations, sensitive to the linguistic alternatives appropriate to those situations. Moffett (1967) notes that the task of the school is to build on and add to the social competence that children bring to school. Teachers can encourage and structure opportunities for school talk that promotes continuing development toward mature language. He further notes that few classrooms accomplish this task. On too many classroom doors is the invisible sign, Abandon Speech All Ye Who Enter Here.

Social interactions that have general application in society, such as persuasion, explanation, cooperative idea building, and the like, should be part of a curriculum of communicative competence. More specific social interactions that have special, defined language forms also need to be included: panel discussions, letter writing, job interviewing, check writing, and childcare.

Communication in social contexts tends to integrate language because of its very nature—there is an exchange between two or more parties. Some social contexts require primarily writing and reading (letters, for example); others involve primarily speaking and listening (discussion). Other social situations are more complex, combining several kinds of language modes, as will be detailed in the following sections.

*Principle Three: Maximizing interrelationships
between the language arts.*

The third principle to guide integrated curriculum planning is to maximize the intrinsic interrelationships between the various modes of communication. These interrelationships are enhanced when language is interrelated in teaching, and diminished when it is not (Lee and Rubin, 1979). We can keep in mind, as Smith reminds us in the introductory statement of this article, that the problem is not to create relationships in the child's mind; the child already approaches language in an integrated manner (unless he or she has been taught otherwise). The problem is to create relationships in *instruction* that support the child's integrated learning.

How are the different language arts related? The mental processes of production and reception create one basic kind of interrelationship. Listeners and readers share similar processes as they "receive" external cues and create mental patterns in response to these cues. Similarly, writers and speakers share a common set of mental processes as they search for symbols to express ideas and feelings. An integrated program can take advantage of reception similarities by asking children to listen for the same kinds of contextual information that they will later read. Production similarities will encourage transfer of descriptive skills practiced orally to later written descriptions. But schools cannot expect the same kind of transfer between listening and speaking—differences between ability to understand Standard English and ability to use Standard English are indicators of the wide gulf between the processes of listening and speaking.

Another connection cuts across the reception/production relationship. The linguistic differences between the two great communicative systems of English—written and verbal—create close connections between reading and writing, and between listening and speaking. ("Listening" is used here to refer to listening to speaking. Listening to written material being read, of course, provides a further bridge between the language arts.) Listeners and readers may, as pointed out previously, share certain common mental processes of reception, but because they grapple with symbol systems so different in nature, they employ very different perceptual and linguistic mechanisms. The act of hearing oral language requires on-the-spot attentiveness to fleeting sounds, bodily movements, and situational cues. It requires knowledge of the sound symbol system, auditory acuity, and sensitivity to endless social variations in the use of this symbol system. Listeners learn about the organization of spoken language, its vocabulary, and how it depends on voice variation, gesture, and the environment for meaning. Speaking uses this same linguistic knowledge.

The act of reading written language requires knowledge of complex aural-visual symbol relationships and sensitivity to long-lasting cues of spatial placement, punctuation, word choice, and discourse organization. Printed material is not as loosely organized as conversation is; it is tightly structured and densely packed with information. More formal words, especially those that define relationships between ideas, are used. Students learn these linguistic forms as they read and write. Thus writing advances reading ability, and vice versa.

The language arts have a dual relationship—they are connected in one way by process similarities and in another way by linguisitic similarities. Figure 1 shows these connections.

As we seek ways to maximize the natural relationships between the language arts, we must keep in mind that adults may need rigid models (such as below) in order to understand these complex relationships. Children, however, do not experience integration in this manner. Children experience interrelationships between the language arts fluidly, not according to a theoretical model, and whatever approach a school chooses should allow for and encourage this fluidity.

In summary, the three principles we have proposed work together to provide a foundation for curriculum planning. When communication effectiveness is placed at the center of the goals of instruction, instruction becomes imbedded in cognitive, expressive, and social contexts which capture children's drives to act on and learn about their world. In this "language-in-use" curriculum similarities in the processes of producing and receiving language will lead to strategies that encourage children to move fluidly between many avenues of expression, between talk, writing,

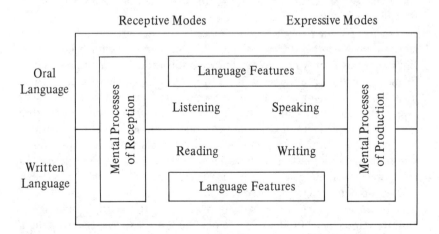

Figure 1. Dual connections between the language arts.

movement, and art. The common linguistic base of reading and writing, and of speaking and listening, leads to other connected strategies that build on the contributions of one mode to another.

In the next section we offer a range of instructional models. These models reflect a variety of professional viewpoints from which schools can choose according to their circumstances and needs.

## Where Does Integration Take Place in the Curriculum?

Integration of the language arts curriculum can take place at three different points: for each of the language arts separately, among the language arts, and across the curriculum. In this section we will discuss each of these three kinds of integration, giving examples of how each kind might look in operation.

### Single Language Mode Integration

How can one language mode by itself be considered integrated? Sometimes children concentrate primarily on one language mode and its special functions and skills. Because these activities are grounded in meaningful communication instead of being fractionalized into isolated subskills, they can be considered to be integrated. This kind of integration is important in and of itself, but it is also fundamental to broader integration across the language arts and across the curriculum. A language arts curriculum made up of long lists of minute competencies cannot be successfully united with other subjects. Two different approaches to single language mode integration are suggested as examples of the possibilities in this area.

*Teacher-planned single activity model.* Teacher preselected objectives can initiate an integrated activity if the children are genuinely engaged. For example, a fourth grade teacher used this model to create a situation to meet specific grade level writing objectives. She set up a center that included a model form of a business letter, stationery, and books listing free and inexpensive materials. The children wrote letters requesting items they liked. Pairs of children proofread each other's letters, using the model. Off went the letters, and soon in came a stream of maps, games, kite-making plans and other appreciated items. This activity represents an integrated single language mode in a social context which originated in teacher-predetermined objectives.

*Workshop model.* In a writing workshop the work originates in children's interests and ideas. We might call it an "experience curriculum" in limited form. Teachers predetermine the time schedule (long spans of time) and the language mode (writing), but allow the sequence of specific objectives to depend on what and how the children choose to write. Donald Graves, a consultant to a writing project of this type, describes some of the results. We paraphrase his report.

"Thank God for Amy," said Graves (1979) as he recalled the explosion of composing that occurred in a New Hampshire classroom. Amy had been to a wedding the weekend before and came to her first grade class longing to perpetuate the experience in writing. But the teacher was too busy that morning for the taking of experience story dictation. Amy began to render her experience into writing by herself as best she could, spelling with the seven consonant sound-letter correspondances that she knew.

"Well, what do you think of this, Dr. Graves?" asked the teacher, showing him Amy's attempts.

"Ah, Amy is inventing," said Graves, and proceeded to explain the developmental research that tells us that children can do this kind of spelling quite naturally if not hindered in their attempts. He went on to add that if as many as three consonant sounds are rendered in a word, the probability is high that the word can be read back by the child at a later time, and that it can be read by other children. When the children saw some examples of invented spellings in compositions that other first grade children were creating, the egocentric lure of telling about their own lives and being able to have it in permanent form was irresistible. Writing took off all around the classroom "workshop."

Only a few objected. "My mother will kill me if I don't get every word spelled right!" cried one child, longing to join in the adventure that his peers were pursuing. "I'll talk to your mother," soothed the teacher. "I'll explain that the story you select for publishing will be typed with correct spelling, and that your invented spelling won't spoil you as a speller." And so it came to pass that by midyear, the least number of books created by a child in this first grade class was twenty-four, and this low number was by a child who did not speak until age four.

Many small skills and processes were integrated as children's experiences were rendered into written composition: letter formation, word separation, positioning on paper, spelling, punctuation, selection and elaboration of content, and anticipating audience response. The children made practice for themselves as they wrote and revised their stories with a persistance that they would never have tolerated from even the most winsome (or punitive) of teachers. (Of course, as the children wrote, they spoke and listened to each other, and over time, their insights into the nature of writing spilled over into their reading. We will discuss these extensions in the next section, integration among the language arts.)

We often believe that child selected activities can be effective only in the primary grades, when children are task-oriented and objectives are not as complex as in the upper elementary grades. But the experience of schools does not bear out this negative view. We could have easily taken a writing workshop example from an older age group: for example, the program described by Yatvin in Haley-James (1981).

## Integration among the Language Arts

Integration takes place among the language arts in many ways. We can only suggest some examples here that seem especially important to us, and that represent a wide variety of alternatives. We suggest five categories of approaches: the Communication Exchange Model, the Mode-Switching Model, the Vicarious Problem-Solving Model, the Personal Problem-Solving Model, and the Long-Term Integration Model. These various approaches are not interchangeable. They provide different language learning opportunities for children, and all have a place in an integrated curriculum. They involve children in all of the language contexts identified above: in cognitive contexts, in which children collect, categorize, analyze, and evaluate ideas; in social contexts, in which they take on social roles to communicate with others; and in expressive contexts, in which they produce and receive personal and artistic messages.

*The communication exchange model.* Much of the time communication is integrated by engaging in activities that spontaneously use many modes of expression. Playing house or store leads to persuading and entertaining, to evaluating, to agreeing and disagreeing, to sign-making and sign-reading. Similarly, discussion, project planning, role playing, puppetry, Readers Theatre, and Language Experience Approach reading naturally bring into play integrated speaking, listening, reading, and writing. These activities are not new to the elementary curriculum. Many of them extend back as far as the 1920s and 1930s in well-elaborated form. But in recent years workbook exercises have taken their place, perhaps because it *looked like* children were learning skills when they completed a direct exercise that named a specific skill. Perhaps recent classroom research studies and new observational evaluation methodologies will help teachers identify important learnings that are taking place in context, so the importance of communication exchanges will be recognized by parents and administrators who now doubt their worth.

*Vicarious problem-solving model.* Often children can be encouraged to attain higher levels of thinking and communicating when teachers provide more complex supportive structures for expression. In a problem-solving approach teachers suggest certain communicative structures that maximize opportunities for individual reflection, peer sharing, and large group sharing. The quest begins when children find a meaningful problem or challenge; they feel it is their very own to explore and to solve in multiple ways; they can feel powerful, capable, and confident in the process. Integrating body, mind, and language to this end energizes the classroom; joy replaces boredom and apathy (Lundsteen 1976; Lundsteen and Tarrow, 1981). Problems can arise from children or from teachers, but the important point is that the children take over—they feel it is their own problem. Consider the following example of vicarious problem solving in a first grade class.

> The challenge was triggered by the children's book *Sam* (Scott, 1967). The teacher structured this challenge by reading the story to a group of ten children, stopping at the crisis point. In this crisis point the boy Sam, after successive frustrating attempts to find a family member to play with him, "sat right down by his father's desk and cried and cried and cried." The ten children adjourned to their tables and art materials to symbolize their thoughts, feelings, and impressions of the story. In the meantime, the teacher and an aide invited individual children aside to confer about their ideas. Here the children were briefly encouraged to speak about Sam, his difficulties, his larger problem, what missing information they might need, what they would suggest Sam do, and if they had ever felt a bit like Sam. Some children, referring to their pictures, wrote captions or advice.
>
> After all children had had the prediscussion experience, the teacher called them (some thirty minutes later) with their pictures to a small group discussion. As the teacher guided this total group with much the same questions as before, fresh ideas emerged, flowing from the prediscussion experiences. Finally, a group "Some Advice to Sam" list emerged.
>
> A powerful "integrator" in this just-described activity was the problem-solving focus. The children cared about Sam and wanted to find a way to help him. This motivating force—empathetic problem-solving—served to muster almost all thinking and communicating processes with an intensity and duration that no isolated, artificially imposed drills could capture. Teacher-structured alternation between individual and group idea development seemed to serve the group well. Later, further integration took place. When a "Sam" puppet family appeared in the classroom corner, children spontaneously reenacted the problem episodes and alternative resolutions. The copy of *Sam* became a book-time favorite, its successive rereadings contributing to the children's reading attitudes and abilities.

The "Sam" episode is a compelling example of teacher-stimulated language experience in cognitive and social contexts. The children were of primary age. Let us turn now to an example of similar alternation between group and individual expression, but at an older age level and emerging from a child-centered source.

In the *Sam* sequence children used all the language arts in cognitive, social, and expressive contexts. The "writing workshop" approach to composition has been developed to include similar problem-solving mechanisms. Here, the focus is on writing itself as a problem to solve. In the Brooklyn, New York program children engage in four different kinds of conferencing as they write, revise, and edit: content, process, evaluation, and editing conferences. They also critically examine library books and magazines for models of the features of good writing.

*Personal problem-solving model.* Moffett (1973) provides a description of on-the-spot curriculum planning which used spontaneous contributions from children's lives to integrate objectives and activities from all the language arts. In terms of the curriculum approaches described at the beginning of this chapter, this sequence could be called an "experience curriculum" approach.

The children were upset about a recurrent problem in their lives: petty stealing of personal items like pencils, erasers, and rulers. Feelings ran very high. Teachers recognized what Moffett called a "burning issue." They met together to plan structured interactions to help the children progress beyond informal discussion of the problem. They had in mind how the children could best solve their real life problem. They also had in mind how to meet upper elementary level language arts objectives through an unusual occurrence which impelled growth and refinement of communicative abilities. They did not fit the immediate social responses of the children into a predetermined language arts sequence. Rather, the reverse. They selected and combined various communicative situations appropriate to the children's current levels of attainment which best served the children's pressing social needs.

The session started with discussion groups. Teachers proposed that the groups produce some ideas about how stealing occurs and what might be done about it.

As Moffett related the satisfying results:

> In each group a scribe was appointed to record whatever ideas occurred. . . . Armed with their notes, the eight or nine scribes met as panelists before the rest of the class. Actually, these meetings were not so much true panels as a series of reports, but the remarks of the scribes could be compared for similarities and differences, and some interaction did take place among panelists. Afterwards, the teacher asked the rest of the class to comment on the panel. Some disagreement came out as well as an occasional new idea.
>
> At this point each of the two classes decided on a second phase of action: one was to make posters about stealing and the other to prepare a publication about it. The class doing the publication brainstormed in the small groups for five minutes about items that

might go in it. After scribes reported these ideas at the panel, the whole class refined and pared them down to eight items, . . . [such as] what-to-do-if-you-don't-want-something-stolen.

Some children were to explain the campaign to other classes to whom the publication was to be distributed. Two children wrote the survey questionnaire and two others compiled it with the teacher. Participation in the brainstorming was total, and every child wrote an article, even those who were hitherto "nonwriters." The articles were read in the small groups, the good but not necessarily best ideas were singled out in discussion, and the papers were revised. Thus, through rewriting and proofreading in the groups, final copy was produced. Then each group discussed these and selected one for the publication. . . . After distributing the posters and newsletter to other classrooms, the participating children went in pairs to garner reactions to their ways of dealing with stealing. The small groups discussed these reactions, and their scribes compared notes at a panel that stimulated a final class discussion about actually implementing a campaign in the school.

Probably no adult of sound mind would have thought up in advance such an intricate rigamarole. . . . the participating teachers had the courage to pursue (the) bare notion of small-group discussion wherever it needed to go, the wit to improvise and orchestrate activities, and the sensitivity to play by ear with the children.

*The mode-switching model.* Not all integration is as complex as the two previous models. Sometimes integration may be as simple as encouraging (or allowing) children to move fluidly from one form of expression to another, from talk to writing to art or movement, for example. Children may be able to solve problems of production in one mode of expression more easily than in another. Once the problem is solved, children may be able to transfer their gains to the other mode. Fluency and confidence that is gained during oral Sharing Time can transfer to writing if the teacher creates similar structures for the two tasks (Busching, 1982). Listening can provide an avenue for comprehension abilities also used in reading. Role playing can illuminate ideas students are struggling to express in writing. Conferencing all during the writing process helps free up new ideas and focus them into coherent prose. Curriculum planning will be required to remove instructional restrictions (such as requirements for all children to write at the same time according to uniform criteria) and to create time and resource structures for consciously planned connections between the receptive and productive modes of expression.

Another kind of integration between the language arts is the recognition that experiences in one mode will develop abilities to be used eventually in another mode. For example, the books that young children hear and read provide models of written discourse that exert influence on their writing many years later. A school program can provide consciously planned sequences of listening to and reading important kinds of writing: not just fiction in the primary grades, and little or nothing in the upper elementary years. Students need to read and listen to essays, newspaper articles, informative description and narration as well as poetry and fantasy throughout elementary and middle school. Children need many exposures to different types of writing before they are asked to read them, and especially before they are asked to write them. Recent editions of basal reading series have broadened their offerings, perhaps in response to a recognition of integration of reading and writing. But all texts with controlled vocabularies create difficulties for young writers. Children learn models of weak, sometimes unintelligible writing from these texts. An integrated curriculum of the future will be one in which these poor writing models are eliminated, or at least deemphasized, and a conscious program of exposure to all kinds of writing continues throughout the grades.

## Integration across the Curriculum

If we believe that language is learned through use, we are inevitably led to making connections between language arts instruction and instruction in other subjects. Neither efficiency nor effectiveness is served by learning to read and write from 9:30 to 11:00 and learning about history and geography from 1:30 to 3:00. When we look at actual school programs, what we see in many schools is even worse. Instruction is not just fractionalized: science or social studies may be crowded out because the school day has been eaten up by excessive practice time "needed" for reading and writing out of context. In this section, instead of providing model approaches as we did in the two previous sections, we will discuss, first, planning problems of integrating language arts across the curriculum, and second, implementation problems of these curricula.

## Planning Problems

Not all unified curricula are equally valuable. Just as a magnificant mosaic can't be made from inferior stones, trivial learning does not become worthwhile just because it is joined with other trivial learning. Similarly, learnings that are randomly glued together do not create worthwhile child experiences. So curriculum planners face two kinds of conceptual problems when constructing (or selecting) quality integrated learning experiences: problems pertaining to selection of the "pieces" that are to be stuck together and problems pertaining to selection of the adhesive that creates the whole. The historical approaches to unified curriculum building that we reviewed in the first section of this article—correlated subjects, multi- and interdisciplinary, and nonsubject oriented—represent different attempts to solve these problems. We will offer some additional guidance in this section for the selection of content (the "pieces") and for the selection of unifying structure (the "adhesive").

*The learnings to be integrated must be of worth in themselves.* Applied to language arts, this guideline points the way to units of *communication,* not units of knowledge about language. Dwelling on "the sound of" /a/ during a unit on apples does not make this activity any more valuable than dwelling on "the sound of" /a/ at any other time. And in a similar way, when Native American ideographs and designs are copied during a social studies unit with little regard for their authenticity or original place in a particular tribal culture, nothing has been contributed to children's understanding of Native American culture or the nature of symbols. The curriculum guide may loftily claim that "integration of content learning with symbolic representation" has taken place, but in actuality nothing of value has taken place.

To build unified sequences of study, teachers must begin with worthwhile elements: quality literature, historical and scientific processes of major importance, and significant concepts and important communication events.

*The connections between the subjects in an integrated curriculum must be worthwhile.* We suggest that connections between the language arts and other subjects are based on the need for communication. When children actively pursue understanding, they have a need to find information, to move from one level of understanding to another, to express and examine new learning, and so forth. Communication, in its variety of form and function, is intrinsic to the search for meaning. These intrinsic relationships between content and communication can serve as a guide for integration across the curriculum.

As stated earlier, the form of language is sensitive to the function it serves. In an instructional sense, this principle can be translated to mean that it is extremely difficult to develop a form of language in a false context—in an artificial imitation of its function. Perhaps the reason why the science and social studies curricula mentioned earlier (SCIS and MACOS) achieved success as settings for language learning was because they are based on careful consideration of the intrinsic conceptualizing and verbalizing processes needed in such studies. Unfortunately, too many commercial and teacher-made programs are pasted together in what might be called the you-heard-a-story-now-illustrate-it approach. If the subject is birds, children listen to bird poems, learn bird songs, write about bird topics (factual and fantasy), read bird books, and illustrate everything. These artificial collections of activities may capture children's surface attention, but they do not create purposeful connections needed for meaningful education.

Example of Subject-oriented Integration across the Curriculum

Two ingenious English teachers, one a historian and the other a drama specialist, combined objectives from their two traditional subjects to create a novel approach derived from the work of Dorothy Heathcote (Fines and Verrier, 1974). Fines and Verrier led children to put themselves into a historical setting or incident, not to *re-enact* it, but to *live in it* on their own terms. The adults created a mood, a setting, or an incident by using *realia,* storytelling, role playing, or by taking the children into an actual environment. When the children had "entered" the scene, they took over. We can see this process at work in the following actual example:

> Verrier was asked to work with a class of children who had had little previous experience carrying out the responsibilities of group drama. Not knowing what to expect, they gathered around expectant but giddy. Verrier placed them physically into the scene by asking them to form a circle of chairs to make a "coroner's court." He then related in dramatic voice the events of the past evening, when he was awakened in the middle of the night by the shrill cry, "Murder!" followed by a garbled tale of tragedy. He recalled the lantern-lit trek to a muddy lane. No identification of the victim, save one. Out of his pocket came the evidence, an amulet on a leather thong, worn by . . . whom?
>
> "Look well on it," and the court, now serious, looked well on it.
>
> "And I do not know to this day which of our women here it was that woke me."
>
> A pause. . . . Time to give the action to the children.
>
> Would they take it? Sometimes the children were ready—sometimes "integration" between their knowledge, their questions, and their interests had taken place, and the drama took off. Other times, they were not ready and another activity emerged. As children dug more deeply into historical life and became more adept at handling the historical process, drama alternated with study over long stretches of sustained work.

What are the values of historical dramatics? Why should language arts be learned in this context? As Fines and Verrier note, one can only sketch the many-sidedness of the contributions of this kind of drama to language, attitude, social, and conceptual growth. We can mention drama as a powerful catalyst for inquiry. It helps children focus on an area of study that is concrete; it helps define questions that will reveal that area more thoroughly. It demands a range of thoughtful answers—no single snap answer will satisfy a group that has lived history. It requires that hypotheses be tested; it demands that results be examined. Drama also offers practice in democratic living: The children become decision-makers, cooperative decision-makers who must take into account the wills and needs of others.

As for language, in drama, children themselves create situations in which their oral expressive abilities are stretched to the uttermost. The force of the situation demands just the right word choice, tone, and gesture. Reading plays an important role: Children will demand immediate access to books to keep the drama going and to answer questions they themselves have formulated. Writing, in Fines and Verrier's work, "comes in small packages." A letter, a list of instructions, a proclamation to post. But great care goes into refining the wording—the audience is well-known; the authors have a heavy stake in the outcome.

Implementation Problems

Realities of the specific organization and resources of the school play a crucial role in the success of integrated learning. We suggest that these realities be taken into account from the very beginning. A beautiful plan that makes too many demands on teachers will create chaos. A simple plan that is successful will pave the way for further, more elaborate plans. We do not mean to imply that no changes in scheduling or teacher role need occur, but do suggest that these changes be made gradually. Time is an important factor. Long stretches of time to work support integration; brief class periods with frequent changes of children between teachers limit planning flexibility.

Teacher specialty is another important factor that can work for or against integration. Specialist teachers can contribute knowledge to add depth to children's work, but when each teacher holds rigidly to specific processes and information defined by their own field of study, integration is difficult to accomplish. Regularly scheduled common planning times can serve to encourage integrated planning, and a shared commitment to the benefits of integration can serve to dissolve subject area territoriality.

In the following planning situation, teachers in one school agreed on a short-term unit of work which they created together to fit their schedules, resources, and individual learning objectives. They chose to avoid traditional subject boundaries as the basis for their planning, dividing areas of learning into categories of: cognitive (e.g., science and math), affective (e.g., the arts, values clarification), and physical-psychomotor (movement education, handwriting).

*Example of Nonsubject-oriented Integration across the Curriculum*

This unit* started with a child's question about where bread came from:

---

*Thanks to Tommy Jones, Sidney Lanier School, Dallas, for this example.

"Was there a bread tree or a bush?" Over lunch (after a good laugh), several teachers in different grade levels decided they could cooperatively muster a cross-age dialoging experience from this question. Children would raise wheat, make bread, and take a field trip to a bakery. Books and films would contribute background knowledge.

Cognitive development would be served with concepts and generalizations concerning community interdependence, the processes of growing and harvesting, and the chemistry of yeast, and also by the mental operations of problem solving. There would be plenty of chances for integrated listening, speaking, reading, and writing focused by problem solving. Plans (both oral and written), thank-you notes, and reports would be needed. Self-chosen forms of expressing new understandings would be encouraged. Skills of word attack would be taught in this context as reading teachers helped children tackle challenging informational books. Math for measuring ingredients and for dividing pairs of children to fit into four and six passenger cars would emerge.

The possibilities for social integration were abundant. Teamed with younger children, the older ones would gain a sense of audience adaptation and have considerable writing practice as they transcribed the younger children's dictation. And they would grow in responsibility and self-respect as they enjoyed a sense of being looked up to and important. The teachers integrated themselves informally. Each offered to take charge where they felt most comfortable. Some good ideas were dropped because they seemed too time-consuming. The community was integrated with the school as parents joined forces with teachers and bakery employees to offer a fulfilling education to these children.

Could evaluation take place in this integrative situation? Yes, there were many behaviors to observe and check, indicative of progress in the language arts and other subjects. Was skill learning more long lasting, more easily retrieved at a later date? Probably. Experience was combined with verbalization. Was learning more memorable? More transferable? Better preparation for a changing world? Highly probable.

**Conclusion**

We are not suggesting that every minute of the curriculum be caught up in integrative, cooperative work, but we believe that unified instruction can be used productively much more than is currently the practice in most schools. We urge that language arts first be integrated as its foundation, each individual writing act or reading act having meaningful intention. Then teachers can further unify these communicative acts to create integration among the language arts, and then more broadly across the curriculum. Teachers have many different approaches to choose from. We have suggested a variety of possibilities, and have offered principles of language learning that can serve as guides to select approaches that fit each school's needs.

# 2 Ten Ways to Integrate Language and Subject Matter

Laura R. Roehler
Michigan State University

When planning for instruction, teachers face multiple (and seemingly contradictory) decisions and problems. They must deal with the dramatic increase in the number of subjects and the amount of content to be taught. They must accommodate the back-to-basics movement which advocates more skills instruction and less frills. Meanwhile, they are aware of time-on-task research indicating that student learning is directly proportional to the time spent engaged in a subject matter. This perplexing situation leaves teachers struggling to find time to teach all that is required in all subject areas. Integration of subject matter can provide one solution to this problem.

## What Is Integration?

Integration is a strategy for intentionally combining subject matter so that students are aware of this integration during implementation. Because two or more subject matters are taught simultaneously, the amount of instructional time in a school day can be increased. Additionally, subject matter can be combined to allow one subject matter to aid in the learning of another. As such, integration is both efficient and effective.

## Components of Integration

Integration requires teacher decisions about two important components of instruction: subject matter and levels of instruction.

*Subject matter.* Subject matter found in educational curricula can be divided into (a) the knowledge base of our culture and (b) the language strategies that carry the information of our knowledge base.

The knowledge base incorporates ideas, thoughts, and feelings our culture has deemed useful and worthy. The bulk of this knowledge is

28

contained in printed materials, with schools being designated as major perpetuators of this knowledge base. In the school, this knowledge base is generally developed in the content areas of social studies, science, literature, music, art, and mathematics.

Language strategies are the second major type of subject matter. Language strategies (including speaking, listening, reading, writing, doing, and observing) are the fundamental tools for sharing the knowledge base. These tools provide the ways for information to be communicated and are generally developed in the subject areas of reading and language arts.

In summary, the subject matter of schools includes ideas, thoughts, and feelings drawn from the knowledge base and organized into content subjects, and includes also the language strategies by which the subject matter is produced, sent, received, and understood.

*Levels of instruction.* As subject matter is prepared for instructional activities, two levels of learning should be considered. One level focuses on the initial learning of new information and the other refers to how previously learned information is used. For instance, a student could learn how to punctuate conversation and then use that ability in writing a complete composition. Likewise, a student could learn that Michigan is surrounded by the Great Lakes and then use that information when discussing the recreational facilities of Michigan. Initial learning occurs whenever students meet new material. The focus of initial instruction is on knowing or understanding. (It is important to note that this information can be drawn from either the knowledge base or the language abilities.) After initial learning occurs, the material can be used. It is important to realize that in actual situations the distinction between initial learning and use of learned material is often not as clear cut as is presented in this planning model. Initial learning is often a consolidation of years of past experiences and intuitive understandings; or it may occur bit-by-bit in several successive experiences. Likewise, as skills and knowledge are used, new learning often takes place.

Thus, the two components of subject matter, and the two levels of learning provide the basic structure for subject matter integration. The way these components and levels fit together is explored in the next section.

## The Relationship of the Components of Integration

Purposeful integration cannot occur unless the relationships among components and levels are clear. Language strategies support and assist in understanding a given subject-area knowledge base by providing channels for communicating with the knowledge base. In turn, concepts from the knowledge base are communicated through the use of language strategies. The knowledge base is useless unless it can be communicated from one individual to another, and, likewise, the strategies that are embedded in communication are useless unless there is a knowledge base to be communicated. Clearly, the curriculum of all content areas should include the integrated use of both knowledge base and language strategies.

It is equally clear that subject matter learning includes both the initial learning level and the use level. Students cannot be expected to use knowledge until they have learned it, and learned knowledge is of little value unless it is used. In fact, information that we want to be valued and remembered over a period of time must be used.

Similarly, language strategies have little value except as channels for communicating knowledge. However, if we expect students to use them these strategies must be initially learned. Some language strategies are learned in teacher-planned activities. Teachers instruct for strategies in order that students can use them to increase their knowledge base. Hence, integration also should occur to ensure that learned language strategies are used in the same way as learned knowledge is used.

Concepts from the knowledge base, language strategies, initial learning levels, and subsequent use levels can be combined to form the basis for ten types of integration. These types of integration will be explained and illustrated in the following sections.

## Types of Integration

The components of subject matter and levels of learning can be visualized in terms of a two-by-two classification system that yields four combinations as shown in Figure 1. These combinations are: the initial learning of language strategies, the use of previously learned language strategies, the initial learning of concepts from the knowledge base, and the use

Learning Levels

| | initial learning | subsequent use |
|---|---|---|
| skills | initial learning of strategies | use of previously learned strategies |
| knowledge | initial learning of knowledge | use of previously learned knowledge |

Subject Matter

Figure 1. Combinations of the components of subject matter and learning levels.

of previously learned concepts from the knowledge base. These combinations can be integrated with each other to provide ten possible types of integration.

For example, the various combinations of *initial learning of language strategies* yields the first four types of integration. The initial learning of a language strategy can be integrated: (1) with the initial learning of another language strategy; (2) with another language strategy previously learned and now being used during learning; (3) with the initial learning of concepts from the knowledge base; and (4) with previously learned concepts from the knowledge base.

If we begin with *previously learned language strategies,* this model yields three additional types of integration. The use of previously learned strategies can be integrated (5) with the use of other previously learned strategies; (6) with the initial learning of concepts from the knowledge base; and (7) with the use of previously learned concepts from the knowledge base.

Beginning with *initial learning of concepts from the knowledge base,* this plan provides two types of integration not yet discussed. Initial learning of concepts from the knowledge base can be integrated (8) with the initial learning of other concepts from the knowledge base; and (9) with the use of previously learned concepts from the knowledge base.

Beginning with *previously learned concepts from the knowledge base* provides only one additional type of integration not yet discussed. Use of previously learned concepts from the knowledge base can be integrated with other concepts from the knowledge base to provide the tenth type of integration.

## Ten Examples of the Types of Integration

Each of these ten types of integration will be described with illustrations taken from classroom observational data collected by the Language Arts Project of the Institute for Research on Teaching at Michigan State University.

1. *Initial learning of two or more integrated language strategies.* The initial learning of two or more integrated language strategies results in the learning of new strategies. In a fifth grade classroom the need arose to discuss playground rules as they related to rights and responsibilities. An individual's rights had been infringed by a group of students. The teacher felt this was mostly a management problem but recognized that the discussion opportunity provided the context for initial learning of two new language abilities. She focused on the initial learning of the strategies of active listening and the strategy of speaking with complete thoughts or sentences.

2. *Initial learning of one or more language strategies while using a previously learned language strategy.* The new strategy or strategies are learned while the previously learned strategies provide the means of learning. This type of integration was used in a fourth grade classroom where the teacher had developed a learning activity using "Dear Blabby" letters. The students wrote letters to "Dear Blabby" about a problem they had. The teacher taught them the form of a friendly letter and then instructed them to use their previously learned penmanship strategies when writing their letters.

3. *Initial learning of one or more language strategies while initially learning concepts.* The outcome of this activity is the initial learning of both new language strategies and concepts. Fourth grade students participated in a learning activity about the Mojave Indians. During the activity, they simultaneously learned new concepts about the Mojave Indians and learned a new expressive communication strategy—some Mojave dance steps to Mojave music. Strategies and concepts were integrated during initial learning phases with Mojave Indian information providing the context.

4. *Initial learning of a language strategy while using a previously learned concept.* The final outcome integrates the initial learning of a language strategy with a previously learned concept. Students in a second grade classroom decided to present science plays. Each group chose a play that continued science information they had learned previously. Each group learned how to select players and then how to give a play. Science concepts, previously learned, were used by the students as they learned new abilities of play acting.

5. *Using two or more previously learned language strategies.* The final outcome of this type of activity is the simultaneous use of two or more previously learned strategies during a lesson. Fourth grade students used both their previously learned knowledge of the form of a friendly letter with previously learned strategies of punctuation in order to answer the "Dear Blabby" letters that had been written earlier in the school week (described previously as the second type of integration). The teacher randomly passed out the "Dear Blabby" letters and students wrote an answer as "Blabby."

6. *Using a previously learned language strategy while initially learning a concept.* The final outcome is the learning of new concepts from the knowledge base while language strategies are used. An example of this type of integration occurred in a fifth grade classroom where students were learning about the Mojave Indians. After they had gathered information from maps and books, they shared

their newly learned concepts in a class discussion. The teacher asked them to use previously learned discussion strategies as they shared new information.

Another example of this type of integration occurred in a second grade classroom where the students were involved in a science lesson about fruit flies. As the students learned new concepts about the life cycle of fruit flies, the teacher directed them to use their previously learned strategy of sequencing. Again, new concepts were learned while previously learned strategies were used.

7. *Use of previously learned strategies and previously learned concepts.* The final outcome of this type of activity is the simultaneous use of both concepts and strategies. This type of integration occurred in a third grade classroom where the students were learning about man-made and naturally occurring objects. Using lists that each student had generated earlier about man-made and natural objects, the students put each concept from the two lists into a complete statement. The students were integrating previously learned concepts about man-made and natural objects with the previously learned strategy of generating complete sentences appropriate for generalizations.

8. *Initial learning of two or more concepts.* The final outcome is the initial learning of at least two sets of concepts from the knowledge base. In a second grade classroom, teachers used a cooking activity to focus the initial learning of group responsibility concepts and exact measurement concepts. Students made and baked cookies as a group, deciding on whether the measurements completed by individual students were correct. One group erred in the measurement of ingredients. The teacher helped the class understand why the exact measurements were important and how group decision making about the measurements might have prevented the error. The concepts of group responsibility and exact measurement were initially learned during the single cookie baking activity.

9. *Initial learning of a concept while using a previously learned concept.* The final outcome is the learning of the new concept while the previously learned concept provides the means of learning. In a third grade classroom, students completed a lesson on the ecology problems of Michigan while using previously learned information from science regarding the insolubility of different types of materials. New ecology concepts were learned as previously learned science concepts were used.

10. *Using two or more previously learned concepts.* The final outcome is the *use* of these concepts during the lesson. Students in a fifth

grade classroom completed a lesson using knowledge about both Mojave Indians and folktales. They had previously learned the characteristics of folktales and the characteristics of Mojave Indian life. Using these previously learned concepts, they evaluated a film to determine whether it qualified as a Mojave folktale.

**Conclusion**

Integration of subject matter can provide exciting and interesting ways to increase instructional time in the classroom. Time allocated for one learning opportunity can be doubly used when integration of subject matter is planned and implemented. Successful subject matter integration, however, requires teachers to conceptualize the two components of subject matter: the knowledge base and the language strategies and the two instructional levels: initial learning and the subsequent use of that learning level. This conceptual structure provides better ways to fit subject matter together, thereby increasing both the efficiency and the effectiveness of learning opportunities.

# 3 The Child's Search for Meaning and Language Learning

Judith I. Schwartz
Queens College, City University of New York

It was once believed that the world was a great, buzzing confusion to the infant who, helpless and weak, lay waiting to be imprinted with the indelible mark of experience. This *tabula rasa* conception of the very young human organism has been dramatically altered over the last twenty years or so, as research has found remarkable competence even in the youngest child. To cite some examples: the fetus can hear even before birth (Appleton, 1975); neonates can see quite well (Mauer and Mauer, 1976); and infants can learn to modify their responses (e.g., Gregg, et al., 1976; Dodd, 1972; Rheingold, 1956). Not only is the infant susceptible to environmental influence, it has the power to influence the environment as well (Lewis and Rosenblum, 1974).

The infant comes into the world biologically programmed to learn. Advanced sensory capabilities heighten the infant's ability not only to respond to, but to arouse the nurturing responses of caregivers. Survival of the human infant is dependent upon the care of others. The patterning back-and-forth between infant and caregiver is a mutual adaptation between the two. Each learns to recognize and understand the other's signals and sequences of specific behaviors necessary to elicit the interaction and trigger modification in the other's behavior (Schwartz, 1980b).

The infant's visual acuity, for example, is adapted to survival through social interaction. Thus, a young infant's near-point visual accommodation is at several inches distance, which is just about where older persons position themselves intuitively for face-to-face contact with the baby (Schwartz, 1980a). The infant's visual and auditory capacities are ideally suited for deciphering and responding to the highly subtle and complex system of facial and vocal cues that permeate human dialogue.

In this way human intelligence begins to act on experience and, to some degree, control it. Human intelligence imposes a grammar of sorts on experience and thus brings order to disorder and creates regularity out of chaos. The mind actively seeks consistencies and patterns from which

35

to induce generalizations: *If these things appear, then that is likely to occur.* The young child learns that by pulling on a string attached to a toy, the toy will move. Likewise, the preschooler induces the rule that *ed* affixed to verbs is a past tense marker, and proceeds to extend this rule even to those irregular verbs where it does not apply.

## Mastering Language

From earliest infancy, the child actively processes experience and imposes meaning on reality. The search for meaning is relentless, but because it is distinctly human, it occurs without duress as naturally as breathing or walking. Children learn to speak as they try to make sense of the language that surrounds them (Smith, 1979). According to Shuy (1981), children's natural language development proceeds from the deep structure level where meaning resides to the surface structure level of external representations of meaning. It is only in school that the process is reversed. The origins of communication may lie in the earliest ritualized turn-taking games such as Peek-a-Boo in which language acts as an overlay to the point-counterpoint action dialogue of the adult and child. Condon and Sander (1974) found a correspondence of 90 percent between the body movement of babies and the structure of adult speech from a frame by frame analysis of films of neonate movements made in the presence of adult speech. Bateson (1971) reported that even infants under two months engage in dialogues with their mothers that show the rudiments of conversational sequencing.

Children process the language they hear and induce from it a latent language structure (Brown and Bellugi, 1964). Toddlers, before their first birthday, produce single-word utterances called holophrases that stand for entire thoughts and are used to accompany action in order to declare, demand, question, or describe a relationship (Menyuk, 1977). Usually, by two years old, children master the propositional nature of language as they start to produce two-word utterances that express logical relationships. As Bryen (1982) observes, the amount of language learning that takes place during the preschool years is quite astonishing. By six years old, children demonstrate the basics of effective communication such as turn-taking, have a syntax that is well-formed and varied, and produce well-developed segmental phonemes and appropriate suprasegmental features such as pitch. In all these accomplishments one can see the power of intelligence at work—noting salient features, observing regularities, hypothesizing relationships, inducing rules, and drawing conclusions. The child's mind is busily exploring, testing, searching, and ordering experience.

Children come to school with what has been called an "effectance motive," the security of knowing their own competence and power to effect change in the environment. Children do not need to be taught that they can learn when they come to school. They know it, because they've *been learning* for the first five or six years of their lives. As Smith (1981) observes, children have an implicit expectation that they can learn, unless experience teaches them otherwise. The search for meaning that characterized the active problem-solving behavior of the preschooler is ready to work on mastering literacy, unless conditions impede it.

Given time, exposure, and the opportunity for active search, young children will discover word structure (Gibson and Levin, 1975). This is amply demonstrated by studies of children's invented spellings. Researchers have found that preschoolers and first graders rely heavily on their understanding of English sounds in beginning writing (Read, 1975; Beers and Henderson, 1977; Beers and Beers, 1980). They will use a letter whose name corresponds to its sound. Where the phoneme-grapheme correspondence is not as regular, the child may use a letter whose sound is closest to the one heard in the word. Read (1980) uses the example of spelling *red* as *rad.* He speculates that this pattern is based upon the child's recognition that the vowel sounds of *bait, bet,* and *bat* are similar. A study of four year olds' knowledge of letters and written words revealed a natural sequence in learning to recognize words that include understanding: that letters are discriminable patterns; that letters provide clues for reading; and that sounds in words are determined by letters (Mason, 1980). Obviously, just as the preschooler induced the latent structure of spoken language, the older child develops a systematic schema for written language from his or her many experiences with print. Imperfect at first, and marked by errors, the child's schema of written language is not random; it is characterized by coherence and internal integrity.

## Engaging the Search for Meaning in Learning Language

The search for meaning is embedded in the child's own social and intellectual development. What are the conditions that can enhance language learning through the use of this unique human trait?

1. *Caregivers and teachers need to acknowledge that the child comes to school with the mechanism for learning built-in and practiced over several years.* Children have "learned to learn" years before they enter kindergarten. While it is true that out of the mix of hereditary and environmental influences, different children come to school with greater or lesser readiness for learning, unless they have

suffered severe physical and/or emotional impairment all children
are ready to learn. This is part of their distinctly human heritage.
Two direct and practical applications of this fact are: the expectation and affirmation by school personnel that children can learn
and will learn; and the use of teaching strategies that actively engage
children in learning.

2. *The teacher or caregiver has a crucial role in facilitating the child's
   search for meaning.* Interface between the immature organism's
   attempts at learning and the mature organism's responses to these
   attempts is necessary if the child is to learn. For example, it is in the
   playful Peek-a-Boo game of infancy when the adult's face disappears
   and then reappears from behind a pillow that the groundwork is
   laid for the baby's understanding of object permanence. Likewise,
   the largely intuitive but nonetheless crucial verbal exchanges of
   toddlerhood in which the adult echoes, expands, and models language for the child provide a superlative training ground for the
   child's growing competence in language production. There is evidence from research that the presence of caring adults who speak
   with children and who listen to them, who answer their questions
   and read aloud to them, is correlated with early success in reading
   (Durkin, 1966). In school, children need teachers who organize the
   environment, plan experiences, and involve themselves with the children sensitively and responsively.

3. *The child will be helped to learn how to read and write if conditions are so arranged that they simulate the way in which the child
   acquired mastery of other skills and knowledge.* The child learned
   to understand and produce the spoken form of language by being
   immersed in a constant flow of language that was used functionally
   and naturally. The child's chances of mastering the written form of
   language will be enhanced if print is a continual presence in the
   child's life and if the consumption of printed material is a natural
   part of each day's activities. In a literate society, children actually
   are exposed to print from the time they're babies: on television
   commercials, street signs, and cereal boxes; in advertising jingles
   and logos. These are highly salient and immediate forms of written
   language, and they ought to be exploited in teaching the child about
   print. Another excellent way to inculcate the child into the process
   of reading is by reading aloud—read books *to* the child, read books
   *with* the child, and take every opportunity to make note of the
   features of print as they occur naturally in everyday happenings. In
   school, making written records for all kinds of experiences—a trip,

a recipe, an invitation, a thank-you letter, a problem in math—provides functional and meaningful opportunities to read and to write. Experiences such as these permit the child's intelligence to operate on understanding print in the same manner that it did earlier in unraveling other kinds of codes in the world.

4. *The child's search for meaning in language will be enhanced: if language is experienced as a whole entity, rather than as discrete units; if language is used functionally rather than for no real purpose; if language is meaningful rather than insignificant; and if language occurs naturally rather than artificially.* Experiences in the child's reality that yielded to the operation of intelligence, that enabled the search for meaning to work had these qualities of wholeness, functionality, meaningfulness, and naturalness. Such experiences bear the necessary consistencies and patterns from which generalizations or rules can be induced. From a study of the developmental patterns and interrelationships of preschoolers' print awareness, Hiebert (1981) concludes that the various dimensions of print awareness are integrally related, and that concentrating instruction on just one aspect such as letter naming provides an overly narrow emphasis. If reading, for example, is taught in isolation from other language functions, then the natural bridges between listening and reading and between speaking and writing cannot be drawn. If, instead, reading develops as a natural consequence out of experiences shared and discussed, written about and listened to, then the child can integrate understandings across all of the language functions. Reading, thus, does not become something to be practiced and drilled in a separate space and time. It is simply another way to extract meaning from experiences that, in this case, have been represented through written symbols.

5. *The operation of intelligence requires the opportunity to explore and experiment.* Indeed, according to Piaget (1952), the origins of intelligence lie in the sensorimotor period of cognitive development in which the child learns about reality by actively manipulating the environment and observing the effect these manipulations have. In a like manner, the child needs many opportunities to explore and experiment with print. These include prewriting and prereading experiences such as painting, crayoning, and reading a story through its pictures. Such quasi-literacy activities have a number of benefits. They permit the child to simulate and practice skills as a preparation for the actual reading and writing experiences to follow; the child role-plays in this exploratory period what she or he needs to

do later on. These experiences also help the child to grasp the concept of symbolic representation: that meaning can be encoded by graphic symbols that persist in time and space and that can be subsequently decoded back into meaning. Even after the child has begun to read and to write, the chance to experiment with printed forms, to manipulate them playfully, will continue to enhance the child's mastery of literacy. Children need the chance to make mistakes, and to review and revise their written work. In this way they can test the validity of their hypotheses about language and refine them as they become more proficient with written language.

6. *The child's search for meaning can either be enhanced or impeded depending upon the degree of discordance, novelty, and ambiguity that prevail in experiences.* For instance, an infant will recognize and even be amused by a figure of the human face in which the features are moderately discordant. If the features are highly regular or grossly discordant, the illustration may not attract the child's attention at all. Experiences with print should be sufficiently familiar to enable the child to perceive similar characteristics and patterns; these are the building blocks of the child's inductions about print. But experiences with print just as experiences of all kinds need to be sufficiently novel to interest and challenge the child and to attract attention. Literacy experiences ought to be not so easy as to bore, nor so difficult as to frustrate. Conditions that operate as baffles to the child's intelligence should be avoided. For example, the terminology of teaching reading ought to be used consistently and associated clearly with its referents. Most beginning readers don't know what a word, a letter, a sentence, or a sound are. They would be helped in their mastery of literacy by the teacher's simple, explicit, and direct use of these and like terms.

7. *The operation of intelligence is facilitated if new experiences contain enough of what is familiar to enable the child to bridge the discontinuity of what is new to what is old.* Applying this principle to reading instruction would mean that the material employed in teaching reading should be personal and familiar enough to allow the child to use mastery of the spoken form in mastering the written form. Individually dictated stories provide an ideal medium for this to occur. These stories are highly engaging because they are part of the child's unique experience. Moreover, the child's observation of the dictation—the actual translation of oral into written symbols— provides a concrete experience with the concept of the representation of orally expressed meaning by written symbols. This is a very

important concept for the mastery of literacy, and one that many, perhaps most, children are unfamiliar with, at least in the early grades. However, because there are very real differences between the spoken and the written forms of language, the child's grasp of literacy will be aided if these personal stories are supplemented by experiences with book language. Children need to hear, see, and read the language of good books. This is real language, too. It is not the stilted, artificial, and boring prose sometimes called "basalese." Only by contact with real print can children understand the peculiarities of print: from typological variations such as allographs to stylistic variations such as poetic inversions.

## Conclusion

All children come to school prepared to *make sense* of what they find there. This search for meaning can be employed in acquiring language competency by creating the conditions and providing the experiences that stimulate rather than impede the operation of intelligence. Acknowledge the vitality of children's intelligence and use it in teaching. Understand the crucial role the teacher has to play in triggering and sustaining learning cycles. Provide experiences with language that are integrated, whole, natural, functional, and meaningful. Make experiences with the written form of language an integral part of all activities. Encourage exploration and experimentation with spoken and written forms. Give children the opportunity to make mistakes and to learn from them. Provide enough of what is novel to stimulate the child's curiosity and to challenge; but enough, as well, of what is familiar so that the child can perceive relationships and experience success. These are ways in which the child's search for meaning can be put to work in mastering language.

## References

Appleton, T. "The Development of Behavioral Competence in Infancy." In *Review of Child Development Research,* vol. 4, edited by F.D. Horowitz. Chicago: University of Chicago Press, 1975.

Bateson, M. "The Interpersonal Context of Infant Vocalization." *MIT Research Laboratory of Electronics Quarterly* 100 (1971): 170–176.

Beers, J.W., and C.S. Beers. "Vowel Spelling Strategies among First and Second Graders: A Growing Awareness of Written Words." *Language Arts* 57 (1980): 166–171.

Beers, J.W., and E. Henderson. "A Study of Developing Orthographic Concepts among First Grade Children." *Research in the Teaching of English* 11 (1977): 133–148.

Brown, R., and U. Bellugi. "Three Processes in the Child's Acquisition of Syntax." In *New Directions in the Study of Language,* edited by E.H. Lenneberg. Cambridge, Mass.: MIT Press, 1964.

Bryen, D.N. *Inquiries into Child Language.* Boston: Allyn and Bacon, 1982.

Condon, W.S., and L.W. Sander. "Synchrony Demonstrated between Movement of the Neonate and Adult Speech." *Child Development* 45 (1974): 456–462.

Dodd, B.G. "Effects of Social and Vocal Stimulation on Infant Babbling." *Developmental Psychology* 7 (1972): 80–83.

Durkin, D. *Children Who Read Early.* New York: Teachers College Press, 1966.

Gibson, E., and H. Levin. *The Psychology of Reading.* Cambridge, Mass.: MIT Press, 1975.

Gregg, C.L., et al. "The Relative Efficiency of Vestibular Proprioceptive Stimulation and the Upright Position in Enhancing Visual Pursuit in Neonates." *Child Development* 47 (1976): 309–317.

Hiebert, E.H. "Developmental Patterns and Interrelationships of Preschool Children's Print Awareness." *Reading Research Quarterly* 16 (1981): 236–260.

Lewis, M., and L.A. Rosenblum, eds. *The Effect of the Infant on the Caregiver.* New York: Wiley, 1974.

Mason, J.M. "When Do Children Begin to Read: An Exploration of Four Year Old Children's Letter and Word Competencies." *Reading Research Quarterly* 15 (1980): 203–227.

Mauer, D.M., and C.E. Mauer. "Newborn Babies See Better Than You Think." *Psychology Today,* October 1976, 85–88.

Menyuk, P. "Language Development: Universal Aspects and Individual Variation." In *Language and Reading Comprehension,* edited by S.F. Winat. Arlington, Va.: Center for Applied Linguistics, 1977.

Piaget, J. *The Origins of Intelligence in Children.* New York: International Universities Press, 1952.

Read, C. *Children's Categorization of Speech Sounds in English.* Urbana, Ill.: NCTE, 1975.

Read, C. "What Children Know about Language: Three Examples." *Language Arts* 57 (1980): 144–148.

Rheingold, H.L. "The Modification of Social Responsiveness in Institutional Babies." *Monographs of the Society for Research in Child Development* 2 (1956): 1–48.

Schwartz, J.I. "Reading Readiness and the Child's Search for Meaning." *Reading Education* 5 (1980a): 50–56.

Schwartz, J.I. "Reconciling Women's Changing Status with Children's Enduring Needs." *Educational Horizons* 59 (1980b): 15–21.

Shuy, R.W. "Learning to Talk Like Teachers." *Language Arts* 58 (1981): 168–174.

Smith, F. "Demonstrations, Engagement and Sensitivity: A Revised Approach to Language Learning." *Language Arts* 58 (1981): 103–112.

Smith, F. *Reading without Nonsense.* New York: Teachers College Press, 1979.

# II  Instruction

Teaching language as a whole and integrated process within meaningful and functional contexts is not a new idea. It was expounded *at least* as early as 1908 in Edmund Burke Huey's *The Psychology and Pedagogy of Reading*. It is an idea that continues to fascinate and capture the attention not only of language researchers and educators (such as Kenneth Goodman and Frank Smith), but writers in allied fields, as well. (See, for example, Bruno Bettelheim and Karen Zelan's *On Becoming Literate: The Child's Fascination with Meaning,* Knopf, 1982). Why then, has the idea not taken hold in classrooms to any appreciable degree? Barren not productive, still rather than dynamic, particularized instead of integrated, forced and artificial in place of free and creative—this is the kind of teaching one too often sees in real classrooms. Why?

A primary difficulty with an integrated language arts program is that beyond its fundamental constructs lies the pressing question of *how do you implement this idea.* Here, one often finds only nebulous and uncertain suggestions. A major reason for this is that an integrated language arts program by its nature resists reduction to the almost ritualized and formulaic routines so neatly encapsulated in "how to" manuals and simplistic made-to-teach recipes. As the articles in section I, Foundations, attest, there is a very strong theoretical rationale for an integrative language arts approach.

In section II, Instruction, the articles are designed to "demystify" the implementation of an integrated approach by describing real programs, tested procedures, and actual language performance. The articles are grouped into the three categories of language integration emphasized throughout the book: integration within one language mode; integration among different language modes; and integration with other subject matter. Although the theme of whole language experiences embedded within meaningful contexts is consistent through all of the articles in section II, the different articles emphasize one or another of the types of integration.

## Integration within One Language Mode

Three articles illustrate how integrative procedures are employed primarily within one language mode. In the first article Eileen Tway looks at writing as a purposeful endeavor. Through the entire span of instruction K–8, the skills of writing are learned in process, as students communicate their ideas. Children's literature provides a cornerstone for the program as reading, speaking, listening, and writing abilities grow together, each enriching the other. Norman Najimy's article continues the focus on writing with his description of Authors and Illustrators, a four-week language arts project in the Pittsfield, Massachusetts, public schools. It clearly exemplifies how a program invested with real meaning and purpose can engage the interest and enthusiasm of children, staff, and parents. Finally, switching the focus to reading, Dorothy King and Dorothy Watson present a strong case for teaching reading as a whole language process in which *meaning* plays the central role.

## Integration among Different Language Modes

Integration across listening, speaking, reading, and writing is illustrated in three articles. Judith I. Schwartz' description of children's experiments with language underscores the central role of play in childhood, and discusses how play *with* language can be fostered in classrooms. Dorris Lee describes in detail how to implement a language experience model in the classroom, which has at its core integration of all the language arts. Finally, Sandra Rietz presents a rich potpourri of song and story games through which intermediate and upper elementary grade children can refine and expand their control over language patterns and forms via playful and noncoercive media.

## Integration with Other Subject Matter

Language as the integrating mechanism for learning about different curriculum areas is emphasized in four articles. Masha Rudman explains the multiplicity of uses children's literature has in broadening and deepening children's understanding of different times, places and peoples. Laura Fortson explains how the integration of the language arts with music, movement, and art experiences helps children to organize their thoughts and to express them in original, flexible, and emotionally satisfying ways. She cites many examples in which such experiences are used as the material for language arts activities. Gayle Rogers shows how all of the curriculum areas are employed purposefully by a class of sixth graders in their study of Native Americans. The expressive and receptive forms of language operate as unifying elements throughout the unit. Betty Jane Wagner's account of a creative dramatic experience shared with nine- and ten-year-olds forcefully illustrates the way in which drama can expand children's thinking and language beyond the immediate circle of their own lives.

# Part One: Integration within One Language Mode

# 4 The Development of Writing in a Language Arts Context

Eileen Tway
Miami University

The development of writing follows the development of speech more closely than many educators have realized. The language arts are usually listed as listening, speaking, reading, and writing, as though there is a chronological order of development. Yet, while the oral language is primary and the written language reflects the oral, in actuality the written language emerges almost as soon as the oral—if the conditions are right. When children are surrounded by a print environment, they begin to relate to graphemes almost as soon as they begin to relate to the phonemes they are hearing all around them.

In fact, one parent recently observed her ten-week-old son, Jed, scanning printed matter in a newspaper and decided to record continued observations of the baby's emerging experiences with print (Lass, 1982). At sixteen months, Jed was scribbling with his finger. At seventeen months, he recognized eight letters, identifying all such letters as B or D. At eighteen months, he recognized twenty letters as letters and could identify the names of fourteen of them. At twenty months, he could spell his name. His mother said, "When at seventeen months he began to point to and call any letter 'B' or 'D', I realized he knew letters were a separate category of visual stimulus" (p. 24).

Although Jed's experiences are not generalizable, current research shows that children go through several developmental stages in writing during the preschool years (Clay, 1979; Temple, 1982; Ferreiro, 1980). When linguists stress that teachers are not the first teachers of language, that children bring a well-developed language to school, it is generally assumed that they are referring to *talking*, not writing. And, for the most part, linguists have been doing just that: focusing on oral language. However, research shows that five- and six-year-olds have acquired substantial knowledge about written language, too (Lavine, 1972; Read, 1971; Chomsky, 1971).

Elementary teachers, then, have a foundation with which to begin the teaching of writing in school. This means that there is no need to wait to start written language experience, but it also means that there is continued need for oral language experiences so that the total language development is ensured. Written language will be sparse if the oral language is neglected, but as the written language expands, the oral language will, in turn, be enriched. The speaking and writing arts are mutually enhanced by this intertwining. Such intertwining will be discussed at greater length later in this article.

If teachers are to understand the development of writing in the school-age child, they need to understand the development that takes place prior to school. The first part of this article will be devoted to early writing in a total language context. Next there will be a discussion of how teachers can foster writing development as part of the language arts program in the primary grades. Finally, there will be a consideration of writing and the other language arts in the upper elementary grades. The important place of literature in encouraging writing development will be a common thread, or unifying element, throughout the article.

## Writing and the Language Arts—Preschool

It appears that writing develops naturally along with the development of the other language arts. Just as children participate in the world of oral language with early attempts such as babbling and single word utterances, they also begin to notice writing and move from random scribbles to directional scribbles, and from unletter-like squiggles to observable separate configurations that resemble letters and that become recurring figures. From this beginning, they discover how to make letters, usually first trying the letters of their name or copying a word from some noticeable place, such as a cereal box. As they progress, children discover that letters stand for sounds, and they will then use invented spellings to write on their own, if not discouraged by unrealistic (for them) adult standards.

Some adults are concerned by invented spellings, believing that they will cause children to acquire poor spelling habits. However, if the invented spelling stage is seen as part of the natural language development process, adults will come to understand its importance in the child's overall language development. Temple, Nathan, and Burris (1982) say that "Children will learn to spell correctly and to write fluently if they are encouraged—but not forced—to express themselves in writing as soon as they feel the urge, and as best they can" (p. 82). The baby who says "mulk" for milk is not reprimanded or discouraged. No one says, "Do not talk yet. You are not ready. Wait until you can say it correctly." Rather, adults are very positive in their encouragement of such early attempts to talk. A parent will say, "Oh, you want some milk," giving the correct pronunciation naturally in the way described by Brown and Bellugi (1966) as "imitation and expansion." The adult provides the model, but not in such a way as to make the child feel "put down" or inferior. In fact, it is quite the opposite; the child is made to feel that such attempted words are real accomplishments.

In the same way, if early writings are given respect and encouragement, the child comes to attach importance to writing. Early writing attempts seem to emerge as satisfying creative acts, but as children come to associate meanings with their creations, they begin to learn more about the use of graphics as meaning-bearing symbols. The oral language environment plays an important part as children begin to associate letter symbols with sounds. They write what they hear; thus comes invented spellings.

Temple, Nathan, and Burris (1982) say that there are two steps in the invented spelling stage: Letter-name Spelling and Transitional Spelling. In the first step, every letter used stands for a sound, and no letters are supplied unnecessarily. However, not all sounds in the message are conveyed by the graphics. Indeed, sometimes only the initial consonant is used to stand for a word. Later, considerably more speech sounds are represented in the invented spellings. This is the transitional stage between early invented spelling and more conventional spelling.

The invented spelling stage may span quite a large portion of the preschool years. Jenny, at slightly over two-and-one-half, knew something about letters and how they were used and for a time chose the letter "H" to spell her name. (See Figure 1.) Jenny was in a prephonemic stage just prior to the letter-name state of invented spelling. At three, Jenny was

Figure 1. Writing sample of a child in a prephonemic stage, prior to the letter-name state of spelling.

closer to a conventional match of letters and sounds and began to try the letters of her name. Brian, at five, was in the transitional state, and very close to conventional spellings, when he wrote the following: "Dear Mom: I am over at Joshis Love fom Brian." (See Figure 2.) Brian's handling of "Josh's" is admirable for one so young; yet he simply wrote what he heard.

By the time most children come to school they have had enough experience with oral language to be capable of writing on their own, using invented spellings. However, they may not know how to make all of the letters yet, and their physical coordination is such that extended writing will usually be difficult, if not impossible. Still, if a child can put two or more related sentences together, that child is achieving written composition. The teacher can help the child supplement and complement written work through providing opportunities for oral composition, for dictation of stories, and for drawing or painting.

The implications for teachers in all of this are great. Teachers are not the first teachers of writing, after all. And children are ready to write from their earliest school days. Yet parallels should be drawn from the conditions and characteristics of early language learning, so that educators do not try to force development nor otherwise act in ways that discourage fledgling attempts. Carl A. Lefevre (1970) gives a "capsule statement of

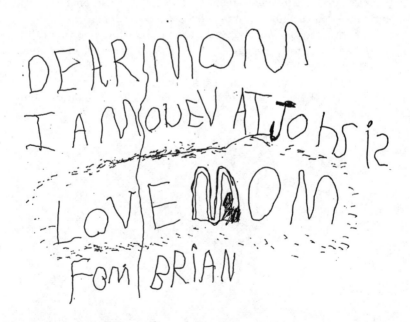

Figure 2. Writing sample from a five-year-old in the transitional state of spelling.

methodology" for teachers when he advises, "The student's language learning in school should parallel his early childhood method of learning to speak his native tongue—playfully, through delighted experiences of *discovery*—through repeated *exposure* to language forms and patterns, by creative *imitation* and *manipulation,* and by personal trial and error, with kindly (and not too much) correction from adults" (p. 75).

A good way for adults to provide experiences for *exposure, discovery, imitation,* and *manipulation* is to read to children from the delightful children's books available today for the very young. Reading aloud to children has been shown to expand language skills significantly, especially when children are encouraged in active response to the literature they hear—through drama, role playing, discussion, and other oral language activities. In addition, greater gains in language development are evident among the younger children, suggesting that the earlier the start to reading aloud, the better (Cohen, 1968; Cullinan, et al., 1974).

Suggested books to read to preschoolers and kindergarteners are as follows:

Flack, Marjorie. *Ask Mr. Bear.* Macmillan, 1932.

Encourage children to talk about birthdays.

Freeman, Don. *Corduroy.* Viking, 1968.

This one can stimulate talk about favorite stuffed animals.

Galdone, Paul. *The Gingerbread Boy.* Seabury, 1975.

Share the old, traditional tales. Encourage children to join in on the refrains.

Galdone, Paul. *The Three Bears.* Seabury, 1972.

Children can retell the familiar story. They can also compare and contrast it with the wordless book, *Deep in the Forest* by Brinton Turkle.

Graham, John. *I Love You, Mouse.* Harcourt Brace Jovanovich, 1976.

This is a good "if I were" story about a little boy saying what he would do if he were each little animal he sees. Another book to encourage "if I were" or "I wish I were" stories is *If I Were A Toad* by Diane Paterson. After enjoying "if I were" stories, it is good to come to a book like *Just Me* by Marie Hall Ets, where the little boy who imitates several different animals finally decides that being himself is best.

Keats, Ezra Jack. *A Letter To Amy.* Harper and Row, 1968.

This can stimulate family letter writing activities.

Swados, Elizabeth. *Lullaby.* Harper and Row, 1980.

Enjoy the rhythmic language.

Wildsmith, Brian. *Brian Wildsmith's Mother Goose.* Franklin Watts, 1964.

Share the rhythm and rhymes of some old favorites and some lesser known nursery rhymes.

Teachers can encourage parents to provide the kind of home environment and experiences that foster natural language development. Parents and teachers can be partners in the teaching-learning endeavor, neither replacing the other's work, but each complementing the efforts of the other. Teachers can work with parents through conferences, newsletters, and parent-teacher-association programs. By encouraging parents to provide a print environment for their younger children as well as their school-age children, teachers will ensure that more and more children have a strong language background when they come to school.

Here is a checklist of "Things to Do" that can be shared with parents:

Provide print environment

Be a model: show children that you enjoy reading and writing

Read to children (very early on)

Use lap technique: hold child while reading, give loving attention and encourage response

Capitalize on real needs for ongoing communication:

Encourage scrawls and scribbling

Print signs like "My Toy Box" and label objects in home

Ask child to dictate a title or caption to you to place under a picture he or she draws

Write bulletin board or refrigerator notes to each other

Encourage letter writing; this can be rewarding

Encourage retelling of stories heard

Keep records on trips, short or long

If parents and teachers capitalize on real reasons to write, writing will develop naturally along with the other language arts. As Lefevre and other linguists stress, there is need for positive support and encouragement; respect for mistakes as signs that children are reaching out for new things to try shows awareness of part of the developmental process.

## Writing and the Language Arts—Primary

Writing in the primary grades is important in its own right as a means of communication, record-keeping, self-expression, and learning through the organization of thoughts on paper. Writing is also being acclaimed by researchers (see especially Chomsky, 1971) as an important route to reading proficiency. Chomsky noted that some children show spontaneous interest in creating words well before they can read, and suggested that children ought to learn how to read by creating their own spellings for familiar words as a beginning. Yet the writing act, important as it is as an art, as a means of communication, and as a route to understanding other people's writing, cannot be completely understood apart from the larger context of all the language arts.

Learning to write not only parallels the process of learning to talk; it is largely dependent on oral language development. As discussed earlier in this chapter, children write what they hear in the language environment around them. Their written vocabulary develops out of the oral vocabulary, the words for which they have acquired meaning. For this reason, it is imperative to maintain a strong oral language program in the elementary school so that children can continue to develop their facility with oral language as the foundation for written language development. The classroom where textbooks and workbooks are the sole materials and only written language is stressed is likely to be barren and unproductive. On the other hand, a classroom rich in language experiences, such as storytelling, drama, discussion, interviewing, group planning, readers theatre, and word play, provides the kind of environment necessary for continued language development, including written language development. It is as Templeton says: Knowledge of word structure is not learned by planned, imposed exercises; rather it is built, modified, and accomodated through the assimilation of many experiences (1980).

One of the best ways to extend children's experiences with words is through reading aloud to them from the best that children's literature has to offer. When children are read to, they are experiencing someone's creative writing; they are gaining a sense of the structure of the different kinds of writing they hear; they are hearing the different ways in which a writer uses words to create an effect; they are hearing the beauty of language at its best in the best of literature; in short, they are learning about writing from excellent models. In turn, as they learn to read, they will want to read some of the favorite books for themselves and they will be primed to read more books, to continue experiencing written language as part of the rich world of language to which they have been introduced.

*Suggested Books for Reading Aloud in the Primary Grades.*

Briggs, Raymond. *Jim and the Beanstalk*. Coward, 1970.

A modern version of *Jack and the Beanstalk* in which the giant is older and more mellow. Comparison and contrast of the two tales are natural.

Duvoisin, Roger. *Petunia*. Knopf, 1950.

A silly goose doesn't understand that having a book does not mean having wisdom until you can really read it. Children will see through Petunia's pretensions and the way they lead to disaster. Other Petunia books are also worthwhile. See *Petunia's Treasure* (Knopf, 1975). It can lead to thinking and discussion of what treasure is most worth having.

Lionni, Leo. *Frederick*. Pantheon, 1973.

One mouse is different from the others. While others gather food for winter, Frederick sits, gathering the sun's rays, he says. When winter comes and the food is eaten, Frederick warms them all with his colorful stories. A good discussion can ensue about different kinds of contributions.

Raskin, Ellen. *Nothing Ever Happens on My Block*. Atheneum, 1966.

Points up the need to be more observant; can be compared to the old favorite, Dr. Seuss' *And to Think That I Saw It on Mulberry Street*.

Sendak, Maurice. *Higglety Pigglety Pop! Or There Must Be More to Life*. Harper and Row, 1979.

Leads to discussion of worthwhile things to do with one's life.

Williams, Barbara. *If He's My Brother*. Harvey House, 1976.

Provides springboard for discussion of what constitutes a reasonable privilege. For example: "If he's my brother, why can't I punch him?"

Zemach, Harve. *Duffy and the Devil*. Farrar, 1973.

The story is reminiscent of *Rumpelstiltskin* and invites comparison.

Zolotow, Charlotte. *Someday*. Harper and Row, 1964.

Stimulates talk about wishes and hopes.

The oral responding, discussion, and even dramatizing that accompany reading aloud to children in the primary grades provide a background of experience with other people's writing—experience that is acted upon and internalized—which makes an excellent springboard to children's own writing. As children grow in writing ability and understanding, they may try to write their own versions of old tales, or to write their wishes and hopes after discussing them. They may write about their own families or about what they observe in their own block or on the way to school. The stories they have heard provide the models and stimulating ideas.

As children write, there is need for positive support and encouragement, just as there was when they learned to talk. "Publishing" children's writing for a larger audience than the teacher (with their permission) will give dignity to their efforts. One way to publish children's writing is to put it into book form. For very young children, collections of their pictures with captions can be put together into a class anthology. Short compositions by individual children can be put into a book with only one line and a picture on each page. Older primary children can make more "ambitious" booklets with more text to a page than captions or one-liners.

*Suggested Books to Use to Encourage Children's Own Books*

Have several books about families available for children to read.

Buckley, Helen E. *Grandfather and I*. Lothrop, 1959.

Buckley, Helen E. *Grandmother and I*. Lothrop, 1961.

Greenfield, Eloise. *First Pink Light*. T.Y. Crowell, 1976.

Berger, Terry. *Big Sister, Little Brother*. Raintree, 1975.

Clifton, Lucille. *My Brother Fine with Me*. Holt, Rinehart, and Winston, 1975.

After hearing or reading several of these books, children can make their own personal family books.

Make a display of books about dreams to invite children's reading.

Baker, Alan. *Benjamin's Dreadful Dream*. J.B. Lippincott, 1980.

Keats, Ezra Jack. *Dreams*. Macmillan, 1974.

Rukeyser, Muriel. *More Night*. Harper and Row, 1981.

Children can make a fantastic story of a dream into a book.

Read myths or "why" stories to children.

Kipling, Rudyard. "Just So Stories" from *Rudyard Kipling's Verse: Definitive Edition*. Doubleday, 1940.

Children can write their own "why" stories.

Many more suggestions, in fact, a whole book full of them, can be found in John Stewig's *Read to Write* (1980). Children's own books can be as simple or as elaborate as the inclination and ability of the author dictate. Such books do not *have* to be elaborate. Simple construction paper or decorated cardboard covers can serve and the book can be bound within the covers by staples or yarn.

It is important, as in all language learning, to have real reasons for writing in the primary grades. Suggestions for teachers, which parallel the suggestions for parents given in the preschool discussion earlier in this chapter, are given below.

*A Checklist of "Things to Do" in the Primary Grades*

> Provide print environment: surround children with books, signs, labels, etc.
>
> Be a model: show children that you enjoy reading and writing
>
> Read to children (They will pick up old favorites to read for themselves later on)
>
> Encourage children to retell stories they have read or heard
>
> Capitalize on real needs for ongoing communication:
>
>> Let children write about families, pets, familiar things
>>
>> Write messages to each other
>>
>> Encourage reports that are current and interesting
>>
>> Write announcements of school events, for bulletin boards, parents, etc.
>>
>> Write about holidays
>>
>> Write real letters
>
> Let children provide storyline for wordless books
>
> Let children predict ending or provide different ending for stories in text or library books
>
> Keep records of events (field trips, pet care, daily schedule, etc.)
>
> Have a Writing Corner with all kinds of materials and a shoebox full of ideas for writing

Writing can help children find their way into learning. It helps children understand more about other people's written work; it gives a firsthand experience with what happens in literature. Writing can be like a conversation with yourself or with others, but with more time to be thoughtful and deliberate than in oral conversations. Beyond the language arts, writing is part of the overall curriculum. For example, writing is important in social studies as children write essays or reports or you-are-there stories about people, places, and events, past and present; it is important in science as children write records of experiments and learn to be better observers.

Finally, writing helps us continue to play with language, as Lefevre suggests students ought to do as part of language learning in school. Children will best learn the conventions for writing through exploration, through all kinds of experiences with writing, where they bump into communication needs for correct spelling, legible handwriting, appropriate form, and so on. And by the intermediate grades, some children will even be playing with the conventions themselves, as Molly, age 10, did in her story, "The End."

The End

Once there was a little girl. Her name was The End. Everybody teased her. They might say, "Once upon a time, the end." The End wished and wished and wished that she had a different name. Then she was pulled forward by a force.

She started going around and around! She was falling, falling, falling. She was falling off the world.

Then she landed on Venus. There were some robots and they said, "We brong you here. We heard you. We will make your wish come true. Now your name is Once upon a Time."

The End

Reprinted from Eileen Tway. "How to Find and Encourage the Nuggets in Children's Writing." *Language Arts* 57 (March 1980): 301.

## Writing and the Language Arts—Postprimary

By the postprimary years, many children have a good start in writing in various modes, for various reasons, and for different audiences. It is apparent according to research that, in general, children of this age have passed through a sequence of broad stages of written language development:

1. scribbling
2. a few letters, words, and garbles (letters and configurations that do not make sense to the reader)
3. a sentence or sentences (not related)
4. two or more sentences that go together in a connected composition

For a more detailed discussion of the stages from beginning writing through the transition to composition, see McDonell and Osburn (1980). The postprimary years are a time for all kinds of composing, both fiction and nonfiction. Once again, though, the conditions must be right. There must be time and opportunity and reason to write.

Recently a math professor visited a public elementary school and, while he saw evidence of math work around the fifth grade classroom he was visiting, he saw no compositions displayed. Believing in the importance of writing as a way of learning, he asked the teacher about the children's writing, thinking that maybe it was filed and the teacher was taking turns displaying work from different areas.

"Oh," said the teacher. "The children can't write. They can't even make sentences. We don't do writing."

The math teacher was as upset as he would have been had he been an English teacher (which unfortunately the fifth grade teacher did not consider herself to be). "If the children do not write," he asked, "how are they going to learn."

It is true that sometimes children come as far as the intermediate grades without much experience in writing. Homes may not have provided such experience and teachers may have been overwhelmed at the children's lack of readiness and failed to start the children with writing experiences at whatever stage they found them. However, with all of the research evidence on developmental stages of writing, it is clear that no matter what the grade level, teachers should let children become involved with real writing at whatever level of competence, and not wait until such time as the teacher feels that children have mastered all the separate skills needed for writing. Only in this way can students make progress, through learning skills in actual writing. The language arts are learned in context, and writing is no exception.

For a "whole" or total language program, where writing is learned in context, oral language experiences need to be continued in the intermediate grades. It is not only all right to read aloud to older children (and to encourage oral response), for example; it is wise to do so, for listening to literature exposes children to language at its best—for modeling, for vocabulary enrichment, for understanding, and so on.

Examples of books to use in encouraging creative and critical perceiving, listening, speaking, writing, and reading in the postprimary grades are as follows:

Arkin, Alan. *The Lemming Condition.* Harper and Row, 1976.
About conformity and the urgent need to rise above it with individual thinking.

Babbitt, Natalie. *Tuck Everlasting.* Farrar, Strauss, 1975.
Deals with problems inherent in the possibilities of life without end. The Tucks have found a spring that gives them everlasting

life on earth, but they also discover the problems of such a life and try to spare the rest of the world. Then a young girl discovers their secret. Considering what she should do about it makes excellent fare for critical thinking; can lead to discussion or writing.

Cooper, Susan. *The Dark Is Rising.* Atheneum, 1973.

A boy with strange powers, able to move in and out of time, sometimes faces the problem of being out of step with time. (Can be compared to *Tuck Everlasting* in this respect.) This book concerns itself with the struggle between good and evil, and can be compared to other such books; for example, Madeleine L'Engle's *Wrinkle in Time.*

Kesteven, G.R. *The Awakening Water.* Hastings, 1979.

[for Grade 6 and up] Set in the future, 1997, this story of life under totalitarianism will help readers picture the extremes of loss of freedom. They will relate to the main character's search for a better way of life. It is another book to kindle discussion of what is most worthwhile in life.

Lewis, C. S. *The Lion, the Witch, and the Wardrobe.* Macmillan, 1950.

This fantasy can lead to speculation as to "worlds as they should be." Children discover loyalty, courage, and faith in the power of "goodness" in the land of Narnia. Students might write their own fantasies of "Other Worlds."

O'Brien, Robert. *Mrs. Frisby and the Rats of NIMH.* Atheneum, 1971.

Rats are given injections that make them extraordinarily intelligent. They learn to read and plan to establish a self-sufficient community. Fascinating issues are raised, with many possibilities for discussion.

Paterson, Katherine. *Bridge to Terabithia.* Crowell, 1977.

A beautiful friendship survives the death of a child, as that child's influence lives on in her friend. A class could discuss Leslie's influence on Jesse and the importance of their imaginary kingdom, Terabithia.

Slote, Alfred. *Tony and Me.* Lippincott, 1974.

Raises questions over different value systems. Can be compared to *When the Sad One Comes to Stay* by Florence Parry Heide. Questions may, in turn, give rise to critical reviews or to personal essays.

Sperry, Armstrong. *Call It Courage.* Macmillan, 1971.

A boy's courage in the face of being different is not only inspirational; it leads to all kinds of considerations of what courage really is. The story has legend-like qualities and could be compared to other legends. Students may try creating and writing their own legends.

Steig, William. *Abel's Island.* Farrar, 1976.

A personified mouse survives for a year on an island after being swept there in a storm, and, in the course of the year, learns a lot about himself. He discovers more substance than he knew he had. Children can be encouraged to think about strengths in their own lives. Of course, children may also compare the story to other "Survival" stories and may want to try writing their own survival-adventure stories.

White, E. B. *Charlotte's Web.* Harper and Row, 1952.

This all-time favorite about a friendship between a pig and a spider can be read on different levels of appreciation: friendship, life cycles, society's values.

White, E. B. *Stuart Little.* Harper and Row, 1945.

A mouse-like child makes friends with a bird; the friends separate; and at the end of the book, Stuart, the Mouse-fellow, starts on a journey to find his friend. Children can discuss what will probably happen. The ending can be compared and contrasted to White's epilogue ending for *Charlotte's Web.* Some students may wish to write a satisfying ending for Stuart Little's search.

Williams, Margery. *The Velveteen Rabbit.* Avon, 1975.

A story, beautifully told, through childhood toys, about what it means to be "real" in this world. In addition to enjoying the beautiful language and thoughts, children may want to try different points of view for the tales they want to tell.

With literature at the core or center of the language program, children's oral and written language will flourish. Firsthand experiences such as field trips, visits with interesting people, examinations of curios and other artifacts, science experiments, etc., will always be important stimuli to languaging, but time limits these firsthand experiences and literature should be *there* in the classroom to extend experience.

Experience with nonfiction is also important, if children are to have models for writing in different modes. Some examples of nonfiction titles that exemplify good writing are listed below:

Fritz, Jean. *What's the Big Idea, Ben Franklin?* Coward, McCann, and Geoghegan, 1976.

Katz, William Loren. *Black People Who Made the Old West.* Thomas Y. Crowell, 1977.

Simon, Seymour. *The Long View into Space.* Crown, 1979.

Steele, William O. *Talking Bones: Secrets of Indian Burial Mounds.* Harper and Row, 1978.

Watson, Jane Werner. *Living Together in Tomorrow's World.* Vineyard Books, 1976.

Although writing will continue to develop naturally in a total language context, teachers need to make some provisions for this development. Teachers need to provide the following conditions:

Prewriting experiences in the classroom with opportunities for brainstorming, for idea gathering, for testing out and organizing ideas

Time and opportunity to write

Teacher and peer response to what is being written

Guidance in revising and proofreading

Opportunities for "publishing" writing for a larger audience than the teacher or classmates

An example of merging these provisions for writing with the overall language program can be shown, using a Writing/Language Project on "Utopia." To begin the project, a teacher reads from books of fantasy or science fiction; such as, *The Lion, the Witch, and the Wardrobe,* or Alexander Key's *The Forgotten Door,* and encourages students to read other similar books. The teacher and students discuss worlds as they should be, or as they would like them to be. The class brainstorms about what "Utopia" would be like. Students select ideas to develop and create their own Utopias. They write the story of their place, and, from there, can go in many possible directions. As teacher and peers respond to what is being discussed and written, many possibilities present themselves. These may be in the form of suggestions or implications for role playing, for predicting the future, for planning for a better future, for getting into problem solving of current world concerns, etc. Some students may write the history of their "world"; others may create a body of literature for their place such as, poetry or legends; still others may create a make-believe newspaper of current happenings in their world. As the Utopias develop, there is opportunity for shaping, revising, and proofreading the final products. The stories may be put in book form for further sharing,

or they may be bound together in a class anthology of "Other Worlds."
See Murphy (1974) for further information on helping students create
imaginary worlds.

In the story excerpt below, Betsy, grade six, has chosen to write an
animal fantasy. She begins her story with an introduction to situation
and place. Her reference to an "unknown place" is a good beginning for
an other-world story.

### Spaz Mouse

Hi, my name is Spaz Mouse. And I am going to tell you the
story of my life. I hope you enjoy it.

I came into this world as a small, gray ball of fluff with no wits
at all. I couldn't move and I didn't have eyes, a nose, or whiskers. I
spent all day riding up and down on conveyer belts. I was only five
inches long and ready for a growth spurt.

And then one day it happened! I started to grow. I grew ears and
eyes and everything all mice should have, even whiskers! But I did
grow one thing that was alien to me. I grew a small, white key
behind my left ear. Finally, I found out what this key was for.

When I was full grown one day the belts stopped. I got very
scared. I saw all my friends being lifted off by a huge giant, having
their keys turned, and losing all control of their muscles, then
coming to a dead stop.

Then it was my turn. I was scared stiff. After it was all over, I
got put in a dark box and got shipped to an unknown place.

Betsy is composing, working her way into a story, in this first draft.
Betsy alternates her fantasy writing with realistic fiction about children her
own age and their problems. Children in the postprimary years of elementary school are ready for all kinds of composing, for different purposes and
different audiences. Children who have been immersed in a print environment through the preschool and primary years are ready for a growth
spurt (like Spaz Mouse) and all kinds of as yet unknown adventures with
writing. It is an exciting world for teachers and students, a world of
intense, enjoyable perceiving, listening, speaking, reading, and *writing*.

### References

Brown, Roger, and Ursula Bellugi. "Three Processes in the Child's Acquisition
    of Syntax." In *Language and Learning,* edited by Janet Emig. New York:
    Harcourt, Brace, and World, 1966.
Chomsky, Carol. "Write Now, Read Later." *Childhood Education* 47 (March
    1971): 296–299.
Clay, Marie M. *What Did I Write?* Exeter, N.H.: Heinemann, 1975, 1979.

Cohen, Dorothy. "The Effect of Literature on Vocabulary and Reading Achievement." *Elementary English* 45 (February 1968): 209–213, 217.

Cullinan, Bernice E., Angela Jaggar, and Dorothy Strickland. "Language Expansion for Black Children in the Primary Grades: A Research Report." *Young Children* 29 (January 1974): 98–112.

Ferreiro, Emilia. "The Relationship between Oral and Written Language: The Children's Viewpoints." In *Oral and Written Language Development Research: Impact on the Schools,* edited by Yetta M. Goodman, Myna M. Haussler, and Dorothy S. Strickland. Urbana, Ill.: NCTE with International Reading Association, 1980.

Lass, Bonnie. "Portrait of My Son as an Early Reader." *The Reading Teacher* 36 (October 1982): 20–28.

Lavine, Linda. *The Development of Perception of Writing in Pre-Reading Children: A Cross-Cultural Study.* Ph.D. diss., Cornell University, 1972. Xerox University Microfilms, 73–6657.

Lefevre, Carl A. *Linguistics, English, and the Language Arts.* Boston: Allyn and Bacon, 1970.

McDonell, Gloria M., and E. Bess Osburn. "Beginning Writing: Watching It Develop." *Language Arts* 57 (March 1980): 310–314.

Murphy, Richard. *Imaginary Worlds.* New York: Teachers and Writers Collaborative, 1974.

Read, Charles. "Pre-School Children's Knowledge of English Phonology." *Harvard Educational Review* 41 (February 1971): 1–34.

Stewig, John. *Read to Write.* 2nd edition. New York: Holt, Rinehart and Winston, 1980.

Temple, Charles A., Ruth G. Nathan, and Nancy A. Burris. *The Beginnings of Writing.* Boston: Allyn and Bacon, 1982.

Templeton, Shane. "Young Children Invent Words: Developing Concepts of 'Word-ness.'" *The Reading Teacher* 33 (January 1980): 454–459.

# 5 Children Writing Books for Children

Norman C. Najimy
Pittsfield Public Schools, Massachusetts

"I liked what I was doing, so I didn't want to quit!" declared Danny B., a fourth grader at Pomeroy School in Pittsfield. Danny was talking to parents who came to school to meet young authors and illustrators. For four weeks Danny had stuck to the task he had undertaken; for four weeks he wrote and rewrote, tossed papers in the wastebasket, started over, sketching layout plans, consulting a dictionary, checking his progress with his teacher, and finally completing what he said was the most important thing he had ever done in school: create his own, original, finished book.

For Danny such stick-to-itiveness was cause for celebration. He had been medically diagnosed as hyperkinetic, incapable of settling down, unable to give his attention to any task for more than a few minutes. Yet on some days Danny did not want to stop working on his book. Now he was describing his experience to people who had come to read the books and talk with the young writers.

The project that so engaged Danny and hundreds of other children in Pittsfield's schools is called Authors and Illustrators: Children Writing Books for Children. For four or more weeks these children learn by doing in a project that brings the arts and skills of language together as an organically functioning unit. They read. They discuss. They invent, write, and rewrite. They consult dictionaries and thesauri. They design and create. They evaluate their own work and their peers'. They practice dramatic reading of their own creations, offering constructive criticism to one another to improve their oral reading. Finally, they share their books with receptive audiences: children in other classes, parents who come to open house to meet the authors and illustrators, and visitors to the school library.

The project does not just happen. It is the result of careful planning and constant alertness by teachers convinced that language is a total experience—not a series of isolated and unrelated exercises done on a handout or workbook page. It is carried on in blocks of time usually allotted to language and spelling and sometimes to reading; the enthusiasm of children involved in the project may also force spilling over into social studies or art or math. It is more than a language project, for it involves design, measurement, peer sharing, and problem solving. Nearly every teacher who has chosen to undertake Authors and Illustrators has reported that even those children who groan when they are asked to open their language texts groan when they are told they must stop working on their books for the day.

## Getting the Project Underway

On day one of the project, scores of children's books—story books, biographies, how-to books, travelogues, etc.—are displayed about the room: on desks, on the window sills, on counter tops, on the chalk ledge. Children browse, then choose two or three books to take to their desks. The teacher initiates discussion with questions like these: Why do you like one of the books you chose? What are these books about? How are the books different from one another? How do you suppose the writers got ideas for their books? As the discussion continues, the teacher jots children's responses on the chalkboard.

The children talk about the subjects of books. "This one is about training wild animals." "Mine's about the sun and some legends about it." "I've got the life of Jackie Robinson." "Here's one about people on another planet." "Look at this one; it tells about different kinds of trees." They see that the subjects of books encompass the whole world.

They talk about formats. "There's a lot of white space." "The pictures in this one are like cartoons." "My book looks like paintings and it's got a gold seal that says Cal-Cald—." "Look at how the words in this one are printed; they look like what they mean." "The printing in this one goes right over some of the pictures." "The book I got is shaped like a whale."

The exploration and talk of books leads to the realization that creating a book requires imagination. It also leads to the possibility that we can be book creators, also. Children respond enthusiastically to the idea. Jan Baran, sixth grade teacher at Morningside Community School, tells of a reticent boy who rarely did any more than was demanded of him: but he retired each day, at his own insistence, for more than an hour on some days, to the broom closet so that he could work on his book. The teacher insisted only that he keep the door open so that he would have fresh air. The result was a book worth showing off and a boy more proud of this product than any he had ever accomplished.

While the enthusiasm is at a peak, children jot down the possible plots, places, or people that their own books could be about. Their themes are as varied as their interests. Al wants to write about two frogmen who save a city from being eaten by a sea monster. Carrie wants to write about animals that are made human by a mad scientist. Jenny plans a story about her pocket calculator (a story based on a real and sad experience). Sam wants to tell about bicycles and Bret has a fish tale to tell. Claire, a bright child, daydreamed and scribbled for nearly all of two sessions before she conceived an idea; her book may be published.

## Ideas into Writing

The ideas incubate until the the next day. Yellow paper (or some type other than the white composition paper that suggests a finished product) is provided. This is for the "sloppy copy"—that phase of writing during which, as the children will say, "We don't have to worry about spelling. We can make mistakes until we get our ideas straight." Children are allowed freedom to play with language, to insert details or change a phrase, to write in the margin or cross out several words or sentences. The sloppy copy stage, which for some children may continue for three sessions or longer, is vital to the success of the project. For the student it is seed-germinating time; for the teacher it is cultivating time.

The laboratory setting for this writing requires that more than one person be available to help the children. In anticipation of the Authors and Illustrators project, parent volunteers or students from a nearby college are recruited to help. The philosophy and process are described to these aides, whose tasks may include giving encouragement to an individual child, playing the role of an audience and asking questions that may lead the writer to providing more specific detail, and alerting the teacher that some child may need special assistance. The teacher is the main resource person, probing to bring forth ideas from the child who says, "I'm stuck," or unobtrusively diagnosing skills needs.

Diagnosis leads to specific, short skills lessons taught at appropriate times. For example, a lesson in sensory language may be taught just before the children begin a "new view" session—that stage of rewriting when the children try to look at their own writing as if they were audience, not writers. Immediately after the lesson children revise some of their verb or noun choices, perhaps checking the junior thesaurus. During the "proofed paper" stage—when children must be concerned about mechanics and spelling—the teacher may teach a lesson in punctuating dialogue, because many young authors are using dialogue in their stories. Instead of assigning a drill sheet, the teacher has the children choose a passage of dialogue from their own writing and, on a practice sheet of paper, punctuate it correctly. Both the teacher and the aide will check each child's skill and lend individual assistance where necessary.

Individual is the keyword for spelling in this project. As they circulate among the writers, the teacher and the aide begin individual spelling lists for each child; each list is composed of words that the child needs. This approach encourages children to try words that they can say or have heard but cannot spell. There is no penalty for misspelling—only assistance to correct the spelling. Like the sloppy copy and the new view, the spelling list goes into the Authors and Illustrators folder which each child keeps through the entire process.

Before creating the actual book, children must write a "presentable product" so that they will have a finished effort to translate into book form. Resistance to this rewriting is minimal, perhaps because children, knowing that their books will be presented to public audiences, want to ensure against botching up the last phase. Many teachers show students photos of manuscripts of authors whom the children know. Some teachers show the students the teachers' own rewrites. This pursuit of quality, declared one parent of a child who was usually content with his first effort, seemed to have a transfer effect upon that child: Peter was, according to his mother, awakened to the realization that it takes work and rework to produce something good, and Peter applied this effort to other work after he had completed his book.

## Designing the Book

Planning the format of the book is a problem-solving process. The teacher introduces the names of concepts the children have already developed through the book-browsing phase of the project. These terms include *title page, copyright sign, publisher, bleed* (picture going off the edge of a page), *graphics* (use of lettering style to emphasize a word or phrase), *superimpose* (having some printing over part of the illustration), and *saddlestitch* (binding the book by stitching at the folds). Children sense some maturity and pride in knowing and using these words in the context of their actual working with them. Children decide (often in discussion with a classmate or with the teacher or aide) what format will best suit their respective books. Will a shape book or a slim book or a regular rectangular one be best for my writing? Should I write on every other page and illustrate the pages between? How many pages will I need?

The last question is answered by the author's dividing the presentable product copy into natural parts. Then the actual book designing begins:

choosing the paper, cutting it to size or shape, overlaying the sheets and folding them if the saddlestitch is chosen. Illustrations and printing are done lightly in pencil so that errors may easily be corrected. Only when the child is ready to make a page final is pen used or color applied. Even at this stage a frustrating problem may arise—but the resourceful teacher or child finds a solution. Chris, for example, had completed six pages of his book before he discovered that he had worked only on the odd-numbered (or right-side) pages and had left all the even-numbered pages blank; but he had copied little more than half his story. He was nearly despondent. So much work and now to start over? "No! Be different." was the solution. "Have the latter part of the book go 'backward'—from right to left." The solution required only a renumbering of the even-numbered pages.

**Oral Presentation**

The books may finally be completed, but the project is not. The next phase focuses on oral language. The real sharing of the product now begins. Throughout the process children have shared their work, reading to one another in a corner of the room and exchanging ideas about how each one may improve the books. But the great sharing now begins. The young authors prepare to read their books to children in kindergarten, first, second, third, or other grades, and to adults.

First, however, they set up a checklist showing what they like about a reader reading to them: showing expression in the voice; having the voice change with each change of speakers in a story; showing the pictures to the listeners, holding the book open and moving it slowly so that everyone can see; speaking loudly enough to be heard; letting the audience see the reader's face; having the reader glance at the audience; speaking clearly. Using the checklist they have devised, the children practice reading their books to the class. The teacher explains the meaning of constructive criticism: pointing out qualities of the reading, suggesting how the oral reading may be improved by referring to the checklist. These dry runs are important, for in the security of their peer group—all of whom share the same experience and purpose—the children are free to practice, as actors before performing for the paying audience.

The authors and illustrators delight in presenting their books to other children in the school; the audiences, especially the younger ones, delight in the attention bestowed upon them and the books read to them. The writers are celebrities. Jay, who usually speaks in monosyllables to avoid embarrassment of stuttering, read his book to many small groups without stuttering. Stacey, whom few believed could complete the project, stood when she read hers, and smiled widely enough to show her malformed teeth when the audience applauded.

## The Open House

The crowning of the project is open house for parents to meet the authors and illustrators. The children review the writing of a friendly letter because they write personal letters of invitation to parents or any other adults whom they wish to come. Again, they draft their letters, revise and edit them, and write presentable products. They also learn how to address an envelope (or review the skill) because the letters are mailed.

Attendance at open house is high. Parents bring the younger siblings; grandparents attend. Sometimes an aunt or neighbor comes. The authors briefly review what they as a class have experienced in this project. Then the visitors circulate among the books and the authors, interviewing the children, listening to a child read, or reading a book and talking about it. At some schools punch and cookies are served, the children hosting the refreshment time.

Says Judy Goetz, teacher at Pomeroy School, "It was a lot of work; but *every* child learned more language than in any other four weeks of the year. And they feel good about it." Karen Rousseau, teacher at Allendale School, declares that her new class, having learned about Authors and Illustrators from the previous class, begins in September asking when they will begin their books. One young author was overheard to tell visitors at open house, "You see, to make a book interesting, you have to use words that make people see and hear." Another author explained, "I worked at it because I knew people were going to read it."

One parent, two years after the child had completed the project, said, "We were sorting out things that we would not take with us when we move away. We came upon Pat's book. It didn't take a second for all of us to agree that we will keep that with us."

Authors and Illustrators: Children Writing Books for Children is a total, integrated language arts project. The investment of time, patience, and resourcefulness results in greater learning and more satisfaction—for both teacher and children—than any ream of workbook pages, any series of isolated lessons in mechanics or spelling or grammar, or any hours of red penciling. And the rewards are lasting.

# 6  Reading as Meaning Construction

Dorothy F. King
Columbia College

Dorothy J. Watson
University of Missouri

Jamie sits looking at a list of words: fat, pat, bat, sat, cat, hat. . . .
Later she sees, "The fat cat sat on the bat. Pat the fat cat."

Josie is waiting her turn in a group whose members are reading
aloud a story in which the words "green," "table," and "wood" appear
ten times each. Later she will do skill exercises in her workbook.

Harold looks at a page with spɷn, baʊl, riɳ, ʃhoʊt, chæɾ, and
tæks on it. Later he will write a story using the symbols he has
learned in school.

Hildy sits on the floor and reads along with her friends and teacher
a story the class has just written. Later she will write a letter to a
friend about the book she has just finished reading.

With such diverse instructional emphases, are all these children going to become readers? It is quite likely they will. One research finding that occurs
regularly is that the majority of children learn to read regardless of, or in
spite of, the teaching method or techniques used. (Weintraub, et al., 1980;
Smith, 1978; Bond and Tinker, 1973; Sipay, 1968; Bond and Dykstra,
1967). This is an amazing finding, given that many methods of teaching
reading are based on mutually opposing, seemingly exclusive, theories.
That is, if one particular theory is effective, its antithesis should not be.

Nonetheless, every day thousands of children become readers. Given
this fact, one might conclude that the method of instruction is unimportant. Nevertheless, we believe that instruction is vital and that a particular
kind of instruction in a particular setting—that is whole language reading
instruction in an integrated language arts program—has much to contribute to making children good readers.

Before presenting this case, one nagging question must be cleared
away: How is it that many children learn to read no matter what their

instructional program? To find out why children become readers we must look at them long before their formal instruction begins. We must investigate their early use of language. From the first day of life, children are communicators with much to make known; through this powerful need to give and receive information, language develops. Oral and written language surrounds children; as it comes to symbolize their meanings, it becomes an indispensable tool for learning.

Fortunately, children easily learn the language conventions that are necessary and specific to their needs and their environments. By age five most children have learned naturally—without formal instruction—the rules of their language (Brown, 1958). No one has said to them, "Now, your sentences consist of two parts; a noun phrase and a verb phrase and through a series of transformations . . ." or "There are eight parts of speech and . . ." Such instruction would be after the fact and given in language that presupposes an ingrained understanding of the rules that children learn in meaningful situations before they enter school.

Useful language derives from meaningful context; children see, hear, and use language in sensible situations of which they are a part. Only when children enter the classroom are they asked to "sit still" for language that is nonfunctional and noncontextual.

Because children see language in meaningful or potentially meaningful contexts they learn that printed language makes sense. Even single words (exit, shoes, K-Mart, women, stop) appear in a context; they are not isolated from world-information. Children learn to respond pragmatically to print as part of a total language-and-living experience.

Initially, then, there are at least two reasons why children become readers: (1) they are language users, and (2) they learn to use printed language naturally in meaningful, useful situations.

These reasons are at once why most children become readers regardless of instruction and also why "instruction" is so vital. It is the prevalence of meaningful print and children's need to make sense of their environments that make all forms of instruction work. There are, however, instructional practices that confuse and dismay the reader. Children may look at spωn during reading, but no other print they come in contact with outside the classroom or reading group is written in this form. We've never seen a ʃhω stœr sign or a notice that scωbee dω wil reetuɾn. If a slate in the kitchen lists "bread, eggs, pepper, milk," that list has meaning and a context. The only place a child sees a list of words devoid of context is in a "reader," on flashcards, on worksheets, or on a reading test.

Children's immersion in functional, purposive print and their natural inclination as language users to derive sense from this print often make methods of instruction look effective when the method deserves no credit. The immersion in meaningful, predictable print and children's natural interaction with it also explain why some children do not associate their real reading ability with the formalized reading instruction of school.

Part of the reason we waste children's time by trying to teach them things they already know or things they don't need to know is that we fail to believe in what we know about children's learning, and we fail to pay attention to our own reading behavior. Before children enter school they have learned millions of interesting things, among which is how to use language meaningfully. We seem to forget this and often treat children as if they were empty boxes into which we must personally place everything learned. We may treat children as if they are inefficient learners (of things they want to know) and teach them confusing and unnecssary information in language-sterile lessons that only get in their way as learners. We may make children's learning to read difficult by removing instruction from anything meaningful to them or by insisting that reading is a self-contained unit that has nothing to do with talking and listening and writing. Because children are active, trusting learners who have so much to learn in such precious little time, teachers must provide instruction that gets mileage from need, context, motivation, and meaning.

To know how to help our students while "staying out of their way," it is necessary to understand the reading process. When we understand the process we can use practices in teaching children to read that promote rather than restrain or stop the process. Thanks to the work of Kenneth Goodman (Allen and Watson, 1976), Frank Smith (1978), and others, we know and can describe what fluent, efficient readers do. Our instructional goal should be to help students move toward these proficient behaviors or to let them practice these behaviors if they already have them.

Like any other behavior, reading cannot be separated from the individuals doing the reading. This important fact must influence our instructional practices. Although children have many similarities, we know they will never suddenly or over a long period of time become alike. Readers approach print with their own unique combinations of language and experience. This experience includes knowledge about the world and things in it, strategies for gaining information, ways of organizing and changing meaning, success in dealing with print, personal attitudes about what risks to take and to what effort and extent the reader will go to make print meaningful.

Confronted with learners with diverse prior knowledge (concepts, schemata, and language), diverse expectations for success, diverse motivations, and diverse personal attitudes toward learning, what will we give them to read? Here again we may forget what we know. Children come to us from a print-rich world, a world full of meaningful, functional print in contexts that are understandable, and a society full of people who are using language in meaningful ways. How far we get from the world in which the children have been learning for years, the world to which they return after school hours, can be marked on this continuum (from De Ford, 1978):

isolated dissected ←——|——|——|——|——|——|——→ functional whole units
parts of language                                          of language

Points on this continuum essentially show different beliefs about language and its users. When we wrench language apart and present only bits and pieces of it (letters, phonemes, syllables, words) to children, there is small wonder that they come to regard reading as something outside their interests and, for some children, outside their abilities—something to be learned because that's what one does in school. Teachers can easily make both oral and written language artificial, meaningless, and confusing by removing listening, speaking, reading, and writing from their purposes (to convey meaning in a context which adds to the meaning) and by separating the processes from each other.

Reading is an active, creative process of constructing meaning. Readers come to print with their individual language competence, experiences, and attitudes. What these backgrounds are determines what meaning the reader predicts the print symbolizes and the amount of print the reader samples. Readers sample very small units of print only when they need to or when they are taught to attend to each and every letter and syllable. Since human eyes can see about an inch of horizontal print at each fixation, construction of meaning will be hindered if a reader takes time to look at everything (Smith, 1978). It simply is inefficient to give attention to every mark on the page as if all marks were of equal importance.

Print reflects the cueing systems available to every reader in meaningful text. These systems are used simultaneously by fluent readers. When a reader uses these systems separately, fluency is broken and reading stops. The systems available are:

1. *graphophonemics.* This system involves the graphic display and its sound relationship. Efficient readers go from the visual array to meaning and tend to use graphophonemic matching as a confirming strategy when the meanings they've predicted do not make sense.

2. *wordings.* This system involves the rules of language, word order, and morphology. Language users rely on their knowledge of this system to confirm whether their predicted meanings are "language correct," that is, "sound like language."

3. *semantics.* This system involves the meanings that readers and writers have in their heads. The closer the language and experience

of the author are to those of the reader, the easier it is for the reader to construct meaning (Y. Goodman and Burke, 1972; King, 1980). If what proficient readers construct does not make sense to them they repredict, resample the print, or continue reading in hopes that the author will provide additional information that will fit their semantic network.

4. *pragmatics*. This system is closely related to semantics but specifically has to do with on-the-page *and* off-the-page context expectations. Efficient readers expect particular language usage, metaphors, inferences, words, ideas, and concepts to appear in certain print contexts and in certain situational contexts.

The constructive nature of reading is evidenced by readers' use of the cueing systems. When efficient readers are in meaningful contexts and have sufficient prior knowledge to allow them to make correct or reasonable predictions, they will sample only lightly from all the visual display in order to form and confirm predictions. When readers are in pragmatically anomalous situations or have little prior knowledge with which to make predictions, then they sample more heavily from the visual display and confirm smaller bits of meaning. Smith (1978) refers to a trade-off between visual (print) and nonvisual (prior knowledge) information. We have added a pragmatic means of support or distraction: situational context.

The reading process begins when readers (with their own background of language competence, experiences, concepts, and attitudes toward themselves as readers and toward reading) approach a print display. Based on prior knowledge, the reader samples the print to the degree necessary, predicts meaning, confirms or rejects the prediction, integrates the author's information, and continues to sample the text in order to construct meaning (Goodman, 1970).

The meaning that readers construct is unique to each individual reader because his or her language and experience is not the same as anyone else's. In constructing meaning readers impose their own language and concepts on the print.

Constructing meaning is not a linear, additive process in which language is read and understood in a word-by-word manner. Rather, it is cyclical—a reader holds meaning or tentative meaning at one time and later revises or confirms that meaning when more information is obtained.

Since readers approach text from individual perspectives and construct individual meanings, they must not be held accountable for obtaining one certain set of meanings from the print unless they are told in advance which meanings or types of meanings they are to "construct." If they are not told, they may not be concerned with what textbook writers or teachers deem important and use as the bases for their tests and assignments.

Through interaction with print, readers develop strategies for constructing meaning; they develop strategies for using the available cueing systems. The strategies a particular reader uses may be reflected in oral reading done for diagnostic purposes. Deviations from print (miscues) are thought to reflect a reader's use of the cueing systems (Goodman, 1967). Studies of these miscues reveal that deviations are not random but reflect purposeful behavior as a reader tries to construct meaning. Far from revealing that a reader who miscues is not thinking or trying, an analysis of oral deviations shows that a reader is relying on a cueing system or systems and is exhibiting strategic behavior in the attempt to construct meaning. An analysis of miscues will show which strategies a reader uses are efficient and which impede construction of meaning.

Reading is not an exact process of reproducing words or meanings. Every reader's miscues are based on personal background and strategy use. This is natural, normal, and to be expected. Accurate word-for-word reading is the exception—and it's abnormal. The construction of meaning is what reading is all about. Miscues are harmful only when and to the extent that they impair fluent construction. When deviations from print change meaning to something that doesn't make sense, either by itself or in the context of the total meaning of the print, then the miscues reveal an inefficient use of strategies.

For example, if the print display is "He petted the horse" and the reader says, "He petted the house" and does not correct, then meaning is lost. Such a reader does not need work with the digraphs *ou* and *or* but with knowledge about what is likely to be petted so that a nonsense prediction like "house" does not occur. If a text display is "The little fellow chased the ball" and the reader says, "The little boy ran after the ball" the meaning is retained. Meanings are personal, as is the language used to express them, and readers who construct meaning use their own language to express meanings.

After two decades of research in reading, Goodman (1976) credits miscue research with making it possible to see strength and order even in beginning readers and in readers of limited effectiveness. Reading, like all language, is patterned and rule-governed. Miscue analysis occurs on the reading of whole, functional text and shows readers as intuitive grammarians, problem solvers, and meaning seekers. A deficit approach to reading that does not allow deviations from print is harmful to readers and subverts their time, enthusiasm, and energy.

We must remember what we know about children's language abilities and the learning process. Our guiding principle should be to capitalize on children's natural abilities and strengths as communicators. Just as our students cannot be dissected into anything less than whole learners whose social, emotional, physical, and intellectual development all interact to make them what they are, neither can their language be wrenched asunder into unnatural parts which occur in artificial situations. A whole-language perspective views language as a system for construction of meaning in reading, writing, listening, and speaking and promotes language use in an environment of functional and interactional language, of natural language.

Research confirms that prior knowledge influences reading efficiency (Chippendale, 1979; King, 1980), that functional whole-language approaches help disabled readers (Jenkins, 1980), and that children learn different things about language and differ in language productions and attitudes depending on the theory of language arts instruction (Watson, 1981).

We need to decide what is important to our students: instruction in which reading gains support from all the language arts and in which the natural abilities of the learner are used in meaning giving situations, or instruction in a reading circle or through workbooks that focuses attention and energy on the mastery of fragments of linguistic information.

## Conclusion

> Jamie sits looking at a list of words: fat, pat, bat . . .
> Josie is waiting her turn in a group . . .
> Harold looks at a page with spɯɔn, baʋl, riɳ . . .
> Hildy sits on the floor and reads . . .

We ask again: With such diverse instructional emphases are all these children going to become readers? Our answer remains the same: It is quite likely they will. But some other interesting things will happen to these children. Jamie, Josie, and Harold will also pass the skills tests at the end of their workbooks, Hildy may or may not. Jamie, Josie, and Harold may be too busy doing "reading instruction" to open a book. They may never find themselves swept up in the mishaps of a bumbling dragon fighting a knight or of a girl and boy finding a special place called Terabithia. Harold may be able to use his knowledge of those never-fail symbols to write stories and not to worry about spelling, but can he find anyone to share them with? He also may not have much fun in the library; it's hard to find anything that looks like "school print." We know Hildy will be a good reader because she already is. She reads her own stories and those of her classmates. She reads professionally authored stories that have predictable language, familiar messages, and repetitious and cumulative lines. She writes notes to herself and stories for her family and friends. She talks and listens and the only nonsense she encounters is the marvelous nonsense of Dr. Seuss or Shel Silverstein. She takes linguistic risks, she makes miscues, she learns from them, and she tries again.

Jamie, Josie, Harold, and Hildy will probably all learn to read, but more is at stake here than reaching an end product. Love of reading, literary heritage, making use of print, success in school, and pride in self—aren't we talking about these too?

## References

Allen, D., and D. Watson. *Findings of Research in Miscue Analysis: Classroom Implications.* Urbana, Ill.: NCTE, 1976.

Bond, G.L., and R. Dykstra. *Final Report of the Coordinating Center for First-Grade Reading Instruction.* (USOE Project X-0001). 1967.

Bond, G.L., and M.A. Tinker. *Reading Difficulties: Their Diagnosis and Correction.* Englewood Cliffs, N.J.: Prentice-Hall, 1973.

Brown, R. *Words and Things.* New York: Free Press, 1958.

Chippendale, E. *A Pycholinguistic Model of Reading Comprehension Based on Language Competence, Reading Proficiency, and Discourse Analysis.* Ph.D. diss., University of Missouri–Columbia, 1979.

De Ford, D.E. *A Validation Study of an Instrument to Determine a Teacher's Theoretical Orientation to Reading Instruction.* Ph.D. diss., Indiana University, 1978.

Goodman, K.S. "Behind the Eye: What Happens in Reading." In *Reading: Process and Program,* edited by K.S. Goodman and O.S. Niles. Urbana, Ill.: NCTE, 1970.

Goodman, K.S. *The Psycholinguistic Nature of the Reading Process.* Detroit: Wayne State University Press, 1967.

Goodman, K.S. "What We Know About Reading." In *Findings of Research in Miscue Analysis: Classroom Implications,* edited by P.D. Allen and D.J. Watson. Urbana, Ill.: ERIC/NCTE, 1976.

Goodman, Y., and C. Burke. *Reading Miscue Inventory Manual.* New York: Macmillan, 1972.

Jenkins, P.W. *The Language Learning of a Language Delayed Child: A Phenomenological Study.* Ph.D. diss., University of Missouri–Columbia, 1980.

King, D.F. *A Psycholinguistic Analysis and Propositional Comparison of the Reading of Selected Middle School Children of Self-Authored and Professionally-Authored Text.* Ph.D. diss., University of Missouri–Columbia, 1980.

Sipay, E.R. "Interpreting the USOE Cooperative Reading Studies," *Reading Teacher* 22 (Oct. 1968): 10–16, 35.

Smith F. *Reading without Nonsense.* New York: Teachers' College Press, 1978.

Watson, D.J. "Teacher-Student Interaction and Student Performance and Attitude in a Whole-Language and a Skills Language Arts Program." Research in progress, 1981.

Weintraub, S., S. Roser, N. Rowe, and W. Hill. *Annual Summary of Investigations Relating to Reading.* Newark, Del.: IRA, 1980.

# Part Two: Integration among Different Language Modes

# 7  Language Play

Judith I. Schwartz
Queens College, City University of New York

I won't go to Macy's
Any more, more, more.
There's a big, fat policeman
At the door, door, door.
He'll catch you by the collar,
And make you pay a dollar.
So I won't go to Macy's
Any more, more, more.

Play and childhood are almost synonymous. When we think of children, we see them at play. We hear them playing, too: chanting jump rope lyrics such as the one above; challenging each other with ritualized insults ("off my case, potato face"); and concocting rhythmic repetitive patterns ("Ramona has a phona, Ramona has a phona") to accompany almost any activity. This language is real; it is alive and purposeful. Children play *with* language—its structure, its sound, its meaning, and its communicative conventions. Children *use* language as an accompaniment to play—in street games like Miss Mary Mack, in their dramatic play, for example. In sociodramatic play, a play theme is elaborated upon by several children who interact with each other behaviorally and linguistically. The imaginative element of this play relies heavily upon language because verbalization helps to direct the play as it symbolizes reality (Flood and Lapp, 1981). Language play permits children to be angry and obstreperous; it lets them defy authority and test reality. And, it does all this *safely* precisely because it is a *play* behavior, a simulation of what is real. In addition, language play provides a free, unselfconscious way in which the child explores, hypothesizes, tests, verifies, and practices with language. Language play can help the child to master language first in its spoken form and later in its written form through such language games as puns, puzzles, codes, and conundrums. It can do this without coercion and with a natural fusion of all the language forms.

In this paper various kinds of language play are described and illustrated, and several ways in which teachers can foster this mechanism for language growth are suggested.

## Kinds of Language Play

### Play with Sound

Both Weir (1962) who taped her two and one-half-year-old son's presleep monologues, and Schwartz (1977) who analyzed 149 samples of language play from children ages six months to ten years, conclude that especially with young children most language play deals with the sound elements of language. Johnson (1928), as a director of an experimental nursery school for very young children more than fifty years ago, found this same phenomenon. Johnson's children composed brief, repetitive chants to accompany some motor activity, as did this four-year-old pretending to scrub clothes against a washboard:

up and down
in and out
up and down
in and out

Sound play is characterized by a strong regular beat or cadence as in this example from a two-year-old:

Doobie doo
Doobie doo
Doobie doo

and this from a six-year-old:

La la la
Lol li pop
La la la
Lol li pop

Sometimes the rhythm persists even in a dialogue. In this example, X and Y are siblings; X is four years old and Y is ten years old.

| X | Y |
|---|---|
| Where you goin'? | To the store. |
| Why you goin'? | To get milk. |
| How you goin'? | I'm walking. |
| When you goin'? | Right now. |
| When I'm goin'? | You're not. I can't take you. |

Playing with sounds is the first manifestation of language play. It begins in earliest infancy with the looming games, tickling, and juggling that adults engage in with babies. Language is incorporated too into very early games such as Peek-a-Boo when the adult may say "I see you" as she peeks out from behind a pillow. Infants revel in the pleasure of their own sounds when they babble. It's likely that the absence of hearing their own voices is what causes congenitally deaf babies to stop babbling, although they begin at the same time that hearing babies do. But, sound play does not end with infancy. Into early childhood and beyond, children continue to delight in the playful manipulation of sounds. And, particularly in the hands of a master like Ogden Nash, even the lowly pun can tickle the fancy of an adult.

> This creature fills its mouth with venum
> And walks upon its duodenum.
> He who attempts to tease the cobra
> Is sooner a sadder he and sobra.
> (Nash, 1973, p. 43)

## Play with Structure

In analyzing the tapes of her son Anthony's presleep monologues, Weir (1962) found a high incidence of what she labeled grammatical practice. Anthony would select a grammatical pattern and substitute words from the same form class or pronouns in one slot of the grammatical frame. In the following example, the first sentence is the frame of the pattern. The full pattern occurs in the second sentence with substitutions, in this case of nouns, in the third and fourth sentences.

I see.
I see dog.
I see house.
I see boy.

Weir believes that this type of language play serves as a systematic practice. And, indeed, it shares the common feature of being *highly repetitive* with practice play in general.

Schwartz (1977) also reported a high frequency of structure play in her data. Invariably the patterns preserved the word order of standard English. The substitutions can be based on either sound or meaning associations. In this example from an eight-year-old, the substitutions are based on sound:

Watch the knicks.
Beat the picks.
Hear the ticks.
Lickety splits.
Hickety lips.

## Play with Meaning

Play with the meaning of utterances occurs less frequently in the language of young children than either sound or structure play. For example,

Schwartz (1977) observed only ten clear instances of it in her data, and most of these were made by children over five. Sometimes a playful variation with the sound of an utterance resulted in an altered meaning that the child perceived and appreciated:

San Diego, Sandiego, Sandi Ego
San Diego, Sandi ego
Eggs aren't sandy.

The *incongruity* of such playful manipulations is one of the prime features of meaning play, and is a characteristic of children's humor in general. Chukovsky (1963) called such play "topsie-turvies." The child inverts the natural order of things and thus distorts meanings. He notes that many such inversions occur in folk literature for children, and argues that when they occur spontaneously in child language they serve to verify the child's knowledge of reality. That may be why meaning play occurs later than sound or structure play. The grasp of semantics continues well beyond the mastery of phonology and syntax. Not until the child knows what is real is she or he ready to be amused by a reverse juxtaposition.

Another kind of play with meaning consists of the inventions of a word or phrase to cover an experience for which a label has not yet been acquired. In the following dialogue between two six-year-olds, *up* is affixed to the verb *sink* in lieu of the unknown word *float.*

> *X:* This sponge is up.
> I can make it sink.
> I can make it sink-up.
> Here's a rock.
> It won't sink-up by itself.
> *Y:* Sink-up rock.
> Sink-up.
> *Teacher:* What did you discover?
> *Y:* He is sinking-up the rock. It won't sink-up by itself.

Note that although the word *sink-up* is invented, it is used in its correct inflected form (sinking-up).

One particular variety of meaning play has been observed in very young children. An eighteen month old spying a big toe sticking out of his all-in-one pajamas calls it "turtle" (de Villiers and de Villiers, 1979). This is a *metaphor*, a figure of speech in which the child overrides conventional category boundaries and brings together objects or events that normally belong to different domains. Kogan and colleagues (1980) believe that metaphor represents a cognitive rather than a strictly linguistic phenomena—a perceptual synesthesia of sensitivity to similarities among visual, auditory, tactile, and other types of sensory stimuli. So, the very early production of metaphors may represent a primitive but fundamentally human way of perceiving the world. Early metaphors are typically the renaming of objects in their immediate presence, based largely upon physical properties and functions (Verbrugge and McCarrell, 1977).

## Play with Rules and Conventions

Play with language that incorporates rules (e.g., Pig Latin) requires sufficiently advanced cognitive development to understand, remember, maintain, and employ the rules of the game. Generally, language games occur when children have entered Piaget's concrete operational stage of cognitive development from about seven to eleven years of age. This type of language play also requires a sufficient degree of social development for the participants to take each other's needs and viewpoints into account. In the following example from a ten-year-old, this is shown by the clear explication, including an illustration, of the games rules: "If I say a name and later on during the game you say it, you're out. Like, if I say Alice and then you say Alice, you're out."

Coinciding with the concrete operational stage of cognitive development is the child's growing competence in literacy. This is when play with written language games begins to be appreciated. There are all kinds of games that fit into this genre: puns, conundrums, puzzles, codes, palindromes, pictographs, and cryptograms, for instance. Moffett and Wagner (1976) describe many of these and illustrate how they may be used. The point, of course, is to remember that this is *play* and whether the medium is speaking or writing, it should maintain the voluntary, self-initiated quality of all play behavior.

In their social play, preschoolers and older children practice with the conventions of social interchange that have their origins in the earliest call-to-response and response cycles of the infant and caregiver. These interchanges are governed by a subtle and complex system of rules, mutual expectations about content and sequence, and rules for regulating exchanges (Schwartz, in press). Garvey (1977) indicates that most of what children know about conversational conventions comes from firsthand experiences of interacting with others in a variety of situations including play. What children do in their practice with the conventions of social interchange is to *violate* the conventions, a distinctly playful device. One such convention is called an *invitation question*: respond and elaborate to a question or assertion about yourself. In this example, one partner (X) repeatedly questions, while the other (Y) refuses to elaborate.

|              X              |              Y              |
|-----------------------------|-----------------------------|
|                             | (Puts on firefighter's hat) |
| Is that your hat?           | Yeah.                       |
| Did you get it from school? | Nope.                       |
| From here?                  | Nope.                       |
| Where? In the car?          | Um, no.                     |
| From you?                   | No.                         |
| From in the . . . other room? | No. Yes.                  |

The social play of preschoolers and older children is rich with opportunities for language play. Some of it consists of ritual insults in which one child can simply repeat the insult made by another, substitute a like phrase for it, or use a different term that is, in some simple way, linked to the insult. Language play dialogues are quite frequent in social play, too. These are characterized by turn-taking characteristics and are often symmetrical enough to have the appearance of a round (Garvey, 1976).

## Fostering Language Play

Play is marked by spontaneity. Beyond the obvious example of learning the rules of a game, teaching in the formal, didactic sense contradicts the nature of play. To teach, to drill, to impose practice and reinforcement may well mark the death of play, both for play in general and for language play in particular.

Language play is an ideal medium for language arts integration because it is natural rather than contrived. As has been observed elsewhere, in natural communication settings the language arts *do* occur together; they are only artificially dissected. Most of the time such fragmentation comes as a result of trying to *teach about* language, rather than *use* language to learn, or to accomplish the tasks of everyday life. Language play resists pedagogical probes by disappearing, self-destructing like the Phoenix when it is so assaulted. In addition to its natural aversion to didacticism, language play's spontaneity, emphasis on process over product, and employment of the child's own language as its central motif actually require the fusion of listening, speaking, reading, and writing.

The many examples of language play cited here illustrate this well:

> listening to and then producing rhythmic chants (listening and speaking)
>
> reciting and elaborating on jump rope chants (listening and speaking)
>
> performing street games such as Miss Mary Mack (listening and speaking)

listening to meaning inversions and nonsense rhymes (listening)

making up rule-governed word games (listening and speaking)

listening to, reading, and then orally composing word games such as puns (listening, reading, speaking)

writing out word games from both set rules (e.g., puns) and from creative invention (writing)

Activities such as these not only provide for integration of the language arts, but require thinking and the opportunity for creative problem solving as well. The nurture and sustenance of language play are more dependent upon qualities of attitude and atmosphere than upon prescriptions and exercises. In the following section, therefore, I will try to answer two questions about attitudes and atmosphere that foster language play: What kind of classroom atmosphere stimulates language play? and When and how should the teacher intervene in language play?

## *What Kind of Classroom Atmosphere Stimulates Language Play?*

Is it facetious to answer this question by saying that a *playful* classroom atmosphere fosters language play? Not really, if by playful one means an atmosphere in which there is not so much tension as to interfere with children's natural locquaciousness and humor. This is the kind of classroom in which dialogue between teacher and children and among children is encouraged. Children and teacher laugh easily and often. Incongruity and diversity are enjoyed, not shunned. Imaginative solutions to problems are sought. Invention and experimentation are prized.

Humor may be one of the strongest mechanisms for survival of the human species, one of our surest defenses against the travesties of fortune. The teacher of this classroom understands this, and demonstrates it by sharing humorous anecdotes, word play, folk literature, jokes, and stories with the children. It is reflected, too, by the teacher's gentle humor in handling interpersonal relations.

Finally, in a classroom where language play flourishes, the teacher stimulates—and values as unique—contributions made by each individual child. Heterogeneity rather than homogeneity is encouraged. Many opportunities are made for sharing oral and written language play. Children are urged to record on audiotape or in writing their own inventions which may be shared later on with classmates. In the classroom that fosters language play, humor in language is sought in both written and oral form from external sources such as folk literature and from within the children's own imagination.

*When and How Should the Teacher Intervene in Language Play?*

Vygotsky (1976) observes that children's play evolves from overt, imaginary situations with covert rules to covert, imaginary situations with overt rules. This characterization of the general nature of play development has parallels in the changes in language play with time. The earliest language play has, besides the intrinsic pleasure it appears to bestow, the function of practice. Later, language is embedded into the symbolic play of the preschooler. It becomes a distinct feature of the make-believe and dramatic play of early childhood. In the intermediate grades, language games with rules begin to predominate as the overt imaginative function of language play recedes.

Vygotsky's trajectory of play development offers useful guidelines on when and how the teacher ought to intervene in language play. Stated broadly, when language play is in its earliest stages of overt, imaginary situations and covert rules, adult intervention should be subtle and indirect. Besides providing and supporting the kind of atmosphere described in the last section, the teacher's role at this point is to support, affirm, and reinforce informally. For instance, if a group of preschoolers begins to chant spontaneously, the teacher has several options that will enhance this language play. She or he may simply smile and listen appreciatively, or gently and softly chant with the children, or unobtrusively tape-record the chant to be replayed later for everyone's enjoyment. The teacher will foster such play, as well, by doing nothing more than permitting the children to proceed without interference or interruption. Another way in which language play can be fostered with young children is by sharing literature that features rhythmic and playful language. Children will spontaneously chant the familiar refrain from Wanda Gag's *Millions of Cats*, for example. With a little encouragement after much exposure to this kind of language, the children will want to compose their own chants.

The wealth of playful language in literature continues to be an outstanding source of stimulation for older children too. Indeed, the repertoire becomes larger as children's increasing knowledge and sophistication enables them to savor the humor of stories such as *The Five Sillies*, puns by Ogden Nash, and Russian and other folk literature that incorporates the absurd. In addition, once children become intrigued by rule-governed language play, the teacher's intervention can become more direct. Now the teacher can play language games with the children— introducing various kinds of games, explaining the rules of the games, and providing the materials necessary to play the games. The teacher's role here is to teach, and then to act as a resource to assist the children when they require this. For example, with an upper elementary grade class the teacher may share a battery of puns. The goal is first to interest the children and then to get them to understand what puns are, how they are constructed, and finally, to compose puns of their own.

Language play is not only a delightful source of pleasure for children, it provides an excellent medium in which to acquire language mastery. Moreover, playing with language engages the language functions of listening, speaking, reading, and writing quite naturally. It's all part of the game.

# References

Chukovsky, K. *From Two to Five.* Berkeley: University of California Press, 1963.

de Villiers, P.A., and J.G. de Villiers. *Early Language.* Cambridge, Mass.: Harvard University Press, 1979.

Flood, J., and D. Lapp. *Language/Reading Instruction for the Young Child.* New York: Macmillan, 1981.

Garvey, C. *Play.* Cambridge, Mass.: Harvard University Press, 1977.

Garvey, C. "Some Properties of Social Play." In *Play—Its Role in Development and Evolution,* edited by T.S. Bruner, A. Jolly, and K. Sylva. New York: Basic Books, 1976.

Johnson, H.M. *Children in the Nursery School.* New York: Day, 1928.

Kogan, N., et al. "Understanding Visual Metaphor: Developmental and Individual Differences." *Monographs of the Society for Research in Child Development* 45 (1980):1.

Moffett, J., and B.J. Wagner. *Student-Centered Language Arts and Reading, K-13.* 2nd ed. Boston: Houghton Mifflin, 1976.

Nash, O. *Ave Ogden: Nash in Latin-Poems by Ogden Nash.* Boston: Little, Brown, 1973.

Schwartz, J.I. "Children's Experiments with Language." *Young Children,* in press.

Schwartz, J.I. "Metalinguistic Awareness—A Study of Verbal Play in Young Children." Paper presented to the American Educational Research Association Conference, New York City, 1977. ERIC Document Reproduction Service, No. ED 149 852.

Verbrugge, R., and N. McCarrell. "Metaphoric Comprehension: Studies in Reminding and Resembling." *Cognitive Psychology,* 1977, *9,* 494-533.

Vygotsky, L.S. "Play and Its Role in the Mental Development of the Child." In *Play—Its Role in Development and Evolution,* edited by J.S. Bruner, A. Jolly, and K. Sylva. New York: Basic Books, 1976.

Weir, R. *Language in the Crib.* The Hague: Mouton, 1962.

# 8 Language Experience

Dorris M. Lee
Tigard, Oregon

Integration of learning includes the conscious attention to the interactions of all four aspects of communication through language. Since one does not talk, listen, read, or write without some content, attention needs to be given to the quality and usefulness of that content. Content needs to be valuable for its literary quality and/or for its contribution to children's understanding of themselves and the world in which they live. Further, integration also needs to include the development of desirable aspects of children's personal competence such as confidence in their ability to learn, responsibility for themselves and their own learning, and establishment of cooperative and mutually respecting personal relationships with peers and adults.

All of this may sound difficult but actually takes less time than simply trying to teach each of the language arts skills separately. And since integrated learning results in more effective competence, content learning and personal development are bonuses. Further, they increase the permanence and usability of the language arts skills throughout the child's life.

Procedures for accomplishing this integrated learning are relatively simple and straightforward. The main requirement is a teacher who has confidence that children can learn and, when they see it as useful to them, want to learn; a teacher who does not need to make every decision or to be the sole authority, who always has to know what is best for each child; a teacher who gets the greatest satisfaction from watching children grow and develop as effective learners and effective human beings with increasing self-direction and responsibility.

These procedures are basically appropriate with learners from pre-school through graduate school. Obviously, the specifics will differ with age, experience, developmental level, personality, and numerous other factors. The general procedures are as follows:

> individuals alone or with others experience something that has personal meaning for them

they talk about the experience, often including its meaning for them, with interested listeners

they record the essence of their experience in some form—art, script, music

they retrieve their thoughts from the recorded form and make the recording available for the retrieval of others

The last three steps may be repeated in any order with that material only or by including other relevant material at each step. The first step, the experiencing, may lead to further experiencing as the discussion and writing develop their thinking and make learners aware of what else they need to know and do. It can also help them decide how best to learn or accomplish it.

## Implementation

Beginning readers are any who can express themselves with reasonable fluency in a dialect understood in their community, and who have shown an interest in books and "what they say."

All children have a host of experiences from which to draw, some pleasant and some unpleasant. The experience that a child offers is the experience that is most useful at that time. Children are provided paper and art materials and encouraged to record their thoughts in color and line. Then as a few have finished their pictures, they meet in groups of three to five with the teacher, Mrs. Reaves.

In turn, each picture is fastened to an easel and the child tells the others what it means. Discussion follows. Mrs. Reaves asks Tommy "What do you want me to write on your picture?" and then reproduces it in clear manuscript writing, says it as she writes it; then, running her hand under it, she says it again. Tommy may "read" it or not as he chooses. The other children then each have a turn. Each has had "center stage," and has expressed his or her thoughts. All have interacted orally, talking and listening; all have observed writing and reading and may have taken part in it. Each has observed "this is what I said and this is what it looks like."

Children make progress by proudly identifying recognized words or phrases in their own stories, those of their peers, or stories in unpublished books. With children who indicate interest, Mrs. Reaves moves into saying each letter as she writes it, rather than just each word; children quickly begin to point out letters that they recognize.

Soon Tommy wants to do his own writing. So, Mrs. Reaves writes his dictated story on a separate strip of paper, and he can then copy it on his picture. When the stories at this stage are kept to one or at most two lines it remains a do-able task. Through watching Mrs. Reaves writing and through his own copying, Tommy soon begins writing on his own. Thus, integrated around each experience, children talk about it, listen to it, write about it, and read it. (More explicit details are presented in chapter 10 of *Children and Language,* Lee and Rubin, 1979.)

**The Environment and Climate**

The classroom needs to contain as many picture books and easy reading books as feasible: materials for recording, including newsprint, crayons, and paints; objects and materials to manipulate and experiment with; and whatever might stimulate a child's thinking, creativity, or imagination. Among these may be displays, mobiles, plants, flowers, terraria, fish tanks, or pets.

The climate a teacher sets is without doubt the single most important factor in children's integrated learning. It accepts each child as he or she is and sets a tone of business-like cooperation. There is discussion of how we will live together so that all can accomplish what they most want to. Each will be responsible for his or her actions and learning. If a problem should arise between two children, they will be helped at first to solve it themselves, then expected to do so on their own. With the youngest children teachers say it takes about a month before this becomes fairly routine. Teachers at the intermediate level report that this routine takes about the same amount of time to establish when children have not previously experienced taking responsibility for decision making.

Plans of all sorts are discussed with the children, and they are encouraged as far as it is feasible to participate in the decision making. A decision they discuss and freely arrive at is a commitment they make. Children are far more likely to carry it out than they are a teacher's requirement they may or may not understand. Besides, they are learning a most important thinking skill that can be a life long advantage.

Self-direction develops when each child participates in establishing purposes and good ways of achieving them. They understand far better their thoughts in relation to what they are doing and why, and they take satisfaction and pride in directing their own activity.

As reading and writing are developed gradually together, several things are important. The first essential is that an accomplishment, however small, be recognized, and errors as far as possible, left uncorrected. No learner at any age at any task will in the early stages perform without error, and we know that whatever is given attention, is learned. So accenting the positive is a very practical as well as more comfortable procedure.

Another important aspect is to be aware of the moments when children need further experiences to stimulate their thinking. These experiences may be provided to individuals, small groups, or the group as a whole according to need. They may take the form of a special activity within the classroom, within the school, within the neighborhood, or a more extended field trip. They may involve materials brought into the classroom, or books on a particular subject of interest. It is important to keep the environment enriched enough to stimulate each child's thinking but stable enough to provide a calm relaxed living space.

It is interesting to note that, as reading and writing continue, reading "thoughts" or "ideas" are gradually becoming more accurate. Writing, which may have had a number of inaccuracies, is also becoming more accurate.

As children mature in their language skills the opportunities for integration expand. One occurs when three or four children choose to read copies of the same story, providing a common experience. They then discuss among themselves their reactions to the story, its plot and characters as well as the writing. Initially this will be on a simple level: discussing incidents and reacting to them, identifying the favorite character, and saying whether or not the story was fun to read.

With more such experience, the children may point out the main elements in the plot, note any similarity to another story they have read, decide which characters were like real people, and characterize the writing more specifically. If they had read other stories by the same author, they might make various comparisons. This is the second phase of a language experience integrated program with the reading of the story being the experience.

The third phase may be to choose to write something based on the book. This might vary from writing a new ending to the story or working up a skit of one of the incidents, to writing a story of their own using a similar writing style, using the plot with different characters, or writing a sequel to the story. Any of these might involve one or all of the group. Here as elsewhere, writing is a most effective learning procedure when it is a response to one's own experience.

Another opportunity for integration occurs when the group as a whole, or a committee, is learning about some aspect of their world through science, geography, history, and/or any other aspect or combination of aspects. Students talk about what they already know about it, decide how they can find out more through printed material and perhaps an interview of appropriate people. They collect the needed information, discuss it, and prepare it for oral or written presentation to the whole group. This can be carried out very simply at the first grade level, or at a fairly sophisticated thinking level by upper grade children who have had previous experience with this type of learning.

## Spelling

Children's writing stories of their own or researched reports raises the question of spelling, a subskill of writing. In integrated learning, spelling needs to be developed in connection with and out of the needs of each child's writing. If correct spelling is to be of importance to children, it must deal with the words the child wants to write at the time. Group spelling lessons, no matter how the words are selected, are worse than a waste of time. Children see them as an irrelevant task, and the useful learning is minimal. Most children, particularly those who read widely, get their ability to write words correctly from their reading. Correct spelling, whether it be by children or adults, depends on two factors, kinesthetics and perception. That is, familiar words are put on paper by the motion of the fingers without conscious attention to the letter, and they are monitored by the eyes: does the word look right?

When children are beginning to write, they are aware that they do not know how to write some of the words. They will ask the teacher or a friend for assistance. To encourage more independent learners, a teacher's first response would then be to ask the child to find the word somewhere. Places to look are in the stories of other children, on charts or lists of words around a theme which have been developed and made available to children (these might be family relatives, words related to holidays, or to experiences or activities of the group), or in books with which the child is familiar. Older children may find help in the dictionary, though not necessarily. A word too difficult to locate may be written on a slip of paper made available for children to take to the resource person.

Younger children should work at learning to write correctly not more than one or two or at the most three words at a time. And they need to be those words the child feels it is most important to learn at that time. The word or words can be clearly written with a felt pen on a slip of paper which some children like to tape to their desks or tables. It is readily available as needed and can be covered with a book or paper when children are ready to test their learning. They write the word as needed in what they are producing, and immediately check its accuracy. When they have developed confidence that they will always be able to write it correctly when needed, the word is removed and another of the child's choice put in its place. When this plan is followed, time is not wasted "learning" words they already know, and words are correct in their written work, not just on tests.

## Reading

One of the essentials in helping children learn to read is to be thoroughly aware of what reading really is and what it is not. It is not, as many would have us believe, saying words in sequence as they appear on the printed page. Rather, it is understanding the thoughts of another, as they have been recorded. One implication is clear: it is not important that every word be vocalized in order as recorded. The oral reading of educated adults seldom meets that criterion. It is important that the reader show understanding of the main thought of the passage. Two useful criteria are: reading (1) must make sense and (2) must sound like language. These two guides help children recognize when they have made a mistake that distorts meaning.

Another essential is that children select the material they read. What individuals select they are far more committed to than what someone else selects for them. They want to find out what the material can tell them, what meaning it has for them, as different from wanting to get it finished at the behest of someone in command. "Covering" material results in minimal learning compared with selecting what they want to find out about.

Oral reading is important, but it is a separate skill that has only a partial relationship to silent reading. The latter is a far more important goal as it describes most reading that one actually does independently of a teacher. The purpose of oral reading is to convey orally meanings that have been expressed in written form. The most effective way to provide experiences in reading orally is to have each child select something for this purpose, read it orally in private until satisfied with the interpretation, then have the opportunity to present it to a group of attentive listeners. If children do this once a month, they progress faster in their ability to read orally than if they read "around the circle" from a common text every day.

The question of phonics needs to be raised. Teachers using the integrated approach find that children learn phonics by reading, not the other way around. As children read and write, most discover for themselves the sounds represented by the various consonants and to some extent the vowels. When chidlren do not seem to be able to do this on their own, they need to be led to discover the relationship through questioning

Take two words with the same beginning letter or sound which the child knows, and ask him or her to say them. What is alike about them in looks? In sound? Then take another word beginning with the same letter and ask how to say that word. The key question then is "How do you know?" This helps children to analyze and come up with relationships they understand because they have discovered them.

When phonics is discovered naturally, sometimes unconsciously and sometimes with assistance, it becomes what it needs to be—a tool, used when needed, often below the level of awareness—and never assumes a distracting or unnecessary importance.

When dealing with vowels it is important to recognize that when a vowel is short and in an unaccented syllable there is no way by which anyone can identify the vowel by sound. All such vowels take the schwa sound, the indeterminate "uh," indicated in dictionaries by ə. We all learn which vowel to write in words, such as *develop* and *formidable,* by recall of one kind or another, not by phonics.

### Individual Conferences

The individual help children need on more than an incidental basis can be given most effectively through conferences. Since the materials children at any stage of development read are what they have individually selected on the basis of interest, it is only occasionally that more than one is reading the same material at the same time. Even when several are reading the same material, the skills they are developing and the help or direction they need are most likely different. Individual conferences can be set up in various ways, three or four times a week for beginners to once or twice a week for more mature readers. The procedure and purpose for the conference needs to be discussed with the children and their suggestions incorporated as far as feasible. Children may sign up for a conference on a chart or a special spot on the chalkboard at the agreed upon intervals and when they are "ready." Being "ready" means either that they feel they have accomplished what they and the teacher decided on as next learnings at their last conference, or they are having difficulty in accomplishing this learning.

At conference time the teacher sees that everyone else's questions are answered to clear an undisturbed time, perhaps three to ten minutes, for undivided attention. This is possible to the extent self-direction has been achieved and appropriate materials and activities are readily available. Following are sample conferences for students in first through sixth grades.

## First Grade

Paul, in first grade, had read several books in addition to his own and his classmates' stories. He brought another book to his conference with a puzzled look on his face. Mrs. Reaves asked how he liked his new book. "It's all right, I guess, but I don't understand this. It doesn't make sense." Mrs. Reaves suggested he begin at the top of the page that bothered him and read it to her. As he read, his face suddenly cleared. "Oh," he said, "I read that word wrong before." Then he had another problem. He couldn't figure out a certain word. Mrs. Reaves suggested he read the sentence up to the word, skip it, and then read the rest of the sentence. Then she asked what he thought the word could be. Paul looked thoughtfully off into space, then he tentatively made a suggestion. Mrs. Reaves asked him to read the sentence using that word then asked "Does it make it sense?" and "Does the word look as if it could be that word?" When she got affirmative answers to both questions, she said, "You have used two ways to solve your problems, what you can do when something doesn't make sense, and what you can do when you can't figure out a word." Paul was eager to get back to his table, and he continued reading with increased confidence. Mrs. Reaves noticed that he wrote the word he had figured out, adding it to his personal dictionary.

## Second Grade

Sam brought the book he was reading to the conference. He was about half through it and was enjoying it thoroughly. Miss Cummings asked what he especially liked about it, and he indicated it was the fun the children were having and the crazy things their dog, Sunny, did. At Miss Cummings' invitation, he told some of the children's activities and the dog's tricks, which was enough to assure her that he was understanding at least most of the story. So she next probed, "What do you think may happen next?" His projections were sufficiently consistent with his previous accounts to give further evidence of his understanding. It did not matter at this stage if he read every word correctly. Far more important was his eagerness to read and his pleasure in it, and that he read with reasonable understanding. Children learn to read by reading, especially when they enjoy it. Together, they set the goal for the next conference for Sam, to report how right he had been about what happened next. Also, they would talk about the next book he had chosen to read. Miss Cummings asked Sam to make a list of the words that described the crazy things that Sunny, the dog, did. She explained that these words could help him with his writing about his own dog.

*Third Grade*

Elaine brought to the conference a book on wild animals in the United States which her group was studying. They wanted to find out which animals needed protection. Mr. Rada asked her if she found the book helpful. She said it was interesting to read, but it didn't tell her what she was looking for. She had looked at some of the other books Mr. Rada had brought in for the project and could not find anything in them either. He asked her how she had tried to find the information. She told him she had looked in the table of contents and read about some of the animals. "How else do we look for special information we want?" "Oh, I remember now, the index!" She quickly turned to the back of the book, but then looked puzzled. "What do I look for?" "What information do you want?" "Which animals need protection." "Which of those words might be a good one to check?" "Protection?" "Try it." "It isn't in here." "What did we say animals that need protection are called?" "Oh, endangered. Here it is—endangered species. Oh, thank you, now I can find what I need." She returned to her table and soon was checking the index in other books as well. Elaine was to make a wall-chart of endangered species for her class. She was responsible for the list only. Her group would illustrate the chart.

*Fourth Grade*

Belinda came for her conference bringing her book. First she told briefly the theme and told about the main characters. Miss White asked if she thought they were the kind of people she might know some day. Belinda considered, then said, "Well, I think I might know Carl, but I can't imagine anybody like his mother!" Miss White asked, "Why?" Again Belinda paused. "I guess it's because she's never happy or never sad and she doesn't care what Carl does!" This assured Miss White that Belinda was not only thinking of characters as people, but was aware of the feelings they exhibited in relation to her own. Since the group had begun focusing on authors and authorship, Miss White asked, "What do you know about the author?" Belinda told of other similar books he had written which were listed in the front of the book. She said she had read two other of his books and chose this one because she had liked the others. Together they decided it would be a good idea to find out more about the author's life and perhaps why he decided to write the kind of books he did. Belinda said that if she found enough information, she would like to write a short biography for the class library, and then her friends could get the same information.

*Fifth Grade*

Sarah wanted to talk about an article she had been reading in her study of volcanoes. She had to work hard to understand the information given, but her intense interest kept her at it steadily. Also she wanted to be sure she really understood it to prepare for meeting with the group who were studying volcanoes. Each had taken a reference to read and report on and they were to meet for discussion tomorrow. Mrs. Gill listened to ideas Sarah felt she understood and then questioned one of them. "Where did you find that information?" Sarah looked through the article, located a paragraph and read it aloud, but stopped midway. "But, this sentence doesn't agree with the one up here." Mrs. Gill suggested that she read both sentences to herself. Suddenly Sarah said, "Oh, I see now. I didn't read this correctly. I should have read it again when the two sentences didn't fit." Then Mrs. Gill helped her to list the ideas she would report to the group by getting the main thought from each paragraph or group of paragraphs. Sarah indicated she would like to prepare an outline for her presentation to the group.

*Sixth Grade*

Jerry brought the book he had been reading to his conference and talked with Mr. Rubin about the story. Topics they covered included a brief story line, the main characters and their relationship to each other, and the contribution of each to the story, that is, the purpose for which the author introduced each. These topics were then applied to the story Jerry had been writing and to his introduction and development of characters. Jerry read a short passage aloud which illustrated a point he was making. Mr. Rubin checked Jerry's understanding of two or three of the more unusual words in the story and asked him to illustrate how he might use them. They decided that Jerry needs to be more aware of words with which he is unfamiliar and talked about getting the meaning of such words from context. Jerry decided that for the next conference he would give more thought to how characters are used and list words whose meaning he has gotten from context.

## Record Keeping

It is important to keep appropriate records of what transpires during a conference. Students may want to keep some record of what has taken place as well as plans for follow-up or next steps, depending on their maturity and writing ability. Teachers, however, will need to devise some means for writing down pertinent information regarding a conference. Perhaps a file for each child that can be kept chronologically where, at a glance, data from several conferences can be seen. Loose-leaf notebooks and file cards have both proven to be useful. The important information to record is not a "good-better-best" rating, but rather the specific learning noted and concepts or skills that are needed but have not yet been learned.

## Evaluation

The usual type of testing is quite inappropriate for understanding children's progress in reading. The conference is surely the single best means, but the cloze test has value when a paper and pencil test is desired for individuals or the group. Such a test can be devised easily by anyone by starting with a reading selection with difficulty appropriate to the maturity of the readers. It is retyped replacing each fifth word with a blank of consistent length and long enough for a child to write in a word. As many copies as needed can then be made.

Children as individuals or groups can then take a copy and attempt to fill in the blanks. Their success depends upon the meaning they derive from groups of words and their implicit understanding of the way language works. They will usually be able to tell the part of speech that was omitted, the tense of a verb, whether a word is singular or plural and, thus, the actual word or a synonym through context. Children who cannot respond adequately to such material indicate they tend to be word callers rather than readers. This means they do not understand what reading is, but have been led to believe it was the ability to say each word in sequence on a printed page gaining only minimal meaning from the process.

When children in the middle or upper grades are having difficulty in reading, the most useful diagnostic device is miscue analysis (Allen and Watson, 1976). It is built on the basis that effective reading depends on the accurate identification of the fewest cues needed to interpret correctly the meaning of the passage. Less effective readers either miss essential cues or pick up inaccurate ones. Miscue analysis can be used informally with any material to help identify a child's difficulty.

## Conclusion

Language experience is a most natural and effective way for integrating not only language skills, but also content, with the personal development of thinking skills, self-direction, and responsibility. The program can be developed gradually, but only when it is, as a whole, consistent with what is known about children and their learning will there be optimum results. This does not mean teachers' programs need to be identical, for each teacher as well as each child is a unique person. What is important is that basic principles be implemented.

## References

Allen, David P., and Dorothy J. Watson, eds. *Findings of Research in Miscue Analysis: Classroom Implications.* Urbana, Ill.: NCTE, 1976.

Bartnick, Robert, and Genevieve S. Lopardo. "The Cloze Procedure: A Multi-Purpose Classroom Tool." *Reading Improvement* 13 (1976): 113–117.

Braun, Carl, Allan R. Neilson, and Robert Dykstra. "Teacher Expectation: Prime Mover or Inhibitor?" In *Reading Interaction,* edited by Leonard Courtney, pp. 40–48. Newark, Del.: IRA, 1976.

Cohen, S. Alan, and Thelma Cooper. "Seven Fallacies: Reading Retardation and the Urban Disadvantaged Beginning Reader." *The Reading Teacher* 26 (1972): 38–45.

Foerster, Leona M. "Language Experience for Dialectically Different Black Learners." *Elementary English* 51 (1974): 193–197.

Gomberg, Adeline Wishengrad. "Freeing Children to Take a Chance." *Reading Teacher* 29 (1975): 455–457.

Gomberg, Adeline Wishengrad, ed. *Miscue Analysis: Applications to Reading Instruction.* Urbana, Ill.: NCTE, 1973.

Gove, Mary K. "Using the Cloze Procedure in a First Grade Classroom." *Reading Teacher* 29 (1975): 36–38.

Lee, Dorris M. and Joseph B. Rubin. *Children and Language: Reading and Writing, Talking and Listening.* Belmont, Calif.: Wadsworth, 1979.

Mickish, Virginia. "Children's Perception of Written Word Boundaries." *Journal of Reading Behavior* 6 (April 1974): 19–22.

O'Hare, Frank. *Sentence-Combining: Improving Student Writing Without Formal Grammar Instruction.* Urbana, Ill.: NCTE, 1971.

O'Hare, Frank. "Making Sense of Reading—And of Reading Instruction." *Harvard Educational Review* 47 (1977): 386–395.

Weber, Rose-Marie. "First Graders' Use of Grammatical Context in Reading." In *Basic Studies in Reading,* edited by Harry Levin and Joanna Williams, pp. 160–162. New York: Basic Books, 1970.

# 9  Songs, Singing Games, and Language Play

Sandra A. Rietz
Eastern Montana College

Both adults and children play with language and with literary form. The human need to "self entertain" through play, in this case language and literary play, has aided the development of literature (Pellowski, 1977, p. 10) and continues to aid in the language development of children.

The act of doing the (oral) literature is the act of playing a game with language, literary form, and human behavior as objects of the play. Primitive forms of language/literary games consist principally of repetitious play (Pellowski, 1977, p. 15) with the features of the language itself. More sophisticated stories and songs play with larger literary features within story or song grammars and provide playful commentary on human circumstance. The game nature of the practice of the oral literature ensures safety for learning both language forms and human content within story or song and eliminates the need to tell language rules in order to achieve language learning. Through active involvement with language and literature, children learn to control language and develop increasingly sophisticated expectations for the behaviors of language and literary forms. The abundant varieties of language play games, literary form and content games available in oral literature present a rich collection of language manipulations from which children can develop language and literary maturity.

Though the literature acts primarily as a tool for the development of access to language—it does not *teach about* language or literature—playing the language/literary games of song and story does require a certain focus of attention upon the object of the play. Continued repetition of the language and grammar of the literature can lead, eventually, to readiness to examine the language and literary forms of story and song in order to know *about* them. For each specific language skill given as a teaching objective in any language teaching sequence at any level, a story or song can be found to do the job, a story or song which will provide, in addition, a safe, holistic, enjoyable means for learning language control.

The literature offers language and literary play at many levels of sophistication. While younger children enjoy repetitious language play, very probably for its predictability, and use it to develop control over language form, older children are attracted to a more subtle play with story form and literary content, and are more inclined to use language as a vehicle directed to achieving larger literary ends.

Songs and stories can be sorted into roughly defined categories of play type. These categories can then be used to aid in the selection of appropriate literary play and language development experiences for children. (See list of titles and categories following text.)

**Songs and Singing Games**

Many language games sing and dance a play with language features and patterns, substitutions within patterns, pattern expansions, and pattern inventions. Play with the entire form of the song and the dance focuses participant attention on *game* rather than on *language,* control over the language of the game being the necessary means to successful play. Game types include no-change-repetition-of-pattern-play, invention and substitution play, question/answer play, cumulative play, whole story play, counting play, and nonsense and "awful" play.

*No-Change-Repetition-of-Pattern-Play*

The "make a bridge and don't get caught" types of pattern repetition play can be very exciting for participants. "How Many Miles to Bethlehem" (Richards, 1974) is typical. Participants choose partners and march hand-in-hand clockwise in a circle. At one point in the circle, couples march under a bridge (two people with hands joined to make an arch). All players sing:

> How many miles to Bethlehem? (Charleston, New Orleans, etc.)
> Four score and ten.
> Can I get there by candle light?
> Yes, and back again.

> LU LU LU LU LU LU LU LU
> LU LU LU LU
> LU LU LU LU LU LU LU LU
> LU LU LU LU LU.

The bridge catches whichever couple is under the arch and holds them while the second verse is sung.

> Open the gate and let me pass.
> First you must pay.

> I have no gold, what shall I do?
> Turn and go away.

The bridge releases its captives, who turn back and form a second bridge.
All remaining couples march while singing a second round of the chorus
and begin the song again. When all couples have been caught and turned
to bridges, the original bridge turns, pulls each bridge in turn under and
through all of the remaining bridges, then leads a wind-the-clock exercise.
This game offers much language repetition and much excitement, while
question/answer transformation is practiced. "A Hunting We Will Go"
(Richards, 1973) provides repetitious practice of inverted pattern and
compound sentence construction.

Many pattern repetition games use the choose someone from the circle
type of play and encourage dramatic creativity. In "The Tide Rolls High"
("Sailing in My Boat," Seeger, 1948), players practice compound construction and commands while selecting one player at a time to leave the big
circle to march in the center. In "Oats, Peas, Beans" (Jones, 1980), players
form a circle with the "farmer" in the center. While the farmer walks in
one direction, other players circle in the opposite direction singing:

> Oats, peas, beans, and barley grow.
> Oats, peas, beans, and barley grow.
> Can you or I or anyone know
> How oats, peas, beans, and barley grow?

All players stop, sing and act out:

> First the farmer plants his seed.
> Then he stands and takes his ease.
> Stamps his feet and claps his hands
> And turns around to view the land.

Players begin circling with the third verse.

> Waiting for a partner.
> Waiting for a partner.
> Open the ring; select one in,
> And then we sing and dance again.

At "select one in" the farmer chooses a partner to circle inside the big
ring. The game continues until all players in the outside circle have joined
the inside circle. The song language contains several basic patterns: a
question and a compound construction, commands, noun plurals, and a
variety of verb forms.

Songs and dances which belong in the no-change category provide
game frames of reference in which simple, short verses can be repeated
at length while player attention is given to the movement of the game.

The usually simple language forms quickly become predictable and controllable.

## *Invention and Substitution Play*

A variety of songs invite player participation in language invention games. Players are presented with given structures into which language can be inserted. Invention and substitution games focus player attention on language form, since play requires language manipulation as well as repetition. Choosing appropriate games from this category requires examination of the language requirements of the game. One very primitive substitution type is "I Love My Shirt," a song that requires noun substitution into direct object function (I love my _____.) repeats use of "I, me, my" in proper locations, builds a compound construction, and utilizes the "es" inflection on the third person verb. "By'm Bye" (Seeger, 1948) requires whole clause construction and basic pattern expansion using where, when, why, how, and adjective embeddings. Players might decide, for instance, that they would like to sing about elephants sitting in a bathtub taking a shower because it is hot outside, that the elephants are old, leathery, wrinkled, smelly, and green with blue spots. The invented line might look like this:

> Old, leathery, wrinkled, smelly, green and blue spotted elephants
> sitting in the bathtub taking a shower because it is hot outside . . .

Such a lengthy invention is coached and written before it is sung, allowing for editing and play with words and imagery in process. "Deep Blue Sea" makes a game of plot invention. Players not only invent single line verses, but also create entire story line. Successful play with story necessitates a bit of borrowing from the supply of stock verses provided from previous generations of players. Begin with:

> Deep blue sea, baby. Deep blue sea.
> Deep blue sea, baby. Deep blue sea.
> Deep blue sea, baby. Deep blue sea.
> It was Willie [what] got drownd[ed]
> In the deep blue sea.
>
> It was sad when the boat went down. (repeat three times)
> (repeat last line)
>
> Cry for him with tears of pearl. (repeat three times)
> (repeat last line)

Three stock verses are sufficient to suggest setting and problem for additional verses. Second grade inventions often include sharks, whales, and Charlie Tuna.

Willie sank to the bottom of the sea.
Charlie Tuna came swimming along.
Charlie ate Willie and was good enough for Starkist.
Charlie and Willie ended up in a can.
I bought the can and made a sandwich.
I ate the sandwich, and it made me [sick].
I returned the can to the grocery store.
I will never eat tuna anymore.
Deep blue sea, baby. Deep blue sea.

Unlike adults, children do not feel compelled to marry Willie to the first mermaid that happens along.

Invention and substitution play in patterns provided by the song itself restrict players to a practice of a highly repetitive nature, and allow players to learn to manipulate syntactic and semantic content according to the rules (structures) of the game.

### Question/Answer Play

With games of the question/answer type, players practice who/what/when/where/why and yes/no questions, invent voices appropriate to song characters, chant in groups, and improvise mime. Most such songs alternate question with answer, some allow partial invention of the answer, or, at minimum, single word substitution into given answers. The level of sophistication of question/answer games seems more a matter of level of humor presented in the story line than of difficulty of constructions repeated. "Who's That Knocking on My Window" (Seeger, 1948) lacks plot altogether, and its simple repetition of only two lines makes it a primitive game of this type. The questioner (person or group) asks the title line; the answer is "_____ knocking at my window. _____ knocking at my door." "There's a Hole in the Bucket" (Richards, 1973) and "Henery, My Boy" tell funny stories in question/answer format, and allow individual players or groups of players to take parts, invent voices, and mime actions. Both simple and more mature question/answer games draw player attention away from language form. The content of the answer is the focus, whether the answer requires no more than a single word substitution or is part of a story line which builds to a punch line ending.

### Cumulative Play

Cumulative games provide building sequences for add-on repeat-back memory play. In many cumulative songs, items added into a growing list of names, actions, or locations to be remembered in order are structurally identical. Players chant lists of nouns, adjective noun sequences, strings of prepositional phrases, or remember long chains of clauses. Difficulty of a cumulative game, in addition to level of humor, might be measured by the manner in which additional elements are built into the sequence to be remembered. Simple cumulative play lists structurally similar or identical items. "The Wind Blow(s) East" (Seeger, 1948) plays with lists of adjective/noun combinations. "When I First Came to This Land" is a collection of repeated clauses conforming to the "And I called my _____, _____ pattern. (And I called my duck, out of luck.) The result of simple cumulative play is a compounding of many elements in a string.

More complicated cumulatives build the addition of new items in the list into one larger pattern. Rather than players repeating a growing compound construction, they continue to expand a pattern from within by adding new elements into the structure with each new verse. "The Ladies in the Harem of the Court of King Caraticus" is a crazy quilt nonsense expansion game that begins as a simple subject-verb pattern. The finished product includes prepositional phrases, embedded clauses, embedded adjectives, dependent clauses, a variety of verb forms, and remains one construction. The joke (for the game is a joke) is carried syntactically and semantically.

1. The ladies in the harem of the court of King Caraticus were just passing by. (repeat four times)

2. The noses on the faces of the ladies in the harem of the court of King Caraticus were just passing by. (4)

3. The boys who put the powder on the noses on the faces of the ladies in the harem of the court of King Caraticus were just passing by. (4)

4. The scintillating witches put the stitches in the britches of the boys who put the powder on the noses on the faces of the ladies in the harem of the court of King Caraticus were just passing by. (4)

5. If you want to see the witches put the stitches in the britches of the boys who put the powder on the noses on the faces of the ladies in the harem of the court of King Caraticus, you're too late, [cuz] they just passed by.

Tongue twister cumulatives, humorous add-ons, and memory sequences that can also be adapted to dramatic play appeal to older children. Memory work in a cumulative game which expands a single pattern from within is more difficult, the language forms less predictable than those in a simple compounding cumulative game.

*Whole Story Play*

Songs that tell whole stories introduce children to play with plot and to
repetition of language forms which manage to contain story line within
the structural restrictions of song cadence. Appropriate story songs for
younger children are those which are structurally repetitious, which can
be danced and mimed. "Old Roger" (Gomme, 1967) is an excellent
example of the integration of dance, mime, and simple, highly predictable
language forms. In "Old Roger," players stand in a circle, sing with hands
folded across chests, and bow to the beat of the music. Three players in
circle center act out the cues sung to them by those in the circle. One of
the three plays Old Roger, who is "dead"; one is an apple tree; one is an
old lady. Children customarily play the game until each person in the
circle has had the opportunity to be one of the three in the center. The
entire song must be repeated for each new set of center players. The game
itself compels the language repetition. The storytelling in "Old Roger" is
less a focus than listening and doing in the center.

Older players prefer songs that tell stories in more complicated and
less predictable language forms, and story songs that deliver a punch line,
an observation about human behavior (preferably funny), credible characters, and a series of events worth attending to. "Logger Lover" (Best,
1955) tells the story of a man who wanders into a town, orders a cup of
coffee from a six foot seven waitress, then proceeds, unwillingly, to listen
as she describes her love affair with a logger who froze to death when the
outside thermometer registered a minus 1000° F. The song lends itself
well to dramatic play, readers theatre, improvisation, choral reading, and
prose story writing using the verse as an expansion starter. Although
humorous, such story songs can serve as points of focus for examining
ballad form, and, perhaps, as models for ballad creating.

*Counting Play*

For younger players, counting songs and games are serious work. Children count within the frameworks of repetitious and predictable language
forms. In general, counting songs for young children, while a form of
play, are not funny. Older children play with counting, since they are
quite capable of counting, in songs whose only purpose is nonsense. Such
frivolous, ad-nauseum counting games ("Ten in the Bed," "One Hundred
Bottles of Beer," Best, 1955) remain one of the wonders of the children's
own oral literature and will be sung with or without the blessings of adults.

*Nonsense and "Awful" Play*

"Awful" songs, songs which amuse children greatly and (some) adults to a
lesser extent, are those that qualify as "gross" (child definition of the

word). These songs contain play elements that fit all of the above listed categories; however, their content and language is often silly, nonsensical, sometimes accomplishes nothing other than endless repetition for the sake of endless repetition. Songs that fit here are games allowing children to play with the act of playing, and to develop through such play, the awareness that literature is a form of play with dimensions of language and with aspects of human behavior. As bizarre as the contents of such games may seem to the adult, "awful" play does represent an important step in the development of ability to play with language and literary form. "Awful" play draws player attention to language and literature as objects.

## Story Games

Play within story is often identical to that within song or singing game. In the story, however, the play is found embedded in story grammar. Players understand, usually without instruction, that the story is a game, and that within the general play that is the story, play of a more specific nature can occur. Specific elements of language play can be found throughout a story, but the selection of a story is best made by examining the nature of (language) play within the "event sequence" or the problem-solving part of the story grammar.

In the event sequence, many stories present play types that can be classified in much the same manner as the list of play types in songs and singing games. Event sequence play can be described as repetition of single event type play, repetition/substitution in single event type play, cumulative sequence play, no repetition sequence play with single problem and more than one problem plots.

### Repetition of Single Event

The single event repetition story accomplishes solution of the problem by repeating the same attempt at problem solving again and again. *The Gunniwolf* (Harper, 1967) repeats a running event until the girl escapes the wolf. In *The Hedgehog and the Hare* (Watson, n.d.), rabbit and hedgehog run the same race, up and back and up and back, until the rabbit gives up. Stories of this type can be shortened or lengthened to suit the tastes and endurances of different audiences by simply adding extra repetitions of the event into the story. The language of each repeated event is identical, making a story form whose behavior is very predictable.

### Repetition/Substitution in Single Event

Stories of the repetition/substitution type repeat events within the story in language that maintains a similarity and predictability from one event to the next. However, within each new event, some substitutions of characters and actions may occur. In *The Wide Mouth Frog* (Schneider, 1980) the frog meets five different animals as he journeys along toward a solution to his problem. He behaves in the same manner with each new animal that he meets, but each new animal answers the frog differently. In "The Red Fox and the Walking Stick" (Ginsburg, 1973), fox repeats his actions and language five times over, each time with a different person or persons and each time with slightly different results. In such stories, some story language is predictable, and some surprise changes are also predictable. Listeners can learn expectations for the changeable shape of story within the confines of overall repetition.

### Cumulative Sequence

Cumulative stories build add-on and, often, repeat back sequences into the problem-solving efforts of the character or characters. The play of the entire story becomes as much a focus on remembering the series of items in the add-on list as a play with plot. *Fat Cat* (Kent, 1972) presents a series of simple sentences for audience participation. ("And the cat said, 'I ate the pot. I ate the stew, And, now, I am going to also eat you.'") Cumulative play presents language that young children can learn to control in a story grammar that the children can learn to predict and expect.

### No Repetition Sequence

In the no repetition sequence story, the problem-solving behavior of the character or characters, while predictable in that listeners have learned some expectations for story shape, does not repeat itself. Each new attempt at problem solving is different from all others, however logical all of these separate attempts might be when taken as a whole. Such stories, depending upon content, tend to have a more adult appeal and tend to focus play on overall shape of plot, on characterizations, on dialogue or description, and on human behavior. Experience with a variety of stories of this general type can aid the development of expectations for the behavior of story as a literary form.

### Two Problem Stories

Some stories present a plot in which more than one problem develops. In some stories ("The Sly Fox," Ginsburg, 1973) more than one problem occurs simultaneously, and the character must solve all problems in order that any of the problems reach a resolution. In other two or more prob-

lem stories, problems occur in sequence ("The Monkey and the Crocodile," De Roin, 1975). No sooner has the character solved one problem
than another appears. Stories containing more than one problem are
more appropriate for children who have learned the predictability of
story shape and plot behavior, and who are ready to play with complications and sophistications of story grammars. Stories that present highly
predictable, repetitious language, and those that aid memory of and control of language forms are most appealing to younger children. Humorous
sophistications, puns, punch lines, funny morals, complications of story
structure, surprise language, surprise endings, and elements that contribute
to awareness of self, others, language form, and story behavior are important additions to stories for older children and for adults.

**Language Development and Literary Play**

*Songs and Singing Games*

No Change—Repetition of Pattern Play

All of these songs and singing games provide pattern repetition play
without invention or substitution in pattern. Many of the songs do allow
for nonlinguistic invention, i.e.: dramatic play and movement.

>(make a bridge and don't get caught types)
>
>Milking Pails (Gomme, 1967)
>Where Has My Little Dog Gone? (Cano, 1973)
>A Hunting We Will Go (Richards, 1973)
>London Bridge
>Maple Swamp
>I'm Going Down to Town
>How Many Miles to Bethlehem? (Richards, 1974)
>
>(choosing games)
>
>The Tide Rolls High (no source) see Seeger, 1948: Sailing in
>  My Boat
>Come and Follow Me (Richards, 1973)
>The Juniper Tree (Seeger, 1948)
>Walk Along John
>Skip to My Lou

The Closet Key

Green Gravel (Gomme, 1967)

Three Dukes-A-Riding

Poor Mary Sits-A-Weeping

The Farmer in the Dell (Cano, 1973)

Oats, Peas, Beans (Jones, 1980)

(circle/dramatic play games)

Such a Getting Upstairs (Seeger, 1948)

Jimmie Rose, He Went to Town

Adam Had Seven Sons

All around the Kitchen

Scraping up Sand

Roll that Brown Jug

The Little Pig

Johnny Get Your Hair Cut (Richards, 1973)

Throw in a Stone

Come and Follow Me

Invention and Substitution Play

All of these songs and singing games allow invention and substitution of language into given functions or structures. Patterns into which substitutions are made are repeated. In addition, many of the songs also provide opportunity for dramatic play and movement invention.

(single word substitutions)

I Love My Shirt (no source) (noun into object slot)

Mary Wore Her Red Dress (Seeger, 1948) (adjective/noun into object slot)

Circle Left (Richards, 1973) (verb and verb/adverb or verb/noun into object slot)

Frog's in the Meadow (noun/proper name into subject slot)

Here We Are Together (noun into object of preposition function)

Sally Go round the Sun (noun/proper name into subject slot)

Down Came a Lady (Seeger, 1948) (noun/proper name into subject slot)

Jim Along Josie (noun/proper name into subject slot and/or verb)

Here Sits a Monkey (noun/proper name into subject slot)

Adam Had Seven Sons (verb/adverb or verb/noun into object slot)

Clap Your Hands (verb and/or noun into object slot)

All around the Kitchen (verb and/or noun into object slot)

Little Bird, Little Bird (noun into subject slot)

(phrase, line, whole pattern substitutions)

I Got a Letter this Morning (Seeger, 1948)

This Old Man

Toodala

By'm Bye

What Shall We Do When We All Go Out?

Oh, Oh, the Sunshine

Juba

Hop, Old Squirrel

Do, Do, Pity My Case

(whole plot/story invention using given pattern)

Skip to My Lou (Seeger, 1948)

The Train Is A-Coming

When the Train Comes Along

Deep Blue Sea (no source)

The Tide Rolls High (no source)

Question/Answer Play

Who's That Knockin' at My Window? (Seeger, 1948)

How Old Are You?

What Shall We Do When We All Go Out?

Billy Barlow

Did You Go to the Barney?

Blow Boys, Blow

There's a Hole in the Bucket (Richards, 1973)

The Button and the Key

Milking Pails (Gomme, 1967)

What Shall We Do with a Drunken Sailor? (Best, 1955)

Henery My Boy (no source)

Cumulative (add on-repeat back) Play

Many of these songs and singing games repeat simple pattern with substitutions provided in the text. In the starred songs (*), singers can invent
and substitute words and/or lines within given structure.

*The Wind Blow East (Seeger, 1948)

*By'm Bye

*Bought Me a Cat

On this Hill (Richards, 1973)

Mommy, Buy Me a China Doll (Zemach, 1966)

Drummer Hoff (Emberley and Emberley, 1967)

The Green Grass Grows All Around (no source)

*You Can't Have Any of My Peanuts

There's a Hole in the Bottom of the Sea

*When I First Came to this Land

The Ladies in the Harem of the Court of King Caraticus

*The Ford Song

*The Barnyard Song

There Was an Old Lady

*Come and Follow Me (Richards, 1973)

*She'll Be Comin' round the Mountain

*Old MacDonald

(cumulative—nonsecular)

The Twelve Days of Christmas (no source)

The Twelve Apostles

Whole Story Play

These singing games introduce whole plot within song/game framework.
The first seven songs listed present plot along with repetitious pattern and
some substitution and/or invention (add "Deep Blue Sea"). The language
in such games is highly predictable in form. Some of the songs, most
notably "Old Roger," include dramatic play and opportunity for invention of movement. The remaining songs in the list present language,
humor, and game at more sophisticated levels, and also lend themselves
well to many related interpretive activities.

There Was a Man and He Was Mad (Seeger, 1948)

Billie Barlow

She'll Be Comin' round the Mountain

Hush Little Baby

Go Tell Aunt Rhody (Richards, 1973)

Old Roger Is Dead (Gomme, 1967)

The Riddle Song (Best, 1955)

Frog Went A-Courtin' (Seeger, 1948)

John Henry

The Fox Went Out on a Chilly Night (Best, 1955)

Patsy Ory Ory Aye

E- Ri -E Canal

Logger Lover (The Frozen Logger)

Old Blue

My Grandfather's Clock

Counting Play

By'm Bye (Seeger, 1948)

Down by the Greenwood Sidey-O

Down Came a Lady

This Old Man

The Tide Rolls High (no source)

One Wide River to Cross (Emberley, 1966)

(And for older singers who are less interested in counting than nonsense and general foolishness: "Ten in the Bed," "One Hundred Bottles of Beer," and more. See Best, 1955.)

Nonsense and "Awful" Play

My Bonnie (Lies over the Ocean) (Best, 1955)

The Hearse Song

The Ship *Titanic*

Clementine

Throw It out the Window

Johnny Vorbeck

Who Threw the Overalls in Mrs. Murphy's Chowder?

The Pig and the Inebriate

Pink Pajamas

Ol' Joe Clark

*Story Games*

Event Sequence Play—Repetition of Single Event Type

In these stories, the event sequence consists of one event repeated a given or chosen number of times. The language in the event is repeated again and again in each retelling of the event.

> The Gunniwolf (Harper, 1967)
>
> The Hedgehog and the Hare (Watson, n.d.)
>
> The Little Boy's Secret (Harrison, 1972)

Event Sequence Play—Repetition/Substitution in Single Event Type

These stories also consist of one event repeated again and again. However, within each repetition of the same event, some detail or details are changed. The first three stories on the list represent primitive stories of the substitution type. In each new repetition of the event, a character name is changed. With the last repetition of the event, outcome also changes. Otherwise, event language remains identical for each repetition. The last stories in the list (especially The Jack Tales) contain changes from event to event which are more complex. Nevertheless, the structure of each repeated event remains the same.

> The Wide Mouth Frog (no source)
>
> The Five Chinese Brothers
>
> The Three Billy Goats Gruff
>
> The Red Fox and the Walking Stick (Ginsburg, 1973)
>
> The Miller, the Boy, and the Donkey (Wildsmith, 1969)
>
> The Three Goats (Literature Committee, 1950)
>
> The Brementown Musicians (Plume, 1980)
>
> The Foolish Frog (Seeger, 1961)
>
> Jack in the Giant's New Ground (Chase, 1943)
>
> Jack and the Bean Tree
>
> Jack and the Bull
>
> Jack and the Robbers
>
> Jack and the Northwest Wind

Hardy Hardhead

Old Fire Dragoman

## Cumulative Sequence Play

The Old Woman and Her Pig (Literature Committee, 1950)

The Gingerbread Man

Fat Cat (Jack Kent, 1972)

The Judge (Zemach, 1969)

The Pancake (Literature Committee, 1950)

Why Mosquitoes Buzz in People's Ears

## No Repetition Sequence—Single Problem Plot

All stories contain "problem" as a necessary part of story structure. It is the "problem" in the story that initiates character activity and plot. Many stories contain only one "problem." In such stories, the solutions that result from the action of the characters are solutions for the one "problem." The listener or reader can safely predict that all action in the single problem story will be focused on the single problem.

The Giant Who Was Afraid of Butterflies (Harrison, 1972)

The Giant Who Threw Tantrums

Sop Doll (Chase, 1943)

The Two Donkeys (Wolkstein, 1979)

Everyone Knows What a Dragon Looks Like (Williams, 1976)

Abiyoyo (Seeger, 1961)

## No Repetition Sequence—Double Problem Plot

In stories that contain more than one problem, character action is focused first on the solution of one problem, then upon the solution of the other(s) in turn, or, character action can be focused on both problems (all problems) at once.

Double and multiple problem stories require the listener or reader to predict story structure of a branched type and to hold in memory and properly associate the correct action with the correct solution to the correct problem.

Jack and the Varmints (Chase, 1943)

Soldier Jack

The Monkey and the Crocodile (De Roin, 1975)

The Sly Fox (Ginsburg, 1973)

No Repetition Sequence—Epic Type

   Gilgamesh
   The Iliad/Odyssey
   The Adventures of Strong Vanya

## Bibliography

Best, Dick, and Beth Best, eds. *Song Fest.* New York: Crown Publishers, 1955.

Bishop, Claire. *The Five Chinese Brothers.* New York: Coward, 1938.

Bone, Margaret B., ed. *Fireside Book of Folksong.* New York: Simon and Schuster, 1947.

Cano, Robin B., ed. *Game Songs.* Boston: Houghton Mifflin, 1973.

Carmer, Carl, ed. *America Sings.* New York: Alfred A. Knopf, 1942.

Chase, Richard, ed. *The Jack Tales.* Boston: Houghton Mifflin, 1943.

De Roin, Nancy. *Jataka Tales; Fables from the Buddha.* Boston: Houghton Mifflin, 1975.

Emberley, Barbara. *One Wide River to Cross.* Englewood Cliffs, N. J.: Prentice-Hall, 1966.

Emberley, Ed, and Barbara Emberley. *Drummer Hoff.* Englewood Cliffs, N. J.: Prentice-Hall, 1967.

Galdone, Paul. *The Three Billy Goats Gruff.* Boston: Houghton Mifflin, 1973.

Ginsburg, Mirra. *One Trick Too Many; Fox Tales from Russia.* New York: Dial Press, 1973.

Gomme, Alice B., ed. *Children Singing Games.* New York: Dover Publications, 1967.

Harper, Wilhelmina, ed. *The Gunniwolf.* New York: Dutton, 1967.

Harrison, David. *The Book of Great Stories.* New York: American Heritage Press, 1972.

Jackson and Bryan, eds. *American Folk Music.* Boston: C.C. Berchard, n.d.

Kent, Jack. *Fat Cat.* New York: Scholastic Book Service, 1972.

Landeck, Beatrice, ed. *More Songs to Grow On.* New York: William Sloane, 1954.

Landeck, Beatrice, ed. *Songs to Grow On.* New York: William Sloane, 1950.

Langstaff, John, ed. *Hi! Ho! The Rattlin' Bog: and Other Folksongs for Group Singing.* New York: Harcourt Brace and World, 1969.

Langstaff, John, and Nancy Langstaff, eds. *Jim along Josie.* New York: Harcourt, Brace, Jovanovich, 1970.

Literature Committee of the International Kindergarten Union. *Told under the Green Umbrella.* New York: International Kindergarten Union, 1950.

Lomax, Alan, ed. *The Folksongs of North America.* New York: Doubleday, 1960.

Lomax, John A., and Alan A. Lomax, eds. *American Ballads and Folksongs.* New York: Macmillan, 1934.

Lomax, John A., and Alan A. Lomax, eds. *Folksong USA.* New York: Duell, Sloan and Pierce, 1947.

Lomax, John A., and Alan A. Lomax, eds. *Our Singing Country.* New York: Macmillan, 1941.

Mitchell, Donald, and Roderick Biss, eds. *The Gambit Book of Children's Songs.* Boston: Gambit, 1970.

Pellowski, Anne. *The World of Storytelling.* New York: R.R. Bowker, 1979.

Plume, Ilse, ed. *The Brementown Musicians.* New York: Doubleday, 1980.

Richards, Mary Helen. *The Music Language: Part One.* Portola Valley, Calif.: Richards Institute of Music Education, 1973.

Richards, Mary Helen. *The Music Language: Part Two.* Portola Valley, Calif.: Richards Institute of Music Education, 1974.

Sandburg, Carl, ed. *The American Songbag.* New York: Harcourt Brace, 1927.

Seeger, Pete. *Pete Seeger Story Songs.* Columbia Record Co., C11668, 1961.

Seeger, Ruth C., ed. *American Folksongs for Children.* New York: Doubleday, 1948.

Sweeney, Sister Fleurette. *Experience Games through Music for the Very Very Young.* Portola Valley, Calif.: Richards Institute of Music Education, 1973.

Warram, Margaret. *Experience Games through Music for the Very Young.* Portola Valley, Calif.: Richards Institute of Music Education, 1973.

Watson, Windy. *The Hedgehog and the Hare.* Cleveland: World Publishers, n.d.

Weavers, The, eds. *The Weavers' Songbook.* New York:, Harper and Bros., 1960.

Wells, Evelyn K., ed. *The Ballad Free.* New York: Ronald Press, 1950.

Wildsmith, Brian. *The Miller, the Boy and the Donkey.* New York: Watts, 1969.

Williams, Jay. *Everyone Knows What a Dragon Looks Like.* New York: Four Winds Press, 1976.

Winn, Marie, ed. *The Fireside Book of Fun and Game Songs.* New York: Simon and Schuster, 1943.

Wolkstein, Diane. *The Magic Orange Tree and Other Haitian Folktales.* New York: Knopf, 1979.

Zemach, Harve. *Mommy Buy Me a China Doll.* Chicago: Follett, 1966.

Zemach, Harve. *The Judge.* New York: Farrar, Straus, and Giroux, 1969.

# Part Three: Integration with Other Subject Matter

# 10  Helping Children to Find Themselves and Each Other in Books

Masha K. Rudman
University of Massachusetts

From books that invite children to observe the world around them to books that take them into the past, the use of children's literature can intensify and augment learning in every area of the curriculum. What is more, it can help children to find themselves and each other in a way that leads them to value diversity in cultures and attitudes, and that provides models and reflections of their own lives. Such a multitude of books exists that it is quite possible to combine attention to multicultural education while at the same time integrating literature into the entire curriculum.

The key to successful learning in this arena is in the provision of numerous books, at several levels of difficulty, presenting as many differing approaches and points of view as possible. Teachers and students can serve as partners in the search for these materials; whenever children are called upon to participate in the preparation of a unit or project they feel more responsible for learning it. Ownership is an important factor in learning. Librarians and parents can also be invited to take part in locating books. (A list of book selection aids is appended to this chapter for your use.) Do not restrict the search to books of any one format or genre: poetry, articles, short stories, novels, fantasy, nonfiction, biography—any of these and more can contain material for your topic.

If you are a teacher of social studies, science, or math, you can find all sorts of books that will aid you and your students in the exploration of a theme or concept. No area of the curriculum is inappropriate for integration with children's literature, although it is easier to find materials for some than for others.

History, of course, is one of the most obvious subjects that lends itself to this combination. If the class is embarked on a unit studying the South, or the Civil War, or slavery, such books as *Long Journey Home,* and *To Be A Slave,* by Julius Lester, combined with a book such as *The Slave Dancer,* by Paula Fox, provide an interesting balance. All three of these books represent the problem of slavery as an evil blight, but they provide different perspectives on it, and consist of different formats. This array permits children to recognize that even when books are in agreement over an issue, there can be vast differences in what is learned from them.

This sort of recognition can also help children to acknowledge that their own responses can vary from each other, or can be influenced by each other. Certainly the discussions following the reading of these books will bring out varying responses from students. Peer interaction combined with teacher valuing of differences provides a legitimate context for children to come to their own conclusions, and to learn to respect their own and others' views, even when they continue to differ.

A discussion of the differences in authors' presentations may lead to further research on the authors of the books. What sources did the author use to write the book? From what perspective are some of the other works by this author written? Interested children may want to explore other written materials about the period; compare the information in the book with facts taken from encyclopedias, textbooks, and other works of reference or nonfiction; and perhaps even investigate primary materials from that time.

Another book that helps children to acknowledge the complexity of the issues in the Civil War is *Across Five Aprils* by Irene Hunt. In telling the story of a family struggling to survive the horrors of the war, divided within itself because one brother is fighting for the South and one for the North, this book helps young readers to see that a person who espouses a just cause is not guaranteed to *be* just. The character who decides to fight on the side of the South is not an evil man; and his brother, the soldier in the Union army, is not our favorite character. It is very important for children to understand that issues are not simplistic and that in reading about a situation they must bring their own experiences and judgments to bear.

History is only one of the social studies that literature can help to illuminate and clarify. The settings of books graphically convey a sense of geography in a way that textbooks cannot hope to do. Laura Ingalls Wilder's *Little House* series, Scott O'Dell's *Sing Down the Moon,* Robert McCloskey's *One Morning in Maine,* and *Make Way for Ducklings* are only a few of the books that provide material for geographic exploration. Children can map the movements of the ducklings, the Ingalls family, or the Navajo people. They can compare the terrain from the books' description to what it looks like now, in contemporary times. (Boston may have changed somewhat from the description in the story, even though it is not many years since the events as described took place.) They can discuss how the geography of the setting affected the story, and how geography in general affects our lives.

Most books invite a wide array of investigations and activities. *Julie of the Wolves,* by Jean Craighead George, can be classified as an adventure story, a book that tells us about the geography of Alaska, a book that describes an anthropological problem, a book about Eskimos, a book about wolves and their habits, a book on ecology, a book about a father and his daughter, a book about a courageous heroine, or just a very absorbing story. All of the above are true. And none of the topics needs to be intruded or forced upon the book. It is so well written that none of the separate features stands out. Each issue is an inherent part of the fabric of the story. Nevertheless, each of the issues exists and can be noticed and discussed, depending upon the activities and studies the class is engaged in.

The same author has written a number of books that help children to become more aware of the natural world. (Children are often motivated to read other books by an author they enjoy, and if the author is versatile, this can lead young readers into additional topics.)

All books present their authors' special and personal points of view. When readers understand this they are freed to continue researching on their own, and to weigh all sorts of additional evidence. They may also compare what each of several authors has said about the same topic, add these to other facts they have accumulated, and construct their own current understanding, subject to future new information.

Whenever possible, specific themes should be taught in conjunction with a larger context. Who were the people involved? Which people or incidents seem to be missing? What myths or preconceptions do we have about the people, the time, the events? How many different sets of materials can we find that will help provide a balanced, or at least multiple perspective?

Historical eras have much in common. A study of World War II, like the Civil War, contains much about battles and armies and generals. There are the "good guys" and the "bad guys." The temptation exists to limit the wars' causes to one or two that are obvious. Literature can help readers to recognize that battles involve real people, that the causes of war are many and complex, and that the people on both sides vary in their virtues and sins.

Just as Julius Lester's books help to blast the myth of the passive and happy slave, so too Yuri Suhl's *Uncle Misha's Partisans,* or Gertrude Samuels' *Mottele* counteract the myth of the Jews as passive victims. These two books describe the activities of a band of Jewish partisans, part of the effective underground and resistance movements. Other books, such as *Friedrich* by Hans Peter Richter, tell the story of the Holocaust from the eyes of a German, non-Jewish boy. And Betty Greene's *Summer of My German Soldier* describes a character who is intelligent, likeable, and nonviolent, and who is a former German soldier!

These and other books that describe people of different backgrounds can help children to clarify their own preconceptions, values, and self-images. They do not necessarily have to be set in crises such as war. *Roll of Thunder, Hear My Cry* by Mildred D. Taylor, and *Alan and Naomi* by Myron Levoy, describe, respectively, a black family and a Jewish family in times of stress, but not actively involved in a war.

*I Wish I Could Give My Son a Wild Raccoon,* a collection of accounts by older Americans from varying ethnic backgrounds, presents authentic personal impressions of history and illuminates the particular ethnic perspectives. Charlotte Herman's *The Difference of Ari Stein* discusses through the story line, the differences between orthodox Jews and others. *Nilda,* by Nicholasa Mohr, describes a young Puerto Rican girl and her friends in Spanish Harlem. For a view of contemporary black family interaction, and a fine presentation of information about the tradition of hair-braiding, try reading Camille Yarbrough's *Cornrows.* These are just a few samples of literally hundreds of titles that contain characters and descriptions of cultures other than the majority group.

When a variety of books is presented in conjunction with any topic, and when these books include something about different ethnic groups and indicate that there are different acceptable life styles, children learn about the process of research and the content of whatever theme is under study in a more powerful way than if they were simply exposed to one set of materials. It is also helpful to go beyond the simple reading of the materials, and to engage in activities with the students so that they can experience the information in more than a visual, cognitive manner.

Debates can be useful, entertaining, and informative vehicles for learning about controversial issues. And almost any issue can be fashioned into a controversy. Even such a simple device as finding two students, one of whom likes a book and the other who dislikes the same book, can bring about an effective debate. Role playing—that is, taking the part of a character as though that character were the child, and working through what the young reader would have done, or how he or she would have felt—can multiply the effects of the reading of the book. Acting out a part of the book in order to prove a point can also enhance the reading for the class as well as for the actors. Sometimes a reading aloud by one or several students can have the force of a dramatic presentation if the students select their sections with care. Students may choose to write journals or letters as though they were the characters in the book. They might also do some research beforehand, and construct a page of a newspaper as it might have appeared on a particular day in the time frame of the book. Perhaps, if the books contain descriptions of historical characters, students would enjoy conducting mock trials of people they perceive to have been guilty of crimes, always, of course, ensuring that the trial is a fair one, with adequate representation for the accused. Writing their own biographies of major (or minor) historical figures, and then reading as many biographies as possible of the same person adds more dimension to a study.

Listening to the music of an era, such as war songs, spirituals, popular songs; looking at paintings depicting the events of the time (either during a trip to a museum, or by browsing through art books); searching for poetry, plays, and literary works that portray characters or incidents; creating dioramas as much to scale as they can manage (math skills); researching the costumes of a period and creating dolls, puppets, or a display of the clothing; designing their own bulletin boards, mobiles, backdrops, or murals that help to set the scene in the classroom—all of these help to present the material to be learned in a way that makes it easier to internalize, and more long lasting.

Challenge your students to see if they can discover the math in their research on life in colonial America. (Cooking, farming, daily life all involved mathematics.) Do the same with science, art, music, English. Encourage them to read books with an eye to extending the reading experience into the other areas of the curriculum. Help them to see that learning is an integrated process, reflecting their own lives and experience and understanding. And enjoy.

## Bibliography

George, Jean Craighead. *Julie of the Wolves.* Illus. John Schoenherr. New York: Harper and Row, 1972.
Alaska and all of its complexities provide the setting for this story of survival and change.
Greene, Betty. *Summer of My German Soldier.* New York: Dial Press, 1973. Pb. also.
A young girl's feeling of isolation and rejection forms the basis for the action. The setting is the South; her family is the lone Jewish family in town.
Herman, Charlotte. *The Difference of Ari Stein.* New York: Harper and Row, 1976.

Ari comes from an orthodox Jewish family. His friends, who are also Jewish, have different customs and values. Therein lies the conflict and the story.

Hunt, Irene. *Across Five Aprils*. Chicago: Follett, 1964. Pb. Grosset & Dunlap.

A family's trials and tribulations living on the border between the Union and the South during the five years of the Civil War.

Lester, Julius. *Long Journey Home, Stories from Black History*. New York: Dial Press, 1972. Pb. Grove Press.

Details of the role of black people in securing their freedom. Individual authentic accounts.

Lester, Julius. *To Be A Slave*. Illus. Tom Feelings. New York: Dial Press, 1968. Pb. Dell.

Slaves' own words of what it means to be a slave.

Levoy, Myron. *Alan and Naomi*. New York: Dell Publishing Co., 1977. (Pb)

A story not only of the aftermath of the Holocaust, but also of a young boy and his family in New York City in the late 1940s.

McCloskey, Robert. *One Morning in Maine*. New York: Viking, 1952.

Sal's loose tooth provides the occasion for her interacting with animals and people.

McCloskey, Robert. *Make Way for Ducklings*. New York: Viking, 1941.

The mallard family arrives safely at the Boston Public Garden after negotiating their way through Boston traffic.

Mohr, Nicholasa. *Nilda*. New York: Harper and Row, 1973.

Spanish Harlem in New York City is the setting for this story of a young Puerto Rican girl emerging into adolescence.

O'Dell, Scott. *Sing Down the Moon*. Boston: Houghton Mifflin, 1970. Pb. Dell.

The Long Walk of the Navajo figures in this story of a strong and courageous young Native American woman.

Richter, Hans Peter. *Friedrich*. New York: Holt, Rinehart and Winston, 1970. Pb. Dell.

The time of the Holocaust as seen through the eyes of a young, non-Jewish, German boy.

Samuels, Gertrude. *Mottele*. New York: New American Library, 1977. (Pb)

A young boy whose family has been destroyed by the Nazis joins a band of Jewish partisans.

Suhl, Yuri. *Uncle Misha's Partisans*. New York: Four Winds Press, 1973.

Mottele is one of the heroes of this book, based on the adventures of Jewish partisans in World War II.

Taylor, Mildred D. *Roll of Thunder, Hear My Cry*. New York: Bantam, 1978. (Pb)

Cassie Logan is part of a black family determined to maintain their independence and humaneness despite all pressures to surrender.

Wigginton, Eliot, ed. *I Wish I Could Give My Son a Wild Raccoon*. Garden City, N.Y.: Doubleday/Anchor Press, 1976.

A collection of oral texts by older Americans from such ethnic backgrounds as Eskimo, Native American, Hispanic, and Afro-American.

Wilder, Laura Ingalls. *Little House in the Big Woods* and *Little House on the Prairie*. Illus. Helen Sewell. New York: Harper and Row, 1932 and 1935.

This series describes the adventures of pioneer life in the late nineteenth century.

Yarbrough, Camille. *Cornrows*. Illus. Carole Byard. New York: Coward, McCann and Geoghegan, 1979.

Poetic contemporary tale informing readers about the tradition of hair-braiding, and incidentally providing some black history.

## Additional Titles Containing Multicultural Content

Alexander, Frances. *Pebbles from a Broken Jar*. Indianapolis: Bobbs-Merrill, 1963.

Fables and hero stories from Ancient China.

Belting, Natalia. *The Long-Tailed Bear*. Indianapolis: Bobbs-Merrill, 1961.

Tales from Native Americans.

Belting, Natalia. *The Stars Are Silver Reindeer*. New York: Holt, Rinehart and Winston, 1966.

Series of verses translated from various native people throughout the world. The topic of all verses is how these various groups viewed the heavens.

Brooks, Charlotte, ed. *The Outnumbered: Stories, Essays, and Poems About Minority Groups by America's Leading Writers*. New York: Dell, 1967.

Minorities of past years; minorities of today.

Cultice, Virginia C. *Kivi Speaks*. New York: Lothrop, Lee and Shepard, 1975.

Kivi is an Eskimo boy who tells the story of his family.

Duncan, Jane. *Brave Janet Reachfar*. New York: Seabury Press, 1975.

A Scottish story about a girl who rescues her sheep from a far hill.

Feelings, Muriel. *Jambo Means Hello, Swahili Alphabet Book*. New York: Dial Press, 1974.

Each letter teaches something about African village life.

Feelings, Muriel. *Moja Means One, Swahili Counting Book*. Illus. Tom Feelings. New York: Dial Press, 1971.

Learn to count to ten in Swahili. Illustrations of African village life.

Ficowski, Jerzy. *Sister of the Birds and Other Gypsy Tales*. Nashville: Abingdon, 1976.

Collection of Gypsy tales compiled by Gypsies who live in Poland today. Includes pronunciation guide and sections on the background of the author and on the history of the Gypsies.

Fufuka, Jarama. *My Daddy Is a Cool Dude*. New York: Dial Press, 1975.

Collection of poems depicting urban life in a black community. Deals with both positive and negative aspects of urban black communities.

Huthmacher, J. Joseph. *A Nation of Newcomers: Ethnic Minority Groups in American History.* New York: Dell, 1967.

An informative survey of the treatment that has been accorded representative minority groups in the United States.

Korty, Carol. *Plays from African Folktales.* New York: Scribner's, 1969.

African folktales adapted to play form.

Mangurian, David. *Children of the Incas.* New York: Four Winds Press, 1979.

A thirteen-year-old Ouechua Indian boy living in a village near Lake Titesach describes his family, home, and daily activities.

Matsumo, Masako. *A Pair of Red Clogs.* Cleveland: World Publishing Co., 1960.

A Japanese grandmother reminisces about the time her clogs were new.

Meltzer, Milton. *Never to Forget: The Jews of the Holocaust.* New York: Dell, 1976.

Intensely human but carefully authenticated history of the World War II Nazi extermination of Jews.

Meltzer, Milton. *Taking Root: Jewish Immigrants in America.* New York: Dell, 1977.

Overview of Jewish immigrant life in America during the late nineteenth and early twentieth centuries.

Meltzer, Milton. *World of Our Fathers: The Jews of Eastern Europe.* New York: Dell, 1974.

View of Jewish life in Eastern Europe up to the time millions of Jews migrated to the United States.

Meltzer, Milton, ed. *Women of America Series.* New York: Dell, (See individual titles for year of publication.).

Biographies of women who engage in a wide variety of careers, battles, and enterprises.

Fleming, Alice. *Ida Tarbell: First of the Muckrakers,* 1976.
Fleming, Alice. *The Senator from Maine: Margaret Chase Smith,* 1976.
McKown, Robin. *The World of Mary Cassatt,* 1972.
Phelan, Mary Kay. *Probing the Unknown: The Story of Dr. Florence Sabin,* 1976.
Scott, John Anthony. *Fanny Kemble's America,* 1975.
Sterling, Philip. *Sea and Earth: The Life of Rachel Carson,* 1976.

Musgrove, Margaret. *Ashanti to Zulu.* New York: Dial Press, 1976.

An African alphabet book that mentions twenty-six of the many African tribes and a few things characteristic of each tribe. This was the 1977 Caldecott Honor Book.

Nic Leodhas, Sorche. *All in the Morning Early.* New York: Holt, Rinehart and Winston, 1963.

The author's version of a cumulative Scottish tale of a boy going off to have his corn ground, and the things he encounters on his journey.

Osborne, Leone Neal. *Than Hoa of Viet-Nam.* New York: McGraw Hill, 1966.

Than Hoa is a ten-year-old boy growing up in a Viet Nam village. He is offered a great opportunity by the village mayor. Than Hoa manages to trap a tiger and both he and his little sister are rewarded with the chance to go to school.

Politi, Leo. *Mr. Fong's Toy Shop*. New York: Scribner's, 1978.

A toymaker and his young friends prepare a shadow puppet play for the Moon Festival in Los Angeles' Chinatown.

Price, Christine. *Dancing Masks of Africa*. New York: Scribner's, 1975.

History and illustrations of many of the masks used in daily life by the West African people.

Sakuri, Michi. *Speak for Yourself*. Boston: Houghton Mifflin, 1977.

A Japanese girl living in Hawaii learns the value of her parents' native tongue.

Schulman, Jay, Aubrey Shatter, and Rosalie Ehrlich, eds. *Pride and Protest: Ethnic Roots in America*. New York: Dell, 1977.

Forty-five selections—essays, fiction, drama, and poetry—reflect the cultural diversity of contemporary American society.

Shulevitz, Uri. *The Magician*. New York: Macmillan, 1973.

Story adapted from the Yiddish of I.L. Peretz. Elijah is disguised as a traveling musician who appears in a small town on Passover. An old, needy couple are surprised by his arrival.

Shura, Mary Frances. *Shoefull of Shamrock*. New York: Atheneum, 1966.

The story of an immigrant Irish family living in New York at the turn of the century.

Singer, Julia. *We All Come from Puerto Rico, Too*. New York: Atheneum, 1977.

Photos of Hispanic children and adults at work and play.

Turska, Krystyna. *The Magician of Cracow*. New York: Greenwillow Books, 1975.

Colorful retelling of the Polish legend of the man in the moon.

Volavkova, Hana, ed. Trans. by Jeanne Nemcova. *I Never Saw Another Butterfly*. New York: Schocken, 1964.

Poems and drawings by children in the Terezin concentration camp during World War II.

## Book Selection Aids

Archer, Marguerite P. "Minorities in Easy Reading." *Elementary English* 49 (5) (May 1972): 746–49.

A bibliography.

Baskin, Barbara H., and Karen H. Harris. *Notes from a Different Drummer: A Guide to Juvenile Fiction Portraying the Handicapped*. New York: R.R. Bowker, 1977.

Annotated bibliography including many perspectives on children and handicaps.

132 *Masha K. Rudman*

Bernstein, Joanne E. *Books to Help Children Cope with Separation and Loss.* New York: R.R. Bowker, 1977.

Contains criteria for selection as well as an extensive annotated bibliography.

Carlson, Ruth Kearney. *Emerging Humanity: Multi-Ethnic Literature for Children and Adolescents.* Dubuque, Iowa: William C. Brown, 1972.

Classroom-oriented suggestions for using children's books containing characters of different ethnic and cultural backgrounds. Annotated bibliography.

Dunfee, Maxine, and Claudia Crump. *Teaching for Social Values in Social Studies.* Washington, D.C.: Association for Childhood Education International, 1974.

Suggestions for value clarification in the area of prejudice.

Gillispie, Margaret, and A. Gray Thompson. *Social Studies for Living in a Multi-Ethnic Society.* Columbus, Ohio: Charles E. Merrill Publishing Company, 1973.

A professional methods textbook.

Rudman, Masha Kabakow. *Children's Literature: An Issues Approach.* Lexington, Mass.: D.C. Heath, 1976.

Discussions of issues such as war, death, divorce, sexism, and racism as developed in children's books. Includes activities and annotated bibliographies.

Rudman, Masha Kabakow, and Barbara Lee. *Mind Over Media: New Ways to Help Your Children Learn.* New York: Seaview Press, 1981.

Practical suggestions and resources such as books, magazines, and materials to enhance children's learning.

Sims, Rudine. *Shadow and Substance: Afro-American Experience in Children's Fiction.* Urbana, Ill.: NCTE, 1982.

A survey and analysis of contemporary children's fiction about black Americans published since 1965.

Stensland, Anna Lee. *Literature By and About the American Indian: An Annotated Bibliography for Junior and Senior High School Students.* Urbana, Ill.: NCTE, 1973. Second Edition, 1979.

Extensive list.

Tway, Eileen, ed. *Reading Ladders for Human Relations,* 6th edition. Washington, D.C.: American Council on Education; Urbana, Ill.: NCTE, 1981.

Includes many themes pertaining to self-image and multicultural awareness. Annotated bibliographies.

# 11 Integration through the Arts

Laura R. Fortson
Clark County School District, Athens, Georgia

Combining language arts activities with music and art makes possible a variety of delightful and highly beneficial ways to develop important skills, abilities, and appreciations in children. These activities need not be complicated nor difficult to plan and implement.

Fortunately, teachers do not have to be especially trained in music, art, or linguistics to combine these areas. Teachers need only to be open and adventurous enough to trust themselves and their children, and wise enough to realize the worth of activities that integrate the learning of basic skills with the cognitive benefits and the enjoyment gained through original expression of ideas in various media. A teacher need not be a poet to encourage children to compose short poems or "thoughts," which may be spoken or sung into a tape recorder and later printed on charts for group reading. Nor does a teacher have to be a musician to promote reading through singing songs recorded for children, or to motivate children to respond imaginatively to music. Furthermore, teachers do not need to be artists to furnish—along with the necessary paints, crayons, and paper—the vital supply of encouragement and appreciation that will free children to communicate their thoughts through art.

The teacher's role is to stimulate reflective thinking and imaginative responses. Teachers will realize that the original responses of children, no matter how simple, represent processes of thought and expression which hold deep developmental value for the child. These promote growth that is truly "total" in terms of intellectual, socio-emotional, and aesthetic benefits. Teachers will also realize that simple offerings—a short "poem," "thought," picture or "design," an improvised puppet, or whatever—can be used to stimulate other productive activities. (Figure 1).

Through expressing ideas nonverbally, through art, music, and movement, children develop important skills and attitudes of mind and spirit which are transferable across content lines and which will directly affect later academic achievement. Cassirer (1946), an eminent philosopher and

133

linguist, has pointed out the importance of feeling and imagination as these contribute to thought. He believed that in adults as well as in children there is constant interaction between nonverbal thought rooted in personal experiencing, and verbal or logical thought, which is directly influenced by language. Both facets of thinking are necessary at all intellectual levels and are dynamically interrelated—each mode enriching or clarifying the other. Through nonverbal as well as verbal expression children practice flexibility in thinking and problem-solving behavior. They produce ideas and elaborate upon these. They grow in their ability to discriminate and to make critical judgments, and they become more fluent in the expression of ideas and feelings.

When participating in pursuits that combine the original use of language with other modes of creative expression such as art and music, children are involved in what some brain researchers term "whole-brain activity"—the type of integrated activity that harnesses the powers of both the left and right brain hemispheres for synthesized functioning (Austin, 1975; Hart, 1978; Sperry, 1975; Williams, 1977). They are involved, although unconsciously, in the processes of synthesizing verbal (or logical) modes of thinking with nonverbal (or imaginative) powers. In such a situation both the child's feeling and intellect are quickened. The child is "focusing all forces" on the immediate experience (Cassirer, 1946). Through such purposeful activity the child advances toward becoming a more fully integrated personality.

For example, the beautifully written story, "Sylvester and the Magic Pebble" was read to primary children. After listening and discussing, the children, divided into groups, dictated summaries of the story to the teacher and aide. These were printed on chart paper by the teacher for group reading. The next day the children recalled the story, read the summaries, and "played out" the story in simple creative dramatics. On a following day the children, in turn, expressed what their own personal wishes might be if they possessed a magic pebble. Boys and girls then painted large pictures depicting their wishes, and printed short descriptive sentences to be taped below each picture (Figures 2 and 3). The pictures, sentences, and summaries were later used as material for small-group language arts and reading activities in which children discussed sentence construction and punctuation. They also participated in word-recognition games in which initial word elements were substituted to form rhyming words, and they substituted a variety of word- and phrase-cards to alter sentence meanings and to add humor to the "wish situations." On another day the children enjoyed an improvised game of "Guess My Wish," in which groups of three or four children pantomimed a sentence under a present on display while classmates guessed the action and read the appropriate sentences (Figures 4 and 5).

The foregoing activities, all inspired by one story, offered many opportunities for teaching basic language arts skills, and they offered additional opportunities also extremely important for the development of academic competencies. The activities invited children to organize their thoughts through nonverbal as well as verbal modes and to express these in original, flexible, and emotionally satisfying ways. Through painting and through pantomiming their "wishes," children were engaged in problem solving and in idea production, and were developing beginning powers of decision-making and critical judgment as they decided which ideas or feelings they wished to express and how this might be done. At the same time, children were enjoying the type of social interaction that leads to emotional health. They were gaining a constructive type of self-esteem as they saw their original ideas, written expressions, and pictures being used both for teaching purposes and for group pleasure.

Boys and girls are eager to learn to read what they themselves or their friends have said. Their original compositions are to be valued not only as creative expressions with important developmental value for the individual child, but also as most effective teaching materials. Songs can be used in this manner. Tony's song, which was hardly more than a chant, was sung into a tape recorder during recess. When printed on chart paper by the teacher, Tony's song furnished appropriate material for group reading and language arts activities. The natural repetition of words and the expression of shared interests that occur in compositions make these suitable materials for use with primary children. Both vocabulary controls and meaning are naturally built in (Figure 6).

Bobby's song, "I Like to Bounce My Ball" was so simple and rhythmic that children could follow the beat through bouncing an imaginary ball, and a few children were even able to bounce a real ball as the song was sung (Figure 7).

Jennifer began humming her original melody as she was writing sentences in a language arts activity. The words followed, on the playground, and the song was tape-recorded. Classmates read and sang Jennifer's song when it was printed on chart paper (thereby learning valuable first grade words), but they also enjoyed moving to the rhythmic pattern of the song and pantomiming a tragic situation.

As children read original "poems," chants, or jingles that they or their classmates have composed, and use them to focus on word recognition, sentence meaning, or sentence construction, they are learning important language arts and decoding skills. They are also learning in happy, natural

Figure 1. The words to Lori's song were sentences she had printed to go with her picture. When asked if she would like to sing the sentences into the tape recorder she spontaneously added the melody. Soon the class was singing and clapping Lori's song. Later the melody was transcribed from the tape to large, ruled chart paper by a parent who had studied music—and language arts, reading, art, and music were happily combined.

Figure 2. Ideas are shared, and enthusiasm and confidence are generated when children paint in a group. Such large-group activity is easily manageable when sets of soup cans, placed in cigar boxes, are used to hold the tempera paint. Several brushes are placed in each can so that children may select and use a desired color and then return the brush to the proper can.

Figure 3. Shonda, age seven, at first needed to copy her dictated sentences from large-scale models printed by her teacher. A few months later she was managing the large printing and spacing herself, and was asking daily to paint, draw, and print. Shonda's excellent progress in reading and in creative writing seemed motivated by her desire to paint and draw and to describe in words the meaning of her pictures.

Figure 4. These "picture-sentences" provided highly personal and enjoyable material for reading and language arts activities. Here children are identifying and matching word-cards. Later they will substitute word elements to form new words, and substitute various words and phrases to change sentence meanings.

After hearing "Sylvester and the Magic Pebble" children painted pictures expressing their own wishes and composed sentences to describe their "wish picture." Then they pantomimed the sentences for classmates who must guess the action and read the descriptive sentence.

Figure 5. Here children are pantomiming "wishes" which have been expressed through the large paintings and the sentences beneath. Other children must guess the action, locate the painting and read the appropriate "picture-sentences." These particular children are pantomiming the sentence directly behind the smallest child, "I wish to see Frankenstein in a haunted house!"

The pictures and sentences served as materials for language arts and reading activities in which children discussed sentence construction and punctuation, matched duplicate word cards to words in the sentences, substituted initial word elements to form rhyming words, and substituted word and phrase cards to alter sentence meanings. Because they were personally and happily involved in producing these materials, children were eager to read and discuss the sentences and "play with" words and sentence meanings.

Figure 6. Original "poems" of young children seldom rhyme, and their songs are often simple chants (Tony's song uses only five different tones), but these are highly valuable both as creative child-expressions and as high-interest reading and language arts material.

Teachers may wish to encourage very short original songs, for these can be easily read by other children and easily remembered for group singing and rhythmic activities.

Figure 7. There can be no doubt that children are reading with understanding when materials for beginning reading are based upon original child-thoughts. *Child interest and meaning are already "built into" their compositions. Vocabulary controls are also "built into" the short stories and "poems" of boys and girls, for they use words they understand and hear often.* Although ideas are expressed in individual ways, there is natural repetition of words and phrases from poem to poem because these reflect similar interests and shared activities.

Figure 8. *Materials for first book-making.* Some of the "good writing" examples shown above are child compositions, but others are delightful poems found in *Poetry and Verse for Urban Children* (Donald J. Bissett, ed.). Copied and illustrated above are "Sliding" by Marchette Chute and "A Trip" by James S. Tippett.

When a child copies and illustrates a number of songs or poems these will be made into an individual *Song and Poem Book.*

Figure 9. "The Nutcracker Suite" (Tchaikovsky) inspired several language arts and reading activities. After becoming familiar with the music and story, children "danced out" the music in child-like fashion, then painted pictures which, in turn, motivated them to compose and print descriptive sentences.

Because large pictures and large print can be easily seen and read, the pictures, displayed in classroom or hallway, invite children to stop and read. Young "printers" persevere to make their words readable (developing useful skills of coordination and planning), but the natural mistakes in spelling and spacing can add an intriguing element of puzzlement to motivate children to "figure out" what a friend or younger child has printed.

Figure 10. When "all the children in the class" have taken their positions on the board it's time to discuss personal relationships and to learn to recognize the words that describe these. Here children select appropriate pronouns from sets displayed on the floor, match these to corresponding cards on the board, and compose oral sentences using pronouns in a variety of verbal child-situations. Later, the more mature children will write sentences using the pronouns on the board.

ways to appreciate the worth of their own thoughts and the thoughts of others. They are gaining the confidence necessary for expressing ideas in original ways. A year after Bobby composed his song his former teacher happened to enter his new classroom. Bobby spontaneously rose from his seat, ran to the teacher and said, "Remember me? I'm the boy who made the song about the ball—and I can still sing it! Do you want to hear me sing it now?" He forthwith sang the song for his former teacher and the whole class, and everybody enjoyed both the song and Bobby's obvious pride in accomplishment!

Published songbooks with the accompanying sets of records and collections of poetry for children are full of delightful songs and poems that invite children to read or sing and then to respond creatively through written and verbal expression, art, and movement. Often children individually or in groups will wish to add a verse to a favorite song or poem, or alter sentences or phrases to make it more suitable or enjoyable.

Appropriate short songs or poems, when printed on chart paper by the teacher, become excellent material for the teaching of decoding skills (focusing upon rhyming words, repeated phrases, and the like). More importantly, perhaps, songs and poems give children a sense of the beauty of language well-expressed. All too often the lyric quality of language, which children need to experience repeatedly if they are to use language effectively, is missing in the commercial reading and language arts kits and materials.

Besides enjoying reading and singing together from teacher-printed charts such songs as "Bend with the Wind," "Mister Turtle," "Star Light, Star Bright," or "Trot Old Joe" (*The Small Singer,* Bomar), or "Butterfly," "The Old Gray Cat," or "A Little Boy Went Walking" (*Making Music Your Own,* Ginn and Co.), children love to move to the mood of the music. They also like clapping and moving to the meter of appropriate poems, chants, and jingles. Primary children are usually eager to copy the short song or poem from the chart in neat handwriting and to illustrate them with crayon drawings. This is especially true if they are to be compiled later so that each child will take home an individual *Song and Poem Book* to be enjoyed with parents and friends (Figure 8).

Recordings of such favorites as "The Nutcracker Suite" (Tchaikovsky), excerpts from "Hansel and Gretel" (Humperdinck), "Peter and the Wolf" (Prokofiev), "The Sleeping Beauty" (Tchaikovsky), "The Firebird Suite" (Stravinsky), and "Coppelia" (Delibes) can furnish inspiration for language arts activities in which children discuss the musical story and summarize or list the sequential happenings either orally or in writing. If allowed to paint or draw pictures of the plot or musical mood (as the recorded music is replayed), children will organize their thinking, use imagination, and exercise powers of recall and creative expression through a different media. Furthermore, children will produce, organize, and elaborate upon ideas in yet additional ways if they are encouraged to dramatize or "dance out" in childlike fashion the music and plot, or suitable sections of these.

Varying types of recorded music will elicit varying kinds of oral or written responses. After listening attentively, boys and girls may verbalize or write descriptive words or sentences that express the mood of the music or describe how the music makes them feel. Again, it is beneficial to encourage children first to move freely to the music or express the mood in pantomime, then paint pictures to portray the mood or ideational content of the music, and finally write descriptive sentences or captions to be attached to the pictures.

Language arts learning centers and bulletin boards can come alive for children if teachers will abandon those stenciled cut-outs, patterns, and teacher art, which discourage and even inhibit expression, and start using the original art work of children. Children's art can be imaginative and delightful, and most effective for motivating learning if teachers will only encourage, accept, and use it joyfully.

Figure 9 shows a bulletin board planned with first graders that was used in a variety of ways to teach both word recognition and sentence composition skills. Children first made cardboard figures of themselves to be displayed on the board along with word cards of personal pronouns the children were encountering in reading lessons. Then each child composed a paragraph stating in short complete sentences name, sex, age, home address, and favorite activities. Before these were displayed as "good writing" beneath the cardboard figures, the paragraphs were used for a game of "Guess Who Is Who." Children, in turn, drew a paragraph from the collection and read it, omitting the child's name. Classmates enjoyed guessing which child fit the information read, and then guessing which figure represented the child. Sometimes it was difficult, yet amusing, to try to match the correct self-portrait to the child.

Bulletin board activities on subsequent days facilitated word recognition skills as children, in response to teacher questions, selected the correct pronouns and matched these to the corresponding pronoun cards on the board. Language arts competencies relating to idea production, verbal fluency, and sentence construction were promoted as children composed oral sentences using pronouns to substitute for names of classmates or familiar objects. For example, the teacher would ask, "How could you use pronouns to say, 'Jenny gave some of Jenny's cookies to Josh and

Beth'?" Children would answer, "*She* gave some of *her* cookies to *them,*" or "*They* got *her* cookies," or "Then the cookies were *theirs!*" After each oral sentence the first graders would point to the pronouns they used (Figure 10).

Language, music, and art can be combined in many natural ways because these modes of expression have much in common. Each can be used both for communicating *responses to ideas and situations,* for *generating and stimulating new ideas,* and for *enlarging or altering concepts.* Together they can be used by elementary teachers to effectively develop skills and communicate ideas which are at the same time useful, yet aesthetic in quality—serving practical academic ends while also enriching the child's spirit and undergirding emotional health. When used together, language, art, and music can enhance child learning so that boys and girls, while learning basic competencies, will also grow in their abilities to respond in flexible, imaginative, and joyous ways.

## References and Suggested Reading

Arieti, Silvano. *Creativity: The Magic Synthesis.* New York: Basic Books, 1976.

Austin, James, "Chase, Chance and Creativity." *Saturday Review,* 9 August 1975.

Cassirer, E. *Language and Myth.* New York: Dover Publications, 1946.

Fortson, Laura R. "Rethinking Curricular Integration in Terms of Child Benefits: The Role of Language Arts." *Language Arts* 54 (April 1977): 378–383.

Fortson, Laura R. "A Creative-Aesthetic Approach to Readiness and Beginning Reading and Mathematics in the Kindergarten." Ph.D. diss., University of Georgia, 1969.

Hart, Leslie A. "Brain-Compatible Teaching." *Today's Education* (November/December 1978).

Maslow, A. *The Further Reaches of Human Nature.* New York: Viking Press, 1972.

McReynolds, Paul. "The Three Faces of Cognitive Motivation." In *Intrinsic Motivation: A New Direction in Education,* edited by H.I. Day, D.E. Berlyne, and D.E. Hunt. Toronto, Canada: Holt, Rinehart and Winston, 1971.

Sperry, Roger. "Left-Brain, Right-Brain." *Saturday Review,* 9 August 1975.

Vygotsky, L. *Language and Thought.* New York: John Wiley and Sons, 1962.

Williams, Roger M. "Why Children Should Draw: The Surprising Link between Art and Learning." *Saturday Review,* 3 September 1977.

# 12  Native American Studies

Gayle L. Rogers
Evanston, Illinois

After reading some of the rich literature about native Americans, including some of their eloquent speeches, I met with the science and social studies teachers, and out of our dialogue came a unit on native Americans that included not only language arts, science, and social studies, but music, art, and drama as well. Almost by accident, I discovered a way to ignite an interest in native Americans. The spark was the fascination with animals my sixth graders had developed in science class. The powerful role of animals in the myths and rituals of native Americans proved to be a natural bridge between science class and language arts. Thus, animals became the focus that illumined a culture which might otherwise have seemed strange and remote.

## Preparatory Activities Focused on Animals

In language arts class I taught research skills, but instead of going through this often dull task in isolation, I related the information the students needed to the interesting animal study they were doing for science. Since the animal study began with a list of animals important to native Americans, one of which was the eagle, I put the word *eagle* on the chalkboard, and in a column next to it listed adjectives describing the eagle's characteristics. Some students joined in, and I wrote down their suggestions. Then, in another column next to the adjectives, I asked the class to help me list verbs that indicated an eagle's precise movements. We stopped to pantomime an eagle's action to stir up more action words. Then we added other columns for food, shelter, sounds, mating, personality traits, physical description, and exercise. They debated which category was best for some of the words until vivid images of the eagle evolved into precise words and phrases.

The next day the students worked in small groups selecting one of the animals, brainstorming, and listing all the words they could associate with their chosen animal. The lists on the board provided a start, but dictionaries and thesauri were in great demand. A lively competition among groups for the most extensive lists continued for two days. Then the students began the task of paring down their list to the most precise words; these were put into columns as we had done with the eagle the day before. The columns provided a way for the students to organize their notetaking as they began to work on their science research reports.

In language arts class, daily journal writing reflected the images of the animals, some emerging as poems. One spelling-vocabulary lesson was to select three to five of the animals, list all the adjectives and verbs applicable to them, and then using a dictionary or thesaurus, list one synonym and one antonym for each adjective and verb. Vivid animal drawings decorated these lists, and animal stories began to bud in their journals; poems flourished. In science class the students continued their research on their chosen animal and eventually wrote a report on its adaptation to its environment. Films such as one of an eagle in flight stimulated their interest.

At this point, I mentioned to the class that I wanted each person to be thinking about one animal that could be the central character of a story. I felt they weren't yet ready to write, however, so I told them that their Sustained Silent Reading of library books was to include a book with an animal in it. I mentioned many of the best-loved books with animal characters, and I read aloud a portion of Sterling North's *Rascal.* Each student then read at least one short story, such as "Old Yeller and the Hogs," "The Gift" from Steinbeck's *The Red Pony,* or "To Build a Fire" by Jack London. With one class I had been reading London's complete *The Call of the Wild.* Our senses were saturated with animal images.

After reading their stories or books, the students listed words they found by categories:

| | |
|---|---|
| A. Animal Description | B. Setting Description |
| 1. Physical Characteristics | 1. Time |
| 2. Movements | 2. Place |
| 3. Emotions | 3. Food |
| 4. Sounds | 4. Shelter |

We discussed the idea of character development, plot, and setting. We showed how writers give tiny hints of a main problem early in a story to prepare the reader for its full revelation later.

Finally, they had enough animal involvement, information, and vocabulary to center on one animal as the focus for a story. I asked them to discuss together in small groups and then write an Animal Story Plan.

First they listed synonyms for their animal and its roles in their story. They listed setting details, using the animal's habits and habitat, which they had learned in their science research. Then they listed other characters and briefly mentioned their involvement with the main animal. They outlined a plot, planning how they would begin their story, then the major problem the main character would encounter, and, finally, the possible ways the problem might be resolved. After I saw their Story Plans, I gave them one week to submit a minimum of two pages. At this point, many students were ready to hand in a completed story; some had fully illustrated theirs. By the end of the next week every one of my 120 students had written a well-planned short story, and they had been in school only six weeks!

Some of their stories were made into illustrated books to be shared with classes of younger children; some were dramatized with costumes, lighting, and sound effects on the stage for all the children on our team. Some added poems to their short stories. To provide further stimulus for poetry writing about animals and nature, I followed the philosophy of Kenneth Koch in *Rose, where did you get that red?*, and read famous poetry. In this case, I read William Blake's "Tyger, Tyger, burning bright," and after discussion, gave Koch's assignment. Their directions were: "Write a poem in which you are talking to a beautiful and mysterious creature and you can ask it anything you want—anything. You have the power to do this because you can speak its secret language."

## Integrated Study of Native Americans

Now the students were ready to appreciate the native Americans' close relationship to Mother Earth and Father Sky and Brother Snake as we read myths, tales, and a biography rich in Indian spiritual kinship with animals and their environment. Each child read one book, *The Light in the Forest* by Conrad Richter, *Sing Down the Moon* by Scott O'Dell, *Ishi* by Theodora Kroeber, or *Indian Tales* by Jamie de Angulo. While reading they kept charts of words they found for Topography, Vegetation, Food, Customs and Traditions, and Indians' Closeness to Nature. They wrote a title and one or two discussion questions for each chapter. Each book was assigned a day for discussion. The children brought richly involved imaginations to these discussions. They wrote a dream one of the characters might have had, made a map of the characters' journeys, and voluntarily created many illustrations. Their daily journal writing reflected involvement, with stories and poems often including Indians and animals.

At the same time in social studies, these native American enthusiasts were studying the history and culture of the Indians. In art class, students studied the symbols in Indian art work, such as those woven into baskets and blankets, often reflecting the Indians' identification with the animal world. The students made a large mural of an Indian face in values of grays and black to hang in the hall outside our classroom. In drama class, they were reading native American myths, learning of the Indians' spiritual kinship with nature and animals, and creating masks to dramatize their own original myth of the creation of the world. This dramatization clearly reflected the students' understanding and growing closeness to the natural powers being affected adversely by the intrusion of technology. In music, students enjoyed films and records of native American music. The teacher took the animal short stories the students had written and guided them to write original songs to accompany their stories.

Two memorable experiences for all our team were cooking and eating American Indian foods. Recipes were researched by our Home Arts teacher for a Thanksgiving Feast. We went to the forest preserve and to the native American displays at the Field Museum of Natural History, and made a visit to the zoo. On a trip to a forest preserve we found animal tracks in the snow. A final testimony to the students' enjoyment was the many times I heard different students say to each other, "When you finish reading *Ishi,* I want to read it," or "When you are done with *Indian Tales,* I want it."

Finally, I offer one student's achievement, which epitomizes the goals of integrated studies. The child wrote verse questions to a peacock, and imaginatively later incorporated her poem into an animal story where animals and an Indian strike a bargain to use the peacock's glorious tail feathers in a ritual dance. Her writing was testimony to the richness which results when children have a wealth of stimuli on a theme.

### The Indian and the Peacock

One spring day a Peacock strode into a clearing with his fan of a tail spread wide for all to see.

"You have a very beautiful tail, very beautiful tail," twittered the sparrow.

"Oh how I wish I had a tail like yours; it's so beautiful," the rabbit said in an envious tone.

The timid field mouse stammered out, "Yyyour tail iiis beautiful, oh Peacock," and scuttled away.

Then the inquisitive raccoon chanted:
Oh Peacock, Peacock where did you get those eyes?
Are they eyes of a demon?
Are you a demon's son?
Or are they eyes of God,

and you an angel be?
When you spread your fan out
wide to let us all see,
Does the purple depth of the
center signal that you're a demon?
Or does the green around the
edge suggest the earth's creator?
Where did you get those eyes, oh Peacock, Peacock?

The Peacock held his head higher, and strutted around singing:
I am a Peacock,
And Peacocks give no secrets.
Where I got my eyes,
Is not for you, Raccoon,
Admire me everyone,
For I am splendid.
I am a Peacock,
And Peacocks give no secrets.

And as he left the clearing he said to Rabbit, "And as for you rabbit, being a Peacock isn't all fun; I'm constantly hunted for my feathers."

Peacock continued this kind of life, going to the clearing on Tuesdays, Thursdays, and Saturdays and eating and "keeping house" on Mondays, Wednesdays, and Fridays. On Sundays he worshipped the Great Spirit like everybody else.

One day an Indian came to Peacock's house; Peacock was sweeping his house with a pine branch. "Oh Peacock. Lord of Eyes will you allow me to pluck a single feather from your fan? I should like to have one in my dance next moon."

"Why should I? What would I gain, and how do I know you won't take more than one?"

"Oh Peacock Lord of Eyes, I wouldn't lie to you."

"Anyway it's next moon, and you can wait. Come back when the sun has gone under the earth and come back up in the east. Then I shall tell you my decision."

The Indian went away disappointed, and Peacock went to Wise Owl. "Wise Owl, you know everything and I wish your advice," began Peacock. "An Indian wishes to have a feather of mine. He wants to pluck one from my fan for a dance. But how am I to know that he will pluck just one?"

"What would he give you in return?"

"Nothing."

"I see . . ." And Wise Owl went deep into thought. Peacock waited patiently well into the night. Finally, just when Peacock was about to tell Wise Owl that he was going home, Wise Owl opened his eyes.

"I have it!" he cried with excitement.

"The Indian shall make a hat that fastens on his head tightly. The top shall have a bowl shape in which you will sit with your fan out wide. He may have a whole fan not just one feather. He will also provide your food, water, and shelter."

The next morning the Indian came and Peacock told him his idea. (He did not mention that Wise Owl had thought it up.) The Indian liked it and helped Peacock pack up his belongings. The tribe loved his dance and Peacock got to show his feathers. Peacock and the Indian liked it so much that Peacock stayed with the Indian for good.

# 13 The Expanding Circle of Informal Classroom Drama

Betty J. Wagner
National College of Education

Informal classroom drama—activities that are largely improvisational (as opposed to performances of scripted plays), including creative dramatics, educational drama, or role playing—is one of the most widely heralded and yet the least practiced of the modes of integrating the language arts with one another and with the content areas. Despite a half-century tradition of drama as a means of educating children, there are still far too few elementary teachers who have had even a single college course in drama.[1] Rarely is a course in drama a requirement for elementary teaching, and even a drama elective often gets crowded out of undergraduate student schedules because of increased state requirements in other areas of the curriculum. Another adverse pressure is the shrinking enrollments in elementary education, which make loosening up of requirements less likely as college or university faculty vie to fill up the classes they teach.

Accountability pressures and the "back-to-the-basics" movement have crumpled arts programs of all kinds, and with tightening school budgets this situation seems unlikely to reverse itself. Too many teachers, including some who have used drama in the past, find themselves backing off into the safe workbooks where meaningless, contextless bits of information about language are parceled out. That way children have "work" to take home to anxious parents, teachers have concrete proof that something is getting mastered, and administrators assume they have clear evidence that the school is accountable to the public; at least textbooks have been adopted and data is available for assigning grades to children. What is happening, of course, is that the learners seldom have a chance to break through to achieving the real goal of language instruction: speech or writing that exhibits depth of perception, clarity of observation, and eloquence of expression.

There is some good news among all these gloomy facts, however. The rebirth of interest in writing, characterized by Bay Area-type writing projects that have sprung up across the country in the past decade, has sparked a fresh look at oral language. In many of these projects, participants are discovering the power of role playing as prewriting. They are reading highly respected theorists such as James Moffett and James Britton, both of whom strongly endorse classroom drama as one of the most effective means to language growth. Teachers are discovering that their own and their students' best writing emerges out of the ooze of expression as Britton has convincingly illustrated.[2] Improvised drama is one way to expand the area of this ooze, to help children find new contexts for expressive language. In the process, pressure is applied to craft language beyond its first informal utterance. A child participating in a drama is challenged to produce clear focus, apt response, sensitive adult attitude, appropriate affective phrase, precise vocabulary, or convincing argument. Often the maturity of the language evoked in the drama astonishes teachers. When this language is taken to paper, the quality of the writing leaps upward.

## A Demonstration Unit

This chapter demonstrates a way to move from improvised drama, an oral art, to writing, and then on to reading. Almost any broad unit of science or social studies content will necessarily evoke all of the language skills and will provide rich opportunities for classroom drama. To illustrate, here is how a colleague, Ruth Tretbar, and I used drama in the Baker Demonstration School of National College of Education to introduce a group of eight- and nine-year-olds to a social studies unit on Brazil and a science unit on water. We decided to approach both of these subjects through a single situation in which a team of Brazilian engineers were building a dam down river from the valley that the Moqui Indian tribe had for generations called their home.[3]

The drama began with the establishment of tribal life. The class was divided into small groups, each of which became a different family in the tribe, and we began the drama by improvising waking up and starting the routine tasks of the day. We kept the pace slow at first so the children could have time to sense the rhythm of the tasks they had chosen to enact. No information was given beforehand; we were interested at this point in helping them believe they were Indians; too many facts might have taken their mind away from the focus needed for belief. Anything they imagined at this stage—unless it was a gross anachronism—was allowed to grow from inside the children. Slowly—almost at life rate—the children improvised routines of washing, building fires, hunting or fishing, preparing food, eating, or caring for the young. The movements were largely pantomime as the group concentrated on exploring what it must be like to be Indians. Only after this slow-paced building of belief were they ready to plan a group event that would symbolize the life of the tribe.

We chose to build a huge council fire. Ruth and I, in role as adult members of the tribe, fed in image-building questions and directions, such as, "Who is responsible for the twigs?" "Let's all break these into small pieces so they will burn quickly." "Now, where is the flint to strike the spark?" Then we all went out to chop down the big trees to get the large trunks to keep the fire burning all night. Ritualistically, we labored together chopping and then dragging huge tree trunks. Again the pace was slow, the breathing heavy. Together we built up the fire—twigs, small branches, the heavy trunk, and, finally dried leaves and berries. We kept working on that fire until everyone was in a rhythmic, primitive panto-mime. Oddly enough, nothing seems to help children believe in a drama more effectively than to stop talking and start moving to the cadence of a group task. If language comes too soon, it sounds thin and chattery. Nonverbal knowing comes before the language of conviction.

Now the group felt like a tribe, and it was time to introduce the conflict. The next day's drama began on the banks of the river, where tribe members energetically faced the challenge of fishing with huge spears they had sharpened. The fishing was intense; but as they worked, Ruth and I started musing about the fact that someone had seen white men down river cutting down trees with big noisy axes and throwing them into the sacred river. Slowly it dawned on the tribe that if the white men blocked the river their homeland would be flooded. What were they to do?

As they pondered their plight, the boy who was in the role of Ashew, the tribe's chief, pulled out a fish that had twenty-five fins. All gathered around to look. Our witch doctor declared it to be a bad luck fish. I wondered aloud about this evil omen. Several tribe members had suggestions; to each, the chief answered in stereotypical laconic Indian sentences. One girl caught the rhythm of his remarks in her story written later:

It was a sad day for the Moqui tride when Achew caught a evil fish With 25 fins in the Amazon River some porle said Let's trow the fish in the River. The chif said no bring bad luck to river. Some said Burn it witch Docter said. Bring bad luck in Eir old witch Docter found a book, The siad if you tuoch eye balls evil spirits willcome

So no one touched the eyeballs. The tribe hesitated and wondered. They finally decided to risk burning the fish, but that was not the end of their troubles. Again to quote from a child's paper:

We started to get wood and, We made a circle With, stones around The fire So the fire would't spread and we Waited and waited and when thie fire Went out the bones were still there

With those bones was fear. The tribe softly walked back to their tents to think about their fate.

The next day the white men came. (They were two volunteers who left their tribal roles temporarily and, after our coaching, returned.) From them, the tribe heard the worst. They were going to have to leave the valley they loved. After the white men left, I stood up in the role of one of the mothers of the tribe, and, holding my baby in my arms, said, "The ghosts of our fathers still fish in this sacred river. I shall not live to see our children grow up away from the power of this tribe." I pressed the group to sense the desperation of a people who could not imagine living without the symbol of their heritage—in this case, a sacred river. They began to pick up the challenge my somber decision posed.

"Maybe we could move somewhere else."

I shook my head slowly. "But our children would never know this valley."

"It's not fair; we'll have to kill them," another tribesman asserted, sharpening his spear.

As we talked, the river slowly rose. The tribe backed up reluctantly, gathering their baskets and spears as they watched the water inch toward their homes. One brave warrior refused to move and stood resolutely as the water rose around him. Soon he was swimming in defiance of the flood.

Then the two white men returned, not hostile or armed, offering us another valley, just as good, but one that would not be flooded. The tribe members were visibly relieved. We decided to go.

After a long and arduous journey we arrived at the new valley. To help the children explore what a people do to make sense of what happens to them, I had pressed each one to bring along one thing we could show our children and grandchildren to let them know what our life had been like in this sacred Amazon River valley.

When we had at last settled in the new valley, we found a cave we decided to make our sacred gathering place. After we built our council fire, the chief called each member of the tribe to come up, say his or her tribal name, and hang onto the cave wall the one item he or she had brought to remind the tribe and its children of our sacred valley. I reverently hung up on the wall the old feathered ceremonial robe of our first chief. Then Little Kitten, one of the oldest women of the tribe, came up with a necklace of snake bones that had belonged to her great, great grandfather, the first chief, and on it we discovered an amulet that had great power. As each child hung a treasure on the cave wall, I amplified the gift by saying, for example, "This is Blue Flower, bringing for our tribe a magic stone from the Sacred Amazon so the River God will bless us in this new valley."

In a drama like this, children become symbol makers, putting together a make-believe world that reverberates with significance. When they talk or write about this world, their language has conviction. We asked the children to write an account of their experiences, a record that could be kept for their children's children. Here is Blue Flower's story:

My name is Blue Flower, and This is about the time A Chew found a fish that brought bad luck. We thought about how to make the fish's bad luck not get us. Then some white men came to our valley and told us our valley would be flooded and so we moved.

It was a long way to The place the the white men took us to. We went through mud and sand and rivers and we stopped in another valley that had berries and apples. The fish were very good and we asked the white men if we could stay in that valley they said OK.

So we set up a cave and we wrote the things we wanted our babies to know

about that valley. Opa, little flower
and Blue flower made a bed for our
baby. After that we loved our valley
for many years, and we never moved
away from that new valley.

On a later day, we asked a group of children to pretend to be anthropologists who came to find out about the Moqui tribal life. The rest of
the class went back to their rituals of home and cradle building, fishing,
hunting, basket weaving, picking berries, and rocking babies. Then the
anthropologists went among them and asked questions. When they left
the tribe, they wrote their accounts of what they had seen and heard.
Their stories were better edited than the first person reports; it was as if
assuming a scholarly role provided a pressure for neatness and correctness. Here is the first paragraph of one anthropologist's five-page account
of the history of the tribe:

# The Moqui Tribe

Once there was a tribe that
lived on the tip of the Amazon
River, and the tribe had to fish and
hunt for their food. so one day they
were fishing for their food and one
of the tribe members called for the
witch Doctor. and the witch Doctor came
runing over to the tribe member and said
"What do you want?" the witch Doctor
said. and then the member of the
tribe said "this is a bad Luck fish is it
not?" he said, hm said the witch Doctor
and then he said it is a very Bad Luck
fish you have to hold By the tail
Like you are now. Do not move while

I go get the Chief of the tribe-I will
Be Back soon." So the witch Doctor
came Back with the Chief and they
came to a council meeting in the
village. the witch Doctor was holding
The fish now. the witch Doctor ~~spo~~
spoke up and said "we have to Burn
this fish!" ...

In this account, the writer is further removed from the events. The tone is more formal and the language use more conventional. By putting the first person account and a third person history side-by-side, children can see the differences between the two and begin to recognize that each rhetorical situation calls for a different casting of one's material.

After the drama was over, the teacher focused on gathering more information. The child's urge to learn, to find out, to read had been fanned by the drama. They made a list of questions:

What do the Moqui eat?

Do they have clay pots?

Do they plant things?

Do they fish with spears or nets?

How do they make baskets?

What do their homes look like?

How do you start to build a dam?

What keeps a dam from being washed away?

Why do people build dams?

Now they were hungry for facts. They relished correcting each other's conceptions of tribal life as they had shown it in the drama. As long as a teacher places no value judgment on the wrong guesses a group makes during a drama, that experience can function as a Directed Reading Thinking Activity, priming the class to look for answers in their information sources. Adult as well as children's books become accessible now because of the children's interest. They often pore over illustrations that answer their questions.

A final activity might be to recreate the life of the tribe in a more tangible and accurate way than was done in the initial improvisation. Now students could use artifacts or clothing they have made based on illustrations or other information sources. They might decide to put on an authentic play for another class; at this point the goal would not be (as it had been for the improvised drama) to forge student interest. Instead, it would be to show an audience what they now know about the Moqui Indians. The loss in dramatic discovery would be compensated for by the gain in specific information. Both are valuable—an improvised drama based solely on the children's imagination of what a particular situation might be like, and a play that is a conscious simulation of a real situation. For young children, however, improvised drama works best for it is closer to the natural mode of response to the world that characterizes preschool play. Children seem to enter with gusto into the lives of other human beings through role play.

Dramatic activities provide a natural mode for evoking a child's tacit language. Since what makes language good in a drama is not different in kind from what makes language good in a written composition, both forms of expression are enhanced by their integration. Good writing is writing honed for a particular audience and purpose. (This is one of the assumptions on which the National Assessment of Educational Progress based its development of the Primary Trait scoring system for evaluating writing.) The test for good language in an improvised drama is the same as for writing: does it achieve its purpose? Both demand that the language user stay in role, elaborate appropriately, use language relevantly, provide coherence, choose words precisely, and craft discourse for a desired rhetorical effect.

Both improvisation and writing are ways to learn to think. Children think as they act to solve problems—in real situations or in drama. By using language they simply make their thinking visible, and as they reflect on what they have said or written, they have a chance to see its effect.

Children's minds are a bit like flashlights, probing the darkness and picking out what interests them, what fits with what they have seen before; they ignore the rest. They will not likely hear or read what they have not first seen and touched in that tiny circle of their awareness. Drama is a very effective way to expand their circles of light, making it possible for them to integrate ever wider spectrums of human experience. The wider their awareness, the fuller their experience, out of which can come expression—both oral and written. Children have an engaging interest in what they have struggled to express. Producing and receiving language inside one's circle of awareness is the most powerful tool for learning that human beings possess. Informal classroom drama is one of the most effective ways to stimulate such language.

## Notes

1. Although the number of colleges and universities that offer course work in child drama has increased slightly in the past two decades, they have by no means kept pace with the expansion in other areas. In 1982, 252 theater departments reported offering at least some course work in child drama (sometimes Children's Theater rather than informal classroom drama). See Lin Wright and Rosemarie Willenbrink, "Child Drama 1982: A Survey of College and University Programs in the United States," *Children's Theater Review,* January 1983. They report on 500 responses received to 1500 questionnaires sent. If all future elementary teachers had courses in drama for children in each of these institutions, the problem we face would be much easier to solve. What is more likely the norm is that elementary education majors have only a session or two in a Language Arts Methods class; this is not enough to turn out teachers who are comfortable with dramatic techniques.

2. James Britton, et al., *The Development of Writing Abilities, 11–18,* Macmillan, New York, 1975; *Language and Learning,* Harmondsworth, England: Penguin Books, 1970; Coral Gables, Fla.: University of Miami Press, 1970.

3. R. Baird Shuman, University of Illinois at Urbana-Champaign, introduced us to this dilemma, a real one taken from a newspaper account.

# III Issues

Language arts instruction, particularly in the case of literacy, seems always to be at the center of controversy. While professional organizations such as the National Council of Teachers of English support an integrative and developmental approach to teaching, other individuals and groups espouse plans that are reductionistic and fragmentary. Accountability and its offshoot, the assessment of small increments of learning, has led to renewed vigor in the call for skills-drills approaches to instruction. An integrated language arts model is at total variance with the latter; thus, it is particularly subject to criticism. How does an integrated language arts approach assess children's performance? What do parents, teachers, and administrators think of such a plan? Does an integrated language arts plan provide for the needs of underachieving children and those whose primary language is not English? This section addresses just these questions.

Susan G. Bennett discusses the shortcomings of standardized assessment of achievement in the language arts and offers guidelines for the development of more appropriate evaluation procedures. Jerome Green enumerates the potent forces that impinge upon decisions administrators make about the kind of language arts programs schools endorse, and then offers specific suggestions to school personnel that can help implement integrated language arts programs. The significance parents have in both their children's learning and the success of an integrated language arts program is highlighted by Lynne Rhodes and Mary Hill. Their suggestions, incorporating specific activities and materials, can be highly effective in informing and involving parents in the language arts program, by helping parents to complement the program at home. Beverly Busching describes how to make more mature language accessible to underachieving children through procedures that involve graduated levels of teacher support and task difficulty and sustained group participation. Celia Genishi observes the congruence between research on mono- and multilingual children through its interactive and developmental view of language acquisition and use, and notes that one key to successful classroom practice is the integration of social and task dimensions. Laura Roehler gives a personal account of an inservice program designed to help teachers integrate language arts instruction. Creative drama was the primary vehicle for instruction, while multicultural education composed the content of specific lessons.

# 14 Integrating Language Arts and Assessing Linguistic Performance

Susan G. Bennett
University of Texas at Austin

In the late 1950s and early 1960s, significant numbers of primary school children were missing one item on a widely used standardized test—much to the surprise of the test makers. The item required the children to circle the appropriate picture of a breed of dog when the examiner mentioned the "correct label." Finally, someone thought to ask a group of children why they did not circle the long-haired dog when the breed collie was named. Quite logically the children responded that the picture represented a Lassie Dog—a response perfectly correct given the popularity of the Sunday evening television show watched by thousands of children each week!

Twenty years later similar problems plague most measures of linguistic performance. Not only do present assessment devices still commonly take language competencies out of context (that is, they confound language knowledge with language usage) but also, they evaluate bits and pieces, small portions, and isolated skills *related* to language fluency but not synonymous with language proficiency. These practices affect both students' feelings about themselves and the ways the language arts are taught in our schools. Nonetheless, the emphasis placed on assessment and evaluation in every facet of education today is far-reaching and influential. Imperative, then, for each teacher and educator is an understanding of the information tests can and cannot provide, specifically what strengths and weaknesses are shared by commonly used linguistic performance assessments, and the effects testing has on instruction.

## What Linguistic Performance Tests Tell Us

Human communication is the most complex of behaviors. As such, language is a tool, a vehicle for expression. When purposes for language are removed, whether they be utilitarian, artistic, or personally satisfying, the

167

meaning of language is dramatically altered. As Walter Loban says, "To reduce power of language to such mechanics of written language as spelling, punctuation, and capitalization is a dangerous oversimplification. These are *not* the true fundamentals of language . . . . A perspective that begins with errors of mechanics rather than with a more complete picture of desirable accomplishments seldom reaches to the really important aspects of language ability—interest, pleasure in doing or using, organization, purpose, and other crucial integrating and dynamic patterns of performance" (1976, p. 45). To test language out of context, removed from a purpose, is as William Jenkins writes, to assess something "significantly different from reality. Many children, in fact most, are able users of language in a variety of contexts. On the playground, interacting at home, solving problems in and out of the classroom, children are using language in a myriad of successful ways. However, the test writers . . . apparently would like to palm off the notion that recognizing an error in spelling, capitalization, or punctuation in an exercise is the same thing as having the ability to use language correctly. This is not the case, and most alert educators know it" (1976, p. 53).

What then do most linguistic performance tests measure and, if not language competency, why have they reached such importance? In schools all over the nation, why do teachers wait apprehensively for standardized test results, fearful that their students are "operating below average"? By considering the ways our society tries to solve many of its problems—close scrutiny—we can understand how standardized testing has assumed such an important role in education.

Throughout history, humans have tried to explain their world and themselves. One of the most successful methods of investigation has been to break a large, complicated structure, concept, or idea down into its smallest, most concrete parts. Usually this procedure works quite well, but sometimes investigators have been unable to reconstitute that which they took apart; in the rebuilt construct, the whole was "greater than the sum of the parts." Undaunted persons chose to examine the pieces of the whole more and more closely until the phenomenon had lost its identity and integrity. This process has occurred in the study of human communication. In order to understand language more fully, we have broken down the communication act into tiny pieces that are observable but no longer represent the larger process. Not only have we separated reading, writing, speaking, and listening, but also we have divided each of the four language arts into separate, isolated, measurable skills. Certainly that may be imperative for the study and dissection of a human behavior, but is it advisable, or even adequate, for *evaluating* a human behavior?

What then are the values of the tests students are so often asked to complete? What do they tell us about a child's ability to manipulate language and to communicate successfully with others? Figure 1 compares three tests widely and currently used in public elementary schools: the California Achievement Test; the Comprehensive Test of Basic Skills; and the Metropolitan Achievement Tests. Many of the strengths and weaknesses of these tests can be generalized to standardized, or norm referenced, tests in general.

In each case, two assumptions have been made: (1) that test performance and test-taking ability are indicative of the child's power in using written and oral language; and (2) that there is a direct relationship between the knowledge tested and the skills critical for effective reading, writing, speaking, and listening. Not only should it be clear by now that these assumptions are faulty, but also that the effect this thinking has on curricula and instruction is far-reaching and damaging.

## The Effects of Testing on Instruction

Historically, American teachers have been looked upon with a certain awe. In their charges were the hopes of the future. Teachers provided the keys to assimilation for thousands of immigrants, to skills for advancement for the poor, and to opportunities for the formerly disenfranchised. With so much faith and responsibility placed in them, teachers have traditionally been sensitive to their failures. All of the advice that "you can't reach every student" does not compensate for the feeling of despair when a student does not succeed. Unfortunately, the more students we have in our classes the more "failures" we are likely to experience. (Strange how we so easily forget our accomplishments.) The American striving for efficiency and constant acceleration has contributed to the teachers' pressures. Out of these concerns has grown the emphasis on competency testing—quality control, performance testing, standardization of the product.

The relationship between testing and teaching is cyclic. Teachers, looking for ways to positively influence larger numbers of students, become like the scientist trying to break larger wholes into smaller, identifiable, and easily measured pieces. Language arts educators with the goals of turning students into life-long readers, well-organized speakers, elegant writers, and attentive, critical listeners can rarely be confident they have achieved their goals. But to set as an objective that all students will be able to identify a noun is attainable, teachable, and measurable in a specific length of time. The teacher, administrator, parent, and student need not wait, perhaps, a lifetime to assess success.

Standardized tests have grown both as a response to the dilemma of measurability as well as a response to the belief that teaching language arts is a hierarchical, step-by-step process whose growth can be easily measured. Success and failure are more often than not measured by the lay public as scores on tests. The powerful back-to-the-basics movement is partly a response to declining test scores—which drives the cycle to spinning faster and faster. Too many student teachers in my methods classes are more concerned with writing behavioral objectives, with devising lesson plans for the teaching of traditional grammar, and with teaching those "skills" addressed in standardized test questions than in the role of the humanities in schools and society, the responses of children to literature, and the encouragement of expressive writing in classrooms. The former are often reinforced by experienced teachers in the field, certainly reinforced by test results, and applauded by administrators and parents. Under these conditions how can we break the cycle and encourage, as Loban says, "instruction that focuses not only upon details but also upon larger adaptations, such as vigor of thought and precise expression of thought and feeling" (1976, p. 45)?

Neither likely nor advisable is the total elimination of any assessment of students' linguistic performance. However, the utilization of criteria suggested by Hook (1976), and summarized below, could result in more appropriate evelation devices, have a positive effect on the development of curricula and teaching methods, and help us to educate individuals who are truly adept communicators.

First, both the teaching and testing of language should include *knowledge of* English and *abilities in using* English. A comprehensive language program, including a testing dimension, needs to include not only grammar, usage, and mechanics, but also practice in effective speaking, listening, writing, and reading.

Second, not only should test items be as free as possible from cultural bias (remember the "Lassie" example), but also should emphasize current standards of language usage. Examples on tests that include unfamiliar, outmoded expressions require the students to complete an unrealistic task.

Third, students should be given opportunities, in both class instruction and testing occasions, to generate rather than recognize appropriate language. Giving students a context and purpose for communicating is a necessary condition for optimum language use.

Fourth, for the amount of time, money, and concern devoted to standardized testing programs, some significant use needs to be made of the results. Presently, the most reliable fact we learn is how well a student or group of students compare to others across the nation on a specific set of tasks. Tests should be able to help improve language curricula, should serve as a diagnostic tool, and imply successful instructional methods.

| Test | California Achievement Test (CAT) | Comprehensive Tests of Basic Skills (CTBS) | Metropolitan Achievement Tests (MAT) |
|---|---|---|---|
| Grade Levels | 1.5–12 | 2.6–12 | 1.5–2.4 - primary<br>3.5–4.9 - elementary |
| Subtests | Reading<br>  Vocabulary<br>  Comprehension<br>Language<br>Mathematics | Reading<br>Language<br>Arithmetic<br>Study skills | Word knowledge<br>Spelling<br>Word analysis<br>Reading comprehension<br>Language (punctuation/capitals) |
| Examiner's Manuals | Extensive, thorough; could overwhelm | Includes directions, scoring procedures, interpreting results, norms | Lengthy, but clear; includes directions for administering, scoring, norming |
| Student Composing | No; neither writing samples nor oral response | No | No; but has students hear the spelling words |
| Sections and Number of Items | Reading vocabulary: 40<br>Reading comprehension: 5<br>Reading in books: 40<br>Capitalization: 30<br>Punctuation: 36<br>Spelling: 25<br>Usage and Structure: 25 | Vocabulary: 44<br>Comprehension: 45<br>Language expression: 55<br>Language mechanics: 55<br>Spelling: 30 | Word knowledge: 50<br>Reading: 45<br>Language: 104<br>Spelling: 50 |
| Modes of Questioning | Matching<br>Multiple choice<br>Following directions<br>Language sections in context of simple sentences<br>Identify initial/final letters of words | Multiple choice<br>Picking misspelled words<br>Punctuating two prose passages | Multiple choice<br>Punctuate sections of sentences<br>True/false (spelling) |
| Usefulness | Can diagnose general strengths and weaknesses | General achievement; survey of individual and group achievement compared to national or local norms | Measures school curricula; gives teacher clue to class standings |

Figure 1. A comparison of three commonly used linguistic performance tests. All three are easily administered and easily taken by students. None is culturally sensitive. Only levels one through three of the California Achievement Test and levels one and two of Comprehensive Tests of Basic Skills are pertinent for this comparison.

Testing has a long way to go before developing a valid, reliable, time and cost efficient instrument satisfying the four conditions stated above. The feasibility of such a test may be unrealistic, but language arts teachers must remain concerned about the implications of testing on curricula, instruction, teachers' roles, and children's school experiences.

## Conclusion

The job of reversing the trend of equating knowledge of language (correct responses to grammar exercises *do not* necessarily transfer to improved writing) with use of language will be difficult. As long as students and teachers are evaluated according to norm-referenced test scores, pressure to teach toward the test will be hard to ignore. In addition, decades of trying to break knowledge into its smallest, "teachable" aspects are nearly impossible to overcome. And expectations by our colleagues in administration and other teaching fields to reduce the language arts to facts, figures, and basic skills will be the most difficult to withstand. But as professionals we must persevere. The language arts are part of the humanities—that which makes us more humane. So significant a part of our lives deserves more respect than breaking it down into a lowest common denominator. Mechanics, conventions, and standard forms need to be put into proper perspective. They are, at most, means not ends. Without the integration of reading, writing, speaking, and listening infused with human emotion and artistic merit, children will be presented with a misleading and inadequate picture of the language arts and human communication. That would be a tragedy for all.

## Bibliography

Hook, J. N. "Tests on the English Language." In *Reviews of Selected Published Tests in English,* edited by Alfred H. Grommon, 76–117. Urbana, Ill.: NCTE, 1976.

Jenkins, William A. "Elementary School Language Tests." In *Reviews of Selected Published Tests in English,* edited by Alfred H. Grommon, 52–75. Urbana, Ill.: NCTE, 1976.

Loban, Walter. "Language Development and Its Evaluation." In *Reviews of Selected Published Tests in English,* edited by Alfred H. Grommon, 45–51. Urbana, Ill.: NCTE, 1976.

*Tests*

*California Achievement Tests (CAT).* Ernest W. Tiegs and Willis W. Clark. Monterey, Calif.: California Test Bureau/McGraw-Hill Book Co., 1970.

*Comprehensive Tests of Basic Skills (CTBS)*. Monterey, Calif.: California Test Bureau/McGraw-Hill Book Co., 1968.

*Metropolitan Achievement Tests (MAT)*. Walter N. Durost, Harold H. Bixler, J. Wayne Wrightstone, George A. Prescott, and Irving H. Balow. New York: Harcourt Brace Jovanovich, 1970.

# 15 An Administrator's Perspective on Integrating the Language Arts

Jerome Green
The Ochs School, New York, New York

## Forces Impeding the Integration Process

Because the English language arts are seldom conceived as an interrelated process or taught holistically, some of the present conditions that impede the integration of English instruction on the elementary level go unrecognized. Most fundamental is the fact that most elementary school teachers do not consider themselves to be teachers of English. Rather they see themselves as teachers of the "common branches" of the primary curriculum. Perhaps the closest they may come to any language arts commitment would be to call themselves teachers of reading—thereby acknowledging several decades of incessant stress on reading instruction, on reading as the basis for evaluating a teacher's and a school's success, and on the primacy of reading as the hallmark of literacy.

This stress on reading has emanated from a variety of sources. State education departments have been mandating courses in reading for elementary school certification requirements; teacher training institutions have been responding with graduate and undergraduate reading specialization programs; school boards and the public at large have been calling for the publication of reading scores to enforce their demands for "accountability"; and more elementary teachers have been flocking to meetings of "specialized" reading associations than to those of the holistically-oriented National Council of Teachers of English, which has endorsed an integrated approach to language.

On the Federal level, Title I compensatory programs have concentrated on remediation in "reading" or "mathematics" but not, one may note with a sense of wounded logic, on "reading and addition" or "language (arts) and mathematics." Children eligible for remedial reading instruction in these programs would be "pulled out" of their homeroom classes and taken to a "reading room" for small group or individualized instruction. This has had the effect of reinforcing a conception of the reading process as a discrete matter rather than one integrated with all the language arts. True, the comparatively recent change in Title I guidelines that permits remediation in reading *and* writing is a step in the right direction. Whether or not these two language processes will be taught within an integrated conception or as parallel activities remains uncertain at this time. In any case, even under the newer guidelines, children in these programs have tended to be moved out of their homerooms, where an integrative language instructional philosophy might be more conducively applied, and into the "special" room where a particular kind of language arts "penicillin" can presumably be administered more effectively by a specialist. The analogy with medicine and the near-extinct family doctor is obvious.

No discussion of the fractionization of English language instruction would be complete without mention of the pervasive effects of judicial intrusions into educational policy-making and pedagogy. Two instances, which span the continent but which also must be mentioned because of their national implications, are the "LAU" decision in California and the "ASPIRA" consent decree in New York. Both deal with the rights of bilingual students, whose native or "dominant" language is not English, and with what their bilingual educational rights and English-as-a-second-language programs should be. Because of the controversy that surrounds bilingual education, as well as related ethnic, sociological, economic, and political factors, the school administrative community has tended to talk warily in this debate. Needless to say, the needs of the non-English speaking child must be met. Some form of bilingual instruction is needed for some children, but to say that they can only be met through programs that tend to isolate or balkanize further the efforts of teachers to integrate the English language arts is certainly disputable. The instructional imperative that guides most foreign language instruction today is "total immersion." If that theory applies to learning Spanish or French as a second language, for example, should it not also work for those learning English?

Finally, the legislative impact of Public Law 94-142, which mandated special educational responses to the needs of the handicapped, must be mentioned in terms of its treatment of learning disability (L-D). Because L-D is usually defined in terms of a child's functioning in (English) language arts below his or her expectancy, and because remediation is usually accomplished in a separate L-D resource room for one or two daily hours while the child continues to be "mainstreamed" or maintained in a regular classroom for the rest of the day, programming problems are added for the "pulled-out" youngsters. Because they are classified as L-D handicapped, the children's language arts instruction is diffused between their homeroom and special education teachers.

## Developing a Climate for Integration

Is it possible to change attitudes and to deal with the school realities that, like them or not, work against the integration of the language arts? Even the head of a school who at heart is a teacher of English and is aware of this fragmentation of language instruction and is sensitive to the desideratum of an integrated approach may look at the situation with discouragement and think of James T. Farrell's novel, *A World I Never Made*. But there are things that can be done to change this "world" and to develop the beginnings of better understanding of the holistic nature of language and its interrelated processes. A good first step in the elementary schools might be to familiarize a school's faculty with the brief but succinct call for dialogue and action expressed in "The Essentials of Education" (Appendix B). Precisely because this statement has been endorsed by all the major subject curriculum professional associations, the highlights of its message demand dissemination: that education is more than easily tested "basics" and "competencies"; that there is an interdependence of skills and content; that understanding, thinking, participating, and communicating persons are the desired products of education, not simply persons possessing isolated skills or tid-bits of information.

A second step to be taken by an administrator would be to follow-up with a parallel document, "The Essentials of English," which has been developed by the Commission on the English Curriculum of the National Council of Teachers of English (NCTE). The essential and critical aspect of language in all learning, thinking, and communication, and the interlocking inseparability of integrated language arts processes are the most important points made in this statement. Both the "Essentials of Education" and the "Essentials of English" statements are available from NCTE headquarters, 1111 Kenyon Road, Urbana, Illinois 61801, and may be reproduced for teachers, parents, and the public at large without limitation.

Membership and participation in the meetings of NCTE or its state and local affiliates, by administrators and teachers, should be encouraged within the school. Membership in NCTE and subscription to *Language Arts* would acquaint one with the breadth of information, services, and publications available that support an integrated philosophy of the language arts. Speakers from NCTE and its affiliates are often available to give talks to faculties or to conduct in-service programs that further this approach.

Finally, because English language facility and understanding is so enmeshed with learning in all curriculum areas, there is no reason why these interrelationships cannot be pursued with other professional organizations, through tandem projects and programs. Professional organizations as well as school subjects need not be islands unto themselves.

## Programs and Pedagogy for Integration

A recent report of the National Assessment of Educational Progress indicated that while more students were learning fundamental reading skills, they were not making equal progress on inferential comprehension. Clearly, the separation of reading skills from "thinking" situations and the stress on one aspect of language to the exclusion of others in meaningful contexts is worth consideration by teachers and administrators. What can they do to establish, enhance, or expand opportunities to integrate the language arts program?

One simple way to start pedagogically is to recommend that, regardless of curriculum content and whenever possible, each lesson should include student involvement in each of the processes of listening, speaking, reading, and writing. This advice would include those particular language arts lessons that may have a listening, speaking, reading, or writing objective as a specific focus. Second, if the school is participating in one of those regularly mandated programs popular in schools such as "Sustained Silent Reading," "Writing Every Day Generates Excellence," or "Story Reading by Teachers to Children," be certain that they include the other language arts aspects in the activity's pedagogical prologue or epilogue.

Another approach to integration of the language arts is through new curriculum developments using this comprehensive involvement of listening, speaking, reading, and writing. For example, units of work in the areas of career choice and education or family living and sex education are particularly appropriate for the language arts teacher. The content of another continuing curriculum interest, global education, is also particularly hospitable to integrated language arts activities.

A third way to encourage integrated language arts activities is through motivation and participatory experiences in and out of school. Class trips to community resources (theaters, libraries, historical or environmental locations, museums and cultural facilities) can be exciting ways to bring the outside world into the school world. If one can arrange for an actual poet or writer-in-residence for a school, or other performing arts activities to be experienced directly by children, the motivational possibilities in all of the language-oriented processes involved are unlimited. Critical thinking, clarified speaking, intelligent writing, accurate reading can be centered on these experiences through both individual and group responses.

Last, but neither least nor most, are those "showcase" activities which administrators use to help remind children, teachers, parents, and the larger public of a school's commitment to the language of our land. Dramatic performances by classes, publications by an individual class or the school, language arts fairs featuring children's work in all aspects of English, and library-media-center-related activities are typical of this approach.

What we do for children as educators must be guided by its usefulness in helping them develop their interests and abilities to their maximum potential. We teachers of English language arts know the central position our responsibility has in the scheme of children's development, and we are well familiar with the concept of educating the "whole child." The whole child includes the child's brain, and although the brain has its hemispheres and sides, its anatomical labels and "matters," it does not identify the language it processes perceptually as listening, speaking, reading, or writing. It amalgamates linguistic symbols and transmits the process holistically as language. We should do no less than what our natural neurological capability does. When we succeed and integrate the language arts, we will have achieved something worth more than words.

# 16 Home-School Cooperation in Integrated Language Arts Programs

Lynn K. Rhodes
University of Colorado at Denver

Mary W. Hill
Westminster College

Parents have always been involved in educating their children. Parents provide the first learning environment in the home, including a highly successful language learning environment. Once the child is in school, parents continue to provide a vital environment that complements the school's language learning environment. In both the school and the home, the child is involved in the process of using language. When the child is a student in an integrated language arts curriculum classroom, this complementary relationship is highlighted even further when the focus in such a program—*using* language to learn about the world—is the same as the way language is used in the home.

It is, of course, in children's best interests for the primary contributors to children's education, parents and teachers, to keep in touch with each other in order to realize fully the strengths that each individual brings to the learning situation. Ideally, this communication should be two way, parents to teacher and teacher to parents. This article, however, focuses on initiating cooperation between parents and teachers from the teacher's point of view. Once communication has been established, parents are encouraged to reciprocate so that an ongoing relationship will be retained between home and school.

For those reasons, the ideas contained in this article are intended both to suggest ways teachers can inform parents about the program their children are involved in and to suggest ways parents can both directly and indirectly complement and contribute to the integrated language arts curriculum. The first section, "Informing Parents," considers an initial meeting designed to establish communication with parents as well as other parent-teacher meetings designed to explore various issues regarding children's written language development. Published material which helps parents to understand children's oral and written language development is also included in the first section. The second section, "Connecting the Classroom Curriculum and the Home," considers how teachers can encourage the direct involvement of parents in the language arts curriculum either through "home projects" or in the classroom.

## Informing Parents

Informing parents about what can be expected in their children's integrated language arts program is an important step. The teacher can assist parents in visualizing the classroom setting and activities, in exploring the developmental progress that can be expected of the children, and in understanding their own vital contribution to language development in everday home activities. Though direct communication between teachers and parents is most effective, this section also includes brochures and articles that can be utilized to inform parents about some aspects of their children's education. If possible, these written materials should be used as a secondary form of communication—to follow or extend the information presented and explored in personal meetings with parents.

### Meeting with Parents

Though individual meetings with parents are certainly important, it is often more efficient for a teacher to meet with the parents of students as a group. Such meetings can serve to establish a common basis for future communication and helps to avoid repeatedly answering the same questions from individual parents about the curriculum program.

Many schools begin the year with an open house, an ideal time for teachers to provide parents with an overview of the integrated language arts program. A slide presentation of classroom scenes from previous years can be invaluable in helping parents to visualize such a program. Everyday activities can be featured in the slides as well as special projects in which the students will participate during the year. For example, the slides can show such activities as everyone (including the teacher) reading materials of their choice, book and writing conferences with individuals and small groups, children working on various projects in learning centers, students writing with one another, children preparing for the Young Author's Conference, etc.

The slide presentation can also afford an opportunity for the teacher to share with parents what needs to be considered in order to help children to become more effective language users. The slides can help illuminate how children become independent readers and writers, how children learn to work cooperatively, how the inevitable and necessary errors in children's work will be handled, etc. Though the aforementioned slides will also illuminate such issues, it is also helpful to include representative samples of work done by students in previous years.

One teacher elicited the help of several sixth graders in taking slides. She makes her slide presentation available twice so that all parents may attend if they desire; it is presented once immediately following school on the day of open house and again in the evening during open house. The teacher invites parents to bring their children because she finds that it helps to establish common expectations within the family and at the same time, provides the children with a concrete idea of their own responsibilities for learning and how the class will function.

Some schools schedule more than one evening for parents to visit school during the year—usually "back to school" nights. The teacher can utilize a part of such an evening to help parents better understand the development of reading and writing or to help them understand how they can encourage reading and writing development at home. Two possible discussions are outlined below; which discussion should be selected for use and exactly how the discussions should be structured depends on the parents' sophistication, the needs of the children, and the teacher's own sophistication regarding language development. If either discussion idea is utilized, however, guidelines should be followed; the idea is to build a discussion on the basis of what the parents already do and know.

Discussion #1

*Topic:* How can parents encourage reading and writing development at home?

*Purpose:* To enable even those parents who do not read with their children to understand that they can encourage reading and writing at home by inviting their children to participate in their own everyday lives and surroundings.

*Initiating participation of parents:*

1. Hand out scratch paper and pencils and ask the parents to jot down everything they have read or written in the last twenty-four hours. In order to make them comfortable, you make a list too, focusing on common everyday instances outside your job as a teacher. If you suspect some parents may be hesitant about writing, provide the option of working in pairs.

2. As the parents make their lists, make comments such as, "Try to imagine the whole day—all over again—in your head. Think about it a bit at a time." Or "I even read my toothpaste tube this morning!"

*Engaging in discussion with parents:*

3. Share the lists. If there is time, compile a list on the chalkboard or overhead that includes different items from everyone's lists. Make a suggestion that individual lists be added to if the sharing sparks a memory.

4. Ask what the parents learned from making the lists and sharing them. Among other comments that may be elicited, common comments will include amazement at both how much they read and write and how unaware they've been about how big a part reading and writing play in their lives.

5. Using either the compiled group list or individual lists, ask the parents to put a star next to those instances of reading and writing where either they already include their children or where they could include their children. A *partial* list from a group of Title I parents who recently were involved in such a discussion included:

| *Writing* | *Reading* |
|---|---|
| telephone messages | street signs |
| grocery lists | the Bible |
| catalogue orders | TV commercials |
| grandma's birthday card | recipes |
| notes on a calendar | directions |

6. Finally, ask the parents to volunteer their thoughts about what adjustments they would have to make in order to include their children in the reading and writing instances they have identified. There was a general consensus in the Title I parent group that just becoming aware of the instances was a major factor but that some activities might also take a bit longer and require more patience if children were to be included.

Discussion #2

*Topic:* What can be understood about reading and writing development by considering the development of other language forms, listening and speaking?

*Purpose:* To enable parents to understand reading and writing development as specific forms of general language development.

*Initiating participation of parents*

1. Ask groups of parents (two to three depending on amount of time you have for conversation) to think together about how their children learned to talk. Ask the groups to focus on commonalities in what they share about individual children's development.

*Engaging in discussion with parents:*

2. Ask each group to volunteer at least one commonality discovered during their conversation and briefly list each on the chalkboard or overhead as it is offered. Likely responses will include: "lots of babbling," "non-stop talking," "asked a lot of questions," "made all sorts of mistakes," "ignored most of corrections," "mispronounced words," "sometimes we'd have to ask two or three times what they meant," "misunderstood us," etc.

3. Ask questions to draw out or clarify observations: "How do you know your children weren't just imitating you?" (to clarify the role of imitation vs. generation of speech rules); "What kinds of things did you and your child talk to each other about?" (to draw out statements regarding the meaningfulness and purposefulness of language); "Why didn't you correct each mistake your child made?" (to draw out statements regarding expectation of eventual success and how over-correction reduces the amount of language a child engages in).

4. Reveal your beliefs that learning to read and write entails much of the same behavior encountered in learning to speak and listen. Use the parents' list and draw parallels where possible between statements about oral language and about reading and writing: "lots of babbling" parallels lot of "scribbling" or pretending to write in young children; "mispronunciations" parallels misspelling in written language, an analogy can be made between the "non-stop talking" and the vast amount of reading and writing necessary to becoming proficient. Encourage the parents to do some of the "translation" as well. (See Goodman and Goodman, 1976; Holdaway, 1979; King, 1975 for discussions on the parallels between oral and written language development.)

5. Summarize by briefly presenting what the discussion means regarding what can be expected in the reading and writing development of the particular age child in your classroom and what the parallels mean for the curriculum decisions made by you for the students.

## Published Materials for Parents

The following list of free and/or inexpensive materials available to parents features children's reading and writing development. The materials were selected based on several important considerations. First, all of the materials support parents' natural use of reading and writing in the home. No special expertise and no special materials are required—only a willingness on the part of the parent to become involved in natural, enjoyable, meaningful, and purposeful reading and writing activities with their children. Second, the materials focus on explaining to parents the important contributions they make to their children's development. Finally, some of the materials (for example, *How to Help Your Child Become a Better Writer*) are especially helpful for teachers who want the support of a professional group in effecting a change in parents' attitudes (in this case, regarding correctness in writing).

> *How to Help Your Child Become a Better Writer.* Available free with a self-addressed stamped envelope or for $4.50 per hundred. May be reprinted without permission. Prepaid requests should be sent to National Council of Teachers of English, Order Dept., 1111 Kenyon Rd., Urbana, Ill. 61801.
>
> > This excellent pamphlet contains suggestions for parents on things they can do at home and what to look for in good school writing programs. Emphasizes that writing develops by doing a lot of writing and that parents' and teachers' foremost focus should be on the content of writing rather than on the proper use of mechanics.

> *Good Books Make Reading Fun for Your Child*
> *You Can Encourage Your Child to Read*
> *Your Home Is Your Child's First School*
> *You Can Use TV to Stimulate Your Child's Reading Habits*
>
> > Single copies are available free with a self-addressed stamped envelope or for $3.00 per hundred from International Reading Association, Order Dept., 800 Barksdale Rd., P. O. Box 8139, Newark, Del. 1971.
> >
> > All four pamphlets emphasize the importance of the natural opportunities parents have in the home to encourage reading.

> *How Can I Help My Child Build Positive Attitudes Toward Reading?*
> *How Can I Encourage My Primary Grade Child to Read?*
> *Why Read Aloud to Children?*
> All are available from IRA (see address above) for $.35 to IRA members and $.50 to non-members.
>
> > Each booklet (twelve pages) emphasizes the importance of parent involvement and the availability of books in the development of reading ability and interest. The third booklet is especially helpful in explaining to parents the major contributions they make to a child's development by reading aloud.

> *Making Connections.* A series of short articles which appeared each month September 1981–May 1982 in *Language Arts,* a journal of

the National Council of Teachers of English. May be reprinted without permission.

Each article in this series contains a "language story" about a child, an explanation of what can be learned from the story, and suggestions for working with children. The articles discuss oral and written language development in young children.

## Connecting the Classroom Curriculum and the Home

In varying degrees and ways, all parents are involved in their children's education. Some parents find it gratifying to contribute directly to the curriculum by volunteering their help in their child's classroom and/or by being partners with their children in doing home projects that extend the curriculum. This section contains suggestions for teachers who want to invite parents to be directly involved with classroom activities either in the classroom or at home.

### *Parent Contributions That Extend the Classroom Curriculum*

Many parents enjoy involving themselves in the projects generated in integrated language arts classrooms. Such projects often reach beyond the boundaries of the classroom and into the home and community. When parents become involved with their children in such projects, the results are often quite interesting, and enrich the classroom curriculum in unexpected ways.

When encouraging parental involvement in home projects, the teacher must be certain that parents understand that such involvement is voluntary. The following sample letter to parents sets such a tone:

Dear Parents,

Our class is beginning a study of insects this week. Over the next six weeks or so, we will be listening to and reading information about insects in our classroom as well as talking and writing about what we observe and learn about insects.

If you are interested in exploring the topic at home with your child, you may find the list of suggested "home projects" helpful. If you and your child think of other home projects related to this topic please share them with our class.

If you and your child elect to do some of these projects together, above all have fun. None of these projects are "homework assignments."

*Home Projects*

1. Accompany your child on insect hunting expeditions. Your child will bring home instructions about notes that could be taken and drawings that could be done as you collect the insects together.

(If you have a camera, you may even want to take some pictures of insects.)

2. Accompany your child to the library to find informational books on insects. You may want to read some of these books to your child.

3. Accompany your child to the library to find stories that have insects as main characters. You may want to ask the librarian for *Cricket in Times Square* as well as other books. You may want to read one or several stories with your child in any way you like.

Other connections can be made between class curriculum and the child's home by considering what unique things families and the larger community can offer to the class. Some home projects which reflect such considerations include the following:

1. Children and their parents can contribute to a directory of community resource people willing to make school presentations.

2. Children and their parents can review favorite TV shows, TV specials, and movies; the child can share the information with the class.

3. Children and their parents can assemble a directory of community field trip possibilities which would be suitable for both family outings and school class trips.

### Parent Participation in the Classroom

Just as parents do not need special expertise to help children with oral and written language learning at home, they do not need special expertise to contribute to children's language growth in vital ways in the classroom. Teachers can utilize parents (and other volunteers) in classroom language activities similar to those in the home. Some suggestions include:

1. Parent reading to children:

   A parent may read to one child or a small group of children. Either the parent or a child may select the material to be read. Then the parent can read to the children just as he or she reads to children at home. No discussion of the story is necessary; the object is to enjoy and appreciate the story for sheer fun.

   Occasionally though, parents who read to children may also want to try some of the following:

   Before reading, the parent and children look only at the pictures, then discuss what the story might be about. As the story is read, the parent may stop occasionally and ask the children to guess what will happen next.

After reading the story, the parent might ask the children reasons why they did or did not like the story; why a particular character was a favorite; or how the children might change the story.

2. Child reading to parent:

   In this activity, the child selects a story to read to a parent. Since the parent plays the role of the audience, the child should read without adult interruption or correction. If the child desires, he or she may use the additional suggestions outlined in the previous activity, parent reading to child.

3. Child and parent reading silently:

   The parent and a small group of children (or a single child) should select reading material of their own choice and read silently for a certain length of time. During this time, each reader should read independently. The child(ren) and the parent can share what they've read if there is time.

4. Child dictating a story and parent acting as a secretary:

   As the child dictates a story, the parent writes it down. The child may draw pictures before or after the dictation to accompany the story. Then the child reads the story to the parent.

5. Parent and child writing and illustrating:

   The parent and a small group of children (or a single child) each illustrate and write a story. Because thoughts during writing are easily interrupted, if anyone asks for help with spelling, the response should be, "Spell it the way you think it should be spelled. We'll talk about it later if you want to." The stories are read to others when completed. Emphasis in this activity is on content of the stories, not on spelling, punctuation, and handwriting.

## Summary

Teachers are encouraged to use the ideas and activities in this article as general guidelines for initiating home-school cooperation. In the suggestions included in this article, the focus has been communication between the teacher and the parents regarding the child's language learning environment. The suggestions included those which inform parents about their child's language learning environment in the school, and those which help parents understand and contribute to reading and writing development in a variety of ways. These suggestions are intended to be adapted to specific teaching situations and schools as a starting point for other ideas which will evolve from teachers and parents as they communicate with each other in the interest of children's oral and written language development.

## References

Holdaway, Don. *The Foundations of Literacy.* Richmond Hill, Ontario: Scholastic Book Services, 1979.

King, Martha L. "Language: Insights from Acquisition." *Theory into Practice* 14, 5 (1975): 293–298.

Goodman, Kenneth S., and Yetta M. Goodman. "Learning to Read Is Natural." Paper presented at Conference on Theory and Practice of Beginning Reading Instruction, Pittsburg, Pennsylvania, April 13, 1976. Also in Resnick and Weaver (eds.), *Theory and Practice of Early Reading.* Hillsdale, N.J.: Earlbaum, in press.

# 17 Low Achievers in Active Language Contexts

Beverly A. Busching
University of South Carolina

The elementary school years are a period of rapid expansion and refinement of language capability. But a significant number of children, for one reason or another, lag behind their peers. Teachers worry when they notice that some children don't speak in groups, can't explain ideas, aren't progressing in syntactic complexity, or are poor writers. Even in classrooms with many opportunities for using language in meaningful social and cognitive contexts, some children may fail to make progress.

Too often our reaction has been to take children with problems out of the classroom into socially isolated individualized "skill drill" lessons which have little connection to actual speaking, listening, reading, or writing. As Yetta Goodman puts it, "In many cases, however, the kids who don't do as well are drilled even more on specifics. . . . Their learning experiences are narrowed and their opportunities for expanding their language in the school setting are poor. Bluntly put, the rich get richer and the poor get poorer. There is little time for talking and even less time for actually writing a story or reading a good book" (1978, p. 43).

How can teachers help the poor get richer? How can shy children be helped to initiate and respond more freely; how can inarticulate children be helped to find the words to express their meanings; how can children who are slow to become literate be helped to acquire these abilities?

## Problems of Low Achievers: Possible Sources

Although we are far from understanding the complexities of language learning, we have strong evidence that surface language problems revealed by tests or observed by teachers are often only symptoms of more fundamental difficulties. Children learn how to use specific skills as they experience communication in many different social and cognitive situations. For example, they learn punctuation as part of a whole "package"

189

or style of communication for particular purposes in particular situations. As young children listen to books and look at them, they absorb a "writing" style of communication that is more formal than conversation, a style that has topic sentences, orderly thought development, and dense presentation of information. They see the punctuation that accompanies this writing. As they write their own thoughts, they gradually become more aware of specific rules by trial and error. Teacher-directed lessons may sharpen punctuation knowledge, but they do not create this knowledge. What may appear to be a set of isolated punctuation skills taught individually is actually part of a whole communication package absorbed over a long period of time.

Specific problems with punctuation can arise because children have not had enough experience with written forms of writing. If children have not had previous receptive experiences with printed material—have not been read to or have not spent time lingering over books by themselves—they may not have developed an intuitive sense of the special organizational structures of writing. If children have not had the chance to write, and to rewrite for a public audience, they may have not built a sense of the connections between ideas and punctuation. Because they have difficulty building mental images of written structures of thought, they can't remember the little marks that signal these structures. As a result, they have difficulty with specific punctuation skills. More isolated punctuation drill may just add to their frustrations. Instructional situations that integrate punctuation practice with interesting reading material and children's own writing may help children make the mental connections between rules for punctuation and actually using it in writing.

One category of underlying problems of low achieving students center on difficulties in managing the whole task of communication, for instance, writing or reading or speaking. A low score on a subskill of an achievement test might be the first evidence to catch the teacher's attention, but the problem is not with the subskill; the problem lies in communicative competence. The child needs help understanding how to go about the broad task of communicating.

Other kinds of problems arise from social relationships. For example, if their errors are over-criticized, children may appear to be unable to learn because they mentally withdraw from the whole instructional situation. Or they may mentally withdraw from textbook exercises because the practice drills have nothing to do with real life and its compelling social rewards.

Children from minority communities often struggle with a different kind of broad underlying language problem. (They may, of course, also suffer from the difficulties discussed above.) The more we learn about how language is used in the many communities across our country, the more we realize that some children are faced with a severe disruption of how they are accustomed to speak and listen, read and write. It is not a matter of specifics, like whether or not they have had opportunities to read books in the home. The differences are far broader. They may not have had any experience with the specialized kinds of communication on which literacy instruction is based. As a result, the instructional situations are confusing and they may withdraw or react inappropriately. Also, they may not know the assumptions about how reading, writing, and speaking are used that majority children generally share, and so they have difficulty learning the skills of this communication. All children, of course, have to learn special school communication patterns, but children from minority subcultures usually have a wider communication gap to cope with.

What are some examples of these differences? We can only hint briefly at some of the variety existing in different communities. All of these examples have been discovered through long term studies of actual interactions. In some communities, children are not expected to converse with adults at all. They talk freely with their peers, but they are limited to brief answers to practical questions or commands with adults. They listen to adult talk, but they have little experience in managing a conversation with adults. In other communities, parents converse with children, but children do not show off knowledge in response to adult questions (What are these things called? That's right!). Children may engage in teasing games or show off talents such as singing or imitations with adults, but they don't demonstrate their knowledge in question and answer sequences with adults. Some obedient minority children have learned to avoid the eye of adults, especially when they are being scolded. Others have learned to expect to work in close contact with adults in situations when school teachers expect independence.[1]

The implications of these conflicts between teacher and child expectations for classroom behaviors are enormous. Teachers constantly monitor and interpret student behavior as indicators of motivation, cooperativeness, and achievement. Demonstrating knowledge through teacher questioning is one of the most used methods of classroom teaching and testing. Looking the teacher in the eye is one of the most common tests of sincerity and honesty. If teachers are not aware of conflicts between their expectations and the student's home interactions, they will naturally suspect problems such as lack of motivation, negativism, or low achievement when the child is signaling something entirely different. They may use this misinformation to make instructional decisions that cut off opportunities to learn before the child is comfortable with the learning situation.

Pluralism is a strength of our multicultural society, and in school it should be recognized and prized. If we are alert to specific differences in local community behaviors we can support the individuality of all children and at the same time help them learn appropriate school communication styles. This will take time and effort, though. How will teachers fit the individual help into their already busy schedule? The strategies suggested below may be of assistance.

## Supporting Participation in Group Interaction

Most importantly, keep children with problems as members of group instructional activities, even when they do not participate or when they participate inappropriately.[2] Being part of the action is basic to learning appropriate behavior. Allow shy children time to sit and watch. Allow them time to use their natural ability to learn how to participate competently. Let them make their hypotheses about what is required, and let them begin to try to communicate based on these hypotheses. They will not always be right, of course. But a certain amount of divergent behavior is part of the social learning process. It rarely disturbs the group unless the teacher over-reacts. You can tolerate the inappropriate behavior while you reward small steps of progress toward competency. Too much or too early correction may teach children that it is safer not to use language at all. Criticism of their silence is even worse—it undermines the confidence they need to begin participating.

Especially damaging are adult criticisms that imply that children cannot improve. ("You're failing reading, do you know that?" "Oh, Henry never has the right answer." "Leonard, why can't you try like the other children do?") At first the child had only one problem—trying to learn. Now there are two: trying to learn and trying to cope with feelings of shame and guilt. How can the child concentrate on learning while filled with anxiety?

I observed a fourth grade teacher who gave her problem students both time and encouragement to work their way through the many frustrations and confusions they faced as they did their instructional tasks. The school achievement levels of all of the children in this class were below grade expectation. Some were very low. It was immediately noticeable that there was very little of the usual belligerence and apathy going on in this classroom. This teacher believed that the children needed a variety of communication contexts just as their more successful peers did, so she put them in the same kinds of situations that more able children enjoyed. They discussed, they did social studies projects, they had free reading time, they wrote and shared their writing. They did not, of course, accomplish these tasks with ease. They had many difficulties. Their teacher gave them time—time to think things out, time to give a better answer, time to formulate a cloudy question. She repeated situations a second and third time so they could capitalize on what they learned from a disorganized first try. The children stayed with the instructional tasks, and their anxieties slowly diminished so they could give their attention to task demands instead of to fear. In the meantime, they received the rewards of belonging to an active classroom group.

Other teachers have utilized art experiences (Eddy, 1977) and science activities (Barufaldi and Swift, 1977; Morgan, A., Rachelson, S., and Lloyd, B., 1977) in similar ways for children who are slow to acquire language abilities.

Cazden (1979) suggests a strategy to give supportive help to children who cannot participate in classroom activities. She observed teachers encouraging withdrawn children by consistently speaking as if the children knew how to behave and respond as pupils. If the teachers did not get an expected and acceptable response, they would interpret a look, a gesture, or silence as if it were at least an attempted response, and would answer it as such. If the response were some kind of verbalization, they would prompt a further response or return with an answer. Thus, the children were receiving practice in appropriate instructional interactions. They were not sent to the corner or placed in a remedial group. The teacher adapted a behavioral modification technique called *shaping* to gradually lead the children in the direction of competence.

I visited a first grade teacher in Virginia who used similar shaping techniques. Ms. Ledden had a very complex and lively opening activity that involved counting, labeling, letter and word distinctions, and sequencing as children looked at the calendar, chose each other for jobs, counted each other, and so forth. A few of the students had great difficulty participating. As I watched her on succeeding days during the Fall, I saw several examples of her shaping techniques. Here are some examples.

> Ms. Ledden guided the students through the opening activities, watching each one very closely. Tom still did not understand how to count off, and missed his turn again. Ms. Ledden looked at him to catch his eye, and casually said, "And Tom is 23." He nodded. On another day, Alice could not count the number of blocks that represented the girls with white socks, so Ms. Ledden encouraged Alice to hold Jane's hand while Jane counted the blocks. "Thank you, Alice and Jane," she said. Jamie jumped up and put the date on the calendar when it was Mariana's turn. "If I let you do it tomorrow will you wait until I call on you?" Ms. Ledden asked him. "OK," he said. "I want you to remember that," she warned him.

The teacher described above worked hard to keep low achieving students in the social roles and intellectual contexts that generate language learning. She did the things that understanding teachers do, such as giving clear, simplified, consistent instructions. She also allowed students who needed it more time. She used shaping techniques to guide students in the right direction, giving hints, prompts, and other kinds of support along the way.

## Gradually Withdrawn Teacher Support

Access to beneficial instructional activities is often not enough. What about children who participate appropriately, but do not appear to be gaining in language expressiveness and maturity? Grace Paley (1978), a teacher in the University of Chicago Laboratory School, and Courtney Cazden (1972) have both observed that interactive situations may not stimulate continued language growth for some children. There is too much opportunity for nonverbal communication and previously known language, and too little incentive to learn new spoken and written forms.

### Retelling Narratives

Gillian McNamee (1979) provides an example of the kind of stimulation that teachers can provide for children who are "stuck" at an immature level of language learning. The child she describes is five years old and has been asked to retell a familiar story.

Retelling can be used to help children learn to follow, anticipate, and create story structure. Most children under the age of six have trouble narrating a story to an adult even when the story is familiar to them. Many children need help with this task well into the elementary years. Joan Tough (1977) found that children from low SES homes had particular difficulty not only sustaining narratives, but in sustaining any extended connected discourse, including descriptions and explanations. Tough observed that less advantaged children tended to name objects, events, or persons rather than explaining meanings or making connections. Tough was not willing to take this difficulty as evidence that the children did not have knowledge of the content or sufficient mental ability to deal with meanings. And when she questioned the children further, she indeed found that they demonstrated the understandings required. They just did not include these descriptions and explanations in their extended monologues.

McNamee agrees with Tough that many children have more knowledge and thinking ability than they exhibit in the classroom. She suggests that if the teacher provides a supportive framework by interacting with the child during a retelling the child can gradually take over more and more of the task. I would like to quote at length a teacher-child exchange which McNamee uses to illustrate how such an interaction might look. This exchange is particularly rich in the variety of kinds of support given by the teacher. Overall, the teacher's role can be characterized as *gradually withdrawn support*.

First the teacher defines the challenge, one she knows is difficult, but possible, for this five-year-old girl. ("Tell me the story of the Five Chinese Brothers.") The teacher is not swayed by Karen's uncertainty and lack of confidence, but moves right into questions which show Karen where she must begin—by identifying the characters. Focusing Karen's attention on highly salient details helps her overcome her anxiety.

> Teacher: Tell me the story of *The Five Chinese Brothers.*
> Karen: I don't know this.
> Teacher: What could the first Chinese brother do?
> Karen: I forgot.
> Teacher: Remember he went fishing? How did he find all the fish?
> Karen: He drank the water.
> Teacher: Right. Now what could the second one do?
> Karen: I forgot.
> Teacher: Oh, remember they tried to cut his head off?
> Karen: That's the one with the iron neck.
> Teacher: And the next brother . . .
> Karen: could stretch and stretch.
> Teacher: Karen, you do remember! You thought you didn't but you do.
> Karen: (her face lights up) I thought I didn't but I do.

In the middle part of the retelling the teacher's questions primarily serve to provide a sequential framework, with Karen providing the content. By the last line below, Karen's confidence is blossoming, and she finishes the story with only occasional hints from the teacher.

> Teacher: Remember the brother they put in the oven so he couldn't breathe?
> Karen: Then he could hold his breath?
> Teacher: Right.
> Karen: Forever.
> Teacher: What happened when the first Chinese brother went fishing? What happened?
> Karen: He drank the water.
> Teacher: Then what?
> Karen: The boy came?
> Teacher: See you do remember!
> Karen: He said: "Can I go fishing?" He kept begging. "OK, I'm going to make a sign for you to come back." Then he drank the water. He made a sign for his hands to come back. And the boy only made faces.

Teacher: What a nasty boy.
Karen:   He thought he was going to burp and all the water came
         out and the boy disappeared.
Teacher: So then what happened?
Karen:   He had to go to the judge.
Teacher: Yeah
(continued to the end of the story)

## Assisted Reading

Gradually withdrawn support can also be used to help students with reading difficulties. Students who fall behind in reading need access to compelling reading material that entices them to enter the reading task with verve and persistence. These readers do not hunger and thirst for meaning from their usual fare: basal readers that they've listened to their friends read over and over. One way to provide compelling reading experiences for poor readers is by what has been called "assisted reading." It takes various forms, but in all of them a mature reader carries part of the burden of wresting meaning from the text. Thus, students can read texts that are at their interest level, and can be exposed to vocabulary at the level of their understanding. Three possible methods are briefly outlined here.

1. *Encourage the child to choose stories or books which are already familiar.* The child can thus anticipate much of the special vocabulary and structure of the text. This of course will only work with material of very high interest to the child, such as favorite library books, poems, or folktales.

2. *An adult or peer reads with the child.* Split up the text by conversational parts or by paragraphs, or in any other way that seems satisfactory. This technique is useful for material which is slightly above the child's instructional reading level, for children who are easily discouraged, for children whose reading rate is so slow that they lose the impact of the story, or as therapy for children who have internalized a word-by-word reading approach.

3. *Put reading material on tape.* Have the printed text available so the child can "read along" visually while listening. Teachers report that children usually do attend to the text as they involve themselves mentally with the story.

## Planning Tasks of Graduated Difficulty

Sometimes a task is too difficult even with adult help. In this case teachers can help by planning *a series of tasks of graduated difficulty* (Cazden, 1979). Grace Paley (1978) describes an example of the planned use of drama in which teachers helped the children with problems work their way through narrations of a series of successively more difficult dramatic episodes. The teachers felt that the kindergarten was generally a good environment for a child with low verbal skills, but it lacked a forceful impetus toward language production growth. Paley says, "(a child) . . . can erect cities out of blocks and paint big murals. He can pour and measure. He can work on a puzzle, sing a song, and classify materials into sets. But to get the child to use more words in longer sentences he must use words within the contexts of action. The action should be so strongly motivated that the child is impelled to speak in order to be part of the action" (p. 320).

Dramatics offers such a challenge: it impells communication and it has rules and standards that children recognize and accept as vital to participation. Dramatics, as Paley explains, separates the serious performing of stories from doll-corner play. In the doll corner, sentences need not be finished. It makes little difference exactly when Daddy comes home or what he says. However, in a dramatization, the point in the story at which the Giant arrives and Jack hides—and the words they say—make a very real difference. If the Giant's wife fails to tell the Giant that it is not an Englishman he smells, how can Jack escape to win all his treasures? The child will feel impelled to learn to say whatever is required. Everyone understands that the story must proceed along a precise logical path.

To help hesitant and inarticulate children gain access to dramatics, the teachers may categorize stories into four levels of complexity from those with few plot elements ("The Three Billy Goats Gruff," "The Carrot Seed") to seven or more plot elements ("Jack and the Beanstalk," "Hansel and Gretel"). After the children are thoroughly familiar with a story (rereadings, discussions, group acting), individual children are given an opportunity to retell the story with the teacher. As an example, here is Donald's first summary of the "Little Red Hen" as he prepares to dramatize:

Donald: The little red hen has five friends, and she is going to bake cookies. And she—I forgot.
Teacher: She found something. What did she find?
Donald: A stick?
Teacher: She found something she could plant.
Donald: Oh, yeah, weeds.
Teacher: Then what did she do?
Donald: Took it to the guard.
Teacher: Took it where? To the guard?
Donald: He gave it back to me, and I make cookies.
Teacher: What did you ask your farm friends to do?
Donald: Will you help me eat the cookies? So she ate them himself 'cause they was bad.

After another dramatization, Donald is able to sustain the narrative with little teacher assistance.

> Teacher: Now, Donald, tell me about the little red hen.
> Donald: One day the little red hen planted the seed and then she cut it and then she rolled it to the—what's he called?
> Teacher: The miller.
> Donald: The miller. Here you go. Give me some flour. No one helped her do all the work. Except the miller. He was good to her. So she says who will help me make the cookies? Not me, says the cat. Not me, says the pig. Not me, says the dog. You all didn't help me in the very first place so I will eat it all up. The end. (end of tape)

Most of the children exposed to a four month program of these dramatic episodes gained in vocabulary and sentence length, and more importantly, became more active participators in classroom interactions. Paley notes that overall class participation was higher, discussion more vigorous, and ideas appeared to be better developed. It was difficult to assign the gains specifically to the exact methods of drama they used. However, whether renewed vigor on the part of the teachers and children caused the change, or whether it was directly a result of linguistic aspects of the drama activities, the benefits were real. Graduated levels of difficulty allowed hesitant children access to a task which would have been too difficult in its most mature forms.

What can we learn from these examples? Certainly, we are reminded of the motivating power of emotional involvement and the potential of children to change and grow. It is sometimes easy just to accept our initial observations of children's low achievement and shunt them off to "special" help. But many of these students are just beginning to learn. Children with problems learn the same way that more able learners do— that is, they learn new language ability when they are in situations that require it. But they encounter more difficulties, and they need more supportive help from adults. They have a variety of communication problems, and they need extra time to devise alternative ways to send and receive messages. Usually, they have acquired anxieties and defensive maneuvers which add to their problems, so they need simplified, repeated opportunities to communicate.

Let's keep these students in the classroom. We can encourage small steps forward with strategies such as gradually withdrawn adult support and tasks of graduated levels of difficulty. Low-achieving children should be challenged but not deterred. The downward spiral of failure can be reversed. It is my hope that teachers will be willing to include children whose progress is slow in active cognitive and social contexts for language learning. It is my hope that teachers will accept the reality that these children will encounter difficulties, and that they will be ready to offer patient encouragement along with planned techniques of support.

## Notes

1. Sources of information about diverse patterns of communication and thought are increasingly available. Some good places to start are Cazden, John, and Hymes, *Functions of Language in the Classroom;* Ward, *Them Children;* and the Winter, 1981, issue of *Theory Into Practice,* published by The Ohio State University.
2. If a "behavior problem" persists—that is, if children continue to engage in hostile or strongly disruptive behavior despite encouragement to change—try to avoid punishments that isolate them. If you feel you must remove them to keep an activity going, make sure they can see and hear what is going on.

## Bibliography

Barufaldi, J., and J. Swift. "Children Learning to Read Should Experience Science." *The Reading Teacher* (1977) 388–393.

Cazden, C. "Peekaboo as an Instructional Model: Discourse Development at Home and at School." In *Papers and Reports of Child Language Development of Stanford University, Department of Linguistics.* Vol. 17. Palo Alto, Calif.: Stanford University, 1979.

Cazden, C.B., ed. *Language in Early Childhood Education.* Washington, D.C.: National Association for the Education of Young Children, 1972.

Eddy, J. "Art Education, the Basics and Beyond." *Art Education* 30, no. 7 (1977): 6–12.

Goodman, Y. "Kid Watching: An Alternative to Testing." *Journal National Elementary Principals* 51, no. 4 (June 1978): 41–45.

McNamee, G.D. "The Social Interaction Origins of Narrative Skills." *The Quarterly Newsletter of the Laboratory of Comparative Human Cognition* 1, no. 4 (1979): 63–68.

Moffett, J. *A Student Centered Language Arts Curriculum.* Boston, Mass.: Houghton Mifflin, 1973.

Morgan, A., S. Rachelson, and B. Lloyd. "Sciencing Activities as Contributors to the Development of Reading Skills in First Grade Students." *Science Education* 61, no. 2 (1977): 135–144.

Paley, G. "The Uses of Dramatics in Kindergarten." *The Elementary School Journal* 78, no. 5 (1978): 319–323.

Tough, J. *The Development of Meaning.* New York: John Wiley and Sons, 1977.

# 18  Integrating Perspectives on Monolingual and Multilingual Children

Celia Genishi
University of Texas at Austin

Recently I was asked to react to a group of research reports in the field of second language acquisition. I had expected to find studies that were strikingly different in theoretical orientation and methodology from studies in first or native language acquisition. Instead, I found a high degree of convergence. These were the topics the researchers addressed: discourse analysis from a sociolinguistic perspective; assessment of language proficiency; assessment of communicative competence; dialect sensitivity; written products as ecologically valid data; the usefulness of grammar rules; and an interactive model of reading comprehension.

If one had to choose a key idea that underlay the second language studies I reviewed, it might be *interaction*: interaction between speaker and listener, between language user and print, between speaker and situation, and between one language-based process and another. An interactionist—and developmental—view of language acquisition and processing seems to integrate research perspectives on monolingual and multilingual children. (For present purposes *multilingual* is used in a general sense to refer to those with competence in more than one language and to children who are becoming multilingual, either at home or in the classroom.) In this paper I discuss how the interactionist, integrative perspective might be extended to the study of multilinguals' acquisition of literacy in the classroom. It is also suggested that researchers consider another kind of interaction, one between task and social goals in classrooms, whether they study monolingual or multilingual children. Finally, I note that the integrative view needs further extension from research to the area of practice.

## Recent Research on the Acquisition of Literacy

The interactionist perspective on language acquisition has already begun to influence research on the acquisition of literacy among monolingual

200

children. This kind of research is often reported in the journal *Language Arts* and may be familiar to many readers. In historical terms, it has ties to research in open education and in early childhood education, which also stress the development of the "whole child." Researchers address questions about the acquisition of literacy, and since the focus is on acquisition, what the child does or thinks is more interesting to the researcher than the adult's teaching techniques. Psychologists who like methodological preciseness and experimentalists in other disciplines find this line of research full of confounded variables, but as Courtney Cazden recently said at a conference on "Communicating in the Classroom" (sponsored by the National Institute of Education, University of Wisconsin, Madison, October 1980) what psychologists call *confounding*, educators call *integration*. Some of these integrative studies will be summarized briefly.

In the early 1970s Carol Chomsky (1972) was one of the first to suggest that oral language and what children know about it are interdependent with writing. She also suggested that the traditional—and revered—sequence of listening, then speaking, then reading, then writing needs reconsideration. Writing, the representation of language in print, may be more natural for children to acquire informally in the preschool years than reading, partly because of children's association of writing with drawing and artistic expression. Others have followed Chomsky's lead and support her with research that shows that children formulate rules about print much the way they formulate rules about spoken language. Ferreiro (1980), for example, used Piagetian methods to study thirty children between three and six years of age in Mexico City and found that young children, regardless of social background and their previous experiences with print, formulated their own rules about how sounds are related to graphemes.

Another recent study by Zepeda-de-Kane (1980) is an investigation of the interactions among drawing, speaking, and writing. Her question was, how does drawing affect the verbalization and storytelling of fifty-five kindergarten children? She found that children told the most elaborate stories about a field trip they had taken after drawing in an unstructured situation. Showing the children a pictorial stimulus or allowing them to color the stimulus before telling the story led to less extensive oral expression.

One of the first researchers to look carefully at the process of learning to write in the primary grade classroom was Graves (1975). One aspect of his extensive study was completing case studies of seven-year-olds engaged in writing episodes. Graves identified three phases of an episode and found that none of these phases was limited to an adult's conventional definition of writing. Children often drew pictures before they wrote or vocalized their messages during the composing phase. Any of the phases could contain interactive behavior when children might question their teacher or peers.

Dyson (in progress) is examining through case studies how kindergartners use oral language in order to gain proficiency in written language. She is identifying interrelationships between children's graphic symbol-producing activities (drawing and writing) and representative oral language. Analysis of data has so far yielded (a) a categorization of oral language functions during composing, (b) a description of components of the processes that precede conventional writing, and (c) a narrative description of the writing style of each of five children, including patterns of oral language use.

One of the most articulate spokespersons for the integration of the language arts is Smith (1981). Like other researchers in literacy acquisition, he believes that the process of reading cannot be understood without an understanding of how children acquire and think about oral language. Because children are predisposed to learn, regardless of the nature of lessons, they will learn about the skills of spelling and writing at the same time that they acquire and use reading skills. In their interactions with all the language arts, children make their own observations and guesses, as long as we present opportunities for them to be engaged in activities that are significant for them.

The research just summarized is based on classrooms for monolingual children, so that there is still need for careful studies of how multilingual children become literate. The concern with children's acquisition of *oral* language, when their native language is not English, has understandably overshadowed an interest in documenting the processes of literacy acquisition. Beginnings have been made from a few vantage points. Fillmore (in press), for example, studies the teaching variables that may affect how well children learn a second language. She analyzes the interaction patterns of teachers and pupils during the whole school day, rather than the "second language lesson" alone. Her careful videotape analyses of children's behavior can be extended to include their behavior as they read and write.

Past, Past, and Guzman (1980) describe a curriculum in a bilingual kindergarten that leads the majority of children in one classroom to become readers by the end of the kindergarten year. Again the focus is not on a single kind of lesson but on the whole curriculum. Field trips and activities like cooking provide the natural experiences that lead to talk, and the teacher often writes the talk down so that it can be read. What is impressive about this kindergarten is not just that it has an integrated language program, but that it is located in an economically poor neighborhood with a large bilingual population. Other programs with goals like those of Past, et al. have been described. These writers' next step might be a detailed analysis of the processes individual children go through as they become readers.

## The Interaction of Task and Social Dimensions

The studies cited focus primarily on the processes involved in children's use of different forms of language. The acquisition of these forms may be viewed as a series of interrelated tasks. Children undertake such tasks in varied situations, and a major dimension of those situations is social. The distinction between task and social dimensions has always been made by sociologists and anthropologists as they analyze social interaction in general. In a given situation, such as a committee meeting, there is usually a set of tasks, or the business agenda, to be accomplished. Since we have all attended such meetings, we know that in addition to this agenda, there is a social one, one that may be responsible for prolonging the meeting from ten to sixty minutes. Individuals accomplish their social objectives by talking first, talking last, or talking most. Or they may choose not to talk in order to assert their superiority or status with respect to others present. In school settings, teachers spend time letting children know who is in charge, children talk at inappropriate times to impress other children, and so on. When social objectives overshadow task dimensions, tasks may never be accomplished. Educational researchers also refer to this dichotomy as one between cognitive and affective components.

In the last ten years researchers investigating language in the classroom have stressed the unity of the social and task dimensions. We cannot understand what students do academically unless we also understand the way they interact socially. It is now a cliché that we must know about children's social and cultural backgrounds outside of school as well as in school in order to help them learn. Since the early 1970s there have been many studies that point out how teachers from the majority culture can misunderstand minority children because of differences in communicative rules.

Within the last five years, there has been a trend toward synthesizing the task and social dimensions in classroom research, particularly in the work of sociolinguists and those associated with ethnomethodology. The work of Mehan (1979), Erickson and Shultz (1977), Dore (1978), and their collaborators has provided a close and careful look at academic lessons and the ways in which they're socially constructed. These investigators have made the point that knowing only the academic content of lessons does not help the student in the role of student unless the social rules of classroom functioning are known as well. Among other features, children must know when lessons begin and end, how teachers ask for information, and how to display appropriately what they know in the unique situation of the classroom.

Only a small proportion of the research on social task dimensions has been based on interactions among multilingual children. An example is the ethnographic report by Carrasco (1979), whose case study of one child provided a basis of collaboration between classroom teacher and researcher. Attention to the social dimension of classroom interaction, which researchers would have the opportunity to observe closely, seems especially important for research in multilingual and multicultural education. First, we are already aware that there may be miscommunications when teachers are unfamiliar with children from minority cultures. Second, we are beginning to see that rules related to children's own views of social situations, including the classroom situation, determine aspects of language use. Studies of code-switching or alternation between dialects or languages, indicate that children who are able to speak a language other than English may choose to speak only English with certain people or in some school settings (e.g., Genishi, 1978; McClure, 1981). Like monolingual children, multilinguals formulate their own rules about when to speak, to whom, and in what ways. In addition, they must choose among languages. The goal for researchers is to take such sociolinguistic rules into account as they study the tasks of reading and writing, for rules that affect oral language choice might also affect how children learn to process print.

## Conclusions

Whether we teach in or study monolingual or multilingual classrooms, what developmental, integrative research tells us is that we may need to redefine "tasks" as we've traditionally thought of them. Social elements, such as a child's general ease with other people, attention to communicative convention among speakers, and level of motivation or engagement enter into success at learning to speak, read, or write. For some students, whether they're in the primary grades or in college, accomplishing an assigned task is sufficient reward. They just want to know what the next task is. For the much larger number of students who have difficulty becoming literate or becoming competent in a second language, we need to be able to reproduce and integrate the motivating conditions that seem to exist as children acquire their first language.

The first conclusion of this paper is that in studying multilingual children from other cultures, we may benefit from the outlook and methods of recent research in the acquisition of literacy in monolinguals. Ongoing studies of bilingual classrooms indicate that a convergence between researchers in "regular" and multilingual settings is just beginning.

A second conclusion is a reflection on the curricula in many kindergarten and primary grade classrooms. The clearest lack of integration in language education seems to exist not among groups of researchers who are interested in language, but between the nature of research and the nature of practice. There are countless studies that suggest that certain situational factors are necessary for language acquisition and learning: a supportive, nonrejecting environment; the opportunity to practice (or make mistakes with impunity); the willingness to make mistakes, etc. All such studies should lead us to conclude that we need to combine task and social dimensions as we teach. Yet what we see in most classrooms is students engaging in the narrowly defined tasks of carrying out drills, writing on worksheets instead of writing about what they know, and practicing grammatical rules.

Perhaps another way to state this is that we still lack a psychology of motivation that teachers can apply in their classrooms. I won't touch upon a crucial part of that psychology, which has to do with mechanisms of learning and memory; but an equally necessary part of that "psychology" must be social. There are social factors that encourage us to talk, factors that researchers like Labov (1970) and Gumperz and Hymes (1972) have been describing for years, although not always in terms of what happens to students and teachers in classrooms. These situationally-bound factors are related to such things as status, power, and saving face. If teachers do not take them into account, children may not activate the psychological mechanisms that enable them to learn a lexicon and rules about language structures and functions. Our task remains one of integration: first, to integrate research on monolingual and multilingual children so that an integrative, developmental perspective is extended to all classrooms, and second, to integrate the social and task dimensions of language education as we work in classrooms.

## References

Carrasco, R. "Expanded Awareness of Student Performance: A case study in applied ethnographic monitoring in a bilingual classroom." *Sociolinguistic Working Paper* #60. Austin, Tex.: Southwest Educational Development Laboratory, 1979.

Chomsky, C. "Write Now, Read Later." In *Language in Early Childhood Education*, edited by C. Cazden. Washington, D.C.: National Association for the Education of Young Children, 1972.

Dore, J. "Variation in Preschool Children's Conversational Performances." In
*Children's Language*, vol. 1, edited by K.E. Nelson. New York: Gardner
Press, 1978.

Dyson, A. Haas. "A Case Study Examination of the Role of Oral Language in
the Writing Processes of Kindergartners." Ph.D. diss. in progress, University
of Texas, Austin.

Erickson, F., and J. Shultz. "When Is a Context? Some Issues and Methods in
the Analysis of Social Competence." *Quarterly Newsletter of the Institute for
Comparative Human Development* 1 (1977): 5–10.

Ferreiro, E. "The Relationship between Oral and Written Language: The Chil-
dren's Viewpoints." Paper presented at the third Impact Conference of the
National Council of Teachers of English and the International Reading
Association, St. Louis, Mo., 1980.

Fillmore, L.W. "Instructional Language as Linguistic Input: Second Language
Learning in Classrooms." In *Communicating in the Classroom*, edited by
L.C. Wilkinson. New York: Academic Press, in press.

Genishi, C. "Language Use in a Kindergarten Program for Maintenance of
Bilingualism." In *Bilingual Education*, edited by H. Lafontaine, B. Persky,
and L. Golubchick. Wayne, N.J.: Avery Publishing, 1978.

Graves, D. "An Examination of the Writing Processes of Seven-Year-Old Children." *Research in the Teaching of English* 9 (1975): 227–242.

Gumperz, J.J., and D. Hymes, eds. *Directions in Sociolinguistics: The Ethnog-
raphy of Communication*. New York: Holt, Rinehart and Winston, 1972.

Labov, W. "The Logic of Nonstandard English." In *Language and Poverty*,
edited by F. Williams. Chicago: Markham Publishing, 1970.

McClure, E. "Formal and Functional Aspects of the Code-Switched Discourse
of Bilingual Children." In *Latino Language and Communicative Behavior*,
edited by R. Duran. Norwood, N.J.: Ablex, 1981.

Mehan, H. *Learning Lessons: Social Organization in the Classroom*. Cambridge,
Mass.: Harvard University Press, 1979.

Past, K.C., A. Past, and S. Guzman. "A Bilingual Kindergarten Immersed in
Print." *The Reading Teacher* 34 (1980): 907–913.

Smith, F. "Demonstrations, Engagement, and Sensitivity: A Revised Approach
to Language Learning." *Language Arts* 58 (1981): 103–112.

Zepeda-de-Kane, F. *Young Children's Drawings as Related to Basic Communication Skills*. Gainesville, Fla.: P.K. Yonge Laboratory School, University of
Florida, 1980.

# 19 Moving toward Integration through Inservice

Laura R. Roehler
Michigan State University

"If you want to really help, help me find more time."

"I can't get through all the objectives I have to teach now, yet every school year brings a new set of objectives for me to teach."

"I feel like I'm going in a dozen directions at once. Nothing really makes sense anymore. If I'm confused, think how the kids must feel."

"We never have time to get into anything in depth."

The above comments are typical of a group of teachers who met with teacher educators to assess our inservice needs. We all felt the need for more instructional time. As we talked further, other needs emerged. We wanted to increase our students' abilities to communicate in writing and to interact constructively with culturally diverse peers and adults. Inevitably, the question of how to motivate students also arose. Ultimately, we decided on the major goal for our inservice: to develop lessons which successfully integrated language arts and multicultural education as a means for efficiently using instructional time and to motivate pupils by integrating creative dramatics into instruction as a means for providing concrete, meaningful experiences.

Once we had our objectives, we thought about how to achieve them. We turned immediately to the university-based teacher educators on our inservice staff who politely turned it back to all of us. We were astounded. We had never known college professors who didn't leap at the opportunity to lecture and theorize! In fact, we were a little put out because we thought that was the purpose for their being on the inservice team. We were supposed to figure out the problems; they were supposed to provide the solutions.

After the shock passed and we had worked together for awhile, we began to think, "Sure, we know some things about teaching and we *can* add that to the inservice model." Over time, the teacher educators and our staff cooperatively developed the inservice program described here.

**Overview of the Inservice Project**

The description of the project includes the setting, the inservice model, and the substance of what we learned about integration.

*The Setting*

All the teachers who participated in the integration inservice are from four elementary schools in a midwestern industrial center. The students in our classrooms ranged from kindergarten to sixth grade. The student population included approximately one-third black, one-third Spanish-American descent, and one-third Caucasian. The teacher educators were from a nearby college of education and included methods instructors, program developers, and program evaluators. The inservice was sponsored by Teacher Corps, a federally funded project.

Sixteen teachers and five university professors participated in the first year of the project while twenty-five teachers and seven university professors participated during the second year. Sessions occurred in an elementary school in a classroom set aside for inservice and, eventually, in the teachers' own classrooms or planning rooms. Initially, participants met twice a week during school hours for a total of six hours, while the teachers' classrooms were being taught by senior intern students from the university's teacher preparation program. Gradually, the inservice sessions moved from class sessions to individual and small group conferences.

*Description of the Inservice Model*

Our jointly developed project was designed to assist us in our understanding the nature of integration and how we could incorporate it into our classrooms. During the first year all participating teachers met in whole group sessions during the first semester. Teacher educators presented examples of how to integrate, observed in our classrooms, and did some team teaching with us to demonstrate how integration could be used. During the second semester, teacher educators assumed the responsibility for small groups of teachers and each week they held individual one-hour sessions in which they helped us plan, implement, and evaluate the integration we tried in our classrooms. These sessions were held in our classrooms or in planning rooms.

*What We Learned about Integration*

What we learned related directly to our goals about developing integrated language arts and multicultural lessons and motivating pupils through creative dramatics. The substance of our experience is discussed here in three categories: our own use of creative dramatics, language, and multicultural education as part of the inservice; the format of the integrated lessons we learned to prepare; and the components of integration and how we learned to relate them.

Teachers moved through a series of inservice sessions where the format was a model of the integrated lessons that we were learning about. First, creative drama was the way we became involved in the lessons. Doing activities before we discussed or wrote about the content of the activities made the learning of the content easier. Second, language provided the means for oral or written interchange. We often read a selection, tried out the content of the selection in one of the various creative drama forms, and discussed what we liked about the creative drama and how we could improve it. Then we completed a follow-up activity, usually in written form. The written work was always shared among the members of the class. Finally, multicultural education provided the content of the lessons. What we talked about, read about, listened to, or wrote about were the basic components of multicultural education—how people are alike and how they are different.

As we became aware of how language arts, creative drama, and multicultural education fit together, we began to focus on the format of the integrated lessons. The format included warm-up activities, focusing activities, and expressing activities. The lessons began with warm-up activities because most of us were initially hesitant about using creative drama; we didn't want to expose ourselves to our peers. Eventually we did, and gradually creative drama became an ongoing element of our teaching repertoire as we, too, used warm-up activities in our classrooms. Sometimes we called them cool-down activities if our integrated lessons were occurring after lunch or recess. Whether they were called "warm-ups" or "cool-downs," they prepared the students for the lesson to come. Warm-ups included finger plays, role playing, acting out parts of a favorite story, trying on characters, creative mental games, and language activities that sharpened the minds.

The format of the integrated lessons we learned to teach were centered on focusing activities. This is where pupils received information. They might hear a story, read a book, watch a role play, see a film, etc. The important element was that the receptive language modes were dominant during this phase of the integrated activity.

After information was received, expressive activities were incorporated. Here, pupils did something with the information we had received. We talked about it; we wrote about it; we acted some of it out. In short, we expressed our ideas, feelings, and thoughts through speaking, writing, and doing. It struck home to us how little of that we do in the classroom. Many teachers think getting the information and taking a test is enough. We learned differently. We found that if we wanted our pupils to remember information over an extended period of time, we should use lots of expressive activities in our integrated lessons. Expressing the information increased everyone's long term retention.

With the format of the lessons (warm-up, focusing, and expressing activities) in place and working, we moved on to the components of integration itself. We found that in order to understand and use integration, it was first necessary to understand the substance of the components we were to integrate. For oui integrated lessons, the components were language, creative drama, and multicultural education. Language consisted of the modes of listening, speaking, reading, and writing. Creative drama consisted of predrama activities such as mirroring, pantomime walks, sense awareness exercises, movement activities, and basic characterizations; fantasy drama activities such as the playing out of scenes, stories, poems, and songs; and human drama activities such as role playing, societal games, socio-drama, and improvisations of human situations. Multicultural education consisted of an examination of the factors that influence the lives of human beings in terms of likenesses and differences that exist. We found that factors that bring about sameness and diversity in peoples' lives include the geographical, economic, social, age, physical, religious, ethnic, and racial elements.

As we discussed and used language modes, creative drama, and multicultural education, the relationships among these components began to emerge. We began to see the natural relationships between language and creative drama. We found that drama made it easier to be motivated to speak about or write down our own experiences about different cultures, whether real or imagined. Not only that, writing and speaking were better under these circumstances, both for our elementary students and ourselves also. Finally, the opportunity to share and discuss shared experiences that were created in the classrooms and critiqued from many points of view provided for the development of thinking abilities and the understanding and appreciation of others, essential to both language development and to multicultural education.

## Summary

Through the inservice project, we developed the elements of integrating language arts, creative drama, and multicultural education. We set up integrated lessons that had warm-up activities, focusing activities, and expressing activities. We developed an understanding of the components of integration and how those components fit together. Finally, we used the integration model in our classrooms with guided assistance provided by teacher educators.

## Effectiveness in Achieving Our Inservice Goals

Naturally, at the end of the two-year inservice, we were interested in determining how effective our experience had been in achieving the goal we had established regarding how to generate more instructional time and attain greater motivation through integration. Two types of evaluation were used, informal and formal.

### Informal Evaluation

The first type of evaluation was informal. The teachers involved discussed the project and its impact. The discussion started when a first grade teacher who was integrating using an outer space theme said, "It's (integration) coming out all the time now, even on the spot. The other day we did exercises by our desks like astronauts might do, and it was right off the top of my head." She concluded by saying, "You've got to come to my room and see our space city. Language arts, creative drama, multicultural education—it's all there!"

We discussed integration as incorporating one subject area into another, nothing is isolated. Language arts can be tied into social studies, science, multicultural education, and creative drama. It can be used in other areas, too. Integration is a cyclical kind of thing rather than a parallel thing. Subjects are combined into blocks. Integration provides more than one means to get to your end. For example, if sentence construction is being taught, there are more ways to convey the concept than just getting up and giving a speech on what a sentence is.

We decided that integration of language arts, creative drama, and multicultural education gets students excited about school and learning. It opens them up and gives them a chance to express themselves. Students get more involved. In fact, their whole bodies are involved, not just their heads.

We felt integration makes it easier to teach. We didn't have time to teach subjects separately. So we put them together and incorporated different areas. As such, we covered a lot more. Students then realized how things are related in real life because they saw it interwoven in the classroom. We have recognized that creative drama is an effective integrating tool not only because students enjoy it, but because it helps them actively remember what they've learned.

For example, one sixth grade teacher used creative drama in an Eskimo unit. The students had to do five different scenes per group from the life of a certain group of people. They wrote it, acted it out, and evaluated it. The teacher reported that in that unit, more than in any other unit, the students have remembered things, even the low ability students. They could refer to specific things, even several months later. Being in it and doing it helped them remember. When students have to do what they've learned, they remember.

We discussed the fact that while integration creates more class time and uses time more efficiently and effectively, it takes more planning time. The skills that need to be covered do not always fit together. Teachers have to think and plan if they don't want to just teach language arts skills for language arts' sake. Creative drama is something the students enjoy and it helps them remember, but it doesn't work for everything. Multicultural education can usually be tied in, at least in terms of how we are alike and how we are different, and language arts fits in all subject areas. It's only logical to integrate these things, but teachers have to find out the best way to teach a certain skill in a certain area. That takes thinking and planning.

There was resounding agreement that we had achieved the two goals we had established. We had developed lessons that successfully integrated language arts and multicultural education, we had a file of them, and we had become more efficient.[1] In addition, creative dramatics has become an established element in our teaching. It was one of the strong ways that we provided concrete, meaningful activities for our students. We used it as a way to move from one subject or activity to another (transitions), as the focus of activities, and as a way for students to express their thoughts, feelings, and ideas.[2]

## Formal Evaluation

In addition to our informal evaluation, the teacher educators involved in the project conducted a more formal evaluation. They specifically wanted to determine which of the participating teachers were most effective in achieving the inservice goals. Toward this end, they trained us in two different ways. One group received the training as described here. A second group received this training and then became "teacher collaborators"—classroom teachers who took on certain teacher education functions by helping fellow teachers to use integration in their teaching. The teacher educator's hypotheses were:

> Teachers who assisted other teachers to integrate subjects would use integration more in their own classrooms
>
> Teachers who assisted other teachers regarding integration would report more use of creative dramatics in their own classrooms
>
> Teachers who assisted other teachers regarding integration would report an increase in self-confidence and professionalism as a result of the experience

To determine the validity of these hypotheses, documentation and evaluation procedures were used throughout the two-year project and included questionnaires, interviews, observations, files of integrated instructional units, activity cards which were completed whenever language arts, multicultural education, or creative drama activities were used in classrooms, and written records of the purposes and results of all sessions. Pre- and post- questionnaires regarding ongoing classroom procedures and knowledge of creative dramatics, language arts, and multicultural education were completed for both groups of teachers. Interviews, conducted by teacher educators trained in ethnographic research, were completed at the end of each school year and periodically throughout the two years. Teachers also recorded how integration was used and files were developed that included all integrated units that were taught in the classrooms. In addition, observations of classroom instruction were completed at the beginning and end of the project by teacher educators to measure the amounts of creative dramatics, multicultural education, and language arts being used and/or integrated in the classrooms of the participating teachers. Records of all interactions (whether whole groups, small groups, or paired sessions) were maintained throughout the entire project including those persons attending, the length of time, the purpose of the interactions, a summary of the interaction, the results of the interaction, and any plans for future interactions.

These data were then analyzed to test the three hypotheses. First, it was found that teacher collaborators *did* use integration in their instructional activities more frequently than the teachers who just received the instruction (significant at the .05 level). Second, it was found that teacher collaborators reported more use of creative drama than the teachers who just received instruction (again, significant at the .05 level). Finally, the interview and questionnaire data indicated that the teacher collaborator group expressed more feelings of professional growth than did the teacher group which received instruction only.

Our informal self-evaluations were in agreement with these findings. Being a teacher collaborator was, most of us felt, the most valuable aspect of our participation in the inservice project. Specifically, going to another school as a teacher collaborator required thinking about what had been learned and how to relate it to a peer. Our skills were tried with new teachers in new classrooms. One teacher added, "Last year was a whole new learning experience for me. This year I was able to share what I've learned with another teacher. Also, I learned from her different ways to do things."

Being a teacher collaborator was a valuable experience because it perfected our skills. For instance, some of us felt we have always done creative drama, but now we had a greater base because we had tried additional ideas. We felt we could articulate our ideas more clearly about learning how you feel and how to express it constructively. And we understood our rationale for doing activities.

Being in other classrooms also helped us become aware of our abilities because the teachers (and especially their students) let us know they thought we were good. We knew we had gained skills, but it was nice to have that positive feedback.

We also received similar benefits from the collaborating sessions. For the collaborating sessions to be successful, planning had to take place. We would decide what to do before the next session, who would be responsible for the different parts of the session, and then we'd plan and prepare. We also set goals for both the collaborator and the new teacher. Learning was not just one way; it was two way.

We identified the following set of characteristics that we felt were important for teacher collaborators:

1. ability to give and receive feedback
2. ability to redirect and stay on task
3. base knowledge of integration
4. ability to physically and psychologically leave classrooms for a period of time
5. ability to determine what someone else is thinking, feeling, or wants done
6. ability to get our partners to try things, avoiding the "expert" role and developing partnership relationships, which contributes to a higher probability of the partner continuing new behaviors
7. ability to develop and try things which were new to the degree that the partners would continue the activity on their own. "Far out" strategies have little carry-over value.

## Conclusion

This is how our inservice project on integration worked. We still use the model we developed and we feel our students continue to be more interested, alert, and involved in our classrooms. They achieve a deeper understanding of the material we present through our integrated activities. We have more spontaneous classrooms, and the students themselves integrate many ideas. These results make the project worth the effort. In addition, however, we discovered that the best integrators of elementary classroom learning activities are the teachers who helped other teachers learn how to integrate. It seems that teachers, too, learn best by expressing, especially when that expression of thoughts, ideas, and feelings is directed toward their peers.

# Appendix A
# Aids to Integrating the Language Arts:
# An Annotated Bibliography

Sandra A. Rietz
Eastern Montana College

Adams, Anne H., Charles R. Coble, and Paul B. Hounshell. *Mainstreaming Language Arts and Social Studies: Special Ideas and Activities for the Whole Class.* Salt Lake City, Utah: Goodyear Publishing, 1977.

Nongraded ideas for all elementary children, designed to include exceptional children within whole class activities. Activities set up for daily use—objectives, preparation notes, and procedures described and illustrated in detail. Total of 180 language arts and 180 social studies objectives presented; each of the 360 activities integrates both language arts and content information. Activities primarily hands-on, child centered.

Bauer, Caroline Feller. *Handbook for Storytellers.* Chicago, Ill.: American Library Association, 1977.

A collection of methods and materials designed for *doing* the oral literature and for introducing written literature orally. Description of props, aids, and "how to" directions given for specific stories and poems. Chapter bibliographies provide an additional source of literary materials for children.

Bissex, Glenda L. *Gnys at Wrk: A Child Learns to Write and Read.* Cambridge, Mass.: Harvard University Press, 1980.

This thoughtful case study follows the author's son as he learns to read and write as part of his daily life at home and, later, in school. His progress is not a steady continuum. The author sees her son's experiences as evidence of the connections between reading and writing and the intentions of the child.

Brown, Rosellen, Marvin Hoffman, Martin Kushner, Phillip Lopate, and Sheila Murphey. *The Whole Word Catalogue.* New York: Teachers and Writers Collaborative, 1972.

Word play activities and "how to's" for oral language play, play with imagery, written language play, play with poetry, and a potpourri of language and literature games.

Butler, Francelia. *Sharing Literature with Children: A Thematic Anthology*. New York: David McKay Co., 1977.

Rhymes, riddles, jokes, language and literary games, folk play, tongue twisters, limericks, folktales, myths, poems, drama, essays, biography, selections from larger works, chosen for "doing" with children. Many book lists. An important on-the-desk reference.

Cardozo, Peter. *The Whole Kids Catalogue*. New York: Boston Books, 1975.

Several hundred content-related activities; gardening, to making-with-junk, to dramatic play, to things to investigate. Directions written specifically for children, adequately detailed and illustrated. Ideal project resource for children who wish to pursue individual interests, or who wish to find out more about topics studied in class.

Cazden, Courtney B., ed. *Language in Early Childhood Education*. Washington, D.C.: National Association for the Education of Young Children, 1972.

Language acquisition and the development of fluency detailed in a series of articles presenting and reviewing language learning research. Presents a foundation for holistic language activities in the classroom.

Chenfeld, Mini Brodsky. *Teaching Language Arts Creatively*. New York: Harcourt Brace Jovanovich, 1978.

Presents students with background, rationale, and procedures for holistic approaches to language development in the classroom. Along with a wealth of activities, Chenfeld deals with the emotional and intellectual climate of the classroom in ways unique among language arts texts.

Coody, Betty. *Using Literature with Young Children*. Dubuque, Iowa: William C. Brown, 1973.

A small book full of practical ideas. How to integrate the literature into the language arts and content area curricula; how to use literature to effect language development. Cooking, puppetry, LEA, Readers Theater, retellings, and much more.

Corcoran, Gertrude B. *Language Experience for Nursery and Kindergarten Years.* Des Plaines, Ill.: Peacock, 1976.

Oral language and activities/dramatic play for language development and for introducing young children to literature. Some finger plays and other oral language plays, plus extensive bibliographies of appropriate literary, art, dramatic storytelling, and music references and materials. Appropriate books to introduce children to environment, family, self-discovery, colors, numbers, language, senses, poetry—all listed by topic. Some language arts and language development background information presented.

Cramer, Ronald L. *Children's Writing and Language Growth.* New York: Merrill, 1978.

A language arts text describing the relationship between oral language acquisition and written language development, and providing methodological notes for talking about writing, independent writing, evaluating writing, spelling, editing, poetry writing. Research studies are briefly reviewed.

Dale, Edgar, Joseph O'Rourke, and Henry A. Bamman. *Techniques of Teaching Vocabulary.* Chicago, Ill.: Field Educational Publications, 1971.

An encyclopedia-like compendium of information about word derivations, word structures, and an excellent collection of word study and word use activities and games appropriate for all grades. Answers teacher and student questions about synonyms, antonyms, homonyms, prefixes, roots, suffixes, figurative language, and more. An important on-the-desk resource.

Emrich, Duncan. *The Hodgepodge Book: Containing All Manner of Curious, Interesting and Out-of-the-Way Information Drawn from American Folklore and Not to Be Found Anywhere Else in the World; As Well as Jokes, Conundrums, Riddles, Puzzles, and Other Matter Designed to Amuse and Entertain; All of It Most Instructive and Delightful.* Englewood Cliffs, N.J.: Four Winds, 1972.

True!

Fadiman, Clifton, and Marianne Carus, eds. *Cricket's Choice.* LaSalle, Ill.: Open Court, 1974.

The best of poetry, short story, folktale, rhyme, riddle, and foolishness

218                                                   *Sandra A. Rietz*

from *Cricket Magazine.* A quality collection of material easily adapted
for a variety of classroom uses: reading aloud, storytelling, Readers
Theater, dramatic play.

Fisher, Margaret. *Who's Who in Children's Books: A Treasury of the
Familiar Characters of Childhood.* New York: Holt, Rinheart, and
Winston, 1975.

Flanigan, Michael C., and Robert S. Boone. *Using Media in the Language Arts: A Source Book.* Des Plaines, Ill.: Peacock, 1977.

Media making activities for children, directions provided. Suggestions
for using media for language development. Lists of stories, books,
records, films, and distributors and suppliers of catalogues and equip-
ment included.

Gerbrandt, Gary L. *An Idea Book for Acting Out and Writing Language,
K-8.* Urbana, Ill.: National Council of Teachers of English, 1974.

A detailed description of small group process-lists of pantomime,
guessing, charade, improvisation ideas, and "writing out" exercises for
coaching open-ended student writing, and for aiding student manipulation of the form and mechanics of written language.

Hall, Mary Anne. *The Language Experience Approach for Teaching
Reading.* Newark, Del.: International Reading Association, 1978.

Explains the rationale and methods of LEA. How to get started, how to
build a sight word vocabulary and decoding ability as students write,
and read their own writing. Carries the methods past beginning reading.

Heilman, Arthur W., and Elizabeth A. Holmes. *Smuggling Language
into the Teaching of Reading,* 2nd ed. New York: Merrill, 1978.

Word games and figurative language games, puzzles, activities for critical
reading, for finding meaning. Includes writing and literature activities.

Hennings, Dorothy Grant. *Communication in Action,* 2nd ed. Boston:
Houghton Mifflin, 1982.

Presents an integrated language arts program. Includes notes about
supportive research studies, extensive explanations, and practical ideas.

Henry, Mabel Wright. *Creative Experiences in Oral Language*. Urbana, Ill.: National Council of Teachers of English, 1967.

Activities and references for choral interpretation, storytelling, creative dramatics, rhythmic movement, reading readiness, and children's theater with narrative descriptions and background regarding language development. Notes on developing the creative dramatics curriculum.

Jacobs, Gabriel. *When Children Think*. New York: Teachers College Press, 1970.

Keeping a journal opens up many new worlds of thought. The author describes the experiences of upper elementary children as he stimulates imaginative thinking through their writing. The selections and conversations show a compelling honesty and range of thought.

Kampmann, Lothar. *Creating with Found Objects*. New York: Van-Nostrand Reinhold, 1971.

A color photograph illustrated collection of art activities using easily found junk. Each activity allows the child a genuine freedom of individual expression. Children's objects d' art beg for talking, writing, dramatic activity. Art activities keyed for age groups grades 1–10.

King, Joyce, and Carol Katzman. *Imagine That! Illustrated Poems and Creative Learning Experiences*. Salt Lake City, Utah: Goodyear Publishing, 1976.

Games, ideas, activities, projects, researchings, plays, poems, pictures, language production starters for children, but written for teachers in quick, clear how-to language. Activities organized into such categories as "Our World," "Senses," "Feelings." Tear sheets provided and duplication of specified pages encouraged.

Landeck, Beatrice. *Learn to Read, Read to Learn: Poetry and Prose from Afro-related Sources*. New York: David McKay, 1975.

The title does not do justice to the variety of singing games, riddles, poetry, folktales, songs, and chants in this collection. Methods for teaching a full range of speaking, listening, reading, and writing abilities while the students enjoy their African (and Hispanic) heritage.

Moffett, James, and Betty Jane Wagner. *Student-Centered Language Arts and Reading, K–13*, 3rd ed. Boston: Houghton Mifflin, 1983.

This new edition of a much-used language arts text and instructional guide is even better organized and more complete than its predecessor. It provides a wealth of individual integrated activities as well as approaches to long-term integrated planning. Traditional objectives are embedded in topics such as word play, dialogue, invented stories, true stories, giving directions, and giving information. Diagnosis and evaluation and special education are covered. One of the best sources for integrated teaching.

Norton, Donna E. *Language Arts Activities for Children*. New York: Merrill, 1980.

One hundred and thirty-four fully lesson-planned language use activities for oral language development, listening, use of literature, media use, and mechanics. Many activities are of the project type; most focus language use on a nonlanguage product and do not make language an object of study.

Piercey, Dorothy. *Reading Activities in Content Areas: An Ideabook for Middle and Secondary Schools*. Boston: Allyn and Bacon, 1976.

Whole language use activities presented in lesson plan fashion, identified for grade level and grouped for subject areas: business, driver education, Speech/English/Journalism, fine arts, foreign languages, health, home economics, industrial/vocational arts, mathematics, physical education, science and social studies. Teacher strategies for developing vocabulary and comprehension included.

Richardson, Elwyn S. *In the Early World*. New York: Pantheon, 1964.

An exceptional firsthand account of rural New Zealand children learning to read and write in association with pottery and print-making, science investigations, and peer-group play. Displays rare insights into the dynamics of individual and group processes of creative endeavor.

Schaff, Joanne. *The Language Arts Idea Book: Classroom Activities for Children*. Glenview, Ill.: Scott, Foresman, 1976.

How-to directions for the teacher for whole language activities, projects, games involving combinations of reading, writing, talking, listening. Much language production and content learning involved. Grade levels given.

Sperling, Susan. *Poplollies and Bellibones*. New York: Clarkson N. Potter, 1977.

A silly dictionary of antique and out-of-use words. Word entries are accompanied by narrative in which all of these strange and delightful bits of a lost vocabulary are used. Fun, and a stimulus to child invented word study, word use, and word play activities.

Stewig, John Warren. *Read to Write: Using Children's Literature as a Springboard to the Teaching of Writing*. New York: Holt, Rinehart, and Winston, 1980.

Ideas for all ages of children, arranged according to increasing complexity where appropriate. Many student responses are included, along with descriptions of suggested procedures. Poetry, descriptions, narratives, character sketches—all kinds of exploratory and finished writing are covered.

Wagner, Betty Jane. *Dorothy Heathcote: Drama as a Learning Medium*. Washington, D.C.: National Education Association, 1976.

This book continues to be the best presentation of Dorothy Heathcote's unique approach to drama as a way of learning. Children are presented with a problem situation to explore through informal drama. As they create roles and actions, they "live" a variety of human situations, expanding and deepening their understanding of themselves and their world. This approach is thoroughly explained. Many problem situations, methods, and samples of student interactions are given.

Wagner, Guy, Max Hosier, and Mildred Blackman. *Language Games: Strengthening Language Skills with Instructional Games*. Darien, Conn.: Teachers Publishing Corp., 1968.

One hundred and sixty usually whole-language games and activities, including many which employ literature, dramatic activity, improvisation, and language intervention. Indices provide procedural notes and categorize activities by general area of language development.

Weeks, Thelma E. *Born to Talk*. Rowley, Mass.: Newberry House, 1979.

A review of young children's language development interwoven with the individual developmental patterns of several young children (one of whom is language disabled). Provides a good review of the contextual influences on language and Britton and Tough's definitions of language functions. A readable and enjoyable approach for nonspecialists.

Whitman, Ruth, and Harriet Feinberg, eds. *Poemmaking: Poets in Classrooms.* Sherborn, Mass.: Massachusetts Council of Teachers of English, 1975.

A form book for poetry writing. Procedures detailed for teachers. Examples and children's poems included.

Wolsch, Robert A., and Lois A. Wolsch. *From Speaking to Writing to Reading: Relating the Arts of Communication.* New York: Teachers College Press, 1982.

A three-stage communication model for older students. Begins with helping students recognize feelings and thoughts, compose orally, then move to written language. Spontaneous forms of expression precede the discipline of predesigned poetic and prose forms. Gives practical suggestions, including adaptions for work-related curriculum.

Zavatsky, Bill, and Ron Padgett, eds. *The Whole Word Catalogue 2: A Unique Collection of Ideas and Materials to Stimulate Creativity in the Classroom.* New York: McGraw-Hill, 1977.

Continuation of *The Whole Word Catalogue,* but much more.

# Appendix B
# The Essentials of Education

Public concern about basic knowledge and the basic skills in education is valid. Society should continually seek out, define, and then provide for every person those elements of education that are essential to a productive and meaningful life.

The basic elements of knowledge and skill are only a part of the essentials of education. In an era dominated by cries for going "back to the basics," for "minimal competencies," and for "survival skills," society should reject simplistic solutions and declare a commitment to the essentials of education.

A definition of the essentials of education should avoid three easy tendencies: to limit the essentials to "the three R's" in a society that is highly technological and complex; to define the essentials by what is tested at a time when tests are severely limited in what they can measure; and to reduce the essentials to a few "skills" when it is obvious that people use a combination of skills, knowledge, and feelings to come to terms with their world. By rejecting these simplistic tendencies, educators will avoid concentration on training in a few skills at the expense of preparing students for the changing world in which they must live.

Educators should resist pressures to concentrate solely upon easy-to-teach, easy-to-test bits of knowledge, and must go beyond short-term objectives of training for jobs or producing citizens who can perform routine tasks but cannot apply their knowledge or skills, cannot reason about their society, and cannot make informed judgments.

## What Are the Essentials of Education?

Educators agree that the overarching goal of education is to develop informed, thinking citizens capable of participating in both domestic and world affairs. The development of such citizens depends not only upon education for citizenship, but also upon other essentials of education shared by all subjects.

The interdependence of skills and content is the central concept of the essentials of education. Skills and abilities do not grow in isolation from content. In all subjects, students develop skills in using language and

223

other symbol systems; they develop the ability to reason; they undergo experiences that lead to emotional and social maturity. Students master these skills and abilities through observing, listening, reading, talking, and writing *about* science, mathematics, history and the social sciences, the arts and other aspects of our intellectual, social, and cultural heritage. As they learn about their world and its heritage they necessarily deepen their skills in language and reasoning and acquire the basis for emotional, aesthetic and social growth. They also become aware of the world around them and develop an understanding and appreciation of the interdependence of the many facets of that world.

More specifically, the essentials of education include, among others, the ability to use language, to think, and to communicate effectively; to use mathematical knowledge and methods to solve problems; to reason logically; to use abstractions and symbols with power and ease; to apply and to understand scientific knowledge and methods; to make use of technology and to understand its limitations; to express oneself through the arts and to understand the artistic expressions of others; to understand other languages and cultures; to understand spatial relationships; to apply knowledge about health, nutrition, and physical activity; to acquire the capacity to meet unexpected challenges; to make informed value judgments; to recognize and to use one's full learning potential; and to prepare to go on learning for a lifetime.

Such a definition calls for a realization that all disciplines must join together and acknowledge their interdependence. Determining the essentials of education is a continuing process, far more demanding and significant than listing isolated skills assumed to be basic. Putting the essentials of education into practice requires instructional programs based on this new sense of interdependence.

Educators must also join with many segments of society to specify the essentials of education more fully. Among these segments are legislators, school boards, parents, students, workers' organizations, businesses, publishers, and other groups and individuals with an interest in education. All must now participate in a coordinated effort on behalf of society to confront this task. *Everyone* has a stake in the essentials of education.

# Contributors

**Susan G. Bennett**, Assistant Professor of English Education at the University of Texas, Austin, received her doctorate in Curriculum and Instruction from the University of California, Berkeley. She is currently serving as Director of the Texas Hill Country Writing Project and Coordinator of the Secondary English/Reading Student Teaching Program and has published extensively in numerous scholarly journals.

**Beverly A. Busching** is Assistant Professor of Elementary Education at the University of South Carolina, Columbia. She has been a consultant on a number of national educational projects and has presented over a dozen workshops dealing with a wide variety of elementary and early childhood education topics. She has also produced several articles and presentations dealing primarily with the language arts and elementary school discipline.

**Laura R. Fortson** is a teacher in the Clark County School District, Athens, Georgia, with over seventeen years experience at the elementary level. She has an Ed.D. in Early Childhood Education from the University of Georgia and has published and presented papers on a variety of pedagogical issues.

**Jerome Green** is Senior Building Principal of The Ochs Public School 111 in Manhattan. He is currently President-elect of the New York City Association of Teachers of English and has served as President of both the New York City Principals Association and the New York State English Teachers. Co-author of *Listening and Speaking in the English Classroom* and contributor to *The Myth of Measurability*, he has written for *Teacher* magazine and other publications, and has spoken at city, state, and national professional conferences.

**Celia Genishi**, Associate Professor in the Department of Curriculum and Instruction at the University of Texas, Austin, received her doctorate in Early Childhood Education: Language and Reading Development Program from the University of California, Berkeley. She has numerous presentations and publications on the subject of bilingual children.

**Mary W. Hill** is Assistant Professor of Education at Westminster College, New Wilmington, Pennsylvania. She has published several articles in scholarly journals and has spoken on the subject of reading and writing at a number of professional meetings.

**Dorothy F. King** received her Ph.D. in Curriculum and Development, including comprehensive examinations in the areas of language arts, reading, special education, and teacher education, from the University of Missouri, Columbia, and is currently Associate Professor of Education at Columbia College, Columbia, Missouri. She has teaching experience in every level of education from preschool through college, including experience in teaching handicapped students. She has numerous scholarly publications and presentations.

**Dorris M. Lee** is Professor Emerita of Education at Portland State University, Portland, Oregon. Her publications include ten books and twenty-three articles that reflect her experience in the elementary classroom, in the university classroom, and as educational consultant for various federal government projects. She has served on the John Dewey Society executive board; as vice president for the American Association of Elementary, Kindergarten, and Nursery Educators; and as president of the International Reading Association, Portland, Oregon.

**Sara Lundsteen** is Professor of English at North Texas State University and Chair of the Board of Directors for the Institute for Creative Studies. She taught language arts at both the elementary and middle school levels. Her publications include ten books, most recently *Guiding Young Children to Learn*, and over 100 articles and reviews in such scholarly journals as *Elementary School Journal*, *Elementary English*, and *California Journal of Educational Research*.

**Norman C. Najimy** is currently Principal at Crosby Middle School, Pittsfield, Massachusetts, and has served as Head of the English Department for the Junior High School as well as Director of English for grades K-12 in the Pittsfield Public Schools. He has served as Regional Chair of the Massachusetts Council of Teachers of English and designed and presented a variety of workshops and presentations on writing and the language arts for a number of professional organizations.

**Sandra A. Rietz** is Associate Professor of Education at Eastern Montana College, Billings, and has taught English at both the elementary and secondary level. She has spoken at over sixty engagements in the areas of storytelling, language acquisition and development, reading in the content areas, composition, and sentence-combining for local, state, regional, and national meetings of IRA, NCTE, and a variety of early childhood organizations.

**Lynn K. Rhodes** is Assistant Professor of Reading Education at the University of Colorado at Denver and is an experienced elementary school teacher. She has spoken at numerous workshops and symposia on the topics of reading and writing and has also published several articles on reading and teaching reading to children with special needs. She has also been involved in recent research dealing with the language arts acquisition of disabled students.

**Laura R. Roehler** presently coordinates the Learning Community Program, an undergraduate teacher education program which focuses on the development of self and group responsibilities within integrated curriculum, at Michigan State University and is senior researcher in the Institute for Research on Teaching, where she has researched integration of the language arts and is currently coordinating research of the teaching of cognitive processes that children use as they read. She has published a basal reading series and a number of articles in such journals as the *Journal of Teacher Education, Reading Research Quarterly*, and *Language Arts*.

**Gayle L. Rogers** is a middle school language arts teacher at Martin Luther King, Jr. Experimental Laboratory Schools in Evanston, Illinois. She is a teacher-consultant for the Illinois Writing Project and has taught workshops for the Illinois Middle School Association and the Illinois Association of Teachers of English as well. She has published several articles on writing and has had several samples of students' writing from her classes published also.

**Masha K. Rudman**, Professor of Education at the University of Massachusetts, Amherst, is Co-director of the Integrated Day Program, editor of the periodical *In Touch*, and consultant to education departments, schools, and organizations across the country in reading, language arts, children's literature, bibliotherapy, informal evaluation, test taking, competency-based education, individualization, open education, and education of the gifted. She has published extensively on a variety of pedagogical issues.

**Judith I. Schwartz** is presently Assistant Professor and Coordinator of Early Childhood Education at Queens College, City University of New York. Her publications include *Window on Early Childhood Reading, Research Papers: A Guided Writing Experience for Senior High School Students*, and *Teaching the Linguistically Diverse* as well as numerous articles in various professional journals.

**Eileen Tway** is Professor in the Department of Teacher Education at Miami University, Ohio, and has taught language arts at the elementary level. She has consulted in a variety of educational settings. Publications include *Reading Ladders for Human Relations, Sixth Edition* and a number of articles in scholarly journals such as *The Elementary School Journal, Elementary English*, and *The Reading Teacher*.

**Betty Jane Wagner** has been a member of the English Department at National College of Education, Evanston, Illinois, for the past eighteen years, teaching composition, children's literature, and language arts methods courses. She is presently Director of the National College Writing Project and Co-director of the Illinois Writing Project. Publications include *Dorothy Heathcote: Drama as a Learning Medium*, *Student-Centered Language Arts and Reading, K–13*, and *Making and Using Inexpensive Classroom Media* as well as a variety of articles in professional journals.

**Dorothy J. Watson** is Professor of Education, Curriculum and Instruction at the University of Missouri, Columbia, has taught in the Missouri public school system, and has worked in inservice teacher education programs in Sierra Leone, Kenya, and across the United States. She is President of the Center for the Expansion of Language and Thinking and her numerous publications include *Findings of Research in Miscue Analysis: Classroom Implications* and *Describing and Improving the Reading Strategies of Elderly Readers*.

Russian-American
Relations
in World War I

# Russian-American Relations in World War I

Benson Lee Grayson

Frederick Ungar Publishing Co.
*New York*

Copyright © 1979 by Frederick Ungar Publishing Co., Inc.
*Printed in the United States of America*
*Designed by Anita Duncan*

LIBRARY OF CONGRESS CATALOGING IN PUBLICATION DATA

Grayson, Benson Lee, 1932–
    Russian-American relations in World War I.

    Bibliography:  p.
    Includes index.
    1.   European War, 1914–1918—Diplomatic history.
2.   United States—Foreign relations—Russia.
3.   Russia—Foreign relations—United States.  I.   Title.
D619.G67          940.3'22          78–21957
ISBN 0–8044–1309–6

79-10020

# Contents

# Introduction

Today, as has been the case since the end of World War II, Russian-American relations significantly affect the world situation. The interests of the two superpowers have clashed repeatedly on every continent and across the broadest spectrum of military, political, and economic matters. Simultaneously, a shared appreciation of the forces affecting both nations has led to a measure of cooperation—to a mutual reduction of tension when crises have threatened to ignite a global conflict, to a constantly changing but still surviving spirit of détente, and to a growth in bilateral commercial ties.

Many of the factors that currently influence the policies of each country with respect to the other antedate the establishment of the Soviet government in 1917. As early as the last third of the nineteenth century, American concern over the treatment of political and religious minorities in Russia increasingly embittered diplomacy between the two governments. Another long-standing area of friction was their rivalry in the Far East, where both powers adopted differing policies toward China and Japan. A third element of continuity involved the Tsarist Empire's desire to obtain the benefit of U.S. technology and goods and the expectation in American business circles of the profits to be gained from expanded trade with Russia.

1

While there is a large body of research on Russian-American affairs during most of the nineteenth and twentieth centuries, the World War I period has received negligible attention. This is understandable, since both nations were directing their primary attention elsewhere. Russia was concentrating on the war, and overwhelmingly its diplomacy concerned three principal allies—Britain, France, and Japan. In America, lack of interest in foreign developments produced a strongly isolationist outlook according to which Russia was regarded at best as a member of one of the warring alliances and at worst as the major foreign power whose traditions and system of government were most alien to our own.

Although many officials in both Washington and Petrograd, as St. Petersburg was renamed after the outbreak of World War I, sincerely wished to reduce points of friction, conflicting considerations, particularly domestic political pressures, sharply reduced the area for compromise. Moreover, 1914–1917 was a period so event-filled that external developments inevitably overshadowed Russian-American efforts at a rapprochement. Further, actual attempts to ease the strain were unsuccessful.

By the start of World War I, both countries were world powers, and the interaction between them was influential in shaping their policies concerning other nations. In the United States, antipathy toward the Tsarist government diminished the sympathy that otherwise would have been extended to the Allies. The state of the bilateral relationship was clearly less important to Russia, where the exigencies of the war would have prevented the Imperial government from carrying out any policies significantly different from those which were pursued, regardless of the state of relations between Petrograd and Washington.

Despite the sparsity of research on this subject, an understanding of Russian-American diplomacy during the war is necessary for full appreciation of the activities of the two governments during the period and even more for the light cast on the potential for developments in our own time. While history does not always repeat itself, the Imperial government's refusal to subordinate other national goals in order to win the benefit of expanded commerce with the United States suggests that we should not be optimistic that the Soviet Union will alter course in favor of increased trade in the future.

# I

## Early Ties between
## the Two Countries

Throughout the greater part of the nineteenth century, relations between Russia and the United States were relatively cordial. While the absence of any serious territorial dispute facilitated the maintenance of friendly ties, the basic reason for harmony was the Tsarist government's policy of supporting America as a counterweight to Britain.

As early as 1809, Count Rumiantzev, the Russian Chancellor, frankly admitted to John Quincy Adams, the first U.S. Minister to St. Petersburg, that it was essential for Russia to back a strong commercial power as a rival to Britain in order to oppose Britain's insistence on the right to control the seas and the maritime trade of other nations. The United States was in an ideal position to serve in such a role, and the Imperial government believed itself to be advancing its own vital interests materially by assisting America, since neither country was likely ever to threaten the other.[1]

The nature of Russia's support of the United States tended to vary, depending on the state of relations with Britain at any given time. This was clearly evident in 1812, when Tsar Alexander I abruptly terminated cooperation with France and allied his country with Britain. On that occasion, Alexander felt he ought not grant Washington trading privileges that were not also extended to his new ally, and so he suspended negotiations with Adams for

5

a commercial treaty, thereby frustrating the American expectation that an agreement was near fruition.[2]

Treaty discussions were resumed at U.S. urging in 1829, but further progress was temporarily delayed by the reluctance of Nicholas, who had replaced his brother Alexander as Tsar in 1825, to negotiate an American treaty that would be displeasing to the British.[3] Three years later, however, Britain and France agreed to support the independence of Belgium jointly, thus nettling Nicholas who opposed that nation's independence. Less inclined, then, to accommodate himself to British sensitivities, he put his signature on the treaty with the United States on December 18, 1832. This document, which was to influence ties between the two countries until shortly before World War I, was predominantly commercial in character. Article I, summarizing the treaty's provisions, stated that the nationals of each country would have the right to live in the other under the same circumstances as the inhabitants.

In a search for new allies during the Crimean War (1854–1856), Russia attempted to win American support in the struggle against Britain, France, and Turkey by offering political and economic concessions. The Tsarist Minister in Washington informed the United States that his government welcomed an increase in trade between the two nations. In a concrete move to strengthen relations, St. Petersburg reduced tariffs on goods Russia could buy from the United States and indicated that it would not object to American annexation of the Hawaiian Islands.[4]

Although the Tsarist government was unsuccessful in securing America's intervention in the war, the United States made no secret of its sympathy for Russia. Secretary of State William Marcy refused to sign an Anglo-French treaty prohibiting citizens of neutral nations from serving in the armed forces of belligerents; such an act, he emphasized, would discriminate against Russia. The American consul in Honolulu even exceeded the norms of diplomatic behavior by alerting the Russians to the Anglo-French fleets' planned attack on the Imperial naval base at Petropavlovsk on the Kamchatka Peninsula, enabling the garrison to beat off the assault.[5]

American sympathy for Russia during the Crimean War was

motivated more by antipathy toward Britain than by attachment to the Russian cause. The Pierce administration deeply resented statements by British Foreign Secretary Lord Clarendon in 1854 which intimated that his nation and France might jointly intervene in the affairs of Latin American countries.[6] Even more resented were blatant efforts by the British Minister in Washington to recruit men, in defiance of American law, to serve in the Crimean War. The United States finally declared the Minister *persona non grata* and obliged him to leave the United States amid such public clamor and strain in Anglo-American ties as to cause speculation that war would break out between the two countries.

The high point of Russian-American relations during the nineteenth century occurred during the American Civil War, when the Tsarist fleet visited New York and San Francisco in 1863. Although St. Petersburg had sent the ships there to have them in a safe place if there were war with Britain, it was widely believed in America that the fleet was under secret orders to assist the Union cause if Britain and France intervened on behalf of the Confederacy. Consequently, the presence of the worships served to strengthen Northern morale, and this has often been cited as proof of Russian friendliness toward the United States.

St. Petersburg made no secret of its support for the North. Tsar Alexander II openly stated that he was very anxious that the United States retain its prewar power and influence. Similarly, the Foreign Minister, Prince Alexander Gortchakov, assured the American chargé d'affaires in St. Petersburg in October 1862 that although Washington had few friends among the great powers, Russia would support the Union and do what it could to prevent the Confederacy's secession from becoming permanent.

Russia's attitude was essentially a continuation of its basic policy of encouraging the United States as a rival to Britain. This objective was clearly enunciated by the Tsarist Minister in Washington, Baron Stoeckel, in February 1862. In a dispatch to St. Petersburg he warned that a weakening of the United States would render it less effective in opposing Britain, which would be disadvantageous to Russia. That Tsarist support was deeply appreciated in Washington was attested by Secretary of State William

Seward, when he requested the American legation in St. Petersburg to inform the Imperial government that Russia "has our friendship . . . in preference to any other European power, simply because she always wishes us well and leaves us to conduct our affairs as we think best."[8]

In 1867 Russia sold Alaska to the United States at a bargain rate, to raise money and because the area would be difficult to hold against British or American expansion. Nevertheless, relations between the two countries deteriorated in the latter part of the nineteenth century. As the United States developed into a big power and as the historic American animosity toward Britain declined in importance, the worth of St. Petersburg's diplomatic backing against London decreased, eventually eroding the very foundation of amity. Equally significant was growing American influence in the Pacific and Far East, where the policies of the United States and Russia came into conflict.

Of all the factors combining to produce estrangement, the most important was the ideological difference between the two countries. As the world's leading exponent of democratic principles, America gradually grew less tolerant of Russia's autocratic government. This disapproval was encouraged by the large numbers of Russian Jews who emigrated to the United States recounting vivid stories of religious persecution under the Tsars.

American criticism of the lack of civil liberties in the Empire came to a head in the "passport dispute," which arose from restrictions that St. Petersburg imposed on American Jews who traveled or resided in Russia. Because they were regarded as a subversive threat, Jews were allowed to live only in certain specified western provinces. Further, the Imperial passport statute required all foreign Jews seeking to enter the country, other than bankers and representatives of large commercial firms, to obtain approval from the Minister of the Interior.[9]

The United States viewed these restrictions as being incompatible with the principle of freedom of religion and argued that the right of free exercise of religion contained in the First Amendment to the Constitution applied to American citizens while they were in Russia. As early as 1873, Secretary of State Hamilton

Fish protested to St. Petersburg that discrimination against American Jews residing in the Empire was a violation of the treaty of 1832.[10]

The problem was compounded by the ambiguous wording of the agreement in question; it could be interpreted to substantiate either the American or the Russian position. The Tsarist government, insisting that no discrimination could occur because it permitted U.S. Jews the same rights it did Russian Jews, rejected Washington's protests.

The American complaints continued nonetheless. John Foster, the U.S. Minister to St. Petersburg, described his duties in 1880 as having little to do other than to ask for leniency in the treatment of American Jews.[11] Ten years later, Congress approved a resolution condemning the Tsarist government's treatment of its own subjects, an act resented in Russia as interference in its internal affairs.

In the face of this criticism, the Imperial government neither responded to U.S. complaints nor made any effort to strengthen its image in America. Following the killing of several Jews in a pogrom at Kishenev in 1903, which drew considerable foreign attention, St. Petersburg rejected an official U.S. request to permit relief supplies to reach the victims. The incident provoked anti-Russian commentary in the United States, and as relations between the two nations worsened, Russian consular agents refused to issue visas to American Jews to visit the Empire.

Superimposed on the strains of the passport dispute was the growing rivalry between U.S. and Tsarist interests in the Far East. In particular, expanding American commercial involvement in China increasingly brought the United States into conflict with Russian activities in that country. This new note of discord could be heard in the instructions Foreign Minister Count Michael Muraviev gave Count Arthur Cassini when the latter was appointed Ambassador to Washington in 1898. The envoy was reminded of the historically well-rooted ties between the two countries, his instructions stressing that the sale of Alaska to the United States for a "paltry sum" was motivated by Russia's objective of strengthening America as a rival to Britain. However,

Cassini was warned to look into the possibility the United States would acquire Canada and to determine whether in this event America would become a competitor for Russia in the north. The Ambassador was also instructed to take energetic action against those U.S. commercial activities in China that would impinge on the Russian sphere of influence there.[12]

Washington, meanwhile, feared that American commerce would be shut out of China if that nation were divided into areas under the control of Japan and the European great powers. To address this problem, in the fall of 1899 Secretary of State John Hay sent similar notes to the six nations having important interests in China—Britain, France, Germany, Italy, Japan, and Russia— asking each country to agree not to interfere with trade entering any treaty port within its sphere of influence in China. Five of the six nations agreed to the U.S. proposal; Russia alone equivocated. Although Hay chose to regard the ambiguous reply from St. Petersburg as signifying acceptance of his note, the incident illustrated the growing divergence between the two nations arising from their impinging commercial interests in the Far East.[13]

The outbreak of the Russo-Japanese War in February 1904 found the United States officially neutral but unofficially heavily pro-Japanese. Washington believed that if Japan were to win, that country would be more likely to respect U.S. interests than would Russia.[14] President Theodore Roosevelt went so far as to warn Germany and France that America would intervene to prevent Japan from losing the fruits of victory, as had happened after the Sino-Japanese War in 1895.[15] Moreover, Roosevelt was acting at Tokyo's initiative when he proposed the peace conference that ended the conflict.[16]

The President's attitude was much resented in Russia, and his general opposition naturally colored the Tsarist attitude toward the United States. Although American sympathy for Japan lessened after the Russo-Japanese War, there was little sentiment in St. Petersburg in this period for a rapprochement with Washington directed against Japan. Instead, Russia joined with Japan to divide northeast Asia into spheres of influence, to the exclusion of the United States. On July 30, 1907, the former enemies signed a treaty agreeing to respect each other's territory, and an accompanying secret convention granted St. Petersburg a sphere of influence in northern Manchuria and Outer Mongolia while Tokyo was to exercise similar control over Korea and southern Manchuria. These agreements and two more secret conventions signed in 1910 and 1912 effectively barred American commercial activity in Manchuria. As early as 1908 the United States Ambassador to China warned that the cooperation of Russia and Japan was rendering futile the attempts by other nations to affect Manchurian developments.[17]

The truth of this assessment was illustrated in January 1910, when Washington suggested to St. Petersburg that the two countries cooperate to prevent Japan from using the Manchurian railways to expand its influence in the region. The Tsarist government rejected the proposal, and the United States was left powerless to attain its objective. The reasons for the Russian decision were frankly stated by Foreign Minister Izvolsky at a Cabinet meeting, during which he pointed out that, "If we reject the American proposal we will call forth the temporary cooling off of American friendship, but America will not declare war on us for this and its fleet will not arrive in Harbin, while in this connection Japan is considerably more dangerous."[18]

The two nations' differences in the Far East served to reinforce the deterioration in relations resulting from the passport dispute. The later issue came to a climax in December 1911 when Congress, under pressure from Jewish groups and other circles in the United States concerned with civil liberties in Russia, began deliberation of a joint resolution calling for abrogation of the 1832 treaty. So important was the matter to Americans that the House of Representatives passed the resolution by the overwhelming vote of three hundred to one. The repeal measure declared that the treaty should be terminated at the earliest possible opportunity, as the United States could not be party to any pact that discriminated between American citizens on the ground of race or religion. The measure maintained that the Imperial government had violated the 1832 agreement by refusing on racial and religious grounds to honor passports issued to American Jews.

Believing that final passage of the resolution would only serve to antagonize the Tsarist government, President Taft did not wait for the Senate to act on the measure but immediately served Russia notice of termination in one year, as provided in the treaty. At the same time he urged that the two countries negotiate a new agreement that would eliminate the source of conflict.

The American action engendered both anger and incomprehension in St. Petersburg. Upon being notified of President Taft's message, Foreign Minister Sergei Sazonov told the American Ambassador, Curtis Guild, on December 15, 1911, that he could not understand how Washington could deliberately sacrifice its commercial position in Russia. Sazonov noted that the United States stood to lose by the action, since it had a potential market of hundreds of millions of dollars in sales to the Empire, while the latter sold relatively little to America.

In retrospect, it is clear that neither government could appreciate the other's depth of feeling on the treatment of religious minorities. Ambassador Guild unsuccessfully attempted to explain that Congress's action was based on an idealistic conviction that it might influence St. Petersburg to abandon restrictions against both Russian and American Jews. He similarly failed to persuade Sazonov that the United States had found that absolute freedom of speech and movement were the most effective means of eliminating the causes of treason and conspiracy.

Sazonov, utterly unconvinced, told Guild that Washington did not appreciate the situation and that what might be true in America was not true in Russia. The vast gulf in thinking that existed in the two nations on the issue was made clear in a counter-proposal put forth by the Foreign Minister in all seriousness (according to Guild): that the Tsarist authorities were prepared to consider arrangements under which Russia's entire Jewish population would be transferred to the United States. He added that Russia's Jews constituted a perpetual menace to law and order as well as to the integrity of the Empire, and that St. Petersburg would never even consider a new treaty that did not accord both nations the right to exclude classes of persons they regarded as undesirable.[19]

In Russia, the U.S. termination of the treaty was regarded as a national insult, and protest demonstrations were held in the capital and other major cities. The conservative Octobrist and Nationalist Parties introduced bills in the Duma to prohibit American Jews from entering the country, to double customs duties on U.S. goods, and to lay a similar increase in fees on American shipping.[20]

The Prime Minister, Count Vladimir Kokovtsov, was particularly incensed, and for the remainder of his time in office he exhibited deep resentment over the issue, asserting repeatedly in the presence of American Embassy staff that his nation had been outraged and insulted by the United States.[21] Ambassador Guild, who previously had been very popular in Tsarist official circles, found the atmosphere in St. Petersburg so unpleasant that he returned to the United States and resigned. Washington in turn responded by leaving the post of Ambassador to Russia unfilled, so that ties between the two countries sank to their nadir in the pre-World War I period.

There was some improvement in subsequent years, but relations between the United States and Russia still remained more correct than cordial. St. Petersburg's position was set forth by Sazonov in a speech to the Duma of April 1912 in which he declared that the nation had always faithfully lived up to its treaty obligations and any assertions to the contrary were false. If the United States wished to negotiate a new agreement, the Empire would not surrender its rights to determine its internal regulations. Concluding on a more optimistic note, Sazonov expressed the hope that Americans' common sense "will make them see the justice of our views, and that the age-long friendly relations between the Russian and American people will not be overshadowed by differences of opinion."[22]

The absence of a formal agreement regulating commerce between the two countries did not have a significant impact on their trade, although the volume remained relatively low. Russian purchases from the United States in 1913 totaled $38 million, in contrast to only $6 million in sales—these amounts representing only 6 percent of Tsarist imports and 1 percent of exports. The

Empire's principal foreign trade partner was Germany, which in contrast purchased 69 percent of all Russian exports and supplied 47 percent of all imports in 1913.[23]

Despite the relatively low level of trade, commercial interests in Russia and the United States believed that potential existed for a considerable increase in volume. Prominent citizens in Moscow organized a Russian-American Chamber of Commerce in 1914, just before the outbreak of war, with Nikolai Guchkov, a former mayor of the city, chosen as president of the group.

In contrast to the private sector, Tsarist officials were slower to forget the bitter feeling from 1911. The Ministry of Finance in January 1914 refused an informal request from a consortium of American and Russian bankers to charter a joint bank to finance bilateral trade, although the proposal was supported by the American Consul General in Moscow and the Moscow Chamber of Commerce. The Ministry justified its refusal on the grounds that relations between the two countries had not yet reached a stage that would warrant such an enterprise.

Meanwhile, in the United States important changes in the political leadership of the country had occurred. The Democratic administration of President Wilson replaced the Republican administration of President Taft in March 1913, ending sixteen years of Republican control. Wilson had served as the reform Governor of New Jersey and as President of Princeton University, but his experience in international relations was limited. He had traveled outside the United States only to Great Britain and briefly to France and Italy. Although the Democratic Party platform in 1912 included a plank approving Congress's action in calling for abrogation of the 1832 treaty, international events played a very minor role in the presidential campaign. Shortly before his inauguration, Wilson remarked to a friend that it would be "an irony of fate if my administration had to deal chiefly with foreign affairs."[24]

The new President selected William Jennings Bryan, one of the stalwarts of the Democratic Party who had run unsuccessfully for the Presidency himself in 1896, 1900, and 1908, as Secretary of State. An idealist, a fervent prohibitionist, and a dedicated advocate of international cooperation to achieve world peace, Bryan had a somewhat greater exposure to international affairs than Wilson, having undertaken a world tour between 1905 and 1907, during which he had visited St. Petersburg. The American press was concerned that Bryan's idealism would prevent him from functioning effectively in office, and the President probably shared these fears but felt constrained to reward Bryan's political support. In any event, Wilson believed that the President should function as the principal architect of foreign policy and thought he could restrain Bryan from unwise actions.[25]

By contrast with Washington, the leadership in Russia remained basically unchanged. In 1914 Tsar Nicholas II, at the age of forty-six, was in the twentieth year of his reign. Although his power had been restricted somewhat following the 1905 Revolution, he retained a large measure of control over the formulation of national policy through his appointment of the Council of Ministers, whose members could be removed at any time at his pleasure.

The Tsar's response to the American termination of the treaty was not specially communicated to the United States, but his reaction was almost certainly the same as Sazonov's. When in 1906 the Council of Ministers had recommended that most of the restrictions against Jews be removed because the measures were easily evaded and they were causing anti-Russian sentiment in the United States, Nicholas rejected this suggestion. His reply to the Prime Minister conceded that there were convincing arguments for approving the proposal but concluded in an interesting illustration of his manner of thinking that "an inner voice keeps insisting more and more that I do not accept responsibility for it. . . . Therefore I intend to follow its dictates."[26]

In 1914 the Tsarist Foreign Ministry was headed by another incumbent of long standing. Sazonov, then fifty-three, had been a member of the Imperial diplomatic service since 1883. After serving abroad in London and Rome, he was named Foreign Minister in 1910. Sazonov was regarded as one of the liberals within the Council of Ministers, with close ties to the British and French Ambassadors and without any strongly anti-American sentiments.

Having been in office as the time of Washington's termination of the treaty, however, he considered the action to be inappropriate and insulting and saw no reason for his country to make concessions to restore friendly relations with the United States.

The Chairman of the Council of Ministers, Ivan Goremykin, was new to office, but he was less important than either the Tsar or Sazonov in framing foreign policy. Goremykin owed his appointment to Nicholas's quarrel with the previous Chairman, Count Kokovtsov, over the Tsar's efforts to curtail the consumption of liquor in Russia. Kokovtsov was serving concurrently as Finance Minister, and he opposed the ruler's prohibitionist policies on the grounds that the government could not afford to lose the revenues raised by the taxes on liquor.[27]

Although the dispute leading to Kokovtsov's departure from office in February 1914 was not related to international developments, the American Embassy in St. Petersburg regarded his replacement by Goremykin as a favorable event. Charles Wilson, the career Foreign Service Officer who served as American chargé during the interval between Guild's departure and the new Ambassador's arrival, commented that Goremykin could scarcely be more hostile to the United States than Kokovtsov, who had been in office during the treaty's termination and never failed to show his deep resentment over the issue. Because Goremykin had not been politically active during the incident, the chargé expected that any feeling of personal resentment he might have toward the affair would be less pronounced than that of his predecessor. Wilson warned, however, that it was not expected in St. Petersburg that Goremykin would play an active role in foreign policy, which function would be left more than ever in the hands of Sazonov. For this reason the chargé doubted that the change in Prime Ministers would significantly affect relations between Russia and the United States.

Goremykin was seventy-five years of age and in poor health at the time of his appointment. Charles Wilson did not know the Chairman personally but had been informed by other diplomats that he appeared very old and feeble, both mentally and physically, and took no interest in any important questions. Wilson therefore believed policy changes would have to await Goremykin's eventual replacement by Minister of Agriculture Alexander Krivoshein, a younger and stronger man, who was rumored to be the designated successor.[28]

In America there was little concern over international relations generally, and especially not over relations with Russia, as the summer of 1914 approached. News about the Empire appeared in the press only occasionally, usually reported factually and unaccompanied either by favorable or critical commentary. Such was the case when the *New York Times* in February 1914 reported only that the Russian Ambassador to Washington, George Bakhmet'ev, had asked to be transferred because of his failure to solve the passport dispute with the United States.[29]

The American government shared the public's wish to avoid involvement in foreign affairs. Washington's policy was stated by Secretary Bryan in instructions to the delegation he was sending in May 1914 to an international conference concerning Spitzbergen: the United States traditionally sought to refrain from interference in European matters.

In the months preceding the outbreak of World War I, little attention was directed in Russia toward the United States. The official gazette, *Pravitel'stvenni Vestnik,* mentioned America infrequently in the months preceding August 1914, less so than Sweden and only slightly more often than Brazil or Argentina. Its commentary varied in tone from objective to mildly critical. A description of the administration of the Philippines, whose takeover by the United States in 1898 had been viewed with suspicion, conceded that America was indeed striving to raise the cultural standing of the inhabitants.[30]

Foreign Minister Sazonov, reviewing Tsarist foreign policy in a May 1914 speech to the Duma, did not even mention the United States or any other country in the Western Hemisphere. By contrast, he covered in great detail the situation in Europe, China, Japan, and Mongolia.[31]

Thus, in the spring of 1914 Russian-American relations could best be described as coolly correct. The ill feeling in the Empire resulting from the termination of the treaty of 1832 and the still unsettled passport dispute had not been overcome. Nor had the differing views of the two nations over their respective interests in the Far East been brought into harmony.

On the other hand, commercial interests in both countries desired an improvement in economic ties. If the replacement of Kokovtsov by Goremykin had not changed Tsarist policy, it had removed from power an individual who felt resentment against the United States. This, then, was the state of affairs when the great powers of Europe were plunged into the chaos and destruction of World War I.

# II

## The Outbreak of War

When on June 28, 1914, the Archduke Franz Ferdinand, heir to the throne of the Austro-Hungarian Empire, and his wife were assassinated by a Serbian nationalist while visiting Sarajevo, the incident did not initially cause particular concern in the capitals of the great European powers. In Washington the Department of State merely prepared its routine message of condolence for President Wilson to send to the Emperor Franz Josef. Indeed, the President's close advisor, Colonel Edward House. was visiting Berlin and London at the time to explore the possibility of establishing an Anglo-American-German *entente*. In a message to Colonel House on July 9, 1914, the President indicated no awareness of the approaching conflict in Europe but congratulated House on the progress of his mission. Similarly oblivious, Raymond Poincaré, the President of France, arrived in St. Petersburg on July 20 to pay an official visit, and the British Ambassador to Russia, Sir George Buchanan, prepared to depart on a leave of absence. He had not only received London's permission but also had purchased tickets for his journey to England.

Meanwhile, on July 2, 1914, President Wilson had moved to fill the post of American Ambassador to Russia, vacant since the resignation of Guild, two years before. For the position he selected George Thomas Marye, a member of the California Bar and a prominent banker in San Francisco and Virginia City, Nevada.

Marye's designation had no relation to the Archduke's assassination—in fact, the American Embassy in St. Petersburg had been instructed by the State Department to obtain Russian approval of the appointment six days before that event, on June 22. In the description of the new envoy furnished by Washington to St. Petersburg, he was described as having been educated in Europe, having traveled extensively, having practiced law, and having served also as Regent of the University of California.[1]

It would have been difficult to anticipate Marye's selection. He had never before held any diplomatic post and at the age of sixty would visit Russia for the first time. Subsequent to his arrival, he explained his qualifications for the position to a journalist with the statement that he had a reputation in the United States for being pro-Russian because he was always interested in the Empire and was familiar with its literature.[2] Despite this limited background, Marye was to become one of the most popular envoys ever to represent America to the Tsarist regime.

The reason for President Wilson's decision in June 1914 to fill the ambassadorial post in St. Petersburg with Marye is not known, but he was probably motivated by domestic American political considerations. Many of Wilson's ambassadorial appointments had been made with the political factor in mind, and Marye had served as Chairman of the Democratic State Committee of California from 1888 to 1893. The timing also appears to have been a result of the replacement of Kokovtsov as Chairman of the Council of Ministers, which engendered hope that the new Chairman would be interested in improving relations with the United States.

Although he was confirmed by the Senate on July 9, 1914, Marye delayed arrangements and did not plan to arrive in Russia until sometime in 1915. The State Department, seemingly unconcerned over developments in Europe, indicated no desire that he take up his post in St. Petersburg more rapidly.

The situation, meanwhile, had become ominous. On July 23, 1914, the Austrian government delivered an ultimatum to Serbia, the small kingdom that included Sarajevo, which Russia had pledged to protect, demanding far-reaching concessions in response to the assassination. The Austrian note was so harshly worded that the head of the Austrian Foreign Minister's Chancellery commented that "no state possessing the smallest amount of national pride or dignity could accept" the demands.[3]

On the following day, Russian Foreign Minister Sazonov met with the British and French Ambassadors to obtain their governments' views and then attended an urgent meeting of the Council of Ministers. After the Tsarist government unsuccessfully attempted to obtain an extension of the time limit in the ultimatum, the Council of Ministers on July 25, 1914, ordered a mobilization of the military forces designated for action in case of war against Austria-Hungary. On July 28, Austria declared war on Serbia and on August 1, 1914, Germany declared war on Russia.

The first indication from the American Embassy in St. Petersburg as to the seriousness of the situation came on July 25, when the chargé alerted Washington that diplomatic and political observers considered events most serious, with Russian intervention inevitable if Austria declared war against Serbia.[4] On the following day, July 26, the Minister of War, General Vladimir Sukhomlinov, confirmed this, informing the American Embassy that he considered hostilities between his country and the Austrian Empire virtually certain. Vienna's declaration of war on Serbia on July 28, 1914, provoked a strong reaction in St. Petersburg. The Russians felt they must come to the aid of their fellow Slavs, and three days later chargé Wilson informed Washington that "the whole country, all classes, are unanimous for war." As the Russian mobilization was expected to put the nation's railroad system into disorder, the Embassy began advising all American tourists to leave the country while it was still possible to obtain transportation.

Charles Wilson also alerted the State Department to the likelihood that Austria and Germany would ask the United States to look after their interests in Russia in case of war. Recalling that American relations with Russia had been strained by Washington's acting as a protecting power for Japan during the Russo-Japanese conflict, he strongly advised against assuming this task again. Despite the chargé's warning, Washington did accede to the anticipated requests. Although Foreign Minister Sazonov, upon receiving formal notification of this development on August 3, 1914, assured Wilson that he was confident the United States would carry out its responsibilities in "the most friendly neutral spirit," it was obviously not a situation conducive to any improvement in relations between the two countries.[5]

With the declaration of war, most of the hitherto divided elements in the population rallied in support of the Tsarist government. On Sunday, August 2, 1914, over five thousand people gathered in the Winter Palace to see Nicholas issue the proclamation of war in accordance with ancient Russian tradition. In the presence of the French Ambassador, the only foreigner permitted to attend the ceremony, government officials, military officers, and members of the Duma and the State Council, the crowd listened as the Tsar repeated word for word the oath taken by Alexander I in 1812 during the Napoleonic invasion that he would not make peace until the last foreign soldier had left Russian territory.

In the United States, reaction to the outbreak of war was sharply negative. The closing of the New York Stock Exchange on July 31 caused dismay in financial circles, while uncertainty over the fate of thousands of Americans stranded in Europe became a national concern. In an attempt at reassurance, President Wilson held a press conference on August 3 at which he stated that there was no cause for alarm, and that the United States would handle the financial and economic dislocations without any material difficulty.

The American government also undertook a last-minute effort to prevent the conflict. On August 4, 1914, President Wilson dispatched messages to the heads of state of France, Great Britain, Russia, Austria, and Germany, offering his services as a mediator. Although all declined the offer, St. Petersburg's reply was the coolest in tone. Charles Wilson was not even accorded the courtesy of presenting the U.S. note to the Tsar. Instead, when the chargé called at the Foreign Ministry on August 6 to request an audience with Nicholas, Sazonov told him that Austria, which had started the war, was the only nation where a change in policy could bring about an immediate end of hostilities.[7]

The Tsar was not in St. Petersburg, however, and no formal response was given to the U.S. proposal. By August 16, 1914, no further Russian answer had been received, and Secretary of State Bryan instructed the American Embassy to inquire discreetly whether one might be expected. On August 26, 1914, twenty days after delivery of the President's note, Sazonov finally met with Charles Wilson to give him the Tsar's reply. Thanking President Wilson for his humanitarian sentiments, the Russian note explained that the Imperial government had not desired the war, was acting only to defend its territory from attack, and believed it premature to contemplate the possibility of peace.[8]

On August 5, 1914, a Russian mob attacked the German Embassy in St. Petersburg and did great damage. As the United States had accepted the responsibility for protecting Berlin's interests, Charles Wilson called at the Foreign Ministry to protest the incident. Sazonov expressed his apologies, and all further such demonstrations were prevented by the Tsarist authorities. However, as the American chargé had warned, the United States once again had been placed in the uncomfortable position of looking after the interests of Russia's enemies.[9]

Meanwhile, the State Department notified Ambassador-designate Marye that the crisis in Europe made his early departure for St. Petersburg desirable. He therefore hurriedly took his oaths of allegiance and of office on August 1, 1914, in San Francisco and promptly left for Washington where he made arrangements to sail for England on August 14. In the interim, on August 10 he was able to meet at length with George Bakhmet'ev, the Tsarist Ambassador to the United States, at the Ritz-Carlton Hotel in New York. There, Bakhmet'ev commented that he did not think it wise for Marye to leave immediately for his post, since the position had been allowed to remain vacant for two years. Under the circumstances, Marye's arrival in the Russian capital after the United States had assumed responsibility for the Austrian and German interests would make him appear to be the representative of the Empire's enemies rather than of America. He expected the war in Europe to last only a few months, and Bakhmet'ev advised Marye to postpone his departure until the conflict was over.[10]

Aboard a return train from New York to Washington, Marye met President Wilson's secretary, Joseph Tumulty, and Senator Ollie James of Kentucky. When the Ambassador-designate broached the subject, both men urged careful consideration of the Russian Ambassador's suggestion. Marye believed that Bakhmet'ev was merely expressing his personal opinion, but he related the conversation to Secretary of State Bryan who decided to request amplification from the Tsarist government. The Russian reply was unenthusiastic, stating only that the Tsar had informed the Ministry of Foreign Affairs that Marye's presence was not at all necessary if he preferred to delay coming, but if he should decide to come, Nicholas would receive him cordially, provided that he happened to be in Petrograd (as the Russian capital had been renamed.)[11]

After considering the situation, Marye concluded that his presence in Russia would have a beneficial effect on relations between the two countries, and he made preparations to sail on September 9, 1914, the earliest date on which accommodations were available. Although the more cautious Secretary Bryan had counseled further delay, Marye's decision to go was justified shortly by Ambassador Bakhmet'ev, who told him on August 31 that he had changed his mind about the duration of the war and had recommended to Bryan that Marye assume his post as soon as possible. Marye noted in his memoirs that the Ambassador's action relieved him of some embarrassment, as he no longer had to explain to the Secretary of State why he wished to leave for Russia at once.[12]

Marye discussed Bakhmet'ev's call with Bryan, suggesting that he and the Secretary meet with the President to obtain any last-minute instructions Wilson might have in mind. The meeting took place, but the President made no substantive comments, leaving both the manner of travel and the course of action to be followed after his arrival in St. Petersburg to Marye's discretion. This absence of specific directions was probably due not to any great confidence by either Wilson or Bryan in Marye's ability but to uncertainty as to how the war would affect diplomatic ties between the two countries. Both men obviously intended to send detailed guidance to the Ambassador as soon as the situation became clearer.

Before leaving for his post, Marye met with Jacob Schiff, Louis Marshall, and Herman Bernstein, who had been among the leaders in the campaign in the United States for abrogation of the treaty with Russia. After describing the Tsarist government's position, the Ambassador-designate asked for arguments that he could use to negotiate a new and more satisfactory agreement. Marye was disappointed at the response, concluding that the replies he received dwelt on the impossibility of the United States accepting discriminatory treatment of its citizens but that they did not show how Russia could be induced to waive the right to legislate its own internal affairs.[13]

Meanwhile, as part of his effort to preserve American neutrality, President Wilson on August 5, 1914, had delivered a message to the country warning that there must not be the slightest violation of U.S. neutrality in favor of either of the opposing forces. Off the record, however, the President favored the Allied position. Writing in his diary after seeing him on August 30, 1914, Colonel House noted that Wilson "goes even further than I in his condemnation of Germany's part in this war and almost allows his feeling to include the German people as a whole rather than the leaders alone."[14]

The President went even further in an off-the-record interview with a reporter of the *New York Times*, commenting, "As for Russia, I cannot help sympathizing with its aims to secure natural outlets for its trade with the world, and a proper settlement should permit this." In this regard, the President was more sympathetic to Russia than was Colonel House, who warned Wilson that, "the saddest feature of the situation to me is that there is no good outcome to look forward to. If the Allies win, it means largely the domination of Russia on the continent of Europe; and if Germany wins, it means the unspeakable tyranny of militarism for generations to come."[15]

As might have been expected, the entry of Russia into World

War I caused important and far-reaching changes in that country. The initial reaction of the government and people was to close ranks against the foreign enemy. After receiving word of the outbreak of hostilities on August 2, 1914, the Tsar summoned a special session of the Duma to explain the situation, a move praised in liberal circles as a manifestation of constitutionalism. On August 8, 1914, the Chairman of the Council of Ministers, Goremykin, told the Duma that the Tsarist government had not desired war and had done all it could to prevent one. He was followed by Foreign Minister Sazonov, who praised Great Britain and France for allying themselves with Russia.

When the officials completed their speeches, all of the party leaders in the Duma indicated their support of the war effort. Alexander Kerensky, the opposition deputy and the future Prime Minister in the Revolutionary Government that followed the overthrow of the Tsar, pledged his energies to the national defense. Even the Socialist deputies absented themselves from the chamber rather than vote against the defense appropriations requested by the government.

The first surge of national feeling was soon crushed by a massive defeat on the battlefield. The Allies were aware that the war plan of the Central Powers called for concentrating their forces to defeat France before the slower Russian mobilization could be completed, and to forestall this, Petrograd hurriedly completed its mobilization. On August 14, 1914, the Tsarist armies began a large-scale advance into West Prussia to relieve the German pressure on France.

The advance into Prussia was short-lived, however; in late August the Germans dealt the Russians a massive defeat at the battle of Tannenberg, inflicting more than one hundred thousand casualties. On August 30, 1914, Foreign Minister Sazonov told the French Ambassador that the Russians had suffered "a great disaster" and that their losses had been "ghastly." The defeat caused a feeling of pessimism to spread over the Russian capital.

In such circumstances, the subject of relations with the United States was hardly an object of primary importance to the Tsarist government. Nonetheless, in the fall of 1914 Petrograd indicated that it was interested in improving relations with Washington if this did not require any concessions on Russia's part. The Russians realized that the road to victory would be a long and arduous one and that friendly relations with the United States could be helpful.

Shortly after he became Secretary of State in 1913, William Jennings Bryan formulated a policy of negotiating "Treaties for the Advancement of Peace" with all the important world powers. These pacts provided for the establishment of bilateral commissions which would attempt to resolve peacefully any dispute arising between the United States and the signatory power. On September 15, 1914, an incongruous time considering that Europe was in the middle of a world war, Bryan dispatched notes to Russia, Belgium, Germany, and Austria, asking those nations to conclude treaties with the United States, after earlier having sent similar requests to Great Britain and France.

The Russian government was the first among those addressed by Bryan to signify acceptance of the American proposal. On October 1, 1914, Ambassador Bakhmet'ev signed a treaty for his government in Washington. The haste with which the Russian government moved in this regard suggested that it gave some importance to improving ties with the United States. Ambassador Bakhmet'ev explicitly stated this idea during the signing ceremony, declaring that Petrograd's agreement to the American proposal was a product of its desire to give proof of good will and friendship to the United States.[16]

The Russian press was no less sanguine in its treatment of the accord. One influential newspaper, the *Russkiia Viedomosti*, declared that the agreement was particularly significant since France and Great Britain had also signed such pacts with the United States. Reverting to language which had been prevalent during the period of harmonious ties prior to and during the American Civil War, the newspaper described the treaty as an outgrowth of the historic friendship between Washington and Petrograd.[17]

In August of 1914, meanwhile, the first efforts were made to lead the United States into financial involvement in the war. A few days after the start of hostilities, the influential New York banking firm of J. P. Morgan and Company was asked by the French government to act as its representative in the United States and to help raise a loan for France of 100 million dollars. The company in turn asked the Department of State whether it had any objection to this proposal.

Secretary of State Bryan forwarded the request to President Wilson for his decision, accompanying it with a recommendation that the government attempt to discourage American firms from participating in loans to any of the combatant nations, even though this was legal. The Secretary expressed his belief that an American refusal to lend money to any belligerent would tend to shorten the war. If the United States permitted J. P. Morgan and Company to participate in the loan to France, it could not morally prohibit such aid to other combatants. Bryan feared that the issue would create hostile factions within the country, each supporting one or the other of the warring sides. Finally, as a practical matter, Bryan warned that if large amounts of capital were permitted to flow abroad, the precedent would prove a handicap should the United States need to float loans.[18]

Robert Lansing, the Counselor of the State Department, opposed the position taken by the Secretary, advising instead that since American citizens were permitted to enlist in the armies of the belligerents, there was no reason to prevent the export of capital. In the words of Lansing, "Why should dollars be better protected than people?"[19] Despite this argument, President Wilson accepted Bryan's recommendation, authorizing him to announce to the press that American banks could lend money to the governments of neutral nations, but that the granting of bank loans to any belligerent nation would be inconsistent with U.S. neutrality.

It was at this point, when Wilson had already decided against permitting loans to the belligerents, that the Russian government expressed an interest in obtaining loans from American banks. On October 16, 1914, Count Sergei Witte, former Chairman of the Council of Ministers and a statesman highly regarded in the United States for his skilled performance in the negotiations that ended the Russo-Japanese War, called at the American Embassy in Petrograd.

Count Witte informed the chargé, Charles Wilson, that the Imperial government had asked him to travel to Washington as head of a Financial Commission to obtain loans. Although he did not wish to accept the mission because of his poor health and advanced age, Witte had agreed to do so if the Russian government would meet two conditions. Witte's price was a high one. He told Wilson he would not go unless Petrograd concluded a new commercial treaty with the United States, granting equal treatment to all American citizens residing in Russia, regardless of their religion; and he further insisted on legislation improving the economic and social conditions of the Russian workers. Unless these steps were taken, Witte declared, he felt it would be fruitless for him to seek any financial credit in the United States.[20]

Witte's conditions were so strong that it is unlikely that he seriously expected the Tsarist government to accept them. Not only was he requesting a complete about-face in the matter of the passport dispute, but his demand for an improvement in workers' rights would have required a fundamental reorientation in Russian economic and political policies.

Petrograd, for its part, may well have urged Witte to head the mission to the United States primarily to get him out of the country. Witte made no secret of his opposition to Russian involvement in the war, and he conducted a campaign in political circles calling for an immediate peace. According to the French Ambassador, more than a month before his call at the American Embassy Count Witte told him that the war was madness, that victory for the Allies was questionable, and that even if this occurred, it would result in the downfall of the Tsarist government. Since Nicholas was rumored to be "mortally afraid of Witte" and to lack the courage to speak to him directly, the proposed mission to the United States would have provided an excellent excuse for sending the count out of the country.

Regardless of the motivation behind Witte's approach to the American Embassy, it had little immediate effect upon relations between the two countries. Charles Wilson had no detailed instructions on the subject of loans and he was obliged to forward Witte's proposals to the State Department for a reply.

The message containing Count Witte's proposal reached Washington during Secretary Bryan's absence from the capital. Robert Lansing, the Acting Secretary, advised President Wilson that the Russian initiative was of such importance as to require a decision from the President. While aware that concluding a treaty with Russia would be a significant success for the Administration, Lansing felt constrained to warn that the United States would violate its neutrality if it became involved in Russian efforts to raise loans in the United States. The President accepted this point of view and Charles Wilson was instructed to inform Count Witte that America desired the commercial treaty but could not accept the accompanying conditions.[21]

Petrograd, for its part, was primarily concerned with obtaining official approval of the campaign to raise loans in the United States. The proposed commercial treaty would at best have been regarded as bait to obtain American agreement to permit loans, and it is very unlikely that the Tsarist authorities at this juncture seriously considered making any concessions on the passport dispute.

On October 20, 1914, four days after Count Witte's conversation with Charles Wilson, the Russian Ambassador, George Bakhmet'ev, called at the State Department to leave a memorandum stating his government's desire to obtain credits in the United States. The memorandum declared that Petrograd was obliged by the war to increase dramatically its purchases in the United States but did not have sufficient dollars. Russia, therefore, wished to issue short-term notes to cover the deficit and asked whether Washington would have any objections.[22]

Significantly, the memorandum, which unlike Witte's comments was a statement of official Russian policy, did not refer to the possibility of negotiating a new commercial treaty. In the exchange of views, both Russia and the United States appear to have been under the illusion that the other was ready to make concessions in order to improve relations.

The State Department made no formal reply to the memorandum, preferring to handle the matter informally. The Russian request, however, had arrived at an opportune moment. In September 1914, the French government had asked the National City Bank of New York for $10 million in credits to help finance the purchase of goods needed for the war. The Bank in turn urged Secretary of State Bryan to permit the measure on the grounds that these differed from bonds which would be sold to the public and that the credits would be used to cover purchases of American goods.[23]

As in the case of Count Witte's proposal, the National City Bank's request for approval was forwarded by the State Department to President Wilson for a decision. On October 23, 1914, he advised Lansing that American government policy would permit the bank to provide the credits requested by France, and, accordingly, the American government's tacit approval was given to the extension of a $10 million credit to France. This was followed in January 1915 by a grant of $12 million credit to the Tsarist government from the firm of J. P. Morgan and Company of New York.

The Russian requests for financial credits from American banks provided a significant indication of a considerable increase in the volume of Russian-American trade since the outbreak of the war. Before the rupture of commercial relations with Germany, Russia had conducted the bulk of its foreign trade with that country, while trade with the United States remained relatively insignificant. After August 1914, Russia was confronted with a twofold supply problem. Not only was it necessary to find a new source for the imports formerly provided by Germany, but Russia also needed to obtain many munitions and war goods that the nation's industry was unable to produce in sufficient abundance.

The quantities of goods purchased by Petrograd in the United States were so vast that by December 1914 orders had been placed for enough boots to supply the entire population of the state of Pennsylvania; the number of blankets bought would have covered the island of Manhattan from one end to the other.[24] These purchases contributed to the rapid wartime growth of American industry and also created in business circles the image of Russia as a vast potential peacetime market for U.S. exports.

As the quantity of American imports increased, the Tsarist government devoted expanded attention to strengthening the transportation routes between the two countries. In an effort to expand the traffic between the American Pacific coast and Siberia, a cheaper and quicker route than the customary approach across the Atlantic to European Russia, the freight rates on the Trans-Siberian Railroad were reduced for certain needed goods. The official Russian government gazette noted that the cessation of trade with Germany had caused other foreign commercial and industrial interests to improve their representation in Russia and added hopefully that "American industry is ready to replace in our markets all the goods which we received from abroad."[25]

By the fall of 1914, Russian-American affairs had entered a new phase. Commercial ties had expanded as a result of the increased Tsarist purchases in the United States. Although this country had accepted a responsibility to protect German and Austrian interests in Russia during the war, the move had not produced the feared worsening of relations there. At the same time, Washington was intent on maintaining a strict neutrality in the war, and its primary objective with regard to Russia was the negotiation of a new commercial agreement. This aim remained virtually unattainable, with both nations showing no disposition to retreat from the positions that had led to the termination of the previous treaty. This, then, was the situation that faced Ambassador Marye, when he arrived to take up his post as the first American envoy in Petrograd in over two years.

# III

# Ambassador Marye
# Establishes Friendly
# Relations

Ambassador and Mrs. Marye arrived in Petrograd on October 24, 1914, after a short stop in Great Britain and then a train trip through Holland, Germany, and Sweden. In an interview with newspapermen on the day of his arrival, the envoy proceeded to win a favorable reception with his warmly pro-Russian statements. Marye referred to the "traditional friendship" between the two nations, stressing that Petrograd's action in "defending" Serbia had won the sympathy of the American nation, and he optimistically declared that the interests of Russia and the United States had never differed.[1]

Three days after his arrival, Marye presented his credentials to Foreign Minister Sazonov. Writing subsequently in his memoirs, the Ambassador noted that he had felt well prepared for the meeting on the basis of conversations he had had in Washington with the Russian envoy, who had fully described Sazonov to him. Marye commented in his memoirs that his impression upon meeting the Foreign Minister was very favorable and that "I liked him at once for his friendly, straightforward way."[2]

The Ambassador also took the occasion to raise the possibility of negotiating a new commercial treaty, for the United States the most important objective in relations with Russia. In response, the Foreign Minister avoided a specific commitment concerning the treaty, and instead emphasized his interest in expanding commerce with the United States and in taking advantage of the existing situation to promote direct bilateral trade between the two nations. It is very likely that Sazonov was referring here to the necessity of obtaining and shipping supplies from America to support the Russian war effort.

On October 30, 1914, six days after his arrival, Marye was received by the Tsar amid the splendor of the Imperial Court. The Ambassador was pleased at the lack of delay in his reception by Nicholas, recalling that one of his predecessors had been obliged to wait four months for the privilege. In fact, both the monarch and Sazonov appear to have gone out of their way to create a favorable impression with Marye. Once again, as in his meeting with Sazonov, the envoy was favorably impressed by his host and reported to Washington that his conversation with the Tsar was "extremely pleasant" and had lasted longer than the usual short audiences dictated by protocol.[3]

In his memoirs, Marye was even more complimentary in describing the Russian ruler, commenting that the Tsar was an "earnest, serious, intelligent man," and that he had been surprised by the extent of the monarch's knowledge. The Ambassador added that Nicholas's leading traits appeared to be his sincerity and kindly sympathy, and that he had clearly been sincere when he had tried to preserve peace in Europe. Marye sympathetically concluded that the Tsar's "beneficent plans were blocked by the German Kaiser, and it is interesting to reflect how natural it seems that the proposals should emanate from the one and the opposition from the other."

This favorable impression of the Tsar may have been due, at least in part, to the Ambassador's being a dedicated prohibitionist; Marye was very much impressed by Nicholas's institution of prohibition in Russia. In his memoirs, Marye extravagantly declared that the Tsar's persistence in implementing the measure despite the war entitled him to not only "the gratitude but to the commendation of mankind," and that posterity would accord him "an enviable place in the history of his country if for no other reason than for his suppression of the vodka traffic."[4]

The views expressed by Marye were scarcely objective. His

open espousal of pro-Russian opinions may have been an effort, in part, to establish cordial relations with the Tsarist authorities. If so, he was largely successful in this endeavor. However, the friendly attitude displayed toward him by the Russians did not in general extend to the nation whose government he represented.

Marye devoted the first months after his arrival to becoming acquainted with the country and with the functions of the American Embassy. In addition to the normal functions performed by a diplomatic mission stationed in a foreign capital, the American diplomatic mission in Petrograd was seriously overburdened by the need to look after the many interned German and Austrian nationals, as well as the increasingly large numbers of prisoners of war being brought back from the front to camps in the interior of Russia. Only a few days after his arrival, the Ambassador advised Washington of the Embassy's urgent need for additional personnel to cope with the problem.[5]

Marye also conceived the idea of bringing the State Department up to date on the subject of strengthening commercial ties between the two nations. Possibly as a result of his meeting with Foreign Minister Sazonov, during which the latter had commented on the prewar importance of Germany as a trading partner of Russia, the envoy devoted himself to obtaining data and preparing a report on this subject. On December 14, 1914, he forwarded to Washington his recommendations on how after the war the United States could take measures to prevent Germany from regaining much of the trade with Russia that had been diverted to America.

Possibly because of this preoccupation with the trade report and with the problem of caring for the German and Austrian interests in Russia, the volume of political reporting from the Embassy describing developments in Russia declined sharply following Marye's arrival. An even more significant failing was the apparent lack of any effort by the Ambassador to meet with Count Witte or to learn the reason behind Witte's proposal for talks on a new treaty with the United States.

The next American initiative to improve relations with Petrograd took place in Washington. In part, this choice of locale may have reflected State Department concern with Marye's competence, but more probably it resulted from the particular interest of Robert Lansing, the Counselor of the State Department.

On December 7, 1914, Lansing raised the matter in a meeting with Ambassador Bakhmet'ev, believing that the Imperial government was now prepared to make concessions in order to build closer economic and financial ties with America. Certainly Count Witte's proposals and the memorandum Ambassador Bakhmet'ev had left with the State Department in October on the subject of American credits would have been viewed in this light by Lansing. Again, the timing was probably also a result of the November Congressional elections in the United States, as the Republicans' success in regaining control of the House of Representatives suggested President Wilson might have difficulty in winning a second term in 1916. A foreign policy success, such as a new treaty with Russia, would clearly be of advantage to the administration.

Lansing pointed out to Bakhmet'ev that this country had a very large Jewish population, most of whom were hostile to Russia and its allies. The Counselor stressed that this was a result of the passport dispute. He pointed out that American Jews were influential in financial circles and with the press and that Petrograd should not discount the importance of their impact upon U.S. public opinion.

To these comments the Ambassador replied that he had not considered the issue from such a viewpoint. He noted that the arguments might cause Petrograd to view the matter of the commercial treaty in a new light and urged that Marye be instructed to raise the issue with the Tsarist government.[6]

On the following day, Lansing continued his efforts to reopen negotiations with Russia on a new treaty. In a meeting with the British Ambassador, Lansing suggested that Great Britain might wish to influence its ally to agree to a commercial treaty along the lines urged by the United States. The envoy apparently accepted the validity of Lansing's views, agreeing that a new commercial treaty with Russia would "change thousands of American Jews into our friends," that it would be a "tremendous gain" for the Allies, and that he would so advise London.[7]

There is some suggestion that Lansing's efforts in this area were made at his own initiative and had not been coordinated within the State Department. On December 14, 1914, Bakhmet'ev again saw Lansing and asked him if Marye had yet been instructed to propose reopening negotiations to the Tsarist Foreign Ministry. Lansing admitted this had not been done and said the United States was reluctant to do so without firm indication that this step would be favorably received by Petrograd. When Bakhmet'ev assured him that he was certain the matter could be satisfactorily arranged if it were properly presented to the Imperial government, Lansing pledged that he would immediately raise the subject with the Secretary of State to see if the effort could not be made at once.[8]

The American effort to implement this decision, however, was considerably delayed because of the onset of the Christmas season. In early January, Marye left Petrograd on an inspection trip to Warsaw to observe conditions in Russian Poland. By the time he returned and was able to broach the matter of new negotiations with the Foreign Ministry, the attention of both governments had been diverted to developments in the war. The opportunity, if such had ever existed, was lost in the rush of events.

# IV

## The United States
## Fails to Obtain
## Russian Help
## against Japan

In August 1914, when World War I began, three nations felt a strong need to attempt to prevent the spread of hostilities from Europe to the Far East. The foremost was probably Germany, which realized that it could not quickly reinforce its garrison at the Kiaochow leasehold on the Shantung Peninsula with enough troops to prevent the colony's being overrun by the Allies. China, with virtually no modern military forces capable of withstanding Japanese pressure, feared that any change in the status quo as a result of the war would enable Tokyo to expand its sphere of influence in China. The United States, as the exponent of the Open Door policy, wished to preserve the independence and territorial integrity of China, thus keeping that nation open to American commerce.

The fourth nation significantly affecting the balance of power in the Far East, Russia, had little to gain and potentially a great deal to lose from any increase in Japanese influence in the area. However, even before the war Petrograd had been forced to accede to Tokyo's policy in the Far East. Now, fighting desperately for survival on the Western Front, the Tsarist government had of necessity to follow the lead of the Japanese.

As early as August 3, 1914, the Chinese government urged the United States to seek the belligerents' agreement not to engage in hostilities on Chinese territory or in the areas administered by the foreign powers on the Chinese mainland. This proposal coincided with American objectives, and on August 10 and August 11 Washington informally sounded out the British and German governments on maintaining the status quo in the Far East.

The American initiative, however, was overtaken by rapidly changing developments. Although Germany indicated that it would agree to placing the Far East outside the area of hostilities, Great Britain advised the United States on August 11, 1914, that Japan would enter the war against Germany. On August 15, 1914, the Japanese Foreign Ministry forwarded to the American Embassy in Tokyo the text of the ultimatum that it had that day presented to Germany. The Japanese demanded immediate withdrawal of all German armed vessels from Chinese and Japanese waters and transfer of the Kiaochow leased territory to Japanese control. In an effort to assuage Washington, the Japanese Foreign Minister sent assurances to the State Department that his nation was not pursuing any selfish purpose and was acting strictly in accordance with its alliance with Great Britain. He further pledged that Japan would not seek any territorial gains in China and would carefully respect the interests there of the neutral nations.

The United States replied rapidly to the Japanese ultimatum to Germany, on August 19, 1914, instructing the American Embassy in Tokyo to inform the Foreign Ministry that as a neutral this nation could not officially comment on the merits of either party in the dispute. However, the American response pointedly stated that Washington was pleased at the Japanese assurances that it sought no territorial gains in China and that the Kiaochow leased territory would be restored to China.[1] On August 23, 1914, in the absence of a German response within the time limit stated in the Japanese ultimatum, Tokyo declared war on Germany.

Petrograd officially welcomed the Japanese declaration of war against Germany and in early August had urged Great Britain and France to do their best to bring such a development about as rapidly as possible. Nonetheless, the Tsarist government was concerned that the United States might respond by cooperating with Berlin in order to prevent the expansion of Japanese influence in the Far East. When printing the text of President Wilson's declaration of American neutrality, the official Russian gazette added that the President was known to be opposed to efforts to drag his country into the war on the side of Germany to limit Japanese expansion in the Pacific.[2]

On September 28, 1914, the Chinese government informed the State Department that it had protested the movement of Japanese troops beyond the limits of the Kiaochow leased zone, into Chinese territory. Within Russia, the Chinese protest to Tokyo was regarded as underscoring the likelihood that the United States would now be cooperating with China to oppose Japanese expansion. In the following year, a brochure on the Far East, printed in Moscow, warned that the United States sought to make the Pacific an "American lake" and that in Tokyo government officials were predicting an "inevitable" war between Japan and the United States.[3]

Thus, the entry of Japan into the war on the side of the Allies had introduced a new element in Russian-American relations. In both countries, but particularly in the Empire, it was viewed as a potentially disturbing factor. Moreover, the potential Japanese threat to American interests was to cause Ambassador Marye considerable concern as he struggled to improve American ties with the Tsarist regime.

When Ambassador Marye returned to Petrograd from his inspection trip to Warsaw in the middle of January 1915, he was immediately drawn into dealing with developments in the Far East. Awaiting his arrival was a letter from Robert Lansing written in the beginning of December. The Counselor referred to an article in the *New York American* which suggested that Russia and Japan had entered into an agreement to cooperate in the Far East at the expense of American interests; Lansing asked Marye if the Embassy had any knowledge of the reported understanding.[4]

Marye immediately arranged to see Foreign Minister Sazonov to inquire into the matter. On January 25, 1915, he informed the State Department that he had met with Sazonov and that the latter had admitted seeing the article. Sazonov told Marye that relations between Russia and Japan were cordial, but he flatly denied the existence of any treaty. The Foreign Minister further assured the Ambassador that an alliance between Russia and Japan was not likely as the interests of the two nations in the Far East were dissimilar.[5]

Sazonov's comments were clearly an effort to beguile Marye, since he avoided any mention of the secret conventions of 1907, 1910, and 1912, which divided portions of Chinese territory into Japanese and Russian spheres of interest. Marye, however, was not misled, and in reporting his meeting with Sazonov to Washington, he stated his belief that there was a strong desire on Japan's part to draw closer to Russia. He foresaw that Tokyo would view the defenseless Philippines as a tempting prize for expansion and warned that the actual threat from Japan would depend on "the strength of the American fleet in Pacific waters."

Marye advised that if Japan attacked the United States, Russian assistance for Tokyo would not be likely. "The [Japanese] attack will come, if it does come," he wrote, "before Russia again begins to develop her plans in Eastern Asia near the shores of the Pacific. Her plans in that region were arrested but by no means destroyed by the events of the Russo-Japanese War; they are as confidently resolved upon at this day as they ever were. When the movement to again develop them will begin, will depend upon events the progress of which cannot be foreseen, but when it does begin it will again be opposed by Japan as it was before. This time, however, we may suppose Russia will be prepared to overcome all opposition however energetic it may be and until then Japan will have a free hand, and America should be on her guard."

The Ambassador added that Petrograd might well welcome a war between Japan and the United States in which Russia remained neutral. On sentimental grounds, he noted, the Tsarist government would be pleased to see what it regarded as American sympathy for Japan during the Russo-Japanese War receive such a reward. More practically, Petrograd would be pleased to see Japanese power weakened or destroyed in a conflict with the United States. Marye stressed, however, that assistance for Tokyo would be most unlikely, primarily because of Russian interest in improving financial and commercial relations with the United States. He emphasized that after the war Russia would desire a period of peace. "Her statesmen and her businessmen," he wrote the State Department, "hope to establish between our country and theirs extensive direct and profitable trade relations and they think that in opening up the vast underdeveloped resources of their country it will be very desirable to have the help of American energy and initiative and of American money."[6]

In this detailed, perceptive, and in many ways prophetic analysis of Petrograd's long-range objectives, Marye clearly indicated that his pro-Russian sympathies had not been allowed to color his judgment. Although he probably gave too much weight to the importance Russia attached to establishing closer postwar commercial relations with the United States, this error is understandable in view of the Ambassador's own business background. Moreover, his views were shared by many officials within the American government and similar opinions strongly influenced United States policy long before and after Marye's service in Petrograd. Indeed, throughout this period the State Department viewed relations with Russia almost exclusively in terms of negotiating a new commercial treaty with that nation.

Meanwhile, it was becoming increasingly obvious that whether or not the Tsarist government chose to admit that it was cooperating with Japan in the Far East, Tokyo was using its control of the former German possessions in Kiaochow to extend its influence in China. On December 12, 1914, the American Ambassador in Japan advised the State Department that the Japanese Foreign Minister, in a speech to the Parliament, had denied that Japan had pledged to return the Kiaochow area to China.[7] In doing this, the Foreign Minister was repudiating the assurances he had given the State Department that his nation would not seek any territorial gains as a result of its entry into the war.

Even more was to follow. On January 18, 1915, Tokyo presented to China a list of twenty-one demands. If accepted in toto by Peking, this ultimatum would have established in effect a Japanese protectorate over much of the country. The American minister to China warned the State Department that that nation's acceptance of the demands meant the end of the American Open Door policy for China as well as of Peking's indepedence in political and industrial matters. He added that if China refused to comply with them, Japan might well foment political unrest as a pretext for occupying Chinese territory to restore order.

The State Department reacted with consternation when it learned of the demands. Washington immediately made a direct approach to Japan, asking that the demands be withdrawn or modified, and the British government was asked to use its influence with Tokyo to bring about a satisfactory solution. When it appeared that these efforts had been unsuccessful, Secretary of State Bryan summoned the Japanese Ambassador on March 13, 1915, and delivered a stern note warning that the United States could not regard with indifference the assumption of political, military, or economic domination over China by a foreign power.

The strong stand opposing the twenty-one demands met with some success. On May 6, 1915, the American Embassy in Tokyo informed the State Department that Japan had sent China an ultimatum demanding acceptance of the twenty-one demands, but adding that these had been modified somewhat in response to United States protests.[8]

Bryan, however, remained opposed to the Japanese policy and immediately requested Great Britain, France, and Russia to use their good offices to prevent the outbreak of war between China and Japan. The Secretary's effort was futile in the face of the three nations' interest in keeping Japan on their side as a contributing ally. The British Foreign Secretary, Lord Grey, told the American Embassy in London that since Tokyo had modified the most extreme of its demands, he was urging Peking to yield to the Japanese ultimatum. France and Russia did not even reply to Bryan's request.[9]

In support of the Secretary's effort, Marye on May 2, 1915, called at the Foreign Ministry to deliver the American request for assistance. When the Ambassador raised the subject, Sazonov immediately dispelled whatever faint hope Marye may have had that Russia would join with the United States in protesting the Japanese ultimatum to China. Pointing out that Peking had already accepted the demands, the Foreign Minister declared that Russia in any event could not make any representations to Tokyo, since "Japan is giving us a great deal of assistance and we expect more."

Marye persevered in his effort, warning that Russia had a long and unprotected border with China which might be endangered if Japan began forming and training Chinese military units. The Foreign Minister stated, however, that Russia was obliged by its situation to give greater priority to immediate needs, and that Japan had already given his country four hundred thousand rifles and was promising to supply an additional three hundred thousand. Sazonov added, in an interesting comment, that in any event, "fifty years from now there won't be any China. Some of its provinces may continue to exist as independent states, together or separately, but there will be no Chinese nation as there is now." It was a prediction which Soviet policy-makers today might well hope to echo.

The Foreign Minister's comments revealed that Russia was prepared to acquiesce in the establishment of a large measure of Japanese control over China. Marye predicted that this position would probably be modified when the war was over and Petrograd no longer needed Japanese assistance, predicting that after the war, Russia, Great Britain, and possibly France would protest to Japan over its actions in China and that the United States might well be asked to join with them in this effort.[10]

Despite this optimistic assessment for the future, the blunt fact was that Bryan's effort to force a Japanese withdrawal of the twenty-one demands had failed. On May 11, 1915, he formally warned China and Japan that the United States would not recognize any agreement reached by the two nations which restricted its activities in China under the Open Door policy.[11] In this way Washington put itself on record as reserving the right to act in the Far East if its interests were threatened. But the United States could not avoid noting that no other Great Power was prepared to join with America to curb Japanese expansion. Russia, in particular, so long as the war continued, was prepared to subordinate its relations with the United States to the more important objective of retaining Tokyo's support.

# V

## American Sales
## to Russia
## but No New Treaty

Russia's need to satisfy immediate wartime requirements led Russia to choose relations with Japan over ties to the United States. Ironically, the same need resulted in Petrograd's growing interest in improving ties with Washington. The cause was the Imperial government's view of America as the source for desperately needed war supplies. To establish expanded trade ties between the two nations after the war was considered desirable by some elements within Russia. But, still, this goal was not granted anything like the importance it was accorded in the United States.

Petrograd's urgent need for war materials became evident by the fall of 1914. On December 17, 1914, the Grand Duke Nicholas, Supreme Commander of the Russian Armies, informed Maurice Paléologue, the French Ambassador, that he had been forced to halt offensive operations because of excessive casualties and because all of the reserves of artillery ammunition had been exhausted. When the Ambassador anxiously sought additional information, the Army Chief of Staff on the following day told him that although the loss of life had been "colossal," the primary problem was a lack of rifles. He added that although he and the Grand Duke had been told before the war that there were over 5 million rifles in the Russian armories, they had found them nearly empty. As a result, the Tsarist authorities were attempting to purchase a million rifles from Japan and the United States.[1]

An interesting indication of the state of the Imperial government was a conversation that occurred on December 19, 1914, when Paléologue raised the matter with the Chairman of the Council of Ministers, Goremykin, in the presence of Foreign Minister Sazonov and the British Ambassador. According to the French envoy, Goremykin replied with evasive language and weary gestures. Some days later, when Paléologue accused him of taking the serious military situation surprisingly calmly, he replied, "What did you expect? I'm so old! I ought to have been in my coffin long ago. I told the Emperor so only the other day; but his Majesty wouldn't listen to me."[2]

On February 9, 1915, Goremykin provided the Duma with an accounting of the course of the war, and in an effort to bolster morale, he spoke most forcefully on the gains Russia could be expected to obtain in the hoped-for peace settlement. Foremost of these, he implied, was Constantinople, the Turkish capital and a site long sought to provide Russia with access to the Mediterranean. Turkey had entered the war on the side of the Central Powers in November 1914, and Goremykin asserted that Tsarist troops were already inflicting serious defeats on the Turkish forces.

Foreign Minister Sazonov also spoke, concentrating on the international situation, and with Goremykin he hinted that the nation would obtain Constantinople after the war. His comments also demonstrated the increased importance the United States now had in Russian policy as a result of the war. Unlike his foreign policy review to the Duma in May 1914, during which he made no mention of the United States, Sazonov raised the subject of German propaganda efforts in America. Asserting that German officials were deliberately spreading false reports about maltreatment of Jews in the war zone in order to provoke anti-Russian feeling in the United States, he expressed the hope that Washington would not yield to "this gross deception" and that Russia's "friendly relations with America will not suffer from German intrigues."[3]

The rapid rise in the Imperial government's volume of purchases in the United States had an impact on both countries. In March 1915 the journal of the Russian-American Chamber of

Commerce, an organization founded in Moscow in 1914, raised this point, commenting that American businessmen were convinced that the scope of trade between the two countries would increase greatly at the end of the war. The journal attributed this view to the feeling that anti-German sentiment would continue in Russia after the war and lead to a preference for America as a trading partner, and that the German economy would be so weakened by the conflict as to prevent its reemergence as Russia's primary supplier.

Implicit in the article was the view that the United States expected Russia and the other Allied Powers to emerge victorious from the war, a cheering thought for the Russian reader. The article also stressed that an improvement in political relations between the two countries was necessary to advance commercial relations, since "in democratic America, it is possible to succeed only on the basis of mass public sympathy."[4]

In March of 1915 the United States publicly announced that it would not prevent American banks from granting credits to belligerent nations. Although this had been in fact Washington's unstated policy since October 1914, the announcement was viewed in Russia as being motivated by recognition of the economic advantages accruing to the United States as a result of the war. In commenting upon the policy, the Imperial government gazette noted that the economic outlook for the United States was "bright" and that this was the reason the nation's bankers were in the process of granting more and more loans to Europe.[5]

The extension of American bank credits to Russia was not received with unanimous approval in the United States. The influential New York banker, Jacob Schiff, who had been one of the leaders in the fight to obtain American abrogation of the treaty with Russia in 1911, attacked the granting of credits as the "greatest treason" ever committed in the history of the United States on the grounds that, "Russia has outdone everyone else in her cruelty and inhumanity, and any help given Russia ought to leave America shameful." The comment was reprinted in the Russian press.[6]

In addition to the economic ramifications of the war, military developments began to impinge on American interests. On Febru-

ary 4, 1915, Germany proclaimed the creation of a war zone
around the British Isles and warned that neutral vessels might be
sunk if they chose to sail in the area. America, whose shipping
would have been the most affected, reacted sharply to the announcement, informing Berlin on February 10, 1915, that to
destroy a U.S. vessel or to kill its citizens on the high seas would
be "an indefensible violation" of neutral rights and incompatible
with the friendly relations existing between the two countries.[7]

The strong stand taken by Washington to defend its shipping
was hailed in Russia as evidence of a growing division between
the United States and Germany. The liberal Russian newspaper
*Rech* commented on February 16, 1915, that relations between
the two nations were deteriorating further with every day and
that "yesterday's friends may become open enemies."[8]

On March 28, 1915, the first American life was lost as a
result of a German attack upon a merchant ship, when a submarine torpedoed the *Falaba*, a small British liner. Although this
was an attack upon a British vessel and not upon an American
one, the development caused serious concern in the United States.
The reaction within the State Department was divided. Robert
Lansing, the Counselor, believed that a strong American response
was required, whereas Secretary of State Bryan feared that the
harsh protest note drafted by Lansing would inflame feeling within
Germany against the United States.

Official Washington still had not decided the proper course
to follow when on May 7, 1915, the crisis became much graver
with the sinking of the *Lusitania*, then the largest ship in service
on the North Atlantic, by a German submarine. Almost twelve
hundred persons were lost, including 124 American citizens, and
the event is generally considered to have had a more jolting effect
upon U.S. public opinion than any other single development
before America entered the World War.[9]

One of those deeply affected was Lansing, who commented
shortly after the sinking that it had made him regard Germany as
"utterly hostile to all nations with democratic institutions." The
Counselor resolved that Germany could not be "permitted to win

this war, or even to break even, though to prevent it this country [the United States] is forced to take an active part."[10]

As had been the situation during the *Falaba* incident, Bryan and Lansing differed over the tone to be taken in protesting to Germany. President Wilson, however, agreed with the latter that the protest note should be a stern one. On May 13, 1915, the United States informed Berlin that the sinking of the *Lusitania* was a "violation of American rights" and demanded that Germany "take immediate steps to prevent the recurrence."

In Great Britain, the note of protest was well received, the *Times* of London commenting that both in substance and expression the note recalled "the best traditions of American diplomacy."[11] Petrograd's reaction, however, was much less favorable. *Rech* declared that President Wilson and former President Taft, whom the paper credited with influencing Wilson to soften the tone of the note, had "under-estimated the mulishness and self-assurance of the Berlin political and military supermen." On the following day the paper continued its coverage of the story, asserting that Wilson from the first had conducted negotiations "so meekly that the demands put to the German government were doomed beforehand," and concluding sadly that the hopes raised that the United States would "offer powerful support for the cause of justice and right" were on this occasion futile.[12]

The official Russian comment on the situation was more restrained. On May 14, 1915, Ambassador Marye met with Foreign Minister Sazonov to deliver the text of the American note. The envoy wrote later that Sazonov thought well of the note but stated that Germany would probably try to temporize on the matter and place the blame for it on Great Britain.[13]

Berlin's reply to the American note was received in Washington on May 31, 1915. Lansing believed the response was unsatisfactory and recommended that a stronger note be sent, and he drafted one that was approved by Wilson over the objections of the Secretary of State. Bryan feared that the note would cause a break in diplomatic relations with Germany and might result in America's entry into the war on the side of the Allies. When the note was sent, Bryan resigned as Secretary of State on June 8, 1915, to be replaced by Robert Lansing.

The Russian press received the news of Bryan's resignation with considerable satisfaction; *Rech* commented that the United States must now realize that its previous policy toward Germany had been "shameful cowardice and dangerously humiliating for a great country."[14] The conservative paper *Novoe Vremia* was more critical, stating sarcastically that "one must admire the iron containment of the government of the United States which seemingly does not wish to see that Germany is really conducting a war against the United States."[15] When Marye again saw Sazonov to convey to him the text of Bryan's letter of resignation and President Wilson's reply, the Foreign Minister observed that they were both "excellent letters and reflected great credit on both men."[16]

Soon after this second exchange of notes between Berlin and Washington, the issue of German submarine attacks on passenger ships was overshadowed in importance in both Russia and the United States by new developments. But the submarine attacks were still considered worthy of mention in Sazonov's speech to the Duma on August 1, 1915, which reviewed the international situation. The Foreign Minister declared that the American public had been strongly affected by the sinking of the *Lusitania*, and by the attendant loss of American lives. He added that it was difficult to say if the "harsh sermon" of Wilson would be followed by more decisive action, but nonetheless, "American public opinion is hostile toward Germany, despite any attempt on the part of the latter to placate America."[17]

By the summer of 1915, it had become obvious that Russian-American relations had been significantly affected by the war, with the United States now far more important to Petrograd than before, as the source of war supplies. Despite the American desire to remain neutral, its involvement in maritime commerce, and the German naval blockade had raised expectations in Russia that the United States might become embroiled in the war against Germany.

Washington, however, gave different priorities to the several elements in the matrix of relations between the two countries.

There was great interest in the stimulative effects upon the American economy of the expanded purchases by the belligerent nations; serious public and government concern developed over the dispute with Germany resulting from its interference with neutral shipping; and controversy continued over Bryan's resignation. But of immediate importance to the United States in its dealings with the Tsarist government, as had been the case since 1911, was the negotiation of a new commercial treaty.

The new Secretary of State, Robert Lansing, at the time of Count Witte's discussions at the American embassy had indicated his great interest in negotiating a new commercial treaty with Russia. On June 19, 1915, only ten days after Bryan's resignation and while he was still only Acting Secretary, Lansing instructed Marye to make informal inquiries at the Foreign Ministry on the matter. Specifically, the Ambassador was to determine the Tsarist government's reaction to a suggestion that preliminary discussions be begun between the two countries. Lansing proposed to side-step the old obstacle in the way of a treaty, the question of the treatment of American Jews in Russia, by suggesting that a new agreement follow the general lines of the old one but omit those sections involved in the passport dispute. The instructions to Marye stated that this thorny subject would be left for later discussion with a view toward settling it "in such a way which will be satisfactory to both parties."[18]

Acting on these instructions, the Ambassador saw Sazonov on June 22, 1915. The Foreign Minister stated that his nation would be very pleased to enter into negotiations for a new treaty, and that he was agreeable to the suggestion that the passport dispute be left for discussion at a later date. Sazonov observed that Russia had always held this position; he had informed the American Ambassador in 1911, at the time of the abrogation of the treaty, that the Imperial government was willing at any time to negotiate a new one. The Foreign Minister added that this feeling was stronger now than ever before, as the Russian government and people wanted the United States to take over the place in trade formerly occupied by Germany. Pleased by Sazonov's reaction, Marye advised the State Department that he had every assurance the Foreign Ministry would take up the matter of a new treaty "in a most friendly spirit and with every desire to facilitate negotiations."[19]

When Marye's report reached Washington on July 23, 1915, Secretary Lansing regarded it as extremely important. He advised President Wilson that Sazonov's response seemed to be very satisfactory and that the State Department should prepare a general draft of a treaty which could then be discussed with the Russian negotiators. Lansing pointed out to the President that if a new treaty could rapidly be concluded, "it would be a distinct triumph for the Administration," surprisingly adding that, "of course, the passport question must be included, otherwise there would be no hope of securing Senatorial consent."[20]

The Secretary was in effect completely changing the nature of the American position on the treaty from the proposal Marye had transmitted to Sazonov. Lansing's modification of his original proposal was made little more than a month after his instructions to Marye to reopen the negotiations, and he was obviously aware that just such an insistence that the treaty resolve the passport dispute along the lines desired by the United States had been totally unacceptable to Russia in the past.

Lansing gave no reason for his startling reversal of policy. It is possible that he was led by the unexpectedly warm comments of Sazonov to conclude that Petrograd was prepared to yield more on the issue than he had anticipated when he sent the instructions to Marye. More likely, however, the Secretary worded his initial proposal loosely so that the Russian Foreign Ministry would agree to reopen negotiations, with the thought that the momentum of the discussions or the fortunes of the war might induce Russia to grant more concessions than originally intended.

President Wilson was equally pleased by the prospect of reopening negotiations, and in a note to Lansing on July 29, 1915, he stated that the Russian reaction as reported by Marye was "indeed good news." Wilson urged the Secretary to push for a new treaty and approved his decision to include in the American draft a settlement of the passport dispute, adding that he had no means of estimating Marye's ability or aptitude concerning the difficult task of negotiating a new treaty and for this reason wished decisions on the talks to be handled so far as possible in the State Department, rather than being left to the discretion of the Embassy in Petrograd.[21]

Wilson gave no reason for his lack of full confidence in the abilities of Marye, but his hesitation may have stemmed from doubts that a relatively inexperienced political appointee could grasp the complex issues involved in framing a new treaty. The Ambassador's sympathetic view of the Tsarist government may also have suggested to the President that Marye would not press as hard for concessions on the passport dispute as might be required by domestic considerations in the United States, including the forthcoming 1916 Presidential elections. Again, relations between Marye and the State Department were not particularly good, and this situation intensified under Lansing, who paid much more attention to the administration of the overseas Embassies than had Bryan.

Although both Wilson and Lansing sought a rapid opening of negotiations with Russia, no immediate initiative was taken by the American government. The delay was probably caused by the administrative difficulty in preparing a draft treaty for consideration and by the diversion of the State Department's attention to other aspects of the international situation. However, in the summer of 1915 there were indications that Petrograd might be prepared to accept a more lenient attitude with regard to restrictions on Jews, and Washington undoubtedly believed that a short delay in forwarding proposals for a new treaty would find the Imperial government more disposed to accept the American position in the passport dispute.

On August 1, 1915, the Duma was called back into session. Ambassador Marye attended and found it an interesting and important occasion. Although he was handicapped by his lack of the Russian language, he could sense the "patriotic fervor" that "pervaded the entire assemblage."

The meeting of the Duma was primarily concerned with the startling shortage of ammunition and supplies for the Russian army, which had so concerned the French Ambassador when he had learned of them in December 1914. Marye, however, gave greater emphasis in his report to proposals introduced in the Duma by liberal members to abolish restrictions on the Jews, since a change in policy on this matter would greatly facilitate the conclusion of a new treaty with the United States. The Ambassador stressed in his report to Lansing that since his arrival in Russia he had striven to learn whether Petrograd was preparing to modify its position in the dispute, adding that he was still waiting for his instructions from the State Department so that he could open talks on the new treaty.[22]

Although both the State Department and Marye wished to concentrate on the matter of a new treaty, it was impossible to escape the consequences of the war. In the spring and summer of 1915, the war went badly for the Russian forces; they were forced to retreat eastward, leaving almost three hundred thousand prisoners behind. On June 13, 1915, the French Ambassador noted in his diary that a mob in Moscow's Red Square had insulted the Russian royal family, demanding that the Tsar abdicate and be replaced by the Grand Duke Nicholas, and in early August the city of Warsaw fell to the German armies.

On August 28, 1915, Marye again saw the Foreign Minister, intending primarily to learn whether there was any substance to reports circulating in Petrograd that Germany had offered to sign a separate peace agreement with Russia while continuing hostilities against France and Great Britain. Sazonov admitted that the proposal had been received via unofficial Danish channels, but he emphasized that his reply had made clear that Russia would entertain peace proposals only when they were made to all of the Allied Powers.

The rumors of the separate German peace initiative had become so prevalent that Sazonov was forced to repeat his assurances publicly. In an interview granted to the correspondent of the London *Times* which was printed in the newspaper *Novoe Vremia* on August 31, 1915, Sazonov acknowledged the rumors that there was dissension among the Allies and that Russia was considering making a separate peace; but he declared flatly that there never had existed at any time "the slightest difference of views between the respective headquarters of the Allies."[23]

Also on August 31, 1915, in the face of continued military reverses, the Tsar relieved the Grand Duke Nicholas and personally took over command of the Russian Armed Forces. It was a serious step to take, a measure opposed by the Council of Ministers. Sazonov gloomily pointed out to the French Ambassador the possible consequences of this development: in the likely event of further military disasters, the nation would hold the monarch personally responsible.

Ambassador Marye summarized the latest developments in Russia on August 31, 1915, in one of his infrequent political reports to the State Department. He believed the German military victories in Poland were only "superficial and temporary military advantages" and was more concerned over the "numerous underhand influences, as unpatriotic as they are powerful," which he saw seeking to assist Germany in its campaign to bring about a separate peace with Russia. The envoy observed that before the war many of the high nobility, several of whom held high government offices, were sympathetic to Germany; but probably as a result of the assurances he had received from Sazonov, Marye concluded that the Russian population and army were strong supporters of the war and that the nation would never make a separate peace or agree to an end of hostilities as long as any Russian territory remained under foreign control.[24]

In his diary, Marye was more pessimistic, revealing his regret and concern that the Tsar had personally assumed command of the Russian Armed Forces. He also voiced the suspicion that the removal of the Grand Duke Nicholas had been the work of pro-German elements within the Court.

Meanwhile the United States, which had indicated its desire to reopen discussions on a new treaty with Russia, once again faced a dispute with Germany over maritime matters. On August 19, 1915, a German submarine sank the British liner *Arabic*, and of the forty-four people killed, two were American citizens. In Washington the incident was viewed as very serious. On August

24, 1915, Lansing sent a memorandum to President Wilson discussing the effects of a possible outbreak of war between Germany and the United States over the *Arabic* affair, warning that this might well follow should Washington break diplomatic relations with Germany, "which appears probable."

Berlin averted an immediate worsening in relations with the United States when the German Ambassador in Washington informed Secretary Lansing that no liners would be sunk by submarines without warning. When Marye received word of the easing of the crisis, he described his feeling of relief in his diary, expressing the hope that America "may yet escape being drawn into this horrible war."

Petrograd's reaction, however, was more critical, with the press arguing that the United States had failed to take a strong enough stand with Germany. In fact, Russia clearly was disappointed that Washington had not been drawn into the war on the side of the Allies. The conservative paper *Novoe Vremia* asserted on August 22, 1915, that the sinking of the *Arabic* was an unexpected blow for the American government, which had believed the promises that Germany would not interfere with neutral shipping. The newspaper predicted that President Wilson would appoint an investigative commission to look into the situation in order to give the appearance of taking action, but that he would take no effective action; the article concluded sarcastically that it made no difference to Russia whether America broke diplomatic relations with Berlin, as Russia was "not called upon to safeguard the dignity of the United States."

A subsequent article in the newspaper, on September 8, 1915, warned that once the submarine dispute with Germany was settled, Washington would probably offer to mediate in the war. It asserted that such a move would be helpful to Germany and warned that "just because the United States forced upon us the unfortunate Portsmouth Peace, it does not mean that all subsequent peace treaties will be concluded by means of America's mediation." Europe, the paper declared, "is for Europeans."[25]

The *Novoe Vremia* article was considered by Marye to be an accurate reflection of the response the Tsarist government would give to any proposal by the United States to act as mediator in the war. Commenting on the article, he wrote in his diary on September 8, 1915, that such an offer at that time would have no effect other than to make America very unpopular with the Allies, and he predicted that any such proposal would be promptly and unequivocally declined "with or without thanks."[26]

As the Ambassador understood, Petrograd was clearly opposed to a separate agreement with Germany or to a mediation effort by the United States and the bulk of the Russian population strongly endorsed this position. However, Russian military reverses and the obvious inefficiency and incompetence in the Imperial government revealed by the war had begun to cause dissatisfaction. The period of internal harmony engendered by the outbreak of hostilities was at an end.

# VI

## The Tsar Takes Charge

In the fall and winter of 1915, opposition grew in Russia to those officials whose inept performance was regarded as being responsible for military defeats. To this development the American Embassy in Petrograd and the United States government by and large played only the role of spectator. Petrograd understandably had little time to devote to the relatively unimportant matter of relations with the United States, and this country, in turn, was disposed to wait until the dust had settled before launching any diplomatic initiatives concerning Russia.

On September 16, 1915, seven days after his assumption of the Supreme Military Command, the Tsar prorogued the Duma under circumstances reflecting the state of tension existing within the nation. When the Duma session began in early August, it had been scheduled to last only three days. During the meeting, however, elements of the moderate right, the center, and the left had formed a bloc, urging formation of a cabinet responsible to the Duma rather than to the Tsar and calling for a program of liberal legislation including the elimination of restrictive measures against the Jews.

A majority of the Council of Ministers favored a change in the Cabinet to make that body more responsive to opinion within the Duma. The Chairman of the Council of Ministers, Goremykin, however, opposed any change and after seeing Nicholas on September 12, 1915, returned with instructions to prorogue the Duma and command all Ministers to retain their posts. Two days later, Goremykin transmitted the Tsar's orders to the Cabinet, reportedly horrifying all of the Ministers and causing Sazonov to come close to fainting. Upon leaving the session, the Foreign Minister commented privately that Goremykin appeared to be mad.[1]

On September 15, 1915, the French Ambassador dined with several leaders of the moderate Cadet Party. Paléologue found them appalled at the closing of the Duma and quoted one as stating that if the Court wished to precipitate a revolution, it was going about it in the right way. Possibly as a result of this conversation, the envoy, who was one of the best informed of the foreign diplomats in Petrograd, became very pessimistic over the future of the Tsarist government, stating in his diary that the great hopes which had been entertained when the Duma session began "have already crumbled into dust." He concluded that the establishment of a Cabinet responsible to the Duma was "merely a wild dream" and that "personal power, autocratic absolutism and the occult forces have triumphed."[2]

Marye's appraisal of the situation, however, was far less gloomy. He praised the behavior of the Tsar in encouraging the Duma to make a thorough investigation and exposure of corruption and inefficiency in the government and blamed the assembly for not being content to look into the matters submitted to them by the government and for raising "decidedly radical" measures such as proposals for ministerial responsibility to the Duma, freedom of the press, and the writ of *habeas corpus*. Marye believed, moreover, that the Russian people were not yet ready nor the Duma fit for the first two proposed reform; such changes could be successfully implemented in Russia only if the people were "laboriously and slowly educated up to them."[3]

The views expressed by Marye in his personal diary parallelled his official reporting to the State Department. His unfavorable opinion of the reform measures considered in the Duma probably were due to his isolation in Russia. Unlike Paléologue he had few acquaintances in Russian political circles and his reporting consequently largely reflected his favorable opinion of

the Tsar and his strongly pro-Allied and anti-German sentiments
rather than whatever may have been occurring within the country.

The internal conflict in the Council of Ministers became more
acute on September 29, 1915, when the Tsar summoned the
Ministers to his military headquarters and assailed them for sub-
mitting a petition calling upon him to remove Goremykin from
office or to accept their resignations. He warned that he would
not permit the Ministers to go on strike against the Chairman of
the Council of Ministers and ordered them all to respect his wishes.
Shortly after this meeting, on October 9, 1915, Nicholas removed
from office two of the leaders in the Cabinet revolt against Goremykin, Prince Nicholas Shcherbatov, the Minister of the Interior,
and the Procurator of the Holy Synod, causing the French Ambassador to observe that the Cabinet changes were a "gust of
reaction" and that the Cabinet now only included two members
with liberal views, Sazonov and General Polivanov, the Minister
of War.

Marye was also concerned about these changes, but he clearly
was not well informed about them. Writing in his diary on
October 12, 1915, the Ambassador described the shifts as a fresh
indication of the "restlessness" that had prevailed in government
circles since the prorogation of the Duma. Admitting that he did
not know the reason the Minister of the Interior had been replaced, he speculated that the action might have been due to some
"indiscreet or impudent utterances after his appointment."[4]

The very limited knowledge of developments in Russia revealed by Marye on this occasion was equalled by the general lack
of knowledge concerning America in Tsarist official circles. On
November 25, 1915, Marye had dinner with the French Ambassador, possibly motivating the latter to comment on the state of
Russian-American relations in his diary four days later. Paléologue
observed that he could never have believed that two great nations
"could know and think so little of each other as Russia and the
United States." Russian society, he noted, regarded America as
a "selfish, prosaic and barbarous nation, without traditions or
dignity, the natural home of democracy and the natural refuge of
Jews and nihilists." The United States on the other hand viewed

the Empire as "simply the iniquities of Tsarism, the atrocities of anti-Semitism and the ignorance and drunkenness" of the Russian peasants. Paléologue felt that as a result the United States hardly ever entered into the calculations of the Tsarist regime, adding that the possibility America might play an important role in the future in the war and in determining the resulting peace settlement was an idea which had never entered anyone's head in Russia, and that even Sazonov was "reluctant to contemplate the prospect."[5]

On November 29, 1915, the American Embassy for the first time informed the State Department of the internal frictions within the Tsarist government. Charles Wilson, Marye's deputy at the mission, reported that there were many rumors circulating that Goremykin would resign within the next few days as Chairman of the Council of Ministers and that his departure from office would be welcomed by the Cabinet and by the country generally. He cautioned, however, that Goremykin possessed the full confidence of the monarch, who might refuse to replace him.[6]

The internal opposition to Goremykin as Chairman of the Council of Ministers, however, was too great for Nicholas to withstand, and on February 2, 1916, he removed Goremykin and selected as his successor Boris Sturmer, who had been a member of the State Council since 1904. Sturmer's selection was received with almost universal disapproval. When discussing the appointment with the French Ambassador, Sazonov went so far as to assure him that foreign affairs would not be adversely affected by the new Chairman, stressing that the Minister for Foreign Affairs was responsible only to the Tsar, that diplomatic questions were never discussed by the Council of Ministers, and that the President of the Council would know nothing at all about developments in that field.

Ambassador Paléologue, however, was not reassured by Sazonov's comments, particularly since he felt that the Foreign Minister had attempted to evade further discussion of the matter. The envoy noted in his diary on February 5, 1916, that he had spent the three previous days gathering information on Sturmer from all quarters and that he was worried by what he had learned. Describing the new Chairman as "worse than a mediocrity, with a third-rate intellect, mean spirit, low character, doubtful honesty, no experience and no idea of State business," Paléologue concluded that neither Sturmer's qualifications nor his background fitted him for his new post and that he had in fact been chosen because of his "insignificance" and "servility." The Ambassador ascribed the appointment to recommendations by the Tsarina and by Rasputin, the mystic who had gained influence over her through supposedly providing "miraculous" medical care to her son, the hemophiliac heir to the throne.[7]

Marye's analysis of the situation on this occasion was very similar to Paléologue's, although his telegram to the State Department reporting Sturmer's appointment was terse, stating only that the new Chairman had been born in 1848 and was a member of the "reactionary party." In his private diary, however, Marye commented that Sturmer was "unfit in every way, is universally distrusted and his appointment is a dangerous one," that it was widely believed Sturmer owed his appointment to the influence of Rasputin, and that the change would result in a further decline in the prestige of the monarchy.

During his stay in Russia, the Ambassador never met Rasputin, whom many historians credit with playing a significant role in destroying the public affection and respect for the monarchy. As late as December 1915, Marye commented in his diary that he had heard many stories about Rasputin during his tour in Russia, but that they had been so "queer and weird" that he was at a loss as to know what to think about him. By the time of Sturmer's appointment as Chairman of the Council of Ministers, however, the envoy had concluded that Rasputin's influence was an unsavory one, and he wrote in his diary that Rasputin's power in the palace was "a blight on the Imperial family and is now a bitter scandal." Marye concluded that the Tsarina would not permit anyone to inform her as to the true character of Rasputin and that his influence with her was due only to her belief that Rasputin had restored and was preserving the health of her son, the Tsarevitch.[8]

On February 22, 1916, the Duma opened its new session. As was customary, Sazonov gave a speech reviewing the international scene, his comments revealing the growing, though still secondary importance of the United States to Russia. The Foreign Minister expressed his great pleasure that the "bothersome" efforts of German agents in the United States had not only been unsuccessful but had served to strengthen sentiment hostile to Germany and in favor of the Allies. He added that the interest of American industry in the Russian market had increased and that this indicated that "with the existing friendly political relations between the two countries, closer commercial relations can provide mutual benefits for both countries."[9]

Sazonov was clearly exaggerating the improvement in Russian-American relations that had taken place. In part, he may have hoped to soothe opposition elements in the Duma, who generally favored an improvement in ties with Washington. Nonetheless, the indifference and latent hostility toward the United States described by Ambassador Paléologue had begun to change. Thus, bilateral diplomatic affairs were in a state of flux when in February 1916 Ambassador Marye resigned from his post in Petrograd.

The reason for Marye's resignation in February 1916 has never been definitely established. There was no advance indication or explanation for the resignation in his correspondence with the State Department, and in his memoirs Marye stated only that the resignation was in the possession of the State Department early in February 1916. The President's note of February 17, 1916, accepting the resignation, expressed the hope that Marye's health would permit him to remain in Petrograd long enough to advise the American chargé, who would handle the Embassy until a new Ambassador arrived.[10]

The *New York Times*, in its coverage of Marye's resignation, commented that the development was not unexpected, referring to reports that had been current in Washington for some time that Marye would be replaced because he was regarded as too strongly in sympathy with the Allies. This very well may have been the reason for the envoy's departure from Petrograd, as he certainly made little effort to conceal his sympathy for Russia and the Allies in his reports to Washington or in his public statements, and his position was further weakened in November 1915 by a dispute with the German minister to Sweden over the proper procedures to be followed by the American Embassy with regard to the protection of Berlin's interests in Russia.

Marye's departure was probably also related to internal political developments in the United States since as a long-time leader of the Democratic Party he may well have hoped to play a more active role in the 1916 election campaigns. Finally, although the Ambassador included nothing but the most favorable comments about President Wilson and Secretary Lansing in his memoirs, his relations with them may have become strained. Marye was well aware of and almost certainly opposed the change in his instructions concerning a new treaty, and he could easily have concluded that when the Secretary modified the original American negotiating position on the passport dispute, Marye would appear guilty of duplicity in Sazonov's eyes. On their part, neither the President nor Lansing appeared to have great confidence in Marye's abilities, and their doubts were probably not lost on him.

The envoy alluded to the actual reason for his resignation in a meeting with Sazonov on February 23, 1916. According to the account given by Marye in his memoirs, the Foreign Minister expressed his great surprise and regret on learning that Marye would soon depart, to which the latter replied that his regret was fully equal to Sazonov's surprise, and that "no consideration of health would have induced me to resign during the war, but that political combinations had arisen at home which affected me and that I felt impelled to withdraw."[11] Marye thus specifically denied the official reason given for his resignation as Ambassador, ill health. The "political combinations," he referred to, however, were never made clear.

The departure of Marye, who had created extremely close personal relations with the Tsarist officials, cast a pall over relations between the two nations. Petrograd's chagrin over Marye's recall, as it was viewed there, was heightened by its coming simultaneously with the transfer of Charles Wilson, the career official who had been First Secretary of the American Embassy for four years. Wilson himself believed that the transfer was due in part to his pro-Allied sympathies. In his memoirs, Marye concluded that the transfer of Wilson was only "a piece of thought-lessness" of the State Department, which had not considered the effect it would have on the efficiency of the Embassy nor on the Russian view of the United States, and that Tsarist officials were so convinced Wilson's transfer was a result of German influence in Washington that "it was useless to attempt to disabuse them of it."

The reaction to these changes in the Embassy reached high within the Russian government. Sazonov told Marye that he was particularly disappointed at the latter's departure since he and Marye understood each other so well and that he had hoped that after the war the two could have worked successfully to improve the political and economic relations between the two countries. The Foreign Minister added that he could not understand the thinking of the United States in changing its representatives in Russia so frequently and asked bitterly, "Doesn't your government care anything for our friendship?"

The Secretary of the Ministry of Foreign Affairs told Wilson that personnel at the Ministry regretted his departure and gen-erally believed that it was due to pro-German sentiment in the American government. The Secretary added that "confidentially I tell you that the work of your embassy will not be made easier by that belief."[12]

The Tsar, himself, was concerned over Wilson's transfer, according to a member of the Court who stated that the monarch regretted Wilson's departure as he was a friend of Russia and the Allies. Nicholas observed that the State Department had probably "received its orders from Berlin" to remove Wilson for that reason and declared that the transfer was "only another proof among the frequent ones we receive of complete indifference, to say the least, of America towards Russia." By contrast, the monarch felt that the United States was always extremely careful to defer to the sensitivities of Berlin.

On March 11, 1916, Ambassador Marye and his wife made their farewell calls upon the Tsar and Tsarina at the Imperial Palace. The Ambassador was in a very pleasant humor, previously having been informed by Sazonov that the Tsar would award him the decoration of the Grand Cordon of the Order of Saint Alexander Nevsky, the highest award ever given an American envoy to Russia. Marye's wife was also honored, being received by the Tsarina, an exceptional token of favor, since the Tsarina had not received any Ambassador or Ambassador's wife since the start of the war.

In his conversation with Marye, Nicholas expressed his regret over the Ambassador's departure, suggesting that the United States erred in replacing its diplomats abroad too frequently, removing them just when their experience at an embassy would make them particularly effective. Marye explained that the tenure of any U.S. envoy was indefinite; even if he had not resigned at that time, he would have been obliged to do so if a Republican were elected in 1916 to replace President Wilson.

Marye then turned to the area of Russian-American economic relations, remarking that after the war there would be a period of great business activity in the Empire and expressing the hope that U.S. firms would be permitted to play an important role in this development. In response, the Tsar stated he would be most pleased to see Americans take a prominent part in the commercial activities of his country and he hoped many would come to Russia. On this happy note, the audience ended.[13]

On March 28, 1916, the new First Secretary of the Embassy, Fred Dearing, arrived in Petrograd to replace Charles Wilson, and the following day Ambassador Marye departed for the United States, having served in his post in Russia for over seventeen months. His arrival had found the two nations unable to agree on a new commercial treaty. When he left, the dispute had still not been resolved, and no American initiative had been taken in the matter since President Wilson and Secretary Lansing's agreement in their exchange of notes in July 1915 that one should be made.

In the interim, the sinking of the *Lusitania* and the controversy with Berlin over submarine warfare had won for the Allies a wide measure of support in Washington. Probably even more important, German policy had convinced Secretary Lansing that that country's defeat was essential to the long-range interests of the United States.

These sentiments, however, were not extended to any significant extent to include American sympathy for Russia. On the contrary, growing U.S. concern over Japanese expansion in the Pacific and Russian bitterness over the circumstances of Marye's resignation threatened to strain diplomatic ties between the two nations. Marye had succeeded in establishing more cordial relations with Petrograd than any previous American envoy had ever done, but he was unable to expand the cordial personal relationships into a more friendly attitude toward the United States on the part of the Tsarist government.

In the economic sphere, there had been a significant increase in Russian-American interaction between 1914 and 1916, almost exclusively as a result of the war. However, as the spring of 1916 approached, it was clear that any effort to improve relations between the two governments would be seriously impeded by a mutual misunderstanding of their positions and interests. The United States, the most powerful nation still neutral in the war, was interested basically in maintaining its neutrality, in protecting its shipping from attacks or interference by either side, in increasing its foreign commerce, and in preventing Japan from gaining a dominant position in the Far East. Insofar as a commercial treaty would increase American commerce with Russia, both during and after the war, Washington ardently desired to conclude a new agreement to replace the terminated treaty of 1832. Being itself so interested in the expansion of commerce with Russia, the United States continually overestimated Petrograd's eagerness for a pact and underestimated the various political obstacles involved. And, while desiring to reach a new agreement, the State Department steadfastly refused to compromise its position on the passport dispute or to offer any concessions that might jeopardize American neutrality.

Russia, unlike the United States, was very much involved in the war. It had already suffered severe reverses and was destined to incur many more, and the strains of the conflict had revealed serious fissures in the Russian society, economy, and system of government. Quite naturally, the Imperial government was vitally and almost exclusively concerned with emerging from the struggle victorious, or at least in avoiding defeat until the war could be won by the Allies.

In such a situation, for Russia the matter of relations with the United States was only of secondary importance. So long as it could continue to purchase the needed American goods without the existence of a commercial treaty, Petrograd regarded the conclusion of a new agreement as of minimal concern. Similar considerations dominated Tsarist policy toward the Far East, as the Empire could not and would not join with the United States in seeking to restrain Tokyo's expansion in that area at the cost of jeopardizing the military assistance it was obtaining from Japan. Should the United States insist upon concessions in the passport dispute as the price for a new commercial treaty, Russia obviously saw little in the way of concrete advantages sufficient to compensate for the possible internal opposition such a policy would produce. And there the matter rested, with neither nation appreciating the interests or position of the other, as the new American Ambassador to Russia, David Francis, prepared to depart for his post.

# VII

## The Disillusionment
## of Ambassador Francis

To replace Marye as Ambassador to Russia, President Wilson selected David R. Francis of Missouri, who in August 1914 had declined an offer from the President to serve as envoy to Argentina. Francis, having previously held public office as Mayor of St. Louis, Governor of Missouri, Director General of the St. Louis International Exposition, and Secretary of the Interior in President Cleveland's cabinet, was by his mid-sixties an influential figure in the Democratic Party. Like Marye, he had never before held a diplomatic post.[1]

Francis's appointment was generally welcomed in the American press. The *New York Times* in praising the selection commented that he had been a trusted advisor to President Cleveland. In editorial comment, the paper further expressed the view that while a new commercial treaty with Russia would be desirable, one could be negotiated only if the Imperial government agreed not to discriminate against American citizens. Prophetically, the editorial added that the situation in Russia was similar to that in pre-Revolutionary France and recalled that in France the path from the Estates-General to the Revolutionary Tribunal was not long.[2]

By his own admission, Francis was not especially well qualified for the Ambassadorial post, and in his memoirs he conceded that before being appointed he had only a vague knowledge of

Russia and no acquaintanceship with the language.[3] Interested primarily in negotiating a new commercial treaty, Francis accepted the post under the mistaken impression that he could accomplish this end without difficulty and that the Tsarist government merely awaited an American overture. With the treaty his primary interest, Ambassador Francis was to find his stay in Russia marked by frustration, bitterness, and failure.

The news of Francis's selection as his successor was forwarded to Marye in the same letter in which President Wilson accepted the latter's resignation. Marye accordingly informed Sazonov about the new appointee during his meeting with the Foreign Minister on February 23, 1916. Sazonov's response was scarcely flattering—he commented only that the Tsarist government would probably like Francis as well as anyone after the present Ambassador.[4]

Prior to departing for Petrograd, Francis met in Washington with Secretary Lansing and subsequently with the Russian Ambassador to the United States to discuss the prospects for a new treaty. Both Francis and Lansing were optimistic, viewing the passport dispute as the only possible stumbling block. Francis's optimism, however, surprised the Russian emissary. Calling later at the State Department to discuss the matter with the Counselor of the Department, Frank Polk, Bakhmet'ev commented laughingly that Francis appeared to believe the treaty could be concluded in a few weeks.[5]

The new American envoy left for Petrograd on April 8, 1916, on the steamship *Oscar II*. On the day of his departure he sent President Wilson a letter summing up his reactions and expectations concerning the assignment and revealing what he felt to be the major issues affecting his mission. Characteristically, he observed that while his personal preference would be to return to the United States to participate directly in the 1916 presidential campaign, he felt that the best service he could render to the administration, the Party, and the country would be to negotiate a new treaty.[6]

Francis's interest in a commercial treaty was based largely on what he believed to be the great opportunities for American business in the Empire. He feared that Great Britain would attempt to take advantage of its wartime alliance to become Russia's dominant trade partner. The Ambassador believed Washington should seize the opportunity afforded by increased Tsarist purchases to insure that America retained and Great Britain was denied the position formerly held by Germany in supplying the bulk of Tsarist imports.

The envoy's estimate of the benefits that would accrue to the United States was very optimistic. His letter advised the President that Russia offered a better field for the investment of American ingenuity and enterprise than any other country on the globe. The major problem to be overcome in establishing closer trade bonds, Francis concluded, was the opposition of Great Britain.[7]

The Ambassador's suspicion of London was fueled by a meeting he had held with representatives of leading American banks in New York before his departure. His conversations with officials of the J. P. Morgan and Company banking house led Francis to believe that the firm was thoroughly British in sentiment. He thought that the company looked with suspicion if not fear upon any movement to promote closer trade or social ties between Russia and the United States. He warned that the firm's desire and plan was to have British banks function as the channels for any Russian financing obtained in the United States.[8]

Francis, by contrast, believed that it was vital to involve American banks. If they were able to negotiate directly with the Russian government to provide loans for the purchase of American goods, he reasoned, such an arrangement would contribute both to the development of closer commercial ties and to the facilitation of progress toward a new treaty. He subsequently met with representatives of the National City Bank of New York to encourage such direct dealings with the Imperial government and thereafter jubilantly informed President Wilson that the bank had thoroughly agreed with his plan for direct dealings with the Tsarist bankers.

Optimistic as he was about a new treaty, Francis was under no illusions concerning Petrograd's pleasure to receive him as Ambassador. He was aware of that government's regret over

Marye's departure and of the suspicions harbored by many officials that the change had been brought about by pro-German elements in the United States. He even wrote to President Wilson to explain that his views were not pro-German to any extent whatever and to pledge that at all times his official conduct and public statements would be as carefully guarded and neutral in spirit as possible.

The suspicions in Petrograd that Francis was so intent to dispel, however, were inadvertently strengthened by circumstances. Although married, the envoy left his wife and family in the United States and sailed accompanied only by an old family servant. On board ship, he became friendly with a fellow passenger, Madame Matilda de Cram, who was returning to Russia after visiting America. Unknown to Francis, she was suspected by the Allied counterintelligence services of being a German agent. Despite an apparent lack of hard evidence to support this suspicion, the Ambassador's presence in her company raised Russian doubts about Francis's reliability. Gossip concerning the relationship became widespread when he continued to see the lady for instruction in the Russian language after his arrival in Petrograd. The result has subsequently been described by George Kennan as a "deplorable atmosphere of disapproval and suspicion among some of the ambassador's leading associates as well as among members of the Allied diplomatic missions."[9]

Francis arrived in Petrograd on April 28, 1916. In an interview with the press that same day, he answered a question about the future of German-American relations with the observation that Berlin would probably never permit things to deteriorate to the point where diplomatic ties would be threatened. He actually asserted that there were more than 20 million Germans in the United States who had "so much taken into their possession all commercial businesses" that they would never permit a break in relations as they would then have to liquidate their assets and return home.[10] This remark, so very different from the warmly pro-Russian sentiments expressed by Marye on his arrival, suggested to the Russians that their fears concerning the influence of pro-German elements on American policy were correct.

On the very next day, the Ambassador was invited to call upon Boris Sturmer, the Chairman of the Council of Ministers. The invitation was a departure from normal diplomatic procedure, which called for a new envoy to meet initially with the Foreign Minister. Upon questioning members of the Embassy staff Francis learned that the situation probably derived from the poor relationship that existed between Sturmer and the Foreign Minister. As a result of this discord, they noted, Sturmer frequently insisted upon meeting dignitaries before Sazonov could do so.[11]

Sturmer apparently went out of his way to impress the Ambassador favorably, declaring during their conversation that he was very anxious for his government to establish closer ties with the United States. Although Francis admitted in his diary that the Chairman was "exceedingly cordial," he was not favorably impressed, observing that Sturmer was "as German as his name." The Ambassador further concluded that Sturmer's "mind worked slowly and his temperament was phlegmatic. In short he impressed me as a dull man."

Francis's poor opinion of Sturmer probably influenced the substance of his discussions with the Chairman. Although conclusion of a new commercial treaty was his primary objective, the Ambassador did not even mention the matter in the discussion. Reporting to Secretary Lansing on the meeting, Francis somewhat lamely stated that the omission was due to Sturmer's poor knowledge of English.[12]

Immediately upon concluding his meeting with Sturmer, Francis called upon Foreign Minister Sazonov, who also rapidly surprised and disillusioned him. For, though the Foreign Minister was "cordial, courteous, attentive, candid and responsive," he emphatically told the envoy that the Imperial government was not prepared to negotiate a commercial treaty at that time. Sazonov went out of his way to emphasize that Russia would not conclude a commercial agreement with any country, including the United States, until all of the Allied Powers had reached agreement concerning economic matters.

An angry David Francis recalled to Sazonov that Ambassador Marye had been told previously by Russian officials that the Imperial government desired a treaty and was waiting for proposals to this end from Washington. The Foreign Minister admitted that he had commented in this fashion to Marye, adding, however, that he had heard nothing from the State Department on the matter since July 1915 and that the situation had since changed. Referring to plans of the Allies to hold a conference on economic matters in Paris in June 1916, Sazonov stressed that Russia would not be able to make any commitment concerning the treaty until the meeting was over. He then observed that the United States had been the responsible party in terminating the previous treaty. While this action had engendered no particular resentment in his country, the Foreign Minister went on, it also had not interfered with trade between the two countries, which he expected would continue in the absence of an agreement.[13]

The Ambassador's protests that he had accepted his post primarily to conclude a new treaty left Sazonov unmoved. The Foreign Minister smilingly commented, as Francis informed the Secretary of State, that the duties of the office would be sufficiently onerous without negotiating the pact. In terminating the meeting, Sazonov alluded to the circumstances of Marye's resignation by stating that he had heard rumors that Francis's appointment was influenced by German elements in America. However, because he had checked with Ambassador Bakhmet'ev in Washington and had been assured that such reports were groundless, he condescendingly told Francis that the Tsarist government was wholly uninfluenced by the rumors, which he did not credit.[14]

In his report of the two initial meetings, the Ambassador characterized as surprising and inexplicable Sazonov's comments on the need to postpone negotiations. The envoy's efforts to ascertain the reasons for the change in attitude left him convinced that the alteration was a result of British machinations. Even before leaving Washington, Francis had told President Wilson that London appeared to be attempting to block the establishment of closer American economic ties with the Russians. The Ambassador's fears concerning British influence in this regard were reinforced by Sazonov's comments to him, and on May 2, 1916, he frankly advised the Secretary of State that since arriving in Petrograd he had heard many things that confirmed his worst suspicions. Francis detailed his belief that the Paris economic conference of the Allies had been inspired by the British, who were "making a decided effort to occupy toward Russia the position held by Germany before the war." He added that although Sturmer and Sazonov had stated they favored direct commercial dealings between their country and the United States, London's influence was very strong and was growing.

The Ambassador's suspicions were reinforced once more when he learned from an unidentified acquaintance that the Tsarist Minister of Finance, Peter Bark, was "completely under British influence" and that Sazonov was kept in his post by support from London. "If this is true," Francis reported to Lansing, "and I am not prepared to question it, we can account for Russia's change of front concerning the commercial treaty."[15]

On May 5, 1916, less than a month after his arrival, the Ambassador was received by the Tsar. Francis found the monarch exceedingly cordial, and after presenting his credentials the Ambassador proceeded almost immediately to raise the subject of the commercial treaty. As in his meeting with Sazonov, the Ambassador stated he had come to Russia primarily to conclude a new commercial treaty. When to Francis's surprise and gratification Nicholas replied that Russia also wished to conclude such a treaty, the envoy wisely did not repeat Sazonov's statement nor ask the reason for the contradiction in the two positions. Describing the conversation subsequently in his memoirs, Francis noted that the Tsar's behavior was characteristic, as "the unfortunate monarch was always trying to avoid difficulties."

Ambassador Francis, like his predecessor, strongly favored prohibition and took advantage of the conversation to praise the initiation of prohibition in Russia at the start of the war. Turning then to the rumors that his replacement of Marye was due to pro-German influence in the United States, Francis stressed that this was completely untrue and emphasized that he would be completely impartial concerning the thorny problem of American protection of the German and Austrian interests in Russia.[16]

During Francis's comments, he observed that the Tsar smiled

and nodded affirmatively. When Francis then added that his personal sympathies were with the Allies and that this was well known in the United States, Nicholas indicated his approval and, according to the Ambassador, "said he was confident that such was the case but was delighted to hear it from my own lips."[17]

The Tsar's behavior toward Francis differs sharply from his early reaction when he was told of Marye's forthcoming departure. While it is possible that Marye's description of Nicholas's concern over the resignation was colored by the source, it is more likely that regardless of his real views, the Tsar would adopt a seemingly cordial attitude toward Francis. To do other, certainly, would risk offending the envoy and the government of the most powerful of the neutral nations, to no useful purpose.

Following his audience with the monarch, Francis began a series of formal calls upon the other members of the diplomatic corps. His meeting with the French Ambassador on May 10, 1916, went very poorly, as Francis was not only laboring under the handicap of replacing Marye, who had been very popular in Russia and was a good friend of Paléologue, but also attempted to be as neutral in word and deed as he had pledged to be. His efforts to avoid giving the slightest hint of partiality in the war won the ire of the French envoy. Paléologue noted in his diary that he had attempted to draw out Francis into discussing the war but that the latter evaded all questions or gave noncommittal answers, from which Paléologue concluded that the American conscience was "still insensible to the great moral interests" affecting the world situation.[18]

Francis's efforts at appearing impartial also evoked displeasure in the Russian newspapers. In a press conference in Petrograd, he carefully limited his comments to the forthcoming presidential campaign in the United States and to local events in St. Louis, leading the conservative newspaper *Novoe Vremia* to observe that when a new Ambassador arrives in a country involved in a tremendous war and does not say a single word about the war, "it is obvious that he must have very serious reasons for his silence." The paper, which was often critical of the United States, went on to connect Francis's failure to mention the war to President Wilson, who it implied was acting like Pontius Pilate by attempting to avoid placing the blame for starting the war on the Central Powers.[19]

In pursuit of his objective of strengthening Russian-American economic relations, Francis directly involved himself in the discussions under way between the Tsarist government and American banks. Prior to his departure from the United States, he had met in New York with representatives of the National City Bank of New York, which was heading a group of American financial institutions discussing a proposed loan of 50 million dollars to Russia. In his discussion with the bankers and subsequently with President Wilson, Francis had voiced his interest in seeing the loan agreement concluded. However, in his first meeting with Sazonov, the Foreign Minister had stated that the loan negotiations were stalled by the demand that the Imperial government post collateral for the loan. Both because of the effect this would have on Russian prestige and possibly also because Petrograd could not post the necessary collateral, Sazonov declared that his government would make no loan that required any security "other than the faith or credit of the government itself."

Once again, as had been the case when Sazonov refused to discuss a new treaty until after the Allied economic conference, Francis believed the Russian decision on the loan negotiations was strongly influenced by, if not completely due to, British efforts. His suspicions were reinforced as the result of a conversation with a representative of the National City Bank in Petrograd, who told him that Russia was about to agree to the requirements of the American banks as of March 1916. However, the Russian position had changed, and the banker concluded this could only have been the result of British efforts to insure that "all foreign relations of a commercial or financial character had by Russia should be through London."[20]

The Ambassador's pessimism over the fate of the loan turned out to be unfounded. On May 18, 1916, he was visited by an official of the Foreign Office, J. Korostovetz, who advised that he had been sent by Sazonov and Finance Minister Bark to determine if Francis was personally in favor of the loan. The envoy replied that because of his official position he could not properly comment on the desirability of a loan made by private American banks to a foreign government. However, he then pointed out the strength and good reputation of the National City Bank and its associates and observed that such a loan would strengthen the relations between the two countries as well as expanding trade between them. Korostovetz indicated that Francis's suspicion of the role played by Great Britain might not have been completely without foundation, pointing out that that country had been providing financial support to Russia and might not wish to see Petrograd obtain such a loan from the United States without London's involvement. The Ambassador countered this by stating that there was no reason for any British involvement in the loan and that America had recently provided loans of 500 million dollars to Great Britain and France.

In his report of the meeting, Francis expressed his satisfaction that he had convinced Korostovetz of the soundness of the loan, adding that he was rendering all the assistance he could to its consumation, as he believed it would have a "very beneficial effect on the diplomatic, as well as the commercial relations between the two countries."[21]

The Ambassador became so deeply involved in assisting the efforts of the American group that he permitted the representatives of the National City Bank to use the Embassy telegraphic facilities to communicate rapidly with their headquarters in New York. Lansing quickly put an end to such assistance, notifying Francis that such conduct would be contrary to the accepted rule of international law that neutral governments could not assist belligerents to raise war loans. Francis's plea that his British counterpart was doing all he could to promote British commercial interests was unsuccessful in persuading Lansing to change his position.[22]

The withdrawal of permission to use the Embassy communication facilities did not prevent the National City Bank representatives from successfully concluding the loan agreement. In need of the financing which would be provided in the loan, Petrograd eventually agreed to compromise on the request for collateral, and deposited the equivalent of 50 million dollars in Russian currency with the banks. This was a concession to Russian pride, but it was really not hard collateral since the currency could and indeed did become worthless when the Tsarist government was overthrown.

When the loan agreement was signed, Francis jubilantly notified the State Department of the event on June 19, 1916, citing as evidence of the impartiality he had pledged to maintain the fact that the Embassy had not participated in the negotiations. He added his personal satisfaction that the loan had been concluded and predicted it would improve ties between the two nations, which he feared had been "strained by the embassy's persistent efforts for German/Austrian prisoners and by constant Jewish agitation in America."

The agreement was also very welcome to the Imperial government. Francis informed the State Department on June 26, 1916, that in a meeting with Sazonov that day, the Foreign Minister had expressed his great gratification over the loan and his hope that it would be the beginning of "much larger financial transactions between the two countries."[23] In a public interview with the Petrograd representative of the American United Press, subsequently published in Russia, Sazonov echoed these comments, stating that he "wholeheartedly" welcomed efforts to "reestablish Russian-American trade relations." The Foreign Minister added that he saw no obstacles in the way of establishing cordial relations with the United States and that in this effort he was receiving the full support of Ambassador Francis.[24]

The warmth engendered by the conclusion of the loan agreement, however, did not result in a relaxation of the Russian position in other areas of dispute between the two countries. One such disagreement concerned American proposals to alleviate the hardship imposed by the war on the civilian population of Russian Poland, which had been overrun by the German and Austrian armies in 1915. At the end of 1915, the leaders of the Polish community in the United States urged that the activities of the Belgian Relief Commission, headed by Herbert Hoover, expand its area of activity to include occupied Poland.

Since the territory in question had belonged to Russia at the outbreak of war, that country, as well as Germany and Austria, was consulted by the United States for its views on providing relief to the civilian population. On May 20, 1916, at the instruction of the State Department, Francis met with Sazonov to ascertain informally what method of distributing relief to the inhabitants of Poland would be acceptable to Russia. The Foreign Minister was initially receptive to the American offer, telling Francis that the Tsarist government had no objection to the extension to Poland of the services provided by American agencies to the inhabitants of Belgium, so long as Washington offered acceptable guarantees that none of the aid would be utilized by the Central Powers for their own nationals.[25]

When he next met with Sazonov on the matter, however, the Ambassador found the Russian position had changed. The Foreign Minister declared to him on June 15, 1916, that he could not consider any plan for Polish relief prior to conferring with the other Allied Powers. Sazonov, further, was adamant against accepting the German condition that the police and occupying forces of the Central Powers in the region be permitted to share in the food supplies brought in by the relief agency.

Petrograd was not alone in blocking an agreement to provide American relief supplies to the Polish population; all of the nations consulted by the United States posed mutually unacceptable conditions. On July 20, 1916, President Wilson sent a note to the sovereigns of Austria-Hungary, Germany, Great Britain, and Russia and to the President of France urging them to reconsider and permit the provision of American assistance to Poland. But his appeal fell on deaf ears.

Although Russia rejected the proposal, the Tsar's response was very cordial in tone, stating that he appreciated the humanitarian motives and unselfish attitude of the United States. Nicholas asserted that the Central Powers were responsible for the impasse by placing unacceptable conditions on the proposed provision of relief supplies, and he stated that his government would be pleased to consider any new American proposals when these conditions were withdrawn.[26]

The discussions between the United States and Russia with

regard to Poland did not place any significant strain on relations between the two countries, but the matter did add to the great body of unresolved issues existing between them. The Polish question further required substantial attention of Ambassador Francis, who was at this time becoming deeply involved in the broad range of subjects at issue between the two governments.

In addition to the negotiations for American bank loans to the Tsarist government and the problem of relief supplies to Poland, he was preoccupied with the situation in the Far East, where Japan was continuing to expand its influence in China despite American disapproval. Francis was at the same time deeply concerned over the effect on American commercial relations with the Allies, and particularly with Russia, of the Allied Economic Conference in Paris. Finally, and probably most important, he wished to see progress in his goal of concluding a new commercial treaty with Petrograd.

During his meeting with Sazonov on June 15, 1916, after discussing the matter of relief for Poland, Francis again raised the subject of the commercial treaty, asking the Foreign Minister for his current views on the feasibility of opening negotiations. Sazonov's response was brief and sharp, reminding Francis that the former treaty had been denounced by the United States and not by Russia. While Russia would be pleased to consider a new treaty, Washington's position on the passport dispute was a stumbling block, and the Foreign Minister observed "rather petulantly" that the United States was the only nation with whom Russia had diplomatic or commercial relations "that ever mentioned the subject of the Jews."

In his report to Lansing of this conversation, Francis expressed his deep concern over the effect American relations with Russia would have on the 1916 presidential campaign. He stated that he was expending considerable effort on the matter of the treaty because of its likely appearance as an issue in the campaign, but he feared that opponents of the administration might charge that Wilson had made no effort to alleviate the treatment of the Jews in Russia. The Ambassador suggested that if this charge were raised, the State Department should refer to Sazonov's statement that no treaty with any neutral country would be concluded until after the Paris Economic Conference.[27]

The Conference in question was held in Paris from June 14 to June 17, 1916, attended by representatives of France, Belgium, Great Britain, Italy, Japan, Portugal, Russia, and Serbia. The suspicion and concern Francis had expressed about the Conference were shared by Secretary Lansing, who upon being informed of the forthcoming Conference, on March 10, 1916, warned the American Embassy in Paris that the meeting might result in the nations attending adopting measures unfavorable to U.S. interests. He therefore instructed the Embassy to attempt to learn the results of the Conference, "using every discretion in doing so."[28]

As feared by Lansing and Francis, the Conference did adopt two groups of recommendations affecting American commercial activities. The first provided for the imposition of measures prohibiting trade between the Allies and the Central Powers and restricting, insofar as it could be enforced, trade between neutral nations and the Central Powers. The second group of recommendations called for the establishment after the war of procedures under which the Allied Powers would grant each other favored economic status within their respective countries, to the disadvantage not only of the former enemy states but also of the neutral nations. Among the latter group, of course, was the United States.

When the results of the Allied Economic Conference were given to the press, the French Minister of Commerce, acting as spokesman, attempted to allay the fears of the neutral nations that their interests would be adversely affected. He stated that they had nothing to fear from the new measures, which he characterized as "legitimate economic defense," and he asserted that the Allies were fighting for the destruction of "German economic hegemony," which menaced the neutrals as much as the Allies.[29]

Francis's suspicions that the decisions of the Paris Economic Conference had been shaped by Great Britain and would hurt the United States were not assuaged by the statement of the French Minister of Commerce. Without obtaining the approval of the State Department for his action and proceeding solely upon the basis of newspaper accounts of the Conference, he raised the matter with Sazonov on June 26, 1916, noting that the Conference seemed to have created an offensive and defensive alliance of the Allied Powers, excluding not only the Central Powers but also the neutrals. The Foreign Minister protested that there had been no intention on the part of the Allies "to exclude America from any commercial relations with Russia," and that the recommendations of the Conference were not binding. Francis, however, was not convinced that his fears were unfounded, and in his report to the State Department, he asked for Lansing's views on the Conference and for instructions as to what further steps the Embassy could take in this matter.

The Secretary of State did not appear eager to support the Ambassador's remonstrances, and his reply to Francis was sent by surface transportation rather than by cable and did not reach Petrograd until mid-September of 1916. In cool language, it stated that the State Department did not believe it was the intention of any of the Allies to impose restrictions on American trade. Adding that the Department welcomed reporting from American missions abroad as to public reaction to the recommendations of the Conference, Lansing in effect rebuked Francis for his initiative by leaving unanswered his request for specific instructions to follow up on the matter.[30]

The reaction of Ambassador Francis to this response was not recorded. He probably spent little time resenting it, since by the time it arrived the Paris Conference had long since passed and his attention was diverted to the more immediate problem of the growing internal unrest in Russia. In the interim, the Ambassador was faced with renewed evidence of cooperation between Petrograd and Tokyo in the Far East, to the detriment of the United States.

# VIII

## The Secret
## Russian-Japanese
## Agreement

Toward the end of January 1916, shortly before his departure from Russia and at a time when his resignation had probably already been submitted, Ambassador Marye became concerned over a spate of articles in the press concerning the possibility of a Russian-Japanese alliance. However, he was reluctant to ask Sazonov about the reports, believing that no treaty had been signed and that to broach the subject would only serve to strain his relationship with the Foreign Minister, particularly since the reports were largely translations of articles originating in the Japanese press. On January 27, 1916, Marye gingerly raised the subject with the Foreign Minister and noted happily in his diary that Sazonov had "entirely confirmed" his assumption that there was no substance to the story.[1]

The reports concerning a Russian-Japanese treaty, however, continued to persist, and on April 7, 1916, the American Embassy in Tokyo informed the State Department that the Japanese Prime Minister had admitted in a press interview that Russia and Japan expected to complete negotiations establishing an alliance between the two nations. The State Department instructed the American Embassy in Petrograd to look into the report and to approach the Tsarist government discreetly in order to learn whether such negotiations were in progress. On April 24, 1916, Fred Dearing, who was acting as American chargé prior to the arrival of Ambassador Francis, took up the matter with Sazonov. The Foreign Minister told Dearing that the relations between Russia and Japan were growing "very friendly," but he asserted that there was nothing secret about the *rapprochement* and assured him that there would be nothing in any agreement that might be concluded by Russia and Japan that would in any way infringe upon American interests.

Unlike Marye, Dearing was not convinced by the Foreign Minister's protestations, and he informed the State Department on April 26, 1916, that he strongly suspected Sazonov had not told him the whole truth about the reports of a Russian-Japanese agreement. He noted, correctly, that the Foreign Minister would have no intention of revealing any really sensitive information to him, as under the American Open Door policy toward China, Washington would certainly strongly protest any Russian-Japanese treaty that might restrict its access to China. If a treaty were in prospect, it would clearly be in Russia's interests to keep the matter hidden from the United States for as long as possible.[2]

The accuracy of Dearing's analysis became obvious on July 7, 1916, when the Russian and Japanese governments formally released the text of the convention the two nations had signed in Petrograd on July 3. The public announcement stated that neither signatory would enter into any agreement directed against the other and that they would join together for mutual cooperation and defense if the interests of either of the nations in the Far East were threatened by a third party.

Francis first learned of the new agreement from the Russian press. He was understandably angry, feeling that the Foreign Minister had deliberately deceived him by not mentioning that negotiations with Japan were under way when the two met on June 26, 1916. He immediately cabled the news to Washington. Stating that the treaty was a surprise to him and to many Russians, the Ambassador flatly declared that he did not like it and wished to make his views known to the Tsarist government if the State Department would authorize him to do so.[3]

On the following day, July 8, 1916, without waiting for the receipt of approval and instructions, Francis requested a meeting with Sazonov to discuss the agreement. He was disappointed to be told that the Foreign Minister was not available, since he was away at the front conferring with the Tsar, and that he would not return to Petrograd for several days. Although the Russian government probably wished to postpone the meeting, Sazonov was indeed not in the capital but was meeting with the monarch to discuss a plan to grant a constitution to Poland.[4]

The Department of State, meanwhile, was receiving information from other sources that the Russian-Japanese agreement contained provisions that were being kept secret and that might adversely affect U.S. interests. The American Consul General in Mukden, Manchuria, reported on July 11, 1916, that there were definitely secret provisions to the treaty and observed that the agreement disclosed the weakened position of Russia and was a diplomatic victory for Japan. He predicted that the treaty would result in the strengthening of Tokyo's sphere of interest in the Far East and so weaken Petrograd's freedom of action that it could be considered an unconditional surrender of rights in the face of an ever-increasing Japanese lust of conquest.

Probably as a result of this report, the State Department on July 13, 1916, asked the American Embassy in Tokyo if it had any evidence suggesting there were secret provisions or arrangements that might infringe upon U.S. interests. At the same time, Francis was instructed not to discuss the subject with Sazonov until the State Department determined the line he should follow.[5]

The Ambassador, however, was thoroughly convinced that the agreement would threaten American interests. Unwilling to accept the delay imposed by the State Department, on July 13, 1916, he reiterated his position to the Secretary of State, in a letter stressing that he could not help but believe the agreement was "unfriendly" in spirit toward the United States. He declared that he would inform Sazonov that the treaty would not be regarded in the United States as indicating any Russian willingness to establish closer diplomatic and commercial relations with America and that a more inopportune time could not have been chosen, as it flew in the face of the recent agreement by U.S. banks to provide a 50-million-dollar loan to the Tsarist government.[6]

In accordance with the intention communicated to the State Department, Francis met with the Foreign Minister on 14 July, 1916, and disregarding the instructions of the Department, he raised the subject of the agreement. Predictably, Sazonov assured him that the United States had no reason to be concerned over the agreement, going so far as to assert that Washington would benefit from the treaty, since it would prevent Germany from competing as it had done previously for Chinese trade with the United States, Great Britain, and France.

Sazonov's assurances did little to reassure the Ambassador, who noted that Japan had taken advantage of Petrograd's inability to defend itself to dictate the treaty to Russia. Francis concluded sorrowfully that "although I was unable to prevent it, however, I did express my disapproval of it to Sazonov immediately after its promulgation."[7]

Francis's deep concern was beginning to be shared by the Department of State. Although the American Embassy in Japan was unable to uncover any evidence that the agreement was injurious to the United States, the State Department on August 16, 1916, instructed the Ambassadors in Japan and Russia to communicate official concern over the treaty. The U.S. demarche specifically emphasized the assumption that the signatories still supported the independence and territorial integrity of China, and it requested them to provide confirmation that they remained committed to the principle of the Open Door for China.

Both governments furnished the assurances requested by the the United States, Japan transmitting on September 13, 1916, a formal note to this effect. Russia, for its part, gave its assurances informally, in a meeting Francis had with the Chairman of the Council of Ministers. Sturmer, who in late July assumed the additional post of Foreign Minister, declared that it was the policy of his country to maintain the principle of equal opportunity for the commerce of all nations in China.[8]

Despite the repeated protestations from Petrograd and Tokyo that their agreement did not pose any threat to the United States, the treaty obviously aroused American concern and added to the tensions already existing between the United States and Russia and Japan. Insofar as Russian-American relations were concerned, the new tie represented a setback in Ambassador Francis's efforts to improve relations between the two countries. The agreement was particularly galling to him as it came on the heels of the successful negotiations for the American bank loan to Russia, an arrangement in which he was deeply involved and which he had hoped would herald the beginning of a new period of cooperation between the two nations.

Whether or not the agreement was actually intended to be directed against the United States is difficult to say, since both the public and the secret provisions could have been interpreted either way. Although the signatories insisted that the treaty was intended only against Germany, they would scarcely have said otherwise, regardless of the truth. Moreover, whatever the actual intentions were, the fact that the United States feared its interests were imperiled was sufficient to strain ties with Petrograd.

By the summer of 1916, the optimism Ambassador Francis had brought with him to Russia over the prospect of negotiating a new commercial treaty had almost completely disappeared. It was impossible to avoid the realization that the Imperial government was subordinating other elements of foreign policy to the imperative of avoiding defeat in the war. The secondary importance attached to improving relations with the United States was clear from the refusal to begin treaty talks, from the agreements entered into by Russia at the Paris Economic Conference, and from the refusal to facilitate the provision of American relief supplies to Poland. The Russian-Japanese agreement was only another evidence of the general situation.

This, then, was the situation, when, in July 1916, Foreign Minister Sazonov, with whom successive American Ambassadors had dealt as the principal spokesman and representative of the Tsarist government in the area of foreign affairs, was removed from office by the monarch.

# IX

## Russia's Situation
## Grows More Serious

From the time of his appointment as Foreign Minister in 1910, Sazonov had assumed a broad measure of responsibility in the formulation of Russian foreign policy under the overall and generally loose supervision of the Tsar. Nicholas's selection of Sturmer as Chairman of the Council of Ministers to replace Goremykin in February 1916, however, had weakened the Foreign Minister's position. Sazonov made little effort to conceal the distaste he felt for Sturmer; his attitude stemmed both from his dislike of the Chairman's reactionary views and from apprehension that he wished to take over the post of Foreign Minister. This resentment was apparent to Sturmer, and he retaliated by doing all that he could to undercut Sazonov and restrict his activities and influence.[1]

The situation came to a head in the summer of 1916 in a dispute over the status of Russian Poland, which had been overrun by the German and Austrian forces and was under their occupation. In an effort to retain the loyalty of the Polish subjects during the war and in order to insure that they would remain a part of the Russian Empire after the war, Sazonov urged the ruler to grant Poland a large measure of autonomy. Although Nicholas initially approved the Foreign Minister's draft of a pronouncement and promised to implement it, Sturmer strongly opposed the measure and with the support of the Tsarina succeeded in changing the Tsar's mind. Feeling that under such circumstances he could no longer retain him as Foreign Minister, the Tsar on July 20, 1916, advised Sazonov that he was accepting his resignation on the grounds of ill health.

The news of Sazonov's removal from office reached the French Ambassador that same day, and he immediately met with his British counterpart to discuss it. The two envoys were dismayed at the news since they regarded Sazonov as personally embodying the commitment of the Russian government to remain in the war; the Foreign Minister's ouster might well signify and certainly would facilitate a possible decision by Petrograd to seek a separate peace agreement with Germany. In an effort to reverse the decision, the two Ambassadors simultaneously sent telegrams to their respective military missions at the Tsar's Headquarters, pointing out that at "this decisive moment of the war, anything which could look like a change in the policy of the Allies might have the most disastrous consequences." The ruler, however, refused their request to retain Sazonov as Foreign Minister, and on July 23, 1916, the press announced the resignation of Sazonov and his replacement by Sturmer, who retained his other post of Chairman of the Council of Ministers.[2]

The first word that Ambassador Francis received of Sazonov's replacement was in the Russian newspaper accounts, and he immediately informed the State Department of the development, noting that the Foreign Minister's removal had caused considerable surprise in the capital. Francis stated that the Embassy was attempting to learn the political ramifications of the change and added optimistically that he expected a "pleasant if not cordial official relationship" with Sturmer in his capacity as Foreign Minister.[3]

The envoy's circle of knowledgeable acquaintances was far smaller than that of the British and French Ambassadors and even than that of Ambassador Marye. After failing to learn of Sazonov's removal prior to the announcement of the news in the press, the Embassy then spent two fruitless days of intensive effort after the announcement without being able to obtain any significant details on the change. In a personal letter to the Secretary of State on July 25, 1916, Francis could only summarize the many rumors he had heard, including one alleging that the Tsarina had urged the Foreign Minister to circulate to Russia's allies German proposals for peace. When Sazonov had refused to do so, according to the report, Sturmer had stated he would transmit the German proposals and the Foreign Minister had resigned in protest.

Francis, to his credit, did not accept the rumors as correct, advising Lansing that although Sturmer was regarded as a reactionary, his loyalty to Russia was not in question. The Ambassador concluded, however, on a pessimistic note, giving his opinion that the forced departure of Sazonov and appointment of Sturmer as Foreign Minister was a triumph for the reactionary elements in the Tsarist government and indicated a strengthening of pro-German sentiment.[4]

By mid-August, the American Embassy had obtained a reasonably accurate account of Sazonov's removal, and the Ambassador forwarded this to Secretary Lansing on August 14, 1916. Although Francis correctly ascribed Sazonov's departure from office to a dispute over the proposed promulgation of a statement on Poland, in his letter to Lansing and subsequently the Ambassador referred to Sturmer's takeover of the post of Foreign Minister as a "promotion," apparently mistakenly regarding his earlier position of Chairman of the Council of Ministers as of minimal importance.

In this same letter, Francis submitted his long-range prediction of the future course of events in Russia. The Ambassador was not particularly well-informed as to the situation in Russia and was clearly still greatly influenced by what he regarded as the vast potential for American business there when the war was over. He also had no suspicion that Russia might be defeated or the monarchy overthrown. Nonetheless, the Ambassador's comments were in many ways perceptive. Although he did not foresee a revolution immediately after the war, he warned that if the Tsar did not grant more personal freedom to the population and more power to the Duma, there would be a revolution within a few years.

Francis clearly did not anticipate the extent of the changes that took place in Russia as a result of the Revolutions of 1917. He expected that any restructuring of the regime would be led by the moderate middle-class forces who constituted the Provisional Government after the overthrow of the Tsar and that Nicholas would be replaced by a British-style limited monarch, or at most by an American-style republic. He never anticipated a radical dictatorship which would fail to respect foreign investments and property.

For this reason, Francis's forecast of a revolution did not lessen his enthusiasm for promoting increased American investment in Russia. He advised Lansing that while he did not wish to violate the neutral status of the United States, he believed that Washington should encourage private investment in Russia, recommending this in part because he believed such investments would offset what he feared were the plans of Great Britain and France to capture the trade of Russia after the war. The Ambassador also felt that economic development would hasten the political evolution of Russia and that increased American investment would strengthen the groups working for modernization and liberation and might possibly forestall the impending revolutionary crisis.[5]

The first meeting between Francis and Sturmer following the latter's assumption of the post of Foreign Minister took place on August 23, 1916, when the envoy called to seek confirmation that Petrograd still supported the Open Door policy toward China despite the Russian-Japanese agreement. Sturmer received Francis warmly and assured him that the treaty in no way impaired American interests.[6]

These comments by the new Foreign Minister reflected a change in the tone if not the substance of Russian policy toward the United States. In addition to the conciliatory attitude Sturmer displayed to the Ambassador in their discussion on the Russian-Japanese agreement, the Tsar's reply to President Wilson concerning American relief to Poland, which was probably drafted by the Chairman, was unusually warm in nature.

That Sturmer knew or cared much about the United States is doubtful, and his expressions of friendship for the United States were probably motivated by dislike for Sazonov. The Chairman regarded Sazonov as very closely identified with France and Great

Britain and probably believed that in improving relations with Francis and the United States he was creating a possible counterweight to the influence of Sazonov and the British and French governments.

Despite Sturmer's cordial attitude toward him, Francis never overcame his initial dislike of the Chairman, which was probably reinforced by the generally critical reaction in Russian commercial and financial circles to the ouster of Sazonov.[7]

The Ambassador's low opinion of Sturmer, however, did not stand in the way of his moving rapidly to take advantage of the removal of Sazonov to increase the role of American business in Russia. In addition to his basic objective of negotiating a new treaty, Francis was very interested in encouraging individual American firms to expand their activities in Russia. He personally involved himself in the proposed establishment of a telegraphic cable directly linking that country with the United States and discussed the matter with Sturmer, with Finance Minister Bark, and with the Director-General of the Russian Posts and Telegraph in September 1916. On September 23, 1916, Francis wrote Secretary Lansing that he was pleased that all of the Russian officials with whom he had spoken had voiced support for the project.

The discussions on the telegraphic cable also gave the Ambassador an opportunity for detailed conversations with Finance Minister Bark. Noting in his letter to Lansing that he had previously heard rumors that Bark was in danger of being dismissed as Minister because he was regarded as being wholly under British influence, Francis observed that the rumors of Bark's pro-British sympathies were either baseless or else the Minister was deliberately concealing them from him. He had found Bark to be the most enthusiastic Tsarist official toward the proposed cable, and reported the Finance Minister had stated that British efforts to obtain commercial dominance in Russia were not only not correct but personally distasteful to him.

Francis believed that it was urgent for American business to get a firm foothold when the opportunity existed, and he urged Secretary Lansing to do all that he could to facilitate agreement for construction of the cable project. Although Petrograd appropriated its half of the 6 million dollars required to finance the cable, the arrangement fell through when the American private firms involved failed to approve the agreement.[8]

The Imperial government's receptivity to the proposed cable project led Francis to conclude that the time might be ripe for him to raise again the proposed commercial treaty, and on September 29, 1916, he discussed the matter with Bark. The latter sidestepped the issue, suggesting that the general principles be discussed first with the Foreign Ministry; when these were settled, he assured Francis, the Finance Ministry would be pleased to work out the details.

In accordance with Bark's suggestion, the Ambassador raised the subject of the treaty with Sturmer in the presence of the Deputy Minister of Foreign Affairs, Neratov. Francis was very distressed when the latter told him that the time was "inopportune" to open negotiations on the treaty.[9] In his report to the State Department on the meeting, he made no mention of any comment or reaction by Sturmer to Neratov's statement, suggesting that the Chairman by his silence indicated his reluctance or inability to reopen the treaty discussions.

The reason for the apparent reversal in Sturmer's position on a new treaty is not clear and it is possible that no real change occurred. Sturmer's general statements to the American Ambassador on the subject may not have been intended to convey any serious intention to embark on negotiations in the near future, and Francis may have misinterpreted the Chairman's general remarks.

In view of Sturmer's frequent indications of a friendly attitude toward the United States, it seems more likely that as Chairman of the Council of Ministers he genuinely had been in favor of beginning negotiations on a new treaty. Not until he assumed the post of Foreign Minister would he have realized the extent of the difficulties in reaching an agreement on the passport dispute, and he probably concluded then that it would be preferable to defer negotiations than to have them begin and end in failure.

Sturmer's prestige and influence with the Tsar had also diminished since his initial conversation with Francis on the treaty.

Ambassador Paléologue noted in his diary that reports were circulating in Petrograd to the effect that Sturmer's position in the Council of Ministers had been weakened as a result of the arrest of one of his close advisors on charges of attempting to blackmail a bank. Probably even more detrimental was an apparent cooling in relations between Sturmer and Rasputin. Without the support of the Tsarina, who had given her backing to Sturmer at Rasputin's suggestion, the Chairman's many opponents would have a good prospect of forcing his removal from office. In such circumstances, Sturmer quite probably believed his position was too weak to permit him to make the required concessions on the passport dispute necessary to obtain American agreement to a new treaty.

The Russian government's fear that internal unrest would be the result of a relaxation in the restrictions against the Jews was raised by the Deputy Minister of Foreign Affairs, Neratov, in a meeting with the French Ambassador, when the latter in September 1916 urged Russia to make some concessions in this area, claiming that this was necessary in order to bring the United States to join the Allies. The Deputy Minister reacted forcefully, declaring that any such relaxation was impossible as long as the war continued. He asserted it would raise up the whole country against the government, with the parties of the extreme right accusing Great Britain and France of secretly supporting the claims of the Jews.[10]

It is possible that Neratov raised this objection merely to block a proposal he personally opposed. It is more likely, however, that he and other members of the government sincerely believed a modification in the restrictions against the Jews would bring forth a storm of criticism and opposition to any officials or Minister regarded as being responsible for the change.

On November 11, 1916, Francis again met with Finance Minister Bark, raising the subject of the recommendations of the Allied Economic Conference of the previous June and stating they would be detrimental to Russian-American economic relations. The Finance Minister readily admitted that if put into effect the recommendations would "seriously injure" commercial relations between Russia and any neutral nation. He stressed to Francis his great interest in establishing close commercial and diplomatic ties between his country and the United States and declared that in his most recent meeting with the Tsar he had advocated such a policy. Moreover, he told Francis, Nicholas had given his "unequivocal approval" to this recommendation.

Encouraged by Bark's comments, Francis repeated the statements made by the Deputy Minister of Foreign Affairs to the effect that negotiations for a new commercial treaty would have to be postponed. The Finance Minister declared that he did not agree and saw no reason why negotiations could not begin at once.[11]

The Ambassador was pleased by Bark's statements, though he was naturally puzzled by the differing position on the matter taken by Bark and Neratov. The reason for the conflicting views was never established, and it is possible that the Imperial government modified its position in the time between Neratov's comments to Francis in September and Bark's statements to him in November. It is more likely, however, that Bark, like Sturmer before he became Foreign Minister, was simply unaware of the great gulf that separated the American and Russian positions on a new treaty. The Tsar's reported agreement with Bark that negotiations should be begun was probably a case of the monarch's giving a polite general agreement rather than his hard commitment to the proposal.

In any case, Bark's indication of Russian willingness to open negotiations on a new treaty was never put to the test. His comments to Francis marked the last occasion when the matter was discussed with Petrograd. In the four months left before the abdication of the Tsar and the fall of the Imperial government, both nations were preoccupied with other matters: the American election campaign of 1916 and the rapidly worsening political crisis in Russia.

In the summer and fall of 1916, Russia became more interested in the election campaign in the United States because of the possible effect the vote might have on American policy. Initially, opinion in the Empire favored the Republican Presidential candidate, Justice Charles Evans Hughes, because he was believed to be more willing to take a firm position against German interference with American shipping. On August 3, 1916, the conservative newspaper *Novoe Vremia* contrasted the "manliness and true statesmanship" reflected in the statements of Justice Hughes with the lack thereof in the actions of "the bookish theoretician," President Wilson.[12]

As the campaign progressed, Russian observers came to the conclusion that there was really little difference between the Republican and Democratic Parties as far as their stands on foreign affairs were concerned. *Novoe Vremia* observed on November 8, 1916, that the results of the Presidential election were of little interest to the Russian public and declared that whether Wilson or Hughes won, the foreign policy of the United States would continue to be determined by public opinion, which favored continued neutrality in the war.[13]

The liberal newspaper *Rech*, mistakenly believing that Justice Hughes had been elected President, stated on November 9, 1916, that no significant shift in American policy could be expected.[14] Five days later, after word had been received of Wilson's victory, the paper declared that since no changes had been expected in policy if Hughes were President, the paper was not disappointed in Wilson's election.[15]

Wilson's victory in 1916 meant that the President would remain in office for another four years, but the situation was not paralleled in Russia, where changes in the Council of Ministers were occurring with increasing frequency. The Tsar appointed Alexander Protopopov to the key position of Minister of the Interior at the end of September 1916; Nicholas acted at the insistence of the Tsarina, who had been urged by Rasputin to bring about the appointment. It was a significant choice, since as Minister of the Interior Protopopov was to be responsible for the efforts of the government to quiet internal unrest.

Nicholas was reluctant to appoint Protopopov to the post, and before he finally yielded to the Tsarina's pleadings, he wrote her that Rasputin's opinions of people were sometimes "very strange" and that it was essential to be careful in selecting persons for high government office. Moreover, the Tsar was himself becoming concerned over the frequent changes in the composition of the Council of Ministers, commenting to the Tsarina that "all these changes make my head go round," and that they were not good for the internal stability of the country.[16]

That the internal situation in Russia was deteriorating was becoming obvious. Rumors were prevalent in Petrograd that Sturmer was working to bring about a separate peace with Germany, a view shared by the British Ambassador, who was asked by two members of the royal family to seek to persuade Nicholas to remove Sturmer as Chairman on grounds that he did not command the confidence of the Allied governments. The envoy had decided to take this serious step, so concerned was he over the internal situation in Russia, until warned by the Deputy Minister of Foreign Affairs that this would not be advisable.

The French Ambassador similarly distrusted Sturmer, his suspicions having been reinforced by a report received from a high court functionary on October 5, 1916, that Sturmer and reactionary elements supporting him were planning to assassinate the Tsar or force him to abdicate in favor of his son. The plotters would then name as regent the Tsarina, who would declare the situation facing Russia so grave as to require a withdrawal from the war.[17]

Although the more sensational of the rumors were of doubtful reliability, their circulation was undeniably injurious to Russian morale and the war effort. The situation was exacerbated by a revival of activity by the extreme left. On October 8, 1916, Ambassador Paléologue was told by one of his many informants that the Russian Social Democratic Party and particularly its extreme Bolshevik wing was becoming more active. He noted in his diary that the prolonged war, "doubts about victory, and the difficulties of the economic situation have given revolutionary hopes new life" and prophetically observed that "preparations are being made for the struggle which is believed to be at hand." He noted the great influence being exercised by the Bolshevik leader V. I. Lenin, who was living in exile in Switzerland.

On October 30, 1916, the factory workers in Petrograd went on strike. In a significant indication of growing disloyalty among the troops, two infantry regiments summoned to assist the police in curbing the violence of the workers instead fired on the police. Paléologue was extremely concerned by this development and rushed to see Sturmer, but to his disgust found the Chairman untroubled. The envoy noted that Sturmer stated confidently that while the incident was serious, it would be punished "mercilessly."[18]

To his credit, the Tsar evidenced greater concern over the incident. When the British Ambassador visited the Tsar's Military Headquarters on October 31, 1916, and pressed upon him the urgency of the situation, Nicholas closely questioned him to learn the latest developments in Petrograd. After some discussion, the monarch admitted that the food supply situation was becoming serious, but he believed that the Council of Ministers would be able to rectify the situation.[19]

As was the case with the British and French Ambassadors, Francis noted the developing internal unrest. Although he never had any extended conversation with the Minister of the Interior, he believed him to be the Tsar's "most hated Minister." The Ambassador commented in his diary that Protopopov was rumored to have met with German agents in Sweden while returning from the Allied Economic Conference in June 1916, for the purpose of discussing a separate peace with Germany. Francis also regarded the Minister as being responsible for deceiving the Tsar and Tsarina over the true state of public sentiment. According to the reports reaching Francis, Protopopov arranged for the royal couple to receive letters purportedly from ordinary people pledging their loyalty to the monarchy and urging the Tsar to crack down on internal unrest with an iron hand.[20]

The Ambassador's first report to Washington concerning the worsening internal situation in Russia was sent on November 12, 1916. Francis referred to the strike that had taken place in Petrograd two weeks earlier and described the long lines of people who could be seen waiting outside of shops in the hope of being able to purchase small quantities of meat or sugar. Commenting on reports that recent manifestations of unrest in the food lines and factories had been caused by German agents, he added that there were also rumors that the incidents were being provoked by the government to provide a pretext for concluding a separate peace with Berlin.

Francis by this time had been successful in expanding his circle of knowledgeable contacts in Petrograd and was able to provide more detailed reporting on internal developments in Russia, informing the Secretary of State that every member of the Council of Ministers feared to be removed from office. He noted that the Duma was scheduled to open on November 14, 1916, and that although the newspapers reported that Sturmer would be unable to address the chamber because of illness, the latter was not seriously ill but was seeking an excuse to avoid appearing before the chamber.[21]

That the Chairman's hesitancy in facing the Duma was justified became apparent when the session opened. The leader of the liberal Cadet Party, Professor Pavel Miliukov, made a speech bitterly denouncing the Chairman, accusing him of attempting to negotiate a separate peace, of betraying Russia, of interfering with the movement of supplies to the troops at the front, and of being in the pay of Germany. In ringing phrases, he declared that Sturmer was guilty of treason.

The latter attempted to retaliate by dissolving the Duma and arresting Miliukov, but the Council of Ministers refused to support Sturmer against the Duma. On November 23, 1916, the Tsar dismissed Sturmer from office, both as Chairman and as Foreign Minister, explaining in a letter to the Tsarina that Sturmer had to go as he had lost all public confidence. Nicholas added that in a recent conversation with the British Ambassador, the latter had predicted serious internal unrest in Russia unless Sturmer was replaced.[22]

Francis wrote a long report to the State Department on November 27, 1916, analyzing the results of Sturmer's removal and transmitting the full text of Miliukov's speech, which had not appeared in the Russian press due to censorship. The Ambassador believed that the speech was the primary cause for Sturmer's removal from office, and he was pleased that the Tsar had been obliged to act because of the strength of opinion against the Chairman in the Duma. Francis noted that the development reflected the growing importance of public opinion in Russia and that if the speech had been made before the war it would have resulted in closing the Duma rather than replacement of the unpopular Chairman.

Sturmer's successor as Chairman was Alexander Trepov, who had been Minister of Ways and Communications. As the latter remained in office only six weeks, Francis never had the occasion to deal with him in that capacity, but the Ambassador was concerned by Trepov's reputation as a conservative. In his report to Secretary Lansing of November 27, 1916, Francis noted that Trepov was considered to be the strongest member of the Council of Ministers and was as much of a reactionary as Sturmer. He related an anecdote he had heard: Trepov was a reactionary by conviction whereas Sturmer was only an opportunist.[23]

On December 1, 1916, Francis attended a session of the Duma, the first to be held since the dismissal of Sturmer. The proceedings were disorderly, with speeches by the Ministers interrupted by shouts from the deputies of "Down with the Ministers" and "Down with Protopopov." When Trepov was finally able to make himself heard, he declared that the war would not end until Russia had gained control of the Dardenelles. This policy objective, which had been so strongly supported by the chamber in 1914, received only perfunctory applause, revealing the great increase in popular demand for an immediate peace.

The Ambassador advised Washington that the most significant event of the session was a speech by Vladimir Purishkevich, a member of the extreme right. Although judging by his political views he should have been counted among the strongest supporters of the Tsar, Purishkevich denounced the Council of Ministers for inefficiency if not treason. In a report to the Secretary of State on December 6, 1916, Francis summarized the internal political developments that had occurred in Russia since the opening of the Duma session on November 14, 1916, mistakenly concluding that these events had strengthened public sentiment in favor of continuing the war and had removed all possibility of Petrograd's negotiating a separate peace.[24]

Francis's detailed reporting of political developments in Russia was in marked contrast to the scanty and sporadic coverage given by Marye, and this change was very much appreciated in Washington, where it was becoming increasingly obvious that the United States was about to assume a more important and more active role in international affairs. On January 16, 1917, the Counselor of the State Department, Frank Polk, wrote Francis that he had read the latter's report on the Duma session with great interest, adding that he would be pleased to receive from Francis frequent reports on the political situation in Russia.

The increased American activity on the international scene stemmed from two causes. Domestically, the reelection of President Wilson permitted him to shift his focus away from internal to foreign developments. Secondly, the inclination of the President to attempt to resolve the world situation was strengthened by the receipt on December 12, 1916, of a note from Berlin stating Germany's readiness to enter into peace negotiations with the Allied Powers and requesting the good offices of the United States in passing this information to France, Great Britain, Japan, Rumania, Russia, and Serbia.

Wilson was already at work preparing his own peace proposal when the German note was received; he was planning to urge all the combatants to agree to end the war, and to offer any American assistance toward this end that might be helpful. The President was very disturbed by the German initiative since he believed it would make any plan he put forth appear to have resulted from Berlin's suggestion and therefore greatly reduce the likelihood the Allies would give it a sympathetic reception. Secretary Lansing believed that the German note had created an "atmosphere of hostility" in the Allied nations "toward the arrogant proposals" of the Central Powers and that Wilson would have been justified in immediately abandoning his plan of addressing the belligerents.[25]

The President, however, remained determined to attempt to end the war. On December 18, 1916, two days after the German proposal had been transmitted by the United States to the Allied governments, Lansing forwarded the President's message on the subject, which expressed the hope that the belligerents could find some means of agreeing on a mutually acceptable solution to end the war and offered American good offices to aid the effort.

The President's note to Russia was delivered to the new Foreign Minister, Nikolai Pokrovsky, by Ambassador Francis on December 23, 1916. The wording was virtually identical to that used by Wilson in his notes to the other nations. The President admitted he was "somewhat embarrassed" to make his offer at the same time as the German proposal and emphasized that the American move was in no way associated with that of the Central Powers and that all nations would benefit from an early end to the war.[26]

As Lansing had predicted, the timing of the German peace proposal eliminated any possibility that the Allies would respond favorably to the American initiative. Even before receiving Wilson's note, the Foreign Minister had told the Duma on December 15, 1916—the day after his appointment to the post— that the Allies would reject the German proposal and fight on until the final defeat of the enemy. On December 23, 1916, Pokrovsky met with the Ambassadors of the Allied Powers stationed in Petrograd and agreed that his government would associate itself with the reply to Wilson prepared by the French Premier. The latter, after paying tribute to the sentiments expressed in Wilson's proposal, observed that the President had treated the two groups of belligerents equally. The Allies, according to the French Premier, could not accept this, since they regarded the Central Powers as bearing the sole responsibility for the start of the war.

The Russian press, which in the past had been very critical of the United States for what it regarded as American unwillingness to criticize Germany, initially avoided any comment on Wilson's plan. *Novoe Vremia* on December 22, 1916, observed that the United States had "acted quite correctly" in transmitting the German proposal to the Allies and that Washington had only fulfilled its formal obligation and had "avoided the trap which was baited by German slyness." [27]

The Russian attitude hardened, however, following a press

conference by Pokrovsky on December 26, 1916, in which he declared that Tsarist foreign policy remained unchanged and that the war would continue until final victory. Turning to Wilson's proposal, he observed that the initiative had been taken almost simultaneously with that of Germany and charged that although the German note made it appear that Berlin was suing for peace, in fact it was a military move associated with Germany's desire to show itself as "a proud victor." If Russia were to enter into negotiations in such circumstances, it would be tantamount to admitting this, and Pokrovsky declared that his nation was not defeated and would not indicate that it was.

The Foreign Minister's comments stimulated intense criticism of the American proposal in the Russian press. On January 1, 1917, *Novoe Vremia* alleged that some of the language in President Wilson's note was similar to what had appeared earlier in a German newspaper, implying that the correspondence indicated collusion between the American and German governments.[28] Even the liberal paper *Rech* on December 28, 1916, characterized Wilson's proposals as "premature" and warned that peace negotiations at that moment would "only serve Germany's designs to cause strife, discontent, and mistrust among the Allies" and immeasurably strengthen the Central Powers.[29]

Despite the rash of unfavorable comment about American policy, Francis surprisingly did not consider that the incident had placed any significant strain on Russian-American relations. In describing the new Foreign Minister in a message to Secretary Lansing on January 16, 1917, the Ambassador exhibited no concern over the reaction in Petrograd to Wilson's note nor to the sharp criticism of the United States it had provoked. Francis observed that he was "favorably impressed" by Pokrovsky and that the latter appeared "courageous and sincere."[30]

The Allied response to Wilson followed the lines of the draft prepared by the French Premier, as had been agreed by Pokrovsky in his meeting with the Allied Ambassadors. In the light of this polite but definite rejection of the proposal, its acceptance by the Central Powers on December 26 was inconsequential. The American effort to bring about an end to the war had failed.

Thus, although the year 1916 ended as it had begun, with Washington still intent on preserving its neutrality and Russia fighting desperately to avoid defeat, there had been significant changes in the two countries during the year. In the United States, President Wilson had won reelection to a second term. While his administration was still interested primarily in assuring the nation's continued economic prosperity and neutrality, there was little doubt that the country was moving toward a more active involvement in international affairs. Even an eventual American entry into the war had become a serious possibility.

Unlike the United States, Russia could boast of neither political stability nor progress. In addition to numerous ministerial shuffles during the year, there had been two changes in the position of Chairman of the Council of Ministers, and a third was about to take place. It was obvious that economic conditions in the country were worsening and internal unrest spreading. However, no national consensus had been reached as yet as to which road to follow: whether to withdraw from the war and cooperate with Germany as advocated by many on the extreme right, or to seek popular support for a program of continuing on in the conflict by appointing a Cabinet responsible to the Duma, as was urged by the liberals and supported by Great Britain and France.

With regard to Russian-American relations, little change occurred in 1916. Although Francis's relations with the Tsar were less intimate than had been those of his predecessor, the Ambassador had largely succeeded in overcoming the initial suspicion in Petrograd about the departure of Marye and Francis's arrival. He had further established relatively close bonds with Sturmer and with Finance Minister Bark and Foreign Minister Pokrovsky.

Insofar as the proposed commercial treaty was concerned, it was still blocked by the two nations' basic disagreement over the passport dispute. Despite the Finance Minister's words of encouragement to Francis, it is doubtful if the Tsar, Sturmer, or the latter's replacement Trepov, could ever have accepted Washington's position on the issue as long as the war continued. Similarly, "on Far East policy" the United States and Russia were as far apart as ever.

On balance then, bilateral ties at the end of 1916 were very much as they had been at the start of the war, cool and correct. Any significant extension of sympathy for Great Britain and France to include Russia was blocked by what the American government and people regarded as the arbitrary nature of the Tsarist regime. This characterization was embodied in U.S. eyes in the refusal of Russia to terminate restrictions against the Jews and negotiate a new commercial treaty.

In Petrograd this coolness was reciprocated. Fighting desperately to remain in the war, the Imperial government was far more concerned with maintaining close relations with its allies than with bettering ties with the United States. In any case, it regarded Washington's demands as unjustified interference in its internal affairs and saw little reason to agree to them in return for the likelihood of obtaining only marginally improved relations with the United States. To the Russian press and to a large part of the Russian government, the State Department's efforts to maintain a neutral and impartial stand between the belligerent camps was regarded as undue consideration for the Central Powers. This, then, was the status of affairs as 1917 began, a year that was to see the overthrow of the Russian monarchy and the entry of America into the war.

# X

# The Last Days
# of the Monarchy

The full extent of the popular dissatisfaction in Russia toward the government's conduct of the war became apparent on December 30, 1916, when Rasputin, the close confidant of the Tsarina, was murdered by persons related to the royal family who feared he was leading the nation and the dynasty to its doom. Francis informed the State Department that the assassination had caused great tension in Russia and noted that Rasputin had been killed because of the influence he had with the Tsarina and the belief that he was bringing disgrace on the royal family.[1]

The incident caused great concern on the part of the British and French Ambassadors, who feared it might signal the disintegration of the Tsar's authority and the country's eventual withdrawal from the war. On January 4, 1917, the French envoy met with Count Kokovtsov, who had been Chairman of the Council of Ministers from September 1911 to February 1914, to learn his views on the situation. Kokovtsov was very gloomy, predicting there would be a revolution against the ruler as soon as a military defeat or famine occurred.

Apprehensive over these words, Ambassador Paléologue obtained an audience with Nicholas to express his concern over the course of events. The French envoy, however, found the meeting on January 7, 1917, most unsatisfactory, returning from the audience with the conviction that the Tsar had lost all hope and was "resigned to disaster." [2]

The British Ambassador was similarly disturbed over developments and obtained an audience with the monarch on January 12, 1917. Raising the subject of a meeting of representatives of the Allied Powers that was about to open in Petrograd, he stated in unusually blunt language that even if the meeting succeeded in establishing closer cooperation among the Allies, there was no guarantee the present Russian government would remain in office or that its commitments would be observed by a successor regime. The Ambassador stressed that revolutionary language was being heard not only in Petrograd but throughout the country and cautioned the Tsar that other assassinations might follow that of Rasputin. Finally, the envoy warned that if Nicholas used strong measures to repress the nation, including closing the Duma, he would lose all hope for Russia. In prophetic words he cautioned, "Your Majesty must remember that the people and army are but one, and that in the event of a revolution only a small portion of the army can be counted on to defend the dynasty."

These strong words left the Tsar nervous and agitated but did not succeed in convincing him to reverse his policies and improve relations with the Duma. As the British envoy concluded, "Whatever momentary impression I may have made was not strong enough to counterbalance the adverse influence" of the Tsarina.[3]

The monarch's refusal to adopt a conciliatory attitude toward the Duma was apparent on January 9, 1917, when still another change was made in the post of Chairman of the Council of Ministers. Nicholas accepted Trepov's resignation and named Prince Nicholas Golitzin, who had been head of the commission providing relief to the Russian prisoners of war, as Trepov's successor. The Tsar's acceptance of Trepov's resignation clearly indicated that he was not prepared to accept the British Ambassador's warning. Some time earlier, Nicholas had written the Tsarina that it was "unpleasant to speak to a man one does not like and does not trust, such as Trepov." But first of all, he added, "it is necessary to find a substitute for him, and then kick him out after he has done the dirty work." The Tsar added that he meant to let Trepov close the Duma and then force him to resign, so that the Chairman would bear all the public resentment for the unpopular decision.[4]

Trepov, however, thwarted the plan by refusing to remain in office unless the Tsar ousted Protopopov, the Minister of the Interior, who had become the most unpopular man in the Council of Ministers and whose dismissal was being sought by many members of the Duma. When Nicholas refused to supplant the Minister, Trepov thereupon resigned as Chairman. Francis reported this development to the State Department on January 16, 1917, but gave little detail on the rapidly developing political controversy in Petrograd.[5]

Meanwhile, at the same time as conditions were worsening in Russia, President Wilson prepared to make a new attempt to bring the war to an immediate end. In doing so, he was ignoring the Allied rejection on January 10, 1917, of his earlier attempt, a response his own Secretary of State considered to be a "practical announcement that the Allies intend to continue the war until Germany was defeated and would not consider negotiations for peace before they had won a complete military victory." [6]

Despite the unequivocal nature of the Allied position, Wilson refused to give up his efforts. As Lansing noted, "It was not in Mr. Wilson's nature to admit defeat." The President resolved to find some means of bringing pressure on the Allies to soften their position and prepared a speech that was in effect an appeal to the populations of the Allied Powers over the heads of their governments to urge consideration of a negotiated peace.[7]

Wilson delivered the speech, which Lansing regarded as "one of his most notable utterances," to the Senate on January 22, 1917, urging the need for a peace without delay and declaring that the United States would have to participate in the postwar international system to prevent future conflicts. His call for creation of a world organization of some sort to preserve the peace and his proposal for a "peace without victory" made the speech a very significant statement of American policy, but in terms of bringing an immediate end to the war, it failed. As Secretary Lansing noted, the governments of the Allied Powers and the bulk of their populations were as suspicious of the President's speech as they had been of his peace proposal of December 1916.[8]

In accordance with Wilson's desire to obtain the widest possible dissemination of his speech, American embassies in all of the belligerent nations were instructed to forward copies of it to the respective Foreign Ministries and to the press. In Petrograd, Francis delivered the text to the Foreign Minister on January 22, 1917, reporting to the State Department that Pokrovsky had received him cordially and had given him permission to send copies to the newspapers.

The Ambassador personally was greatly impressed by the President's proposals and informed the State Department on January 23, 1917, that the speech was "truly American," "timely," and "forceful" and would make a lasting impression. In glowing terms he declared he was "proud to have been the Agent by which it was transmitted to this absolute monarchy, where I have the honor to be the representative of this immortal declaration of the independence of humanity." [9]

The Tsarist government never formally replied to the President's speech, a response that was almost certainly to be expected since the regime was desperately devoting all of its attention to the dual problems of stemming the growing internal unrest and maintaining the struggle against the Central Powers. Again, the Russian position on continuing the war until the military defeat of Germany remained unchanged and had been communicated to the United States in reply to President Wilson's earlier peace proposal, and a second negative response would serve little other than to place unnecessary strain on relations with America.

Francis reported the initial and informal reaction to the President's speech in a message to the State Department on January 27, 1917. The general response was to regard Wilson's proposal for a new world order as a "Utopian dream" which could not be realized for many years to come. He noted that the speech had gained widespread attention in Russia and that the most frequent criticism of it dealt with the proposal that the war be settled without victory to either side. Quite naturally, opinion in Russia ran that Germany had been responsible for starting the war and that the settlement proposed by President Wilson would enable Germany to escape the punishment it deserved.[10]

In large part, any extended consideration of the President's peace plan was precluded by the rapid course of events there and in the United States. On January 31, 1917, the German Ambassador informed Lansing that Berlin would begin unrestricted submarine warfare against all shipping in the waters around Great Britain, France, Italy, and the eastern Mediterranean. This was a grave step for Germany to take, as it was in effect a repudiation of the assurances it had given previously that American lives and shipping would not be jeopardized by submarine warfare. Washington reacted strongly to this challenge, on February 3, 1917, formally breaking diplomatic relations with Germany. Even the prospect of an American entry into the war could not be ruled out, since Lansing recommended such a move to the President.

The news that the Americans had ruptured diplomatic relations reached Petrograd on February 3, 1917. By the following day, Francis had still not received any official confirmation of the report, and he frantically cabled Washington for information, commenting that the Russians were very pleased with the strong stand taken by Washington toward Germany and were beginning to regard the United States as an ally.[11]

The Russian government and population were indeed overjoyed at the split between Germany and America and the possibility the latter might enter the war on the side of the Allies. Such a reinforcement would significantly strengthen the Allies and materially improve the prospects for Russia to hang on in the war until final victory.

The first reflection of Petrograd's new attitude toward the United States appeared in the public comments of the Chairman of the Council of Ministers to the President's speech of January 22, 1917. Prince Golitzin declared that the Allies had made many sacrifices to the ideals they defended when they entered the war and could not agree to Wilson's proposal of a peace without victory, but he added that the President's comments showed that he had associated himself with the general principles of the Allies. The overall tone of the Chairman's comments was far more cordial to the United States than was Foreign Minister Pokrovsky's response to the President's earlier peace proposal, and the Imperial authorities insured widespread publicity to the Chairman's remarks by having them reported in the official government gazette on February 7, 1917.[12]

Russian pleasure at the new position of the United States was mitigated by continuing deterioration in the internal situation in Russia. Nicholas, despite the unparalleled representations to him by the British and French Ambassadors on the gravity of the situation, was making no efforts to improve it. On February 18, 1917, the British envoy informed London that the situation was grave and that only the wish of the Duma to avoid action compromising the conduct of the war had prevented an explosion, warning that a predicted scarcity of food and fuel might spark the revolution he feared.[13]

On February 25, 1917, Francis similarly alerted the State Department that the opening of the new Duma session two days later might well be a decisive moment in Russian history, noting that the session was anticipated with "great uneasiness" and that concerted action by the workers to conduct strikes and illegal demonstrations was expected. By March 6, 1917, the supply situation had worsened, and the capital was suffering from a shortage of bread and wood for fuel. The French Ambassador discussed the situation with Pokrovsky that day; he was depressed to note that the Foreign Minister "did not conceal his anxiety" over the situation. Two days later, Paléologue observed mobs in Petrograd shouting for bread and peace, and on the following day, March 9, 1917, the mobs looted bakeries in search of bread. The Cossacks, the Tsar's most dependable military forces, were called to restore order and killed several of the rioters.[14]

Francis made his first report to Washington on the worsening situation in Petrograd on March 9, 1917, when he informed Lansing that there had been demonstrations in the streets by the laboring classes, particularly women unable to purchase food for their families. The Ambassador at this juncture was apparently unaware of the serious nature of the situation, as he transmitted his report to the State Department by surface transportation rather than by cable.[15] Between March 9 and March 14, 1917, conditions in Petrograd continued to worsen as amid much confusion, the troops refused to fire on the demonstrators, and the Council of Ministers found itself powerless to influence the situation. In the vacuum of authority that existed, the Duma established an Executive Committee which organized a Provisional Government, and under pressure the Tsar abdicated. The day of the Romanovs was over.

On March 14, 1917, as soon as telegraphic communications had been restored, Francis sent his first report to Washington on the situation. He summarized the rapid developments of the three previous days during which communications had been suspended: the Duma had refused to obey the Tsar's orders to adjourn, the Provisional Government had been established by the Duma, the Ministers had resigned, and the troops had supported the new government in the capital.[16]

The fall of the monarchy and the establishment of the Provisional Government were very welcome to Francis, who only three days after the Tsar's abdication, on March 18, 1917, asked the State Department for permission to recognize the new regime promptly. In urging this course he declared that the Revolution represented the victory in Russia of the democratic principle of government, of which the United States was a foremost champion in the world, and he stressed that American recognition would be particularly important to the new government and would greatly strengthen it. Finally, he reported that the President of the Duma and Miliukov, the new Foreign Minister, had pledged that they would keep Russia in the war, and he warned that the survival of the new government and the success of the Revolution depended upon the Provisional Government's ability to do this successfully.

On the following day, Francis again cabled to urge support for the Provisional Government. Going even further than advocating immediate recognition, he recommended that the United States strengthen the new regime by providing financial assistance.

In an effort to provide the administration with arguments to use in winning public support in the United States for such a policy, he urged that it was "immeasurably important to the Jews" that the Revolution succeed and warned that great discretion would have to be exercised in any modification of the restrictions against the Jews in Russia since to do otherwise might turn against the Revolution the "anti-Semites who are numerous here."[17]

By March 20, 1917, Francis had still not received a reply to his request for permission to extend American recognition to the Provisional Government. Growing increasingly anxious that opposition to this move might be developing in Washington, he again cabled the State Department pressing for a favorable response. Pursuing his campaign, on March 21, 1917, the Ambassador sent still another message to Washington on the issue, reporting that he had met with Prince Lvov, the President of the Provisional Government, whom he described as "possibly the most respected man in Russia." To bolster his call for a rapid response, Francis warned that Paléologue was reported to have received authorization from Paris to extend French recognition and suggested that unless the United States acted rapidly, it might lose the advantages to be gained by being the first nation to establish diplomatic relations with the new regime.

In reality, Francis' concern was unjustified, as the Department of State agreed with him that the Provisional Government should be accorded recognition and instructed him to do so on March 20, 1917. When the cable reached Francis two days later, it left him overjoyed and he jubilantly telegraphed Washington, "Earnest congratulations. Hearty thanks."[18]

The American envoy was so intent on having the United States be the first nation to recognize the new Russian government that he immediately arranged to carry out his instructions. At three o'clock in the afternoon of March 22, 1917, Francis saw Prince Lvov and in the presence of members of the Provisional Government and of his own staff formally extended American recognition to the new regime. The era of American relations with the Imperial government was over and a new chapter had begun.

# XI

## Conclusions

The rapidity with which the United States extended diplomatic recognition to the Russian Provisional Government in March 1917 indicated how much it welcomed the establishment of a democratically inclined regime in Petrograd. This move was followed two weeks later, on April 2, 1917, by President Wilson's message to Congress requesting that it recognize that a state of war existed with Germany. Despite the conjunction of the two developments, the American entry into the war was only marginally affected by the Russian Revolution. The primary factor in the United States decision was the policy pursued by Berlin, particularly the declaration of unrestricted submarine warfare on January 31, 1917, and the so-called Zimmerman note, which appeared in the American press on March 1, 1917, and indicated that Germany was attempting to incite Mexico to attack the United States in the event of an American entry into the war.[1]

The internal changes in Russia, nonetheless, were an important consideration in Washington's decision to enter the war. Distaste for the Tsarist government had been significant in prompting influential elements in the United States including, but not limited to, Jewish circles to press for strict observance of neutrality and to oppose any assistance to Russia.

The new Provisional Government was hailed by virtually all

elements in the United States. Interestingly, Secretary Lansing stressed the important effect U.S. belligerency would have upon Russia when on March 19, 1917, he urged Wilson to declare war against Germany, commenting that the American declaration of war would encourage and strengthen the Provisional Government. He pointed out that it was democratic in character and that the United States ought to sympathize with it, emphasizing that the new regime was founded on its hatred of absolutism and "would be materially benefited by feeling that this republic was arrayed against the same enemy of liberalism."[2]

The extent of American dislike for the Russian Imperial government may at first glance appear surprising. Throughout the greater part of the nineteenth century, relations between the two nations were relatively cordial, and although they were shaken by the American termination of the commercial treaty, by 1914 they had partially recovered from their low point. Moreover, the outbreak of war resulted in a substantial increase in Russian commercial and financial ties with the United States. In addition to the significant profits that accrued to the United States from this expansion, it created the expectation in Washington and to some extent in Petrograd that the end of the war would see a substantial participation by American business in the Empire's economic development.

Despite these positive factors, American relations with the Tsarist government never improved beyond the stage of cool correctness existing in 1914. In part, this was due to the differences between the two nations over their interests in the Far East. As early as 1899, Russia had been reluctant to agree to U.S. proposals for the establishment of the Open Door policy in China, and this hostility was compounded by Washington's sympathy for Tokyo during the Russo-Japanese War and was further strengthened after the outbreak of the World War. By that time, Japan was regarded as a potential rival of the United States, and Russia was forced by the exigencies of the war to give Tokyo virtually a blank check to carry out its policies in the area. In particular, the United States was concerned by Petrograd's failure

to support efforts to restrain Japan from threatening the independence and territorial integrity of China. However, the differences that existed between America and Russia over their goals
and interests in the Far East were not primarily responsible for
the cool relations that persisted between the two governments.
One indication of this is the rapidity with which Washington
recognized the Provisional Government, despite the lack of any
evidence that the new regime would pursue policies in the Far
East significantly different from its predecessor.

A more serious impediment to any improvement in relations
during the war was the United States' determination to maintain
its neutrality, an objective widely misunderstood in the Empire.
Both the Russian government and the general population held a
grossly exaggerated view of the importance of pro-German sentiment in America and believed that Wilson's policy was strongly
influenced by this factor. What to Washington was a sincere effort
to preserve the nation's status as a neutral, a policy ardently desired by most of the American population throughout the greater
part of the period, was regarded in Russia as extreme reluctance
to avoid alienating Germany. In these circumstances, nothing
would have satisfied Petrograd other than a markedly pro-Allied
attitude on the part of the United States, something neither its
government nor population was prepared to accept.

In America, the most important factor in preventing any
improvement in relations was the strong feeling against the arbitrary nature of the Tsarist regime, a view that became linked in
public opinion with the passport dispute. As such, it became a
matter of importance in American internal politics, as the comments of Secretary Lansing and Ambassador Francis attest.
Washington sincerely felt it could sign no new commercial treaty
which did not settle the dispute along the lines desired by the
United States. Indeed, the Wilson administration felt obliged to
press for a satisfactory solution as rapidly as possible in order
to ward off expected domestic political criticism that it was
tolerating injustice in Russia.

Within the Empire, this attitude was strongly resented. It

was understandably denounced as foreign interference in Russian internal affairs and was attacked throughout the war by those who were in favor of continued restrictions against the Jews. It was also opposed by those who might have been inclined to support some change but who, as the Deputy Foreign Minister indicated to the French Ambassador in September 1916, feared that a violent reaction to a shift in policy might endanger the government's existence.

Thus, any analysis of bilateral relations during the war leads to the conclusion that the two nations were separated by a wall of mistrust and ignorance. Neither could appreciate the limited room for maneuver available to the other as a result of historical and current constraints upon its freedom of action. In these circumstances, no significant improvement in ties was possible short of a marked change such as the overthrow of the monarchy and the establishment of the Provisional Government.

It is difficult to speculate what the course of Russian-American diplomacy would have been had the Provisional Government survived. However, the major irritants, strategic rivalries in the Far East and American resentment over internal Russian policies, continue to impede an improvement in relations today, and despite the optimistic assumptions of Ambassador Francis, Secretary Lansing, and others, it is logical to assume that many of the problems that strained ties before and during World War I would have been difficult to solve in negotiations with the Provisional Government after the end of hostilities.

It is even further afield from the subect of this study to attempt to relate it to current American relations with the Soviet Union. It may be useful to remember, however, that throughout the wartime period the United States expected Russia to agree to concessions in the political area in return for the prospect of significant economic gains to accrue to both nations from an expanded commercial exchange. Today, this nation again seeks a moderation in restrictive internal Soviet policies and looks to a significant increase in economic relations as a possible *quid pro quo*. The circumstances now are of course very different; neither nation then had the military capability to threaten the very survival of the other. Nonetheless, it may be wise not to be over-confident as to the extent of concessions attainable from the Soviet Union as, not for the first time, we seek a détente with Russia.

# Comments on
# Principal Sources

The most valuable source of information for this study was the unpublished documents of the United States Department of State, located in the National Archives in Washington. These documents included the reports of the two American Ambassadors whose service in Petrograd coincided with this period, other communications exchanged between the Embassy in Russia and the State Department, and correspondence between President Wilson and other American officials. All of these throw light on the question of Russian-American relations as seen in Washington, and in the Embassy in Petrograd. They complement the sparse selection of documents dealing with Russia contained in the published papers of the State Department: *Papers Relating to the Foreign Relations of the United States* and *The Lansing Papers*.

Moreover, both American Ambassadors to Petrograd, George Marye and his successor David Francis, published works dealing with their service in Russia. Marye's volume is the more useful of the two because it was based upon his diary which was written at the time the events described took place, and because he omitted many pertinent details from his relatively infrequent reports to Washington. These details, fortunately, are contained in profusion in his book, *Nearing the End in Imperial Russia.* Ambassador Francis's book. *Russia from the American Embassy,* is of more limited value. Not only was his official reporting of developments in Russia much greater in scope and frequency than his predecessor's, but the book was compiled from private letters written by Francis to his family and friends, frequently in very general language.

On the Russian side, material is more difficult to obtain. The Soviets have published very little of significance on Russian-American relations during the war, even though voluminous material on Russian relations with other nations was made public. This may have been due to the relatively low priority accorded relations with the United States by the Soviets following their seizure of power, compared to relations with Great Britain and France. Again, the Soviets may have felt no incentive to publicize this section of the Russian archives, which presumably would not have met the Soviet objectives of showing the United States in a critical light.

The activities of the Russian Ambassador to the United States are also largely obscure. All of the available information indicates that his role was a passive one and that most of the initiatives in Russian-American relations during the war were taken in Petrograd between the American Embassy and the Russian Foreign Office. This situation was encouraged by both American Ambassadors' being forceful men who wished to be fully involved in the course of relations. Possibly, too, Ambassador Bakhmet'ev's having an American wife was regarded by the Russian government as creating divided loyalties; therefore he was not made privy to the sensitive policy discussions.

Fortunately, there is available in the United States the greater part of the runs of three of the most important Russian newspapers: *Rech,* the organ of the liberal Cadet Party, *Novoe Vremia,* a conservative paper, and *Pravitel'stvenni Vestnik,* the official Russian government gazette. Although these papers devoted relatively little space to Russian-American relations, reflecting the secondary importance of the subject in Russia, the occasional editorial comment they devoted to the foreign policy activities of the United States provides an interesting and useful adjunct with which to examine material from other sources.

The Russian Foreign Minister, Sazonov, the French Ambassador, Paléologue, and the British Ambassador, Buchanan, all published books on their experiences in Russia during the period. Although they devote almost no attention to Russian-American relations, their books are useful for the light they shed on the internal and international policies pursued by the Tsarist government.

# Notes

*Chapter One*

1. *The Memoirs of John Quincy Adams,* edited by Charles F. Adams, Philadelphia, 1875, Vol. VI, p. 179.
2. J. Hildt, "Early Diplomatic Negotiations of the United States with Russia," *Johns Hopkins University Studies in Historical and Political Science,* Vol. XXIV, p. 55.
3. F. Golder, *Guide to Materials for American History in Russian Archives,* Washington, 1917, p. 55.
4. F. Golder, "Russian-American Relations During the Crimean War," *American Historical Review,* Vol. XXXI (1926), p. 465.
5. E. Adamov, "Russia and the United States at the Time of the Civil War," *Journal of Modern History,* Vol. II (1930), p. 592.
6. F. Golder, "Russian-American Relations During the Crimean War," *American Historical Review,* Vol. XXXI (1926), p. 464.
7. "K istorii russko-amerikanskikh otnoshenii vo vremia grazhdanskoi voiny v S.SH.A." *Krasnyi Arkhiv,* Vol. XCIV (1939), pp. 97–153.
8. B. Taylor, *The Life and Letters of Bayard Taylor,* Boston, 1884, Vol. I, pp. 401–403.
9. B. Egert, *The Conflict Between the United States and Russia,* St. Petersburg, 1912, p. 8.
10. E. Zabriskie, *American-Russian Rivalry in the Far East,* Philadelphia, 1946, pp. 15–16.

11. M. Laserson, *The American Impact on Russia*, New York, 1950, p. 363.

12. "Severo-Amerikanskiye Soyedinennye Shtaty i tsarskaya Rossiya v 90 godakh XIX veka," *Krasnyi Arkhiv*, Vol. LII, (1932), pp. 125–142.

13. United States Department of State, *Foreign Relations of the United States*, hereafter *Foreign Relations*, Washington, 1899, pp. 128–142.

14. H. Pringle, *Theodore Roosevelt*, New York, 1931, p. 379.

15. E. Morison, *The Letters of Theodore Roosevelt*, Cambridge, Mass., 1951–1954, Vol. IV, p. 1284.

16. T. Dennett, *Roosevelt and the Russo-Japanese War*, New York, 1925, pp. 176–177.

17. Zabriskie, *op. cit.*, p. 137.

18. *Ibid.*, p. 160.

19. *Foreign Relations, 1911*, pp. 696–697.

20. Egert, *op. cit.*, p. 45.

21. United States Department of State, Unpublished Archives of the Department of State, 1914–1917 (hereafter Archives), Dispatch from St. Petersburg of February 14, 1914, File. No. 861.002/34.

22. *Stenograficheskii Otchet Gosudarstvennuyu Dumy*, 1912, pp. 2172–2173.

23. *Vestnik Russko-Amerikanskoi Torgovy Palaty*, Moscow, December 1915, pp. 432–433.

24. R. Baker, *Woodrow Wilson, Life and Letters*, Garden City, N.Y., 1927–1929, Vol. IV, p. 55.

25. R. Curry, *Woodrow Wilson and Far Eastern Policy, 1913–1921*, New York, 1957, p. 17.

26. V. Kokovtsov, *Out of My Past, the Memoirs of Count Kokovtsov*, Stanford, California, 1935, p. 275.

27. V. Gurko, *Features and Figures of the Past*, Stanford, California, 1939, p. 465.

28. Archives, Dispatch of February 14, 1914, from American Embassy in St. Petersburg, File No. 861.002/34.

29. *New York Times*, February 21, 1914, p. 3.

30. *Pravitel'stvenni Vestnik*, March 2, 1914, p. 5.

31. Archives, Dispatch of May 28, 1914, from American Embassy in St. Petersburg, File No. 861.032/5.

*Chapter Two*

1. Archives, Telegram of June 22, 1914, to St. Petersburg from the State Department, File No. 123 M 361.
2. *Russkiia Viedomosti*, October 12, 1914, p. 4.
3. S. Sazonov, *Fateful Years, 1909–1916*, London, 1928, pp. 174–176.
4. Archives, Telegram from American Embassy in St. Petersburg of July 25, 1914, File No. 763.72/2.
5. Archives, Telegram from American Embassy in St. Petersburg of August 3, 1914, File No. 763.72/92.
6. *Foreign Relations, 1914 Supplement*, Washington, 1928, pp. 18–19.
7. Archives, Telegram from American Embassy in Petrograd of August 6, 1914, File No. 763.72119/6.
8. *Foreign Relations, The Lansing Papers,* Vol. I, 1939, Washington, p. 1.
9. *Russkiia Viedomosti*, August 6, 1914, p. 2.
10. G. Marye, *Nearing the End in Imperial Russia*, Philadelphia, 1929, pp. 17–19.
11. Archives, Telegram from American Embassy in Petrograd of August 24, 1914, File No. 123 M 362.
12. Marye, *op. cit.*, p. 22.
13. *Ibid.*, p. 22.
14. A. Link, *Wilson, the Struggle for Neutrality*, Princeton, N.J., 1960, p. 51.
15. Link, *op. cit.*, p. 43.
16. *Foreign Relations, 1914 Supplement*, Washington, 1928, pp. 1–9.
17. *Russkiia Viedomosti*, September 24, 1914, p. 3.
18. *Foreign Relations, The Lansing Papers,* Vol. I, 1939, Washington, pp. 131–132.
19. *Ibid.*
20. *Ibid.*, p. 133.
21. *Ibid.*, p. 134.
22. *Ibid.*, p. 135.
23. Link, *op. cit.*, p. 133.
24. *Pravitel'stvenni Vestnik*, March 18, 1916, p. 5.
25. *Pravitel'stvenni Vestnik*, October 30, 1914, p. 4.

*Chapter Three*

1. *Ruskiia Viedomosti,* October 14, 1914, p. 4.
2. Marye, *op. cit.,* p. 35.
3. Archives, Dispatch from Ambassador Marye of October 30, 1914, File No. 123M361/14.
4. Marye, *op. cit.,* pp. 37–38.
5. Archives, Dispatch from Ambassador Marye of October 28, 1914, File No. 124.613/10.
6. Archives, Memorandum of Robert Lansing of December 7, 1914, File No. 711.612/263.
7. Archives, Memorandum of Robert Lansing, dated December 8, 1914, File No. 711.612/264.
8. Archives, Memorandum of Robert Lansing of December 14, 1914, File No. 711.612/265.

*Chapter Four*

1. *Foreign Relations, 1914 Supplement,* Washington, 1928, pp. 162–172.
2. *Pravitel'stvenni Vestnik,* August 8, 1914, p. 2.
3. Y. Yeleonskaya, *Voina e Kultura,* Moscow, 1915, pp. 34–38.
4. Archives, Dispatch from State Department to Ambassador Marye of December 3, 1914, File No. 761.94/85a.
5. Archives, Dispatch from Ambassador Marye of January 25, 1915, File No. 761.94/87.
6. *Ibid.*
7. *Foreign Relations, 1914 Supplement,* Washington, 1928, pp. 206–207.
8. *Foreign Relations, 1915,* Washington, 1924, pp. 79–145.
9. *Foreign Relations, The Lansing Papers,* Vol. II, 1940, Washington, pp. 424–425.
10. Archives, Dispatch of Ambassador Marye, dated May 9, 1915, File No. 793.94/374.
11. *Foreign Relations, 1915,* Washington, 1924, p. 146.

*Chapter Five*

1. M. Paléologue, *An Ambassador's Memoirs*, London, 1923, Vol. I, p. 222.
2. *Ibid.*, p. 225.
3. Archives, Dispatch from Ambassador Marye of February 13, 1915, File No. 861.032/6.
4. *Vestnik Russko-Amerikanskoi Torgovy Palaty*, Moscow, March 1915, pp. 77–81.
5. *Pravitel'stvenni Vestnik*, March 18, 1916, p. 5.
6. *Ibid.*, March 24/April 6, 1916, p. 1.
7. *Foreign Relations, 1915 Supplement*, Washington, 1928, pp. 94–99.
8. *Rech*, February 5, 1915, p. 1.
9. Link, *op. cit.*, p. 372.
10. R. Lansing, *War Memoirs of Robert Lansing*, Indianapolis, 1935, pp. 19–21.
11. *Foreign Relations, 1915 Supplement*, Washington, 1928, pp. 393–397.
12. *Rech*, May 3, 1915, p. 2; May 4, 1915, p. 1.
13. Marye, *op. cit.*, p. 163.
14. *Rech*, June 28, 1915, p. 3.
15. *Novoe Vremia*, June 23, 1915, p. 4.
16. Marye, *op. cit.*, p. 179.
17. *Novoe Vremia*, July 20, 1915, p. 3.
18. Archives, Cable from Lansing to Ambassador Marye, dated June 19, 1915, File No. 711.612/240a.
19. Archives, Letter from Marye to Department of State, dated June 23, 1915, File No. 711.612/242.
20. Archives, Memorandum from Lansing to President Wilson, dated July 26, 1915, File No. 711.612/242.
21. Archives, Note from President Wilson to Lansing, dated July 29, 1915, File No. 712.612/242 1/2.
22. Marye, *op. cit.*, pp. 242–243.
23. *Novoe Vremia*, August 18, 1915, p. 1.
24. Archives, Dispatch from Ambassador Marye, dated August 31, 1915, File No. 763.72/2161.
25. *Novoe Vremia*, August 9, 1915, p. 5; August 26, 1915, p. 4.
26. Marye, *op. cit.*, pp. 238–239.

*Chapter Six*

1. Gurko, *op. cit.*, pp. 576–577.
2. Paléologue, *op. cit.*, Vol. II, 74–75.
3. Marye, *op. cit.*, pp. 247–252.
4. *Ibid.*, p. 288.
5. Paléologue, *op. cit.*, Vol. II, pp. 110–111.
6. Archives, Dispatch from Charles Wilson, dated November 29, 1915, File No. 861.002/41.
7. Paléologue, *op. cit.*, Vol. II, p. 166.
8. Marye, *op. cit.*, pp. 455–456.
9. *Pravitel'stvenni Vestnik*, February 10, 1916, p. 4.
10. Marye, *op. cit.*, pp. 463–464.
11. *Ibid.*, pp. 325–326.
12. *Ibid.*, pp. 460–463.
13. *Ibid.*, pp. 470–477.

*Chapter Seven*

1. Archives, Memorandum giving biographical data on Ambassador Francis, dated August 25, 1914, File No. 123F/84, 84/1a, 84/16.
2. *New York Times*, February 24, 1916, p. 12.
3. D. Francis, *Russia from the American Embassy*, New York, 1921, p. 3.
4. Archives, Dispatch from Ambassador Marye, dated February 23, 1916, File No. 123 F84/11.
5. Archives, Memorandum of Frank Polk, dated April 19, 1916, File No. 711.612/276.
6. Archives, Letter from Ambassador Francis to President Wilson, dated April 8, 1916, File No. 711.612/247 1/2.
7. *Ibid.*
8. *Ibid.*
9. G. Kennan, *Soviet-American Relations, 1917–1920, Vol. I, Russia Leaves the War*, Princeton, N.J., 1956, p. 39.
10. Archives, Dispatch from Ambassador Francis dated April 29, 1916, File No. 123 F84/23.
11. Francis, *op. cit.*, p. 9.
12. *Foreign Relations, The Lansing Papers*, Vol. II, Washington, 1940, p. 313.

13. *Ibid.*
14. Archives, Cable from Ambassador Francis, dated May 2, 1916, File No. 123 F84/16.
15. *Foreign Relations, The Lansing Papers,* Vol. II, Washington, 1940, pp. 310–312.
16. Francis, *op. cit.,* pp. 14–16.
17. *Ibid.*
18. Paléologue, *op. cit.,* Vol. II, p. 253.
19. *Novoe Vremia,* June 13, 1916, p. 3.
20. *Foreign Relations, The Lansing Papers,* Vol. II, Washington, 1940, p. 311.
21. *Foreign Relations, The Lansing Papers,* Vol. I, Washington, 1939, pp. 148–149.
22. *Ibid.,* pp. 149–150.
23. Archives, Dispatch from Ambassador Francis, dated June 26, 1916, File No. 600.001/25.
24. *Rech,* June 13, 1916, p. 2.
25. *Foreign Relations, 1916 Supplement,* Washington, 1929, pp. 886–891.
26. *Ibid.,* pp. 892–912.
27. Archives, Letter from Ambassador Francis to Secretary Lansing, dated June 16, 1916, File No. 711.612/249.
28. *Foreign Relations, 1916 Supplement,* Washington, 1929, p. 972.
29. *Ibid.,* pp. 974–978.
30. *Ibid.,* pp. 981–982.

*Chapter Eight*

1. Marye, *op. cit.,* pp. 436–439.
2. Archives, Dispatch from Dearing, dated April 26, 1916, File No. 861.48/125.
3. Archives, Cable from Ambassador Francis, dated July 7, 1916, File No. 761.94/99.
4. Archives, Cable from Ambassador Francis, dated July 11, 1916, File No. 761.94/102.
5. Archives, Cable from Acting Secretary of State Polk to Ambassador Francis, dated July 11, 1916, File No. 761.94/102.
6. Archives, Letter from Ambassador Francis to Secretary of State Lansing, dated July 13, 1916, File No. 761.94/107.

7. Francis, *op. cit.*, p. 31.
8. Archives, Letter from Ambassador Francis to Secretary of State Lansing, dated August 29, 1916, File No. 761.94/124.

*Chapter Nine*

1. Sazonov, *op. cit.*, pp. 336–339.
2. Paléologue, *op. cit.*, Vol. II, pp. 301–304.
3. Archives, Cable from Ambassador Francis, dated July 23, 1916, File No. 861.002/43.
4. Francis, *op. cit.*, p. 20.
5. Archives, Letter from Ambassador Francis to Secretary of State Lansing, dated August 14, 1916, File No. 861.002/46 1/2.
6. Archives, Letter from Ambassador Francis to Secretary of State Lansing, dated August 29, 1916, File No. 761.94/124.
7. Archives, Letter from Ambassador Francis to Secretary of State Lansing, dated August 14, 1916, File No. 861.002/46 1/2.
8. Francis, *op. cit.*, pp. 28–29.
9. Archives, Letter from Ambassador Francis to Secretary of State Lansing, dated November 12, 1916, File No. 711.612/252.
10. Paléologue, *op. cit.*, Vol. III, pp. 17–24.
11. Archives, Letter from Ambassador Francis to Secretary of State Lansing, dated November 12, 1916, File No. 711.612/252.
12. *Novoe Vremia*, July 21, 1916, p. 3.
13. *Ibid.*, October 26, 1916, pp. 4–5.
14. *Rech*, October 27, 1916, p. 2.
15. *Ibid.*, November 1, 1916, p. 2.
16. Nicholas II, *The Letters of the Tsar to the Tsarina, 1914–1917,* translated by A. L. Hines, London, 1929, pp. 256–257.
17. G. Buchanan, *My Mission to Russia and Other Diplomatic Memories,* London, 1923, Vol. II, pp. 24–27.
18. Paléologue, *op. cit.*, Vol. III, pp. 50–77.
19. G. Buchanan, *My Mission to Russia and Other Diplomatic Memories,* Vol. II, London, 1923, pp. 26–27.
20. Francis, *op. cit.*, pp. 33–34.
21. Archives, Letter from Ambassador Francis to Secretary of State Lansing, dated November 12, 1916, File No. 711.612/252.
22. Nicholas II, *op. cit.*, p. 296.
23. Archives, Dispatch from Ambassador Francis, dated November 27, 1916, File No. 861.032/9.

24. Archives, Dispatch from Ambassador Francis, dated December 6, 1916, File No. 861.032/10.
25. *Foreign Relations, 1916 Supplement*, Washington, 1929, p. 87.
26. *Ibid.*, p. 97.
27. *Novoe Vremia*, December 9, 1916, p. 5.
28. *Novoe Vremia*, December 19, 1916, p. 3.
29. *Rech*, December 15, 1916, p. 2.
30. Archives, Letter from Ambassador Francis to Secretary of State Lansing, dated January 16, 1917, File No. 861.00/271.

*Chapter Ten*

1. Francis, *op. cit.*, p. 42.
2. Paléologue, *op. cit.*, Vol. III, pp. 137–152.
3. Buchanan, *op. cit.*, Vol. II, pp. 42–50.
4. Nicholas II, *op. cit.*, p. 307.
5. Archives, Dispatch from Ambassador Francis, dated January 16, 1917, File No. 861.00/271.
6. Lansing, *op. cit.*, p. 193.
7. *Ibid.*, p. 194.
8. *Ibid.*, p. 195.
9. Archives, Dispatch from Ambassador Francis, dated January 23, 1917, File No. 763.72119/516.
10. Archives, Dispatch from Ambassador Francis, dated January 27, 1917, File No. 763.72119/517.
11. Archives, Cable from Ambassador Francis, dated February 4, 1917, File No. 763.72/3205.
12. *Pravitel'stvenni Vestnik*, January 25, 1917, p. 2.
13. G. Buchanan, *op. cit.*, Vol. II, pp. 55–57.
14. Paléologue, *op. cit.*, Vol. III, p. 213.
15. Archives, Letter from Ambassador Francis to Secretary of State Lansing, dated March 7, 1917, with postscript dated March 9, 1917, File No. 123F84/35.
16. Archives, Cable from Ambassador Francis, dated March 14, 1917, File No. 861.00/273.
17. Archives, Cable from Ambassador Francis, dated March 19, 1917, File No. 861.00/288.
18. Archives, Cable from Ambassador Francis, dated March 22, 1917, File No. 861.00/294.

*Chapter Eleven*

1. Lansing, *op. cit.*, pp. 226–231.
2. *Foreign Relations, The Lansing Papers,* Vol. I, Washington, 1939, pp. 626–628.

# Bibliography

Adamov, E., "Russia and the United States at the Time of the Civil War," *Journal of Modern History*, Vol. II (1930).

Adams, John Quincy, *The Memoirs of John Quincy Adams*, edited by Charles F. Adams, Philadelphia, 1875.

Baker, R., *Woodrow Wilson, Life and Letters*, Garden City, N.Y., 1927–1929.

Bond, F., *Mr. Miller of "The Times,"* New York, 1931.

Borodin, N., *Severo-Amerikanskie Soyedinennye Shtaty i Rossii*, Petrograd, 1916.

Buchanan, George, *My Mission to Russia and Other Diplomatic Memories*, 3 Vols., London, 1923.

Buchanan, James, *The Works of James Buchanan*, 12 Vols. edited by John Moore, Philadelphia, 1908–1911.

Coolidge, A., *The United States as a World Power*, New York, 1927.

Curry, Roy, *Woodrow Wilson and Far Eastern Policy, 1913–1921*, New York, 1957.

Dennett, T., *Roosevelt and the Russo-Japanese War*, New York, 1925.

Egbert, B., *The Conflict Between the United States and Russia*, St. Petersburg, 1912.

Francis, David, *Russia From the American Embassy*, New York, 1921.

Golder, Frank, *Documents of Russian History, 1914–1917*, New York, 1927.

————, *Guide to Materials for American History in Russian Archives*, Washington, 1917.

————, "Russian-American Relations During the Crimean War," *American Historical Review*, Vol. XXXI (1926).

————, "The Russian Fleet and the Civil War," *American Historical Review*, Vol. XX (1915).

Gurko, Vladimir, *Features and Figures of the Past*, Stanford, California, 1939.

Hildt, J., "Early Diplomatic Negotiations of the United States with Russia," *Johns Hopkins University Studies in Historical and Political Science*, Vol. XXIV.

Kennan, George, *Soviet-American Relations, 1917–1920, Vol. I, Russia Leaves the War*, Princeton, N.J., 1956.

"K istorii russko-amerikanskikh otnoshenii vo vremia grazhdanskoi voiny v S.SH. A." *Krasnyi Arkhiv*, Vol. XCIV (1939).

Kokovtsov, V., *Out of My Past, the Memoirs of Count Kokovtsov*, Stanford, California, 1935.

Lansing, Robert, *War Memoirs of Robert Lansing*, Indianapolis, 1935.

Laserson, Max, *The American Impact on Russia*, New York, 1950.

Lauriat, Charles, *The Lusitania's Last Voyage*, Boston, 1915.

Link, Arthur, *Wilson, the Struggle for Neutrality*, Princeton, N.J., 1960.

Malloy, W., *Treaties and Conventions . . . .* , Washington, 1910.

Marye, George, *Nearing the End in Imperial Russia*, Philadelphia, 1929.

Millis, Walter, *Road to War*, Boston, 1935.

Morison, E., *The Letters of Theodore Roosevelt*, Cambridge, Mass., 1951–1954.

*New York Times*, 1914–1917.

Nicholas II, *The Letters of the Tsar to the Tsarina, 1914–1917*, translated by A. L. Hines, London, 1929.

*Novoe Vremia*, 1914–1917.

Paléologue, Maurice, *An Ambassador's Memoirs*, 3 Vols., London, 1923.

Pratt, Julius, *A History of United States Foreign Policy*, Princeton, N.J., 1955.

*Pravitel'stvenni Vestnik*, 1914–1917.

Price, Ernest, *The Russo-Japanese Treaties of 1907–1916 Concerning Manchuria and Mongolia*, Baltimore, 1933.

Pringle, H., *Theodore Roosevelt*, New York, 1931.

*Rech*, 1914–1917.

*Ruskiia Viedomosti*, 1914–1917.

*Russian Review*, New York, February 1916–February 1917.

Sazonov, Sergei, *Fateful Years, 1909–1916*, London, 1928.

"Severo-Amerikanskiye Soyedinennye Shtaty i tsarskaya Rossiya v 90 godakh XIX veka," *Krasnyi Arkhiv*, Vol. LII (1932).

*Stenograficheskii Otchet Gosudarstvennuyu Dumy*, Third Duma, Petrograd, 1912.

Taylor, Bayard, *The Life and Letters of Bayard Taylor*, Boston, 1884.

Thomas, Benjamin, "Russo-American Relations, 1815–1867," *Johns Hopkins University Studies in Historical and Political Science*, Vol. XLVIII.

United States Department of State, Unpublished Archives of the Department of State, 1914–1917.

————, *Papers Relating to the Foreign Relations of the United States, The Lansing Papers, 1914–1920*, Washington, 1939–1940, 2 Vols.

————, *Papers Relating to the Foreign Relations of the United States, Vol. V, 1899, 1911, 1914, 1914 Supplement, 1915, 1915 Supplement, 1916, 1916 Supplement, 1917, 1917 Supplement I*, Washington, 1914–1931.

*Vestnik Russko-Amerikanskoi Torgovy Palaty*, Moscow, December 1915.

Yeleonskaya, Y., *Voina e Kultura*, Moscow, 1915.

Zabriskie, Edward, *American-Russian Rivalry in the Far East*, Philadelphia, 1946.

# Index